A ▲ 157
POREČ ▲ 166

HUNGARY
Pécs
DRAVA
irovitica
DUNAV
Som
Donji
Miholjac
Beli
Manastir
Daruvar
Osijek
Zrenjanin
Novi Sad
Vukovar
PAPUK
Nova Gradiška
Našice
Dakovo
Vinkovci
Tovarnik
DUNAV
DUNAV
Belgrade
Slavonski
Brod
SAVA
SAVA
edor
SERBIA
AND
MONTENEGRO
Banja
Luka
Doboj
Brčko
Bijeljina
BOSNIA-
RZEGOVINA
MODRAČKO
JEZ.
Zvornik
Valjevo
Travnik
Zenica
DRINA
Užice
Kraljevo
VITOROG
Sarajevo
Kupres
Foča
Pljevlja
ZLATAR
Novi Pazar
Sirij
Imotski
DALMATIA
ČETINA
Makarska
Mostar
SERBIA
AND MONTENEGRO
OF HVAR
Ploče
Metković
D OF KORČULA
Nikšić
HAJLA
LASTOVSKI KANAL
Ston
DUBROVNIK
MLJET
ŠIPAN

D OF HVAR ▲ 230
DUBROVNIK ▲ 234
ISLAND OF KORČULA ▲ 246

ŠIBENIK
As well as its Greco-Roman legacy, it has some fine examples of Renaissance architecture.

TROGIR
The narrow streets of this fortified medieval town are bordered by houses of ocher-colored stone.

SPLIT
2,000 years of architecture and one of the oldest, most grandiose squats in the world – the town's mixed architectural styles developed within the walls of Diocletian's palace.

ISLAND OF HVAR
The campanile of St Stephen's Cathedral in Hvar Town is typically Venetian.

DUBROVNIK
Gothic portraits, Renaissance cloisters, baroque pediments – from its churches to its palaces, this is one of the great cities of Europe.

ISLAND OF KORČULA
Korčula Town has fine architecture and its church has great art.

CROATIA
AND THE DALMATIAN COAST

KNOPF GUIDES

● Encyclopedia section

■ NATURE

The natural heritage: species and habitats characteristic to the area covered by the guide, annotated and illustrated by naturalist authors and artists.

HISTORY, LANGUAGE AND RELIGION

The impact of international historical events on local history, from the arrival of the first inhabitants, with key dates appearing in a timeline above the text.

ARTS AND TRADITIONS

Customs and traditions and their continuing role in contemporary life.

ARCHITECTURE

The architectural heritage, focusing on style and topology, a look at rural and urban buildings, major civil, religious and military monuments.

AS SEEN BY PAINTERS

A selection of paintings of the city or country by different artists and schools, arranged chronologically or thematically.

AS SEEN BY WRITERS

An anthology of texts focusing on the city or country, taken from works of all periods and countries, arranged thematically.

▲ Itineraries

Each itinerary begins with a map of the area to be explored.

★ SPECIAL INTEREST

These sites are not to be missed. They are highlighted in gray boxes in the margins.

INSETS

On richly illustrated double pages, these insets turn the spotlight on subjects deserving more in-depth treatment.

◆ Practical information

All the travel information you will need before you go and when you get there.

USEFUL ADDRESSES

A selection of the best hotels and restaurants compiled by an expert.

PLACES TO VISIT

A handy table of addresses and opening hours.

APPENDICES

Bibliography, list of illustrations and general index.

MAP SECTION

Maps of all the areas covered by the guide; these maps are marked out with letters and figures making it easy for the reader to pinpoint a town, region or site.

◆ Zagorje, Banovina

◆ Zagorje, Banovina

Each map in the map section is designated by a letter. In the itineraries, all the sites of interest are given a map reference (for example: ◆ **C** B2).

The itinerary map shows the main sites, the editor's choices and the places of special interest.

The mini-map pinpoints the itinerary within the wider area covered by the guide.

Podravina, Slavonia ◆

▲ From the Zagorje to the Podravina

1. ZAGREB ★ 2. MEDVEDNICA 3. MONTENEGRO 4. GORNJA BISTRA 5. STUBIČKE TOPLICE 6. DONJA STUBICA 7. MARIJA BISTRICA 8. BELEC 9. ZAJEZDA 10. SLANJEC 11. KUMROVEC 12. MILJANA LUŽAR 13. TRAKOŠĆAN 14. LUDBREG 15. KOPRIVNICA 16. PREDIGRAD 17. KRAPINA 18. TRSKI VRH 19. TRAKOŠĆAN 20. VINAGORA 21. VINICA 22. OPEKA 23. LUDBREG 24. KRIŽEVCI 25. KOPRIVNICA

through the oak, beech and pine forests that cover its slopes. A few miles to the north of Kaptol ▲ 108, a cable car climbs the 2½ miles (4 km) to the top of Sljeme (3,389 ft/1033 m), the range's highest peak. To the west of the mountain, the caves of Veternica, the country's largest cave network, cover a distance of 3½ miles (6 km). The caves have revealed traces of human habitation dating back 40,000 years. The hilltop fortress of Medvedgrad (below, right) is one of the few medieval structures that have survived in northern Croatia. Recently restored, it was built in the 13th century by the Bishop of Zagreb and has an attractive late-Romanesque chapel. The bishop and humanist poet, Ivan Česmički (1434–72), who wrote his famous epigrams and elegies under the name Janus Pannonius, died in the fortress.
GORNJA BISTRA. Several baroque castles stand at the foot of the western slopes of the mountain. Gornja Bistra (1770–5) has the U-shaped layout typical of the late-baroque period. The great oval hall is decorated with trompe-l'oeil frescos.
STUBIČKE TOPLICE. In the early 19th century, Maksimilijan Vrhovec, Bishop of Zagreb, began to build a spa around these famous springs (toplice means 'baths'). The architect K.H. Vestebuy successfully incorporated neo-Gothic, Classical and Biedermeier elements into the buildings.
DONJA STUBICA. The Gothic church of Sv. Trojstva (the Holy Trinity), renovated during the baroque period, houses a pulpit in late-Gothic style and the tomb of Franjo Tahi, the overlord whose cruelty helped to trigger the Peasants' Revolt of 1573.

◆ A A–C1-3

BISHOP VRHOVEC
Maksimilijan Vrhovec had trained in Graz, Vienna and Bologna, gained a degree in philosophy and theology, and become a freemason before being appointed Bishop of Zagreb in 1787, at the age of 25.

He was well-versed in philosophy and founded a printing press. His social preoccupations led him to build a hospital in Zagreb and the thermal baths at Stubičke Toplice. He began landscaping the main park, named Maksimir in his honor ▲ 114, and contributed to the region's economic development.

In summer, Mount Medvednica offers an escape from the oppressive heat of the city. In winter, 'Bear Mountain' is transformed into one of the country's largest areas of ski slopes.

The foothills of the 'Slovenian Alps' lie to the north of Zagreb. Throughout history, this part of the country has always been known as 'Croatia'. Together with the plain to the south of the capital, it escaped Ottoman domination and, like the rest of Christian Europe, experienced an age of feudalism that bequeathed many chateaux, most of which had been renovated by the 18th century. This is also a region of baroque churches which, like the rest of the former Habsburg empire, was deeply marked by the Counter-Reformation. This itinerary starts from Mount Medvednica (Bear Mountain) to the north of Zagreb, and passes through western Zagorje, to the west of the capital, and then northern Zagorje, to the magnificent baroque town of Varaždin. After a brief visit to the Medimurje, Croatia's northernmost region, it returns to Zagreb via the Podravina or 'Drava Valley'.

Mount Medvednica ◆ A A2-3

Mount Medvednica, to the north of Zagreb, has been a nature reserve since 1981 and is the city's ultimate green space. Marked woodland paths lead

116   117

★ The star symbol signifies sites singled out by the editor for special attention.

● ▲ ◆
The above symbols within the text provide cross-references to a place or a theme discussed elsewhere in the guide.

At the beginning of each itinerary there is a reference to the main map section underneath the mini-map.

FRONT ENDPAPER Not to be missed
BACK ENDPAPER Croatia in figures
02 How to use this guide
06 Introduction to the itineraries
07 Authors

● **Encyclopedia**

15 NATURE
16 Landscapes of Croatia
18 The oak forests of Slavonia
20 Kopački Rit nature park
22 Mountain forests
24 Mediterranean forests
26 Marine life

29 HISTORY AND LANGUAGE
30 Chronology
38 The Croatian language
40 The Glagolitic script

41 ART AND TRADITIONS
42 Music and dance
44 Traditional costumes
46 Rural life in eastern Croatia
48 Peasant fishermen
50 Food: 'Štrukli'
52 Croatian specialties

53 ARCHITECTURE
54 Ancient architecture
56 Pre-Romanesque architecture
58 Romanesque architecture
60 Renaissance architecture
62 The villas of Dubrovnik
64 Baroque architecture
66 Rural architecture
68 From Neoclassicism to Modernism

73 CROATIA AS SEEN BY PAINTERS

81 CROATIA AS SEEN BY WRITERS

▲ Itineraries in Croatia and the Dalmatian Coast

99 ZAGREB
106 *The Museum of Zagreb*
116 From the Zagorje to the Podravina
124 *St Mary of Jerusalem, Trški Vrh*
132 Central Croatia
138 *The Plitvice Lakes national park*

141 SLAVONIA
142 Osijek
146 The Baranja Region
147 The Podravina Region
148 Southeastern Slavonia
150 Central Slavonia
151 Western Slavonia

153 ISTRIA
157 Pula
162 Pazin
166 Poreč
167 The Northern coastline
168 *The Basilica of Poreč*
170 Northern Istria

171 RIJEKA
172 From Rijeka to Zadar
176 Trsat
177 The Opatija Riviera
178 *Opatija and early tourism in Croatia*
180 The Cres and Lošinj Archipelago
182 Krk island
184 Rab Island
185 Senj
188 Pag Island
186 *The Velebit*

189 ZADAR
196 From Zadar to Split
198 The Zadar Archipelago
200 *The Kornati Islands*
202 Šibenik
204 The Krka National Park
206 Trogir
210 *Salona, capital of Roman Dalmatia*
212 Toward Sinj

213 SPLIT
216 *Diocletian's Palace*
222 *Ivan Meštrović*
224 Omiš
228 Brač Island
229 Šolta Island
230 Hvar Island
232 Vis Island

233 DUBROVNIK
242 The Southern Dalmatian coast
246 Korčula
252 Mljet
252 Lastovo

◆ Practical information

254 Before you go
255 Croatia from A to Z
260 Festivals
261 Hotels, restaurants and cafés
267 Glossary
268 Addresses and opening times of places to visit
281 Bibliography
282 List of illustrations
286 Index

289 MAP SECTION
A Zagorje, Banovina, Podravina, Slavonia
B Istria, Central Croatia
C Dalmatia
D Zagreb
E Split
F Dubrovnik
G Rijeka
H Zadar
I Šibenik
J Pula

ZAGREB ▲ 100

The historic district of Gradec, whose Sabor (Parliament) is a symbol of Croatian identity, stands opposite the former ecclesiastical town of Kaptol and its cathedral. Below them lies the modern city of Zagreb whose neoclassical, neo-baroque and Art Nouveau buildings date from the 19th and early 20th century.

FROM THE ZAGORJE TO THE PODRAVINA ▲ 116

To the north of Zagreb lies the Zagorje, a region of wooded hillsides famous for its baroque castles – built or renovated in the 18th century – and churches. The town of Varaždin, a veritable treasury of baroque architecture, marks the northern-most point of this itinerary.

CENTRAL CROATIA ▲ 132

The Turopolje region, with its amazing wooden churches and houses, stretches from southeast of Zagreb, along the River Sava to Sisak. To the west of Zagreb, at the foot of the Zumberak hills, lies the beautiful baroque town of Samobor. From Karlovac, to the southwest of the capital, one of three major routes leading to the coast runs through the famous Plitvice Lakes national park.

SLAVONIA ▲ 141

The easternmost region of Croatia is bounded by Hungary, Bosnia-Herzegovina and Serbia. Its fortified towns – Vinkovci, Slavonski Brod, Nova Gradiška – are typical of the Military Frontier of the Austro-Hungarian empire. As well as being regarded as the granary of Croatia, Slavonia is also a rich wine-growing region, especially around Ilok to the southeast of Osijek.

ISTRIA ▲ 153

The most northerly peninsula on the Croatian Adriatic coast shares many characteristics with its Italian neighbor. Away from the coast, the landscapes around Pazin have a decidedly Tuscan feel, while the multicolored façades of the coastal ports – from Umag, via Poreč and Rovinj, to Pula – are reminiscent of Venice.

FROM RIJEKA TO ZADAR ▲ 171

Rijeka stands at the northern end of the Kvarner Gulf which stretches to the steep coastal mountains of Dalmatia in the south. The tourist boom of the mid-19th century, centered around Opatija and the islands of Krk, Cres and Lošinj, was directly linked to the region's mild climate.

FROM ZADAR TO SPLIT ▲ 189

The coastal towns of Zadar, Šibenik and Trogir have some fine examples of Roman, medieval and Renaissance architecture. Offshore, the strings of islands and islets include the famous Kornati archipelago, now almost devoid of life. The inland region, which suffered during the conflict of 1991–5, has managed to preserve its agricultural tradition.

FROM SPLIT TO DUBROVNIK ▲ 213

With Diocletian's Palace at the historic heart of the city, Split stands at the gateway to the extremely popular island resorts of central Dalmatia – Brač, Hvar and Vis. The deeply indented coastline of the Makarska Riviera is dominated by the steep slopes of the Biokovo Mountains.

SOUTHERN DALMATIA ▲ 233

In the shelter of its ramparts, the former city-state of Ragusa, now Dubrovnik, has preserved its heritage as a rich trading center. The island of Korčula, which occupied a strategic position on the maritime route between Dubrovnik and the rival port of Venice, harbors some unrivaled architectural treasures. To the south lie the lush vineyards of the Pelješac Peninsula.

All the information in this guide has been checked by the large team of specialists who were involved in its production.

STANKO ANDRIĆ
Researcher at the Croatian Institute of Historical and Social Sciences. Author of 'Slavonia'.

MARINO BALDINI
Archeologist and art historian. Author of 'Istria'.

VLAHO BOGOŠIĆ
Works at the Institute of Lexicography in Zagreb, and wrote the sections on the Župa and Konlave regions.

BOŽICA BRKAN
Journalist for the daily newspaper *Večerni List*. Author of 'Food' and 'Croatian specialties'.

NENAD CAMBI
Curator of the Archeological Museum in Split and lecturer in Classical and Paleochristian archeology at the University of Split. Author of the sections on Salona, Narona and Issa, areas where he has carried out a number of excavations.

NAILA CERIBAŠIĆ
Musicologist at the Zagreb Institute of Ethnology and Folklore Research. Author of 'Music and dance'.

NICOLAS CHRISTITCH
A historian with a wide knowledge of Croatia due to family connections, he added material throughout the guide and wrote the useful information for travelers in the Practical Information.

STJEPAN DAMJANOVIĆ
Lecturer at Zagreb Faculty of Philosophy and author of a number of works on the Slav language and Glagolitic script. President of the Croatian Committee of South Slavs. Author of 'The Glagolitic script'.

ŽELJKA ČORAK
Art historian, writer and literary translator from French, Italian and English, who has published a monograph on Zagreb Cathedral. Author of 'Zagreb' and 'The Elaphite Islands'.

ALENA FAZINIĆ
Art historian and curator of the Gradski muzej (Town Museum) in Korčula Town. Author of 'Korčula'.

MILJENKO FORETIĆ
Born in Dubrovnik where he has lived all his life. Historian and editor-in-chief for the Matica Hrvatska (MH) cultural organization in Dubrovnik. Author of 'Dubrovnik' and 'The southern Dalmatian coast'.

AGNÈS GATTEGNO
Journalist who contributed to 'Useful addresses'.

NADA GRUJIĆ
Historian at the University of Zagreb. Wrote 'The villas of Dubrovnik'.

JELENA HEKMAN
Editor for the literature department of the Matica Hrvatska (MH) cultural organization. Compiled part of 'Croatia as seen by writers'.

EMIL HILJE
Lecturer in art history at the University of Zadar, specializing in 14th- and 15th-century Dalmatia. Author of 'Zadar', 'The Zadar Hinterland', 'The Zadar Archipelago', 'Rab Island', 'Pag Island' and co-author of 'The Kornati Islands'.

TOMISLAV HITREC
Fellow of the Institute for Tourism in Zagreb and author of a number of works on the history and socio-cultural aspects of tourism. Wrote 'Opatija and Early Tourism'.

KATARINA HORVAT-LEVAJ
Art historian and researcher at the Institute of Art History in Zagreb. Author of 'Baroque architecture'.

RADOVAN IVANČEVIĆ
Professor of art history at the Academy of Fine Arts and lecturer at the Faculty of Architecture (University of Zagreb), Radovan Ivančević has published a number of scientific works and scripted around 100 television programs. President of the Croatian Society of Art Historians in Zagreb, he planned the architecture section and wrote 'Renaissance architecture'.

MILJENKO JURKOVIĆ
Art historian and lecturer at the University of Zagreb. Author of 'Pre-Romanesque architecture' and 'Romanesque Architecture'.

ZORAN KLARIĆ
Geographer and fellow of the Institute of Tourism in Zagreb. Author of the sections on nature parks and reserves, and co-author of 'The Kornati Islands'.

MLADEN KLEMENČIĆ
Geographer and compiler for the Zagreb Institute of Lexicography. Advisor for the 'infomaps' at the start of each itinerary, author of 'The Velebit' and co-author of 'Central Croatia'.

TRPIMIR MACAN
Historian and compiler of encyclopedias and dictionaries for the Zagreb Institute of Lexicography. Editor of the 'History' section of the guide.

AUGUST KOVAČEC
Lecturer in French and Romanic linguistics at the Faculty of Philosophy (University of Zagreb). Author of 'The Croatian language', and one of the main editors for the guide.

ZVONKO MAKOVIĆ
Lecturer in art history and writer. Author of 'From Neoclassicism to Modernism'.

VLADIMIR MALEKOVIĆ
Director of the Arts and Crafts School in Zagreb, author of several publications and designer of the permanent exhibitions in several Croatian museums. Author of 'From the Zagorje to the Podravina' and co-author of 'Central Croatia'.

SOPHIE MASSALOVITCH
Journalist who compiled and updated 'Useful Addresses' for the latest edition of the guide.

ALEKSANDRA MURAJ
Scientific advisor at the Zagreb Institute of Ethnology. Author of 'Arts and Traditions'.

TONI NIKOLIĆ
Botanist and lecturer at the Faculty of Natural Sciences in Zagreb. Author of the pages on natural environments.

SLOBODAN PROSPEROV NOVAK
Arts lecturer at the Faculty of Philosophy (University of Zagreb). Contributor to 'Dubrovnik'.

DANIJEL OREŠIĆ
Geographer and lecturer at the Department of Geography (University of Zagreb). Author of 'The Plitvice Lakes National Park',

Encyclopedia

Nature, *15*
History and language, *29*
Art and traditions, *41*
Architecture, *53*
Croatia as seen by painters, *73*
Croatia as seen by writers, *81*

In the 1920s and 1930s Croatian photography
and painting were dominated by two major
trends – the sense of national identity and
a new social awareness of the harsh
lives of peasants who lived off the land.

Photograph c.1939

Croatia has 1,105 miles (1,778 km) of coastline along the Adriatic. In the past, fishing was one of the country's main sources of livelihood ● *48*.

Photograph c.1890

The soil and climate of Croatia are ideally suited to viticulture, and several different kinds of wine are produced ● 52.

Photograph c.1920

Nature

Landscapes of Croatia, *16*
The oak forests of Slavonia, *18*
Kopački Rit nature park, *20*
Mountain forests, *22*
Mediterranean forests, *24*
Marine life, *26*
Karst, *28*

Landscapes of Croatia

THE SLAVONIAN PLAIN ▲*141*
Most of Croatia's cereals (maize, wheat, barley) come from the eastern plains.

ISTRIAN PENINSULA ▲*153*
The peninsula is a patchwork of eroded forests, meadows, fields of red earth, ancient terraces and vines.

Although small, with an area of 21,908 square miles (56,742 km²), Croatia has a remarkable diversity of landscapes. Fertile plains stretch across inland Croatia, marking the southern limit of the Pannonian Basin, while the narrow and heavily forested chain of the Dinaric Alps links Pannonia to the Adriatic seaboard. The mountains are separated by valleys and fields, in places where the limestone karst is covered with a thin layer of arable soil. The Adriatic coast is also a karstic region dominated by Mediterranean scrub.

HRVATSKO ZAGORJE ▲*120*
This densely populated agricultural region has an undulating landscape where subsistence crops are grown on scattered plots. Vines are cultivated on the south-facing slopes.

GORSKI KOTAR ('WOODED DISTRICT') ▲*140*
The Dinaric Alps are covered with dense forests, mainly beech and fir, that provide refuge for large numbers of wild animals. The region's heavy rainfall is due to the moisture-laden winds blowing in from the Adriatic.

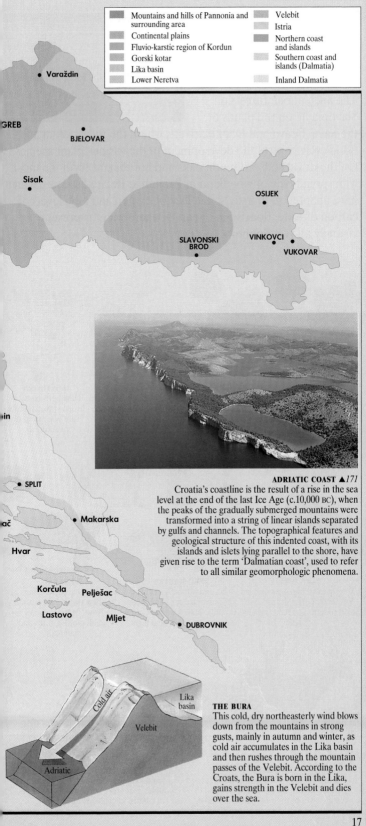

Legend

Mountains and hills of Pannonia and surrounding area	Velebit
Continental plains	Istria
Fluvio-karstic region of Kordun	Northern coast and islands
Gorski kotar	Southern coast and islands (Dalmatia)
Lika basin	Inland Dalmatia
Lower Neretva	

Varaždin

GREB

BJELOVAR

Sisak

OSIJEK

SLAVONSKI BROD

VINKOVCI

VUKOVAR

in

SPLIT

Makarska

ač

Hvar

Korčula   Pelješac

Lastovo   Mljet

DUBROVNIK

ADRIATIC COAST ▲171
Croatia's coastline is the result of a rise in the sea level at the end of the last Ice Age (c.10,000 BC), when the peaks of the gradually submerged mountains were transformed into a string of linear islands separated by gulfs and channels. The topographical features and geological structure of this indented coast, with its islands and islets lying parallel to the shore, have given rise to the term 'Dalmatian coast', used to refer to all similar geomorphologic phenomena.

Cold air

Lika basin

Velebit

Adriatic

THE BURA
This cold, dry northeasterly wind blows down from the mountains in strong gusts, mainly in autumn and winter, as cold air accumulates in the Lika basin and then rushes through the mountain passes of the Velebit. According to the Croats, the Bura is born in the Lika, gains strength in the Velebit and dies over the sea.

The oak forests of Slavonia

The ancient oak forests of Slavonia lie on the plains of the Sava, Drava and Danube rivers, where the river system and flood cycle control the development of the various plant species. On the driest soils, common oaks and hornbeams form the most widespread type of woodland in Pannonia. Related species, which have adapted to marshy soil, a lack of oxygen and high levels of carbon dioxide, flourish in the areas where water is present virtually all year round.

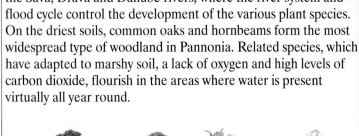

COMMON OAK
The trunk of this deciduous tree can measure up to 8 feet (2.5 meters) in diameter.

COMMON HORNBEAM
The hornbeam, with its slightly serrated leaves, often grows alongside the oak.

GUELDER ROSE
The bright red, inedible fruits remain on the plant throughout the winter.

HAWTHORN
Hawthorn grows in broad-leaved forests, rarely in mixed or pine forests.

BARN OWL
The barn owl builds its nest in lofts and belfries. It feeds on small rodents and hunts mainly at night.

PINE MARTEN
This exceptionally swift and agile creature can climb trees. It hunts small mammals, birds and insects by day and night.

WILD CAT
The wild cat seeks refuge in hollow trunks and disused burrows. It feeds mainly on small reptiles, birds and mammals.

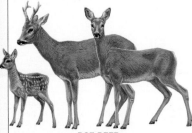

ROE DEER
These live in herds in winter and small groups in summer. They live up to 15 years and the female gives birth to 1–3 fawns at a time.

RED OR COMMON FOX
For a long time persecuted as carriers of rabies, foxes feed on small mammals and birds, insects, carrion and fruit.

Kopački Rit occupies an area of some 68 square miles (177 km²) on a flood plain between the Danube and Drava rivers. In spring, when the river waters seep into the marshes, the area is lush with vegetation and teeming with fish, frogs and insects. This wealth of plant and animal life supports 275 species of birds, including cormorants, gray herons, ducks, moorhens, seagulls, terns and storks. During migration, the marshes harbor several tens of thousands of birds. Willows, poplars, oaks, ash and chestnut trees grow on the more elevated areas of the park.

BLACK STORK
This tree-nesting bird favors marshes and river inlets, where it finds a plentiful supply of food.

GREAT WHITE HERON
A solitary bird that nests in quiet, isolated places. It is a common sight in winter on the marshes of Kopački Rit.

SPOONBILL
The spoonbill nests among the willows, reeds and vegetation on river banks, where its young are protected from predators.

Kopački Rit nature park

Around Lake Kopačevsko jezero, which is linked to the River Danube, variations in the water level have directly influenced the species that have taken up residence.

ROACH
One of the most common species of fish in the waters of the Kopački Rit nature park.

EUROPEAN POND TORTOISE
This tortoise is common in marshy areas, where it hunts frogs and small mammals.

GRASS SNAKE
The grass snake is at home in the water or on dry land, and feeds mainly on amphibians.

CHUBB
This common European freshwater cyprinid fish is a very active predator.

WHITE-TAILED SEA EAGLE
The white-tailed sea eagle nests high in the trees and feeds mainly on fish and small birds.

CORMORANT
The cormorant, with its dark plumage and webbed feet, is a migratory bird. It is an expert diver and excellent fisher.

OTTER
The otter is well adapted to this wetland environment where it feeds on fish, shrimps and frogs.

■ Mountain forests

Even the steepest slopes have been colonized by hardy bushes.

The mountain forests can be divided into several layers, characterized by the type of vegetation. The highest layer is occupied by juniper and black pine, which can withstand heavy winter snows. Below these, at an altitude of 1,800–4,000 feet (550–1,200 meters), lies mixed forest of beech and pine. Further down, hornbeam and oak grow on the inland slopes, while hazel and beech favor slopes facing the Adriatic. These forests are home to many wild animals, some of which – bears and wolves, for example – have become quite rare.

BEECH
The beech is a large temperate tree that favors shady slopes.

WHITE PINE
This conifer can grow to a height of 148 feet (45 meters) and produces erect cones.

MOUNTAIN PINE
A very hardy pine that forms the last link between forest and high mountains.

BLACK PINE
This pine is found in the mountains and along the Mediterranean coast.

BROWN BEAR
Today some 400 individuals inhabit the forests of the Dinaric Alps. They weigh an average of 330 pounds (150 kilos), although a large male can weigh up to 660 pounds (300 kilos).

TIMBER WOLF
These animals live in small, highly organized packs. They hunt deer and small mammals.

WILD BILBERRY
The bilberry flowers in May–July and produces edible berries.

SQUIRREL
The fur of this agile rodent is usually gray, gray- to black-brown, or reddish brown.

WILLOW TIT
It nests in the trunks of dead trees, making its own holes or using those of woodpeckers.

Red squirrel

Thick-billed nut-cracker

Fir tree

Capercaillie

Beech

Martagon lily

Lynx

Pine marten

F.Desbordes 99

23

■ Mediterranean forests

The Adriatic coast has long, hot, dry summers and short, mild winters. Most of the perennial plant species are evergreen. They have adapted to the poor, limestone soil and lack of water by developing a large root system and small, hairy, waxy or linear leaves that reduce transpiration. Mediterranean scrub, a transitional ecosystem between an open (heathland) and closed (oak and pine forest) environment, is the result of the intensive exploitation of the region's forests.

HOLM OAK
Glossy green surface
Downy gray surface
The tree's root system and foliage have enabled it to adapt to the poor soil and lack of water.

ALEPPO PINE
Karst
Clay
The roots of this coastal pine absorb the moisture from pockets of clay trapped in the karst.

MYRTLE
An aromatic oil is distilled from the leaves of this extremely slow-growing shrub.

LENTISC
The lentisc or masti tree is used for coast reforestation since i tolerates saline soil sea mists and drough

ROSEMARY
Rosemary's linear leaves have aromatic and therapeutic qualities.

PHOENICIAN JUNIPER
Both the tree and shrub form have small, soft leaves.

MONGOOSE
This native of Africa, introduced to Croatia via the island of Mljet ▲ 250 feeds on birds and small mammals. Its quick-wittedness an agility also enable it to kill poisonous snakes

PEREGRINE FALCON
The peregrine falcon rears its young in the safety of steep rocky cliffs. It hunts other birds.

OLIVE-TREE WARBLER
Although it merges with the foliage of the scrubland, it is betrayed by its strident and rather raucous cry.

SHORT-TOED EAGLE
This large migratory bird of prey only hunts reptiles, whic it feeds to its single chick.

Aleppo pine

Short-toed
eagle

Rabbit

Holm
oak

25

■ Marine life

0–33 FEET (0–10 METERS)
Water plants develop on rocks along the coast, where light
penetrates and the water is rich in oxygen. Those in the upper
layers can either withstand exposure to the air at low tide or foll
the ebb tide into deeper water. The lower waters provide refuge
spawning grounds for many species due to the decreased amou
of light – 30 percent less at 16 feet (5 meters) – and micro-relief

The Adriatic has little in the way of tidal movement, extremely
blue and transparent waters and average salt levels for the
Mediterranean. In the north and center, the sea is relatively
shallow but, beyond the Palagruža shelf, lie the depths of the
southern Adriatic Basin. Much of its flora and fauna are found
throughout the Mediterranean but a number of endemic species
favor the Adriatic's relative isolation. Most of the living species
are found within the coastal system, which is characterized by the
presence of photosynthetic plants. The type and number of the
various species depend on a range of ecological factors, including
the amount of light, type of sea bed and water temperature.

**NEPTUNE GRASS,
0–33 FEET (0–10 METERS)**
Entire meadows of Neptune grass
(*Posidonia*) develop on the sand or mud of
the sea bed, especially in the central and
southern Adriatic. Because of their high
level of organic production, these meadows
harbor many animal and plant forms. Many
fish species feed and spawn here.

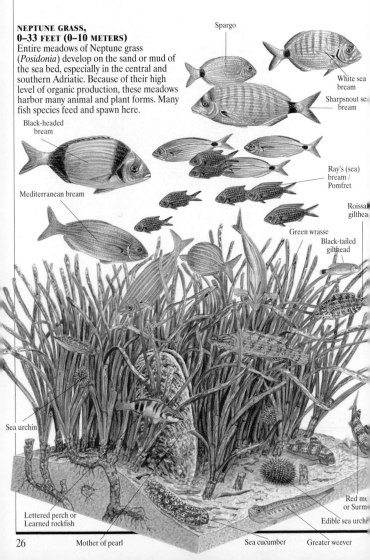

Spargo

White sea
bream

Sharpsnout sea
bream

Black-headed
bream

Ray's (sea)
bream /
Pomfret

Mediterranean bream

Roissa
gilthea

Green wrasse

Black-tailed
gilthead

Sea urchin

Lettered perch or
Learned rockfish

Red mu
or Surm

Edible sea urchi

26

Mother of pearl

Sea cucumber

Greater weever

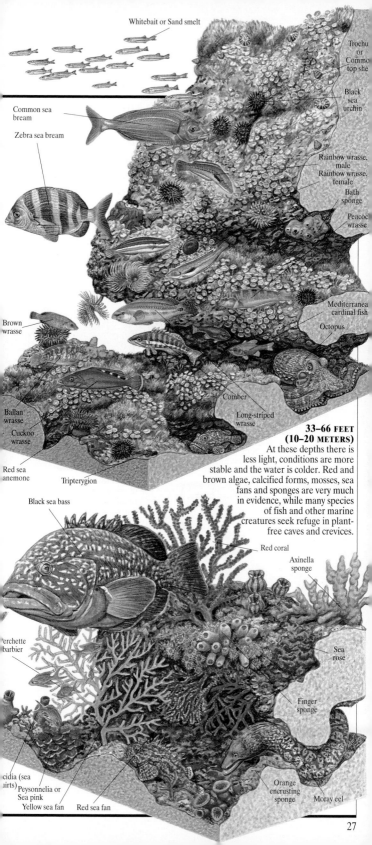

Whitebait or Sand smelt

Trochu or Commo top she

Black sea urchin

Common sea bream

Zebra sea bream

Rainbow wrasse, male
Rainbow wrasse, female

Bath sponge

Peacoc wrasse

Brown wrasse

Mediterranea cardinal fish

Octopus

Ballan wrasse

Cuckoo wrasse

Red sea anemone

Tripterygion

Comber

Long-striped wrasse

33–66 FEET (10–20 METERS)
At these depths there is less light, conditions are more stable and the water is colder. Red and brown algae, calcified forms, mosses, sea fans and sponges are very much in evidence, while many species of fish and other marine creatures seek refuge in plant-free caves and crevices.

Black sea bass

Red coral

Axinella sponge

erchette barbier

Sea rose

Finger sponge

cidia (sea uirts)

Peyssonnelia or Sea pink

Yellow sea fan

Red sea fan

Orange encrusting sponge

Moray eel

◼ Karst

Many of the geomorphologic terms used to describe karstic phenomena – doline, polje, ponor, uvala – are borrowed from Serbo-Croat.

Croatia offers a fine example of classic karst topography, a very distinctive landscape caused by limestone being dissolved in underground water. The Croatian karst has been created in a limestone region dating from the Mesozoic era, which represents 40 percent of the national territory. In the poljes – broad, flat basins enclosed by rocky slopes – the rivers plunge into ponors or sinkholes, re-emerging as karstic springs at lower altitudes as they encounter a less permeable type of rock. A great many of these springs emerge along the coast, sometimes underwater. The chemical process involved in the dissolution of the limestone creates interesting surface formations – lapiaz, for example – and underground systems of caves and chasms.

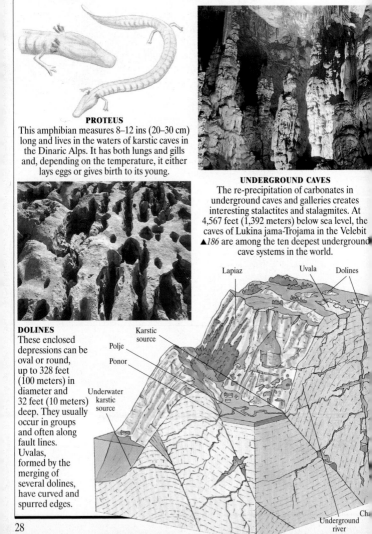

PROTEUS
This amphibian measures 8–12 ins (20–30 cm) long and lives in the waters of karstic caves in the Dinaric Alps. It has both lungs and gills and, depending on the temperature, it either lays eggs or gives birth to its young.

UNDERGROUND CAVES
The re-precipitation of carbonates in underground caves and galleries creates interesting stalactites and stalagmites. At 4,567 feet (1,392 meters) below sea level, the caves of Lukina jama-Trojama in the Velebit ▲186 are among the ten deepest underground cave systems in the world.

Lapiaz   Uvala   Dolines

Karstic source

Polje

Ponor

Underwater karstic source

DOLINES
These enclosed depressions can be oval or round, up to 328 feet (100 meters) in diameter and 32 feet (10 meters) deep. They usually occur in groups and often along fault lines. Uvalas, formed by the merging of several dolines, have curved and spurred edges.

Cha
Underground river

History and language

Chronology, *30*
The Croatian language, *38*
The Glagolitic script, *40*

-6000–2500		-1600–1200	4th century BC
Neolithic Period: sites at Danilo, Hvar, Butmir.		Bronze Age: fortified dwellings (*gradine*).	Arrival of the Greeks and Celt

-8000   -6000   -4000   -2000

-2200–1800	8th century BC
Eneolithic Period: sites at Lasinje, Vučedol.	Illyrian tribes settle in the region.

10TH CENTURY

German Empire
Hungary
ZAGREB
ZADAR
Byzantine
SPLIT
Empire
DUBROVNIK

☐ Northern Croatia
☐ Croatia
☐ Principality of Neretva
▨ Intermittent Croat domination
☐ Byzantine possessions

1358

German Empire
Hungary
ZAGREB
ZADAR
Bosnia
SPLIT
DUBROVNIK

☐ Croatia
☐ Venetian possessions

1606

Austria   *Hungary*
ZAGREB
RIJEKA
Ottoman
ZADAR
SPLIT
Empire
DUBROVNIK

☐ Croatia
☐ Republic of Dubrovnik
☐ Venetian possessions

1791

Austria   *Hungary*
ZAGREB
RIJEKA
ZADAR
Ottoman
SPLIT
Empire
DUBROVNIK

☐ Croatia
☐ Austrian military administration in Croatia
☐ Republic of Dubrovnik
☐ Venetian possessions

1881

Austria   *Hungary*
ZAGREB
RIJEKA
Ottoman
ZADAR
SPLIT
Empire
DUBROVNIK

☐ Croatia
☐ Austrian territory

1918

Austria   *Hungary*
LJUBLJANA
ZAGREB
RIJEKA
Romania
BELGRADE
ZADAR (Italy)
SPLIT
DUBROVNIK
Bulgaria
Albania
Greece

☐ Croatia
☐ Slovenia
☐ Bosnia-Herzegovina
☐ Serbia
☐ Montenegro
☐ Vojvodina
☐ Territory annexed by Italy

6–9 AD The Illyrian uprising is suppressed; Illyrian territory comes under Roman rule.

c.620 Arrival of the Croats.

200	400	600	800

7 The Illyrians are conquered by the Romans.

582 Fall of Sirmija.

c.614 Fall of Salona (Solin).

c.800 Višeslav becomes the first prince (*knez*) of Croatia.

Illyrians, Greeks and Romans

At the beginning of the Bronze Age, the Illyrians, an Indo-European ethnic group comprising several tribes (including the Histri, Dalmatians and Liburnians), settled in the region of present-day Croatia. During the 4th century BC, the Celts merged with the Illyrians or pushed them further south. During the same period, the Greeks founded fortified colonies on the islands of Vis (Issa was the main trading counter between southern Italy and the Illyrian territories), Hvar and Korčula, and on the mainland, in the region of Trogir and Stobreč, near Split. Although the Illyrians borrowed certain commercial, social and cultural practices from the Greeks, they made every effort to limit the latter's expansion. The Romans, on the pretext of coming to the aid of the Greek coastal colonies, in fact set out to conquer the Illyrian territories which they finally subjugated in the early 1st century AD, after more than

200 hundred years of war. In the Roman province of Dalmatia, Greeks and Illyrians gradually became Romanized, especially in the coastal towns, inland urban centers and valleys, while life in the mountain regions remained more or less unchanged. The Romans were great road builders, and urban trade and craftsmanship flourished. They also made a significant contribution in the fields of political and social organization and in a number of economic areas – such as navigation, fishing and the cultivation of vines, olives and citrus fruit. In the 4th century, the Roman Empire was faced with social and religious unrest and invasions from the north. When Theodosus died (in AD 395), the Empire was divided between his sons, with the rivers Danube and Drina marking the

frontier between the Eastern (or Byzantine) and Western Roman Empires. The Western Empire was assailed by various peoples – including Goths, Huns and Ostrogoths – and disappeared altogether in AD 476. The Eastern Empire re-asserted its authority for a time, especially under the Emperor Justinian (527–565), over what would subsequently become Croatian territory.

The early Middle Ages

THE ARRIVAL OF THE CROATS

In the early 7th century, at the end of the Greek and Roman period, the Croats – a Slav tribe whose name (Hrvat) is thought to be of Persian origin – migrated to southeastern Europe and settled in Dalmatia. Although relatively few in number, they were fearsome warriors and successfully established themselves as the strongest power along the Adriatic seaboard. The process by which the Croats merged with other Slav tribes and the Romanized indigenous population marks the beginning of Croatia's history. This history stems from a geographical position at the crossroads of three regions that have played a major role in European history – central Europe, the Mediterranean and the Balkans. In the early 8th century, several early tribal states were founded, the most important being the Croatian state established between the coastal region with its Byzantine towns and the highland region of Gvozd. The Croatian state was inspired by Classical culture and a wealth of Frankish and Byzantine influences, while its early acceptance of Christianity formed a solid basis for the construction of a national identity. The treaty of Aix-la-Chapelle (812) confirmed and continued to reinforce, throughout history, the disastrous division of the Croatian territories. The coastal towns, from Kotor to Zadar, remained under Byzantine control, while the northern Croatian state and Istria came under the aegis of the Frankish emperor.

31

810–823	845–864			1102	1202
Prince Ljudevit Posavski rebels against the Franks.	Prince Trpimir founds the Trpimirović dynasty.			Union of Croatia and Hungary.	The Venetians in Zadar with the h[...] of the Crusaders.
800	900	1000		1100	

| 852 | 879 | 925 | | 1148–1211 |
| Prince Trpimir issues the earliest-known edict by a Croatian prince. | Letter from Pope John VIII to Prince Branimir. | Coronation of Prince Tomislav. | | Dubrovnik signs protection treaties with Italian and Croatian towns and the Ban (governor) of Bosnia. |

The kingdom of Croatia

In c.845 the Croatian prince Trpimir, who had defeated the khan of Bulgaria, successfully established de facto independence while still formally recognizing Frankish sovereignty. In so doing, he founded the Croatian dynasty that ruled until the end of the 11th century. The center of the kingdom lay between Nin, Salona (Solin) and Knin. Some 30 years later, Branimir (879–892) was recognized as an independent ruler by Pope John VIII, who gave his blessing to the new kingdom and thus ensured its allegiance to Western Europe. Tomislav (910–28), recognized as king by the Pope following his victory over the Hungarians, established the kingdom's northern boundary along the River Drava. As an ally of an ailing Constantinople, Tomislav defeated the 'tsar' of Bulgaria

and was ceded sovereignty over Dalmatia by the Byzantine Emperor. Under Tomislav, the political unity of coastal and inland Croatia was established, and reinforced by the creation of an ecclesiastical state placed under the control of the metropolitan see of Split. After a period of dynastic crises marked by territorial losses, the royal power was consolidated under Petar Krešimir IV (1058–75), the most powerful of the Croatian kings. He reconquered the Dalmatian towns, re-established his authority over the region between the rivers Sava and Drava, and incorporated the principality of Neretva into the kingdom.

Petar Krešimir died childless and power passed to one of his dignitaries, the Ban (governor) of Slavonia, Dimitr Zvonimir (1075–89). By supporting Pope Gregory VII and his reforms, Zvonimir not only gained international recognition for the

territorial unity of the kingdoms of Croatia and Dalmatia, but also managed to associate his state with the powerful political community of European states. The direction of this foreign policy guaranteed a period of peace, prosperity and cultural development. Zvonimir also died without an heir, which triggered a serious dynastic crisis. This was finally resolved when the Croatian nobility signed a treaty with the Hungarian Arpadović dynasty to which Zvonimir's wife Jelena belonged, thus giving rise to a close relationship between Croatia and Hungary. Croatia retained its independence but lost international recognition; the Sabor (parliament), representing the nobility, and the Ban were appointed by the king of Hungary.

The late Middle Ages

THE HUNGARO-CROATIAN UNION

By conquering the towns of Dalmatia, Koloman, the first king of Hungary (1095–1116) to accede to the throne of Croatia and Dalmatia, was able to guarantee the kingdom's territorial unity. But his successors, who ruled from Pannonia, were not strong enough to unite the coastal and inland regions in the long term, all the more so since a new power was emerging in the Adriatic – the Venetian Republic.

By 1205, the Venetians had conquered the entire coast and the islands of Croatia and Dalmatia. In 1358, Louis I of Anjou (1342–82), king of the Hungaro-Croatian kingdom, drove out the Venetians and brought most of the Croatian territories under central European power. In the decades that followed, the coastal towns and inland regions enjoyed a cultural revival. It was the most successful

period for Croatian civilization during the late Middle Ages, and represented a decisive stage in the process of unifying the various Croatian cultural groups. Their differences were overcome by the idea of a union based on tradition and the political experience of the early Middle Ages. However, the Ottoman Turks were gradually gaining ground in central Europe and the Hungarian rulers were neither able to

restrain their great vassal states nor preserve the territorial unity of their kingdom. In the first half of the 15th century, Venice reconquered all Croatian towns except Dubrovnik. The conquest of Bosnia by the Ottomans in 1463 left Croatia directly exposed to the Turkish threat – the division of medieval Croatia began with the terrible defeat of Krbavsko polje (in the Lika, south of Plitvice), in 1493.

42	1301 Charles Robert of	1358 Louis I of Anjou	1463	1527 Habsburgs	1593 Turks are
ongols	Anjou accedes to the	drives out Venetians and	Ottomans	accede to the	defeated at the
er Croatia.	Hungaro-Croatian throne.	unites Croatian states.	invade Bosnia.	Croatian throne.	Battle of Sisak.
	1300	1400		1500	1600

48	1416	1493	1573
e Pope authorizes the	Dubrovnik abolishes	The Croatian defeat at	Peasant revolt in
hop of Senj to officiate in	the slave trade.	Krbavsko polje marks the	northern Croatia.
atian rather than Latin.		beginning of Ottoman rule.	

The 16th century – Croatia divided

After the defeat of the Battle of Mohács (1526), most of Hungary was conquered by Suleyman the Magnificent. With Louis II of Hungary (*above*) killed in battle, the Croatian nobility chose Ferdinand I of Habsburg as king of Croatia to ensure the protection of their kingdom and assert its identity vis-à-vis Hungary. However, this did nothing to halt the Ottoman advance. In spite of fierce resistance from the Croatian army and its victory at the Battle of Sisak in 1593 (*below*), the already diminished kingdom was further reduced. By the end of the 16th century, it was one third of its original size: *reliquiae reliquiarum olim incliti Regni Croatiae* ('the remains of the remains of what was once the glorious kingdom of Croatia'). Because of continued Ottoman attacks, the political center of the kingdom was transferred to the relative safety of the northeast, while endless streams of refugees found sanctuary in central Europe or crossed the Adriatic. In the depopulated areas along the borders of the Ottoman Empire, the Military Frontier was gradually established. The Habsburgs used a system of tax exemption to attract large numbers of Christian refugees, with military experience, fleeing from Ottoman rule. These border areas were also placed outside the jurisdiction of the Croatian Sabor (parliament) and Ban (governor). The first groups of Serbs arrived among these refugees. However, just as Croatia seemed definitively divided between three great powers – the Venetians, the Habsburgs and the Ottomans – Dubrovnik was enjoying its golden age.

The increased power of the republic of Dubrovnik, in the 15th and 16th centuries, was not only due to its economic development but also to its strategic position between the Christian West and Muslim East – an asset that the city used to its advantage. Its independence enabled Dubrovnik to become the most powerful spiritual center in Croatia.

| **1671** The leaders of the nobles' revolt against the Habsburgs are executed. | **1683–99** and **1714–18** Wars are waged successfully against the Ottomans. | **1745** Virovitca, Požega a Srem (Srijem) are annex to Croatia. |

1600   1630   1660   1690   1720

| **1667** Dubrovnik is destroyed by an earthquake | **1700** Pavao Ritter Vitezović publishes *Croatia rediviva*. |

The 17th and 18th centuries – torn between Vienna and Pest

During the 17th century, the Habsburgs tried to impose absolute rule and a centralized state in Croatia. The dissent of the nobility reached its height during a conspiracy led by the heads of the two most powerful Croatian vassal families – the governor, Petar Žrinski, and Fran Krsto Frankopan. When the plot failed and the leaders were executed in 1671, the power of the Croatian aristocracy was broken once and for all by the absolutism of Vienna. Following the siege of Vienna by the Turks, in 1683, the whole of central Europe was drawn into a war of liberation, fueled by the deep social unrest that was undermining the Ottoman Empire. Croatia was finally liberated in the early 18th century and, with a view to persuading the Habsburgs to restore Croatian independence while maintaining the prerogatives of the aristocracy, the Croatian parliament attempted a reconciliation with its Hungarian counterpart. However, Hungarian nationalist ideology, which demanded that there be only one language (Hungarian) and a single nation (Hungary) between the Adriatic and the Carpathians, forced the Croats into siding with Vienna once more. Croatian politics were once again torn between the absolutism of the Habsburgs and the increasing power of Budapest.

The 19th century

THE ILLYRIAN PROVINCES

The expansionist policies of Napoleonic France led to the dissolution of the two great Adriatic commercial republics of Venice and Dubrovnik, and the union of Croatian territories south of the River Sava under the name of the Illyrian Provinces (1809–13). Although short-lived, the experience of this rediscovered unity encouraged national integration. The French government introduced major economic, legal and educational reforms during this period. Following the Treaty of Vienna (1815) (illustrated *above* in an 1815 lithograph by J. Zutz), most Croatian states came under Austro-Hungarian control. However, the Habsburgs, driven above all by their ow dynastic interests, did nothing to bring about the states' administrative unification.

7 The Venetian
Republic is dissolved
Napoleon.

1841 The first
political parties
are founded.

1860
The constitution
is restored.

1868 The Hungaro-
Croatian treaty defines
the status of Croatia.

1780   1810   1840   1870   1900   1915

6 and 1780
Slavonski and Hrvatski
ur codes determine the
us of Croatian peasants.

1809–13
The Illyrian
provinces are
established.

1832
Janko Drašković calls
for Croatian unity in
Disertacija ili Ragovor.

1847
The Sabor declares
Croatian the official
language.

1904
Croatian
Peasant Party
founded.

The Croatian National Revival

Under the leadership of Ljudevit Gaj (1809–72), a new generation of intellectuals founded the movement for the national revival of Croatia, known as Illyrianism (*Illirizam*). They advocated the development of a common literary language that would transcend regional characteristics.

On a political level, the movement aimed to unite all Croatian states and, on a cultural level, to unite all southern Slavs. Inspired by the European revolutionary movements of 1848, the Croatian political powers developed a new program that abolished feudalism, established a representative assembly and demanded the unification of Croatian states. Alarmed by the extremism of the Hungarian national revolution, the Habsburgs looked for support within Croatia and appointed a reformer, Colonel Josip Jelačić (1801–59), to the position of Ban. Since it was impossible to reconcile the objectives pursued by the Hungarian revolution with the survival of Croatia, Jelačić used the army to crush the revolutionaries in Hungary. However, instead of unifying the Croatian states, Vienna imposed its absolutism on both the defeated Hungary and Croatia, as well as suppressing Croatia's political institutions (re-instated in 1860).

THE DUAL MONARCHY OF AUSTRIA-HUNGARY

Because of the nationalist demands within his empire, Franz Josef I (1848–1916) agreed to establish the dual monarchy of Austria-Hungary in 1867, with Dalmatia and Istria remaining in the Austrian half while Croatia, under a Ban, was ceded to Hungary. The economic and political crisis provoked by this division of territory was partly attenuated by the Hungaro-Croatian treaty of 1868. According to the treaty, Croatia retained its autonomy and the Croats, unlike other Slav nations within the Hungarian empire, gained political recognition as a nation in their own right. The territory of the Military Frontier was later reincorporated into Croatia in 1881.

DEADLOCK

Because the constitution of the dual monarchy prevented national union, Croatian politicians were forced to consider other solutions. A number of political parties and movements were formed, all with different ideologies. The National Party (*Narodna stranka*) of Bishop Josip Juraj Strossmayer tried to oppose Vienna and Pest, demanding cultural union for all South Slavs. Ante Starčević (1823–96) and his Croatian Party of Rights, disappointed by the failure of the Illyrianist movement and the proposed treaties, favored the formation of an independent Croatian state. In Dalmatia, those opposed to union with Croatia founded an autonomist movement, asserting the Italian nature of their province. The first Serb parties also emerged, secretly supported by the Serbian Orthodox Church and the kingdom of Serbia, claiming Dalmatia for the Serbs. By the late 19th century, a new generation of politicians had succeeded in forming the Croat-Serb Coalition, thus transcending the differences between the main political powers. However, Vienna and Pest were opposed to their plans for the reorganization of the dual (Austro-Hungarian) monarchy into a new federal monarchy and, in spite of an election victory in 1906, the Coalition faced political failure.

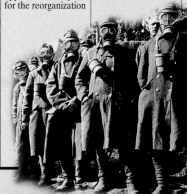

1918 The Kingdom of Serbs, Croats and Slovenes is created under the Karađorđević dynasty.

1929 King Aleksander establishes a dictatorship. Ante Pavelić founds the Ustaše (Rebels)

1941–5 The Independent State of Croatia is li to the Axis powers. The anti-Fascist movement led by the Yugoslav Communist Party.

1915   1925   1935   1945   195

1928 Stjepan Radić is assassinated in the Belgrade parliamentary chamber.

1939 Croat-Serb agreement approves the creation of the Banovina of Croatia.

1945 Croatia forms part of the new Yugoslavia.

The first Yugoslavia (1918–41)

After the start of World War One, the Croats and other dissatisfied Slav states tried to find an alternative solution to the monarchy. The threat of national territory being further fragmented led many politicians to support the idea of a union of South Slav states under the Serbian Karađorđević monarchy. However, at the end of the war (1918) and as an ally of the victors, Serbia was able to impose its own conditions. The Croatian ideal of creating a South Slav state whose members enjoyed equal rights was sidelined in favor of Serbian dominance within the Kingdom of Serbs, Croats and Slovenes. With the dissolution of its Sabor, Croatia lost its legal and political identity after thirteen centuries of history. The new state not only united nations with unequal economic resources, but also with very different historical, religious, cultural and legal traditions. In a bid to resolve the political crisis, the Croats demanded a reorganization of the new union of states that took account of their historical identities. Belgrade responded by imposing a repressive police regime that affected all aspects of public life. The crisis came to a head in 1928 with the assassination of Stjepan Radić, president of the Croation Peasant Party and the champion of federal reorganization. The following year, King Aleksander Karađorđević adopted the name Yugoslavia for the new state and established the 'Sixth of January Dictatorship'. There followed an unprecedented period of military and police repression, and Croatian politics became increasingly radical. Ante Pavelić emigrated and founded a right-wing separatist organization known as the Ustaše (Rebels) who were responsible for the assassination of King Aleksander in Marseilles, in 1943. The Cvetković-Maček Agreement (Sporazum) (1939) – Vlatko Maček was Radić's successor – approved the creation of the Banovina of Croatia, an autonomous Croatian territory within Yugoslavia, which incorporated most of the country's historic territories. However, the agreement (rejected by most Serb politicians) was reached on the eve of World War Two and could not save the Yugoslavia of the Karađorđević monarchy.

JOSIP BROZ, ALIAS TITO
Secretary-general of the Yugoslav Communist Party in 1937, and premier of the Federal Republic of Yugoslavia in 1945, Tito (1892–1980) governed along strictly Communist and national lines. In foreign policy, he distanced himself from the two major East-West political blocs and formed a union of nonaligned states. In economics, he advocated a policy of decentralization. He was elected President of the Republic in 1953 and became president for life when the constitution was revised in 1974, giving greater powers to the six member republics and two provinces.

World War Two

In spring 1941, Yugoslavia was carved up between Germany and her Italian, Bulgarian and Hungarian allies. When Vlatko Maček refused to head a pro-Nazi Croatian state, Zagreb witnessed the instatement of Ante Pavelić, who had the backing of Italy. The leader of the small right-wing Ustaše organization became the 'Polglavnik' (supreme head of the Independent State of Croatia (NDH), which incorporated Croatia and Bosnia-Herzegovina. After decades of Serb terror, there were large numbers of Croats living in this state, even under the aegis of the Axis powers, which were supposed to be the guarantee of their national survival. However, the new puppet government ceded most of Dalmatia to the Italians, introduced racist legislation based on the German model, and made no secret of its intention to eliminate the Serbs by murdering them, converting them to Catholicism or deporting them. Opponents of the regime were murdered en masse in the concentration camps. In June 1941, the first Croatian guerrilla movements were formed. Discontent was rife, stirred up by the outlawed Communist Party of Josip Broz (alias Tito – see right), who formed an armed anti-Fascist resistance movement known as 'the Partisans'. The movement gained strength with the success of the Allied forces in their advances across Europe and, in 1945, the Communists declared Yugoslavia an independent republic and made it a totalitarian state.

ROB NIKADA!

1970 The Croatian Communist Party condemns unitarianism.

1974 New Yugoslav and Croatian constitutions.

1980 Tito dies.

1995 Dayton Accords.

1999 Franjo Tuđman dies.

1965   1975   1985   1995   2005

1967 Declaration on the status of the Serbo-Croatian literary language.

1968 The Socialist Republic of Croatia proposes decentralization of the Yugoslav economy.

1991 Start of the war against Croatia.

1995 Croatian military victories.

Communist Yugoslavia

The single-party regime that repressed all political and ideological opposition attempted to resolve the issue of national identity by imposing a supranational Communist ideology on the six republics – Slovenia, Croatia, Bosnia-Herzegovina, Serbia (including the provinces of Vojvodina and Kosovo), Montenegro and Macedonia. Serbia had the largest population and therefore dominated the government machinery, which led to the gradual 'Serbianization' of the armed forces, police and state bureaucracy. An attempt to redefine the political status of Croatia during a period of crisis within the centralized socialist state ended in failure in 1971. Although it was crushed, the 'Croatian spring' highlighted the inevitability of reforms within the federation. The 1974 constitution, which gave member-states practically equal status, was unable to prevent the progressive break-up of the Yugoslav federation in the years following Tito's death.

End 1991: the Yugoslav army and Serbian militia control 25 percent of Croatia (shelling of Dubrovnik ▲ 235, bombardment of Vukovar ▲ 143). **January 1992:** the international community recognizes Croatian independence.

1992–5: during this period military operations free the occupied territories in southern and central Croatia.

Croatian independence

The economic crisis, unresolved issues of national identity, the erosion of the ideology and the collapse of Communist regimes in Eastern Europe triggered a political crisis in Yugoslavia.

April 22 and May 6, 1990: Franjo Tuđman's Croatian Democratic Union (HDZ) wins a landslide victory in the Croatian national elections and he is proclaimed president.
August 17, 1990: the start of the rebellion by the Krajina Serbs.
December 22, 1990: the Sabor finishes work on a new constitution and declares Franjo Tuđman President of Croatia.
May 19, 1991: a referendum empowers the Croatian parliament to enter into negotiations for a confederation with Yugoslavia or, if these fail, to declare independence.
June 13, 1991: the first overt attacks by the Yugoslav army in Croatia.
June 25, 1991: the Sabor declares Croatian sovereignty and independence, and breaks off administrative and political links with the other Yugoslav republics.

2000: Stjepan Mesic is elected President of Croatia.
2003: Croatia officially applies to become a member of the European Union, and it is predicted that this will happen during the second wave of expansion in 2007.

● The Croatian language

A Southern Slavic language

Croatian, the official language of the Republic of Croatia, belongs to the group of Southern Slavic languages that includes Slovenian, Serbian, Bulgarian and Macedonian. It is written in Roman characters enriched with specific symbols or combinations of letters that have a particular phonetic value. The ethnic minorities (Serbs, Italians, Hungarians, Czechs, Slovaks) can also use their own language within the education sector and certain areas of local administration.

Three dialects

Croatian is divided into three dialects – Chakavian (*čakavski*), Kajkavian (*kajkavski*) and Stokavian (*štokavski*) – based on the three different interrogative pronouns used for 'what?' (*ca?*, *kaj?* and *što?*). Chakavian is spoken in Istria, on all the Adriatic islands north of Korčula and Lastovo, and on a narrow coastal strip that incorporates Senj and then runs from Nin to the mouth of the River Cetina, as well as in the western part of the Pelješac peninsula. Kajkavian is spoken in northern Croatia, around Zagreb, and in certain valleys of the Gorski kotar. Stokavian is spoken in the remaining regions of Croatia, where variations in the pronunciation of the words for 'faith' (*vira*, *vera* and *vjera*) and 'world' (*svit*, *svet* and *svijet*) are used to identify three sub-dialects: Ikavian (*Ikavski*), Ekavian (*Ekavski*) and Ijekavian (*Ijekavski*).

The Stokavian spoken in Slavonia is a mixture of Ikavian and Ekavian, and retains certain archaic features. The majority of Stokavian-speaking Croats use the Ikavian or Ijekavian dialects, with only a tiny minority speaking the Ekavian variant. In the 19th century, the Ijekavian variant of the Stokavian dialect was chosen as the standard form of the Croatian language.

ALPHABET AND PRONUNCIATION

The Croatian Roman alphabet has thirty letters, including three digraphs – *dz* (pronounced 'j' as in 'jungle'), *lj* ('lyeu' as in 'milieu') and *nj* ('gn') – and five letters with diacritical marks – *č* ('ch' as in 'choose'), *ć* ('ch' as in the Spanish *chico*), *đ* ('g' as in the Italian *giglio*), *š* ('sh') and *ž* ('j').

CONSONANTS: *q*, *w* and *x* are only used for foreign names; *c* is pronounced as 'ts' and *j* as 'y'; *b* is aspirate and *s* is always unvoiced.

VOWELS: *e* is pronounced as in 'egg', *u* as 'ou' (in 'you'), while *y* does not exist in Croatian words. Each letter is given more or less the same value, and there are no silent vowels.

- Kajkavian
- Chakavian
- Štokavian-Ikavian
- Štokavian-Ijekavian
- Štokavian-Ekavian
- Štokavian-Slavonian

STRESS
The stress can placed on any syllable, although rarely on the last. Placed at the beginning of a word, it is combined with a falling or rising pitch, which gives rise to tonic accents: short falling, long falling, short rising, long rising (˘ ̄ ˊ ˋ). When the stress is placed on the middle syllables, it is always rising.

Religious literature

When they had settled in Croatia (7th and 8th centuries) and converted to Christianity, the Croats adopted Latin as their religious language. In the 10th century, religious texts in Paleo-Slavonic (or Old Church Slavonic), written in 'square' Glagolitic characters ● 40 also appeared in Istria, on some islands in the northern Adriatic and in parts of inland Dalmatia. In the 11th century, it incorporated elements of the vernacular and gave rise to Croatian Old Church Slavonic. In southern Dalmatia, however, Old Church Slavonic and

vernacular Croatian were written using a Cyrillic script known as 'Bosniak' (*bosančica*) or 'Croatian script' (*harvatsko pismo*). The Croats were the only European Catholics to be authorized by Rome to use a language and script other than Latin for religious purposes. Thus, in the Middle Ages, religious literature was written in three languages (Croatian Old Church Slavonic, Old Church Slavonic and Latin) and three types of script (Latin, Glagolitic and Cyrillic). The Latin (or Roman) alphabet, which was used from the 14th century

onward for texts written in the vernacular, soon superseded the two Slavic alphabets. Even

so, the Glagolitic script, used by the Church, and *bosančica* survived until the 19th century.

A long-lasting reform

During the Counter-Reformation of the late 16th and early 17th centuries, attempts were made to create a common literary language. However, it was not until the 19th century and the Croatian National Revival that the Ijekavian variant of Stokavian was adopted as the

common written language. Despite persistent efforts to 'Germanicize' and 'Magyarize' the language in the 19th century, and the systematic 'Serbianization' carried out in the twentieth, the Croatian language retained its specific characteristics.

Secular literature

The Croats also adopted Latin as their administrative and scholarly language and, between the 15th and 18th centuries, produced numerous scientific and literary texts in Latin (by Marko Marulić, Antun Vrančić, Ilija Crijević and Rušer Bošković, among others). In 1847, Ivan Kukuljević Sakcinski delivered one of the first speeches in Croation to the Sabor and, in the same year, Croatia – one of the last European states to abandon Latin – chose Croatian as its official language. Popular literature was initially written in one of the three Croatian dialects – Chakavian (used by the poets Petar Hectorović in Hvar, and Marko Marulić in Split, and the novelist Petar Zoranić in Zadar), Stokavian (used in the

remarkable Ragusan literature of the late 15th–18th centuries, as well as by the playwright Marin Držić and the poet Ivan Gundulić), and Kajkavian.

● The Glagolitic script

In Croatia, the rectangle replaced the circle, giving rise to the Glagolitic ('square' or Croatian) alphabet.

The Glagolitic alphabet is thought to have been invented in the 9th century by the missionaries Saint Cyril and his brother Saint Methodius for translating the Bible from Greek into Old Church Slavonic and for preaching to the Moravian Slavs. They incorporated Christian symbols – the circle, representing divine perfection, the triangle (the Holy Trinity) and the cross (suffering). The script, which was either never used in other Slav countries or at least only until the 13th century, remained dominant in Croatia until the late 15th century and even continued to be used in certain religious communities in Dalmatia and Istria until the 19th century.

THE GLAGOLITIC SCRIPT AND CROATIAN CULTURE

The oldest surviving Croatian Glagolitic texts date from the 11th century. Most are engraved in stone, like the one on the Baška tablet (Bašćanska ploca), c. 1100 (*below*). The tablet is remarkable for its dimensions and the importance of the text, which makes the first mention of a Croatian king in the Croatian language.

THE GLAGOLITIC SCRIPT AND ROMAN CATHOLICISM

When they converted to Christianity, the Croats used Old Church Slavonic and the Glagolitic script for religious literature, whereas Orthodox Slavs used the Cyrillic script. The Croats were the only European Catholics exempted by Rome from using Latin or the Roman alphabet. They printed their first missal in Glagolitic script in 1483 (*right*).

Arts and traditions

Music and dance, *42*
Traditional costumes, *44*
Rural life in eastern Croatia, *46*
Peasant fishermen, *48*
Food: 'Štrukli', *50*
Croatian specialties, *52*

● Music and dance

Tambura (left).
Gusle, stringed instruments played with a bow, are
used to accompany epic songs in the Dinaric Alps.

Croatia's traditional music and dance are characterized
by very different styles of execution, an extremely varied
repertoire and a wide range of different wind and stringed
instruments. This diversity is the result of the country's
turbulent history, its geographical position at the crossroads
of central Europe, the Mediterranean and the Balkans,
and the different ways of life in its various regions. While
music and dance accompany religious celebrations and
traditional festivals, they are also an important part of
everyday life. Today, folk festivals play a key role in the
preservation and revival of Croatia's cultural heritage.

THE 'TAMBURA'

The *tambura*, a lute-like stringed
instrument that is plucked or
strummed, was introduced by the Ottoman
Turks in the 14th and 15th centuries. In the
19th century, *tambura* orchestras made up
of instruments of varying sizes, shapes and
pitches were formed in Slavonia, then in other
regions and, later, within Croatian émigré
communities. As the principal musical symbol
of national identity, the *tambura* is today the
most widely played instrument in both popular
and highbrow traditional music. An annual
tambura festival has been held in Osijek
since 1961.

THE 'LIRICA' OR 'LIJERICA'

The *lirica* (*lijerica*), a stringed instrument
played with a bow, is an early form of violin.

Typical of southern
Dalmatia, it is played
by a seated musician
who taps out the
dance rhythm with
his foot.

THE 'SOPILA' OR 'ROŽENICA'

This oboe-like instrument is typical of Istria and the Kvarner region. It is always played in pairs – one large and one small *sopila*.

THE 'VRLIČKO KOLO' (*above*)

This typical dance from the Dinaric Alps begins with very slow movements accompanied by a type of singing known as *ojkavica* (beginning with vocal vibrations on the syllable 'oy'). Then the singing stops and the dance gathers speed. Couples break away from the circle (*kolo*) to perform a movement known as the *skoči gori* ('jumping in the air') in which the dancers lift their partner off the ground and then jump themselves – the final part of the movement is known as *u letu* ('in flight'). The various forms of *ojkavica* are also typical of the Dinaric Alps.

THE 'SLAVONSKO KOLO'

When it comes to folk music and dance, Slavonia, Baranja and Srem share the same traditions. The *bećarac*, a rousing song accompanied by *tambura*, is the 'national anthem' of these three regions. The *Slavonsko kolo* is characterized by a series of slow sung movements alternating with rapid dance movements. The dance is sometimes accompanied by a type of bagpipe with two pipes and a single mouthpiece – revived since 1990 – or a solo *tambura* (*samica*), but more usually a *tambura* orchestra.

A TRADITIONAL REVIVAL

The movement for the revival of regional music and dance traditions began in the 1920s. It concentrates on amateur folklore groups and organizes festivals, the most important being the International Folklore Festival, held in Zagreb in late July. The Klapa Festival (for male-voice choirs) held in Omiš in July, successfully combines tradition and modernity.

● Traditional costumes

TRADITIONAL SANDALS
These traditional sandals, which are extremely soft and supple, are made by hand from fine strips of leather.

Traditional costume was still worn in rural areas until the early 20th century. The basic materials – linen, woolen fabrics and coarse cotton – were still produced within the context of the rural economy and nearly all peasant women were skilled in the art of embroidery and lace-making. Different natural environments, economic conditions and historical events led to the development of three types of costume – the Adriatic style of the coastal region and islands, the Dinaric style worn in the central mountains, and the Pannonian style from the plains of northern Croatia – although there were many local and regional variations. Traditional costume is no longer a part of everyday life but is still worn at festivals, where it is a symbol of regional identity.

THE ADRIATIC STYLE

In summer, the women wore a Renaissance-style cotton blouse with a pleated skirt of hand-made wool. In winter, this was replaced by a sheepskin skirt with the fleece worn on the inside. On their heads, women wore a long, narrow scarf which was tied differently, depending on whether they were married, widowed or in mourning. The Mediterranean connection is reflected in the men's costume – long, wide trousers and a long cotton hat reaching to the shoulders.

THE DINARIC STYLE (FOR MEN) IN THE SINJ REGION
On special occasions, the men wore a jacket embroidered with a row of silver hemispheres, disks and rings. Ceremonial weapons – a short rifle and cutlass – hang from their broad leather-and-wool belts. Each year, young men dressed in national costume take part in a traditional contest – *Sinjska alka* ('the ring of Sinj') ▲ 212 – held in the region.

In the mountain regions of central Croatia, girls would wear a red beret, while the women wore a white scarf.

THE DINARIC STYLE (FOR WOMEN)
Apart from the coarse cotton blouse, the rest of the clothes tended to be made of wool, hand-spun by the women and colored with natural dyes before being woven or knitted.
The costume was usually set off by a silver necklace.

THE PANNONIAN STYLE
The costume for both men and women was mainly made of cotton, often decorated with red, blue or black embroidery, depending on the function of the garment. Festival costumes in the Dakovo region are embroidered with gold thread, which looks even more spectacular when set against the black velvet of the women's shawls and men's jackets. The Posavina region is renowned for an excellent quality linen used to make fine fabrics that are often embroidered.

EMBROIDERY
As well as geometric and floral designs, weavers, especially in northeastern Croatia, favor stylized animal designs on wool, and they work on cotton as well as linen fabrics.

RED
The color red had a symbolic and magical significance. In Croatian popular mythology, red is the color of youth and health.

● Rural life in eastern Croatia

Northern Croatia is a region of vast, fertile plains dotted with forests and crossed by slow-flowing rivers – the Danube, Drava and Sava. It is a natural environment that favors extensive and extremely diverse types of agriculture, from the cultivation of cereals (such as wheat and maize) and oleaginous crops (sunflowers) to the rearing of pigs, cattle and horses. The inhabitants are very attached to the land, which generously rewards the time and effort invested in its cultivation. This relative wealth can be seen in the region's costumes, jewelry, food and interior décors. It is also reflected in a tradition of warmth and hospitality and the lavish celebration of weddings and family and religious festivals.

INNER BEING

The code of politeness observed by the inhabitants of eastern Croatia in their everyday lives is deeply rooted in a tradition of hospitali[ty] and based on mutual respect. These principles imbue thei[r] approach to the worl[d] and life in general.

OUTWARD APPEARANCE

The peasants of Slavonia and Srem like their clothes to reflect their wealth, which is why many of the costumes worn by young women and girls are decorated with valuable accessories. Sequins are extremely popular and are worn as earrings or around the neck. When worn as a necklace, they ar[e] linked by threads which are usually red sometimes yellow. Tradition requires that, on the day of her wedding, a young bride's costume mus[t] be decorated with sequins.

DECORATION

Over the centuries, the imagination and creativity of the peasants of eastern Croatia have given rise to an unusual form of artistic expression, based on the decoration of everyday objects. As well as woodwork and textiles ● *44*, the Slavonians have always decorated gourds (squashes). This is done in three stages – carving the designs, coating the gourds in acetic acid, and coloring the surface brown by heating over a naked flame. Some gourds are inlaid with pewter or silver. This art is still practiced today in the regions around Županja and Vinkovci.

SUMMER, HARVEST

In summer, harvest is still the central event of village life. In the past, the men scythed the cereal crops and the women gathered them together and tied them in sheaves. While they worked, they sang songs composed by farmers.

AUTUMN, SMOKING MEAT

The fat, black pigs of Slavonia are usually killed in late November's *svinokolja* (pig slaughter). Most of the meat is preserved as hams, sausages, blood sausage and above all *kulen* (spicy paprika sausage), and hung inside the house or smokehouse (*right*).

AUTUMN, DISTILLING 'RAKIJA'

Each family has at least one plum tree whose fruit is used to make the sweet plum brandy known as *meka rakija* after the first distillation, and the stronger *prepečenica* when re-distilled.

WINTER, WOMEN'S WORK

On winter evenings, the women gather in small groups, in a different house each evening, to spin, weave, sew, embroider and clean the feathers used to fill pillows and eiderdowns.

Today, many of the men from the Adriatic coast and islands sail the seas of the world before returning home to end their days.

Legend has it that, in the distant past, the Croats decided to leave their homeland in the Carpathian Mountains and migrated westward to the land of orange and lemon trees that bordered the Adriatic. Their god Perun, overseer of right and order, helped them by lighting their way. They overcame the aridity of the soil and enjoyed the rich bounty of the sea, and life for the inhabitants of the Adriatic coast continued to be divided between agriculture and fishing for centuries. Over the ages, their constant battle against nature has produced a determined and hospitable people.

FISHERMEN
The bounty of the Adriatic enriched the life of the region's farmers who, after a hard day's toil on the land, used to go fishing with nets they dyed and mended themselves, and hoop nets made from woven branches. In the past, Adriatic fishermen used boats powered by oars (*gajeta*) or sails (*leut*) and usually caught mackerel. Today, the fishermen from the island of Ugljan ▲ 198 fish on the open sea.

SAILORS
The hardships endured by sailors, depicted in popular songs, have not deterred many young men from choosing a life at sea. Over the centuries, myth and reality have become merged in the collective memory.

Peasant fishermen

SHEPHERDS

For Croatians living on the islands and along the Adriatic coast, sheep represent an additional resource. They graze on rocky terrain, feeding on the aromatic plants that give their flesh and milk a very distinctive flavor ● 52. In June and July, shepherds shear their sheep using a technique dating from ancient times. The skins are tanned and used to make clothing and blankets, while the spun and woven (or knitted) wool makes a valuable contribution to the local economy ● 44.

MEN IN SHEEP'S CLOTHING

Between Epiphany and Whitsuntide, the entire coast of Croatia celebrates a pre-Lenten carnival (*karneval*). The trial of the 'carnival king' (a dummy) offers an opportunity to settle the past year's grievances and comment on political and social life. Some carnival practices reflect ancient rites and beliefs, like the strange *zvončari* ('ringers') from the villages around Rijeka ▲ 175 – groups of men wearing sheepskins who walk in step waving clubs and ringing bells to ward off evil spirits.

WINE-GROWERS

In spite of the stony soil, the patient efforts of the wine-growers and the region's dry summers produce some excellent grapes. Once they have been harvested, the grapes are trodden and the must is stored in barrels that have been rinsed in sea water. According to legend, this is the only water that will clean and purify them.

Croatia has at least two gastronomic traditions. Along the Adriatic coast, the food has a distinctly Mediterranean flavor, with grilled and poached fish occupying pride of place. *Pršut* (smoke-cured ham) served with goat's cheese and olives is a favorite hors d'oeuvre. Further inland, the food is influenced by Hungarian, Austrian and eastern traditions. Cooked meats (*kulen*, *krvavica*) are extremely popular, while potatoes and cabbage (sometimes pickled as in days gone by) are very much in evidence. The recipe for *štrukli*, which can be eaten as a sweet or savory dish, comes from the Hrvatsko Zagorje.

INGREDIENTS (SERVES 6–8)

FOR THE PASTRY: 1 lb (500g) plain white flour, a good pinch of salt, 1 egg, 1 tablespoon oil, 1 tablespoon mild vinegar, a little warm water, a knob of butter.

FOR THE FILLING: 3½–5½oz (100–150g) butter 1lb 4oz (600g) cream cheese, 4 eggs, salt, 4floz (10cl) sour cream.

FOR THE TOPPING: crème fraîche.

1. Heap the flour onto a pastry board, make a depression in the center and add the salt, egg and most of the oil. Gradually mix in the flour with a knife.

2. Add the water and vinegar, a little at a time mixing well in and then kneading the dough with your hands until it is nice and smooth.

3. Divide the dough into three balls, coat with oil and cover each with a warm bowl. Leave to rise for 30 minutes.

4. To make the filling, whisk the softened butter together with the cream cheese and eggs (beaten with a little salt). When the mixture is smooth and light, add the sour cream.

Spread a clean tea towel on a flat surface, sprinkle with flour and roll out one of the balls of dough. Stretch the dough even more with your hands so that it becomes very fine. Trim off any thick edges to make a rectangle. Leave to dry for 5–10 minutes.

6. Dot with a little melted butter and spread one third of the filling lengthwise over half the dough. Then roll the dough, starting from the side covered with filling, using the tea towel – the dough is so fine, it will break up in your hands.

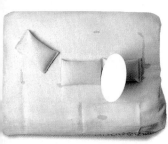

Press the handle of a wooden spoon into the rolled dough at 4-inch (10cm) intervals to make small sausage shapes. Then cut cleanly with the edge of a plate and seal the dough at both ends of each 'sausage'. Repeat the process with the other balls of dough.

8. Plunge the *štrukli* into a pan of boiling salted water for 10–15 minutes and then remove with a slotted spoon.

10. Serve piping hot.

Arrange the *štrukli* in an ovenproof dish, cover generously with crème fraîche and cook in a preheated oven at 350°–400°F/180°–200°C/Gas Mark 4–6, for about 20 minutes.

● Croatian specialties

In Dalmatia, *pršut* – a delicious smoke-cured ham – is a treat not to be missed.

COOKED MEATS

Pork occupies pride of place in Croatian cuisine and Slavonia is famous for its cooked meats. In autumn, the black pigs raised in the region are allowed to roam free in the oak forests to feed on the acorns that give their flesh its delicious flavor. Hams, sausages, blood sausage and *kulen* (spicy paprika sausage) are made and smoked according to traditional methods ● 47.

'PAŠKI SIR'

This ewe's-milk cheese from the island of Pa ▲ 188 is Croatia's best-known cheese. The island's salt-meadow lamb is also considered the best in the country. Both these products owe their distinctive flavor to the Bura, a col northeasterly wind that blows across the Velebitski kanal (Velebit strait), carrying salt to the scrubland on which the sheep graze.

SOUP

In Croatia, meals usually start with a lightly spiced vegetable soup, which may also contain meat or fish.

LIQUEURS

Local spirits include *maraskino* ▲ 193, a clear liqueur (25 percent proof) made from bitter cherries known as *marascas*, and *travarica*, a herb brandy with medicinal properties.

WINE

The vineyards of Istria and Dalmatia, on the Adriatic coast, often produce richly colored, full-bodied wines such as *postup* (red) and *pošip* (white). Further inland, wine-producin centers such as Plješivica, Vinica and Varažd produce lighter wines. Slavonia (Kutjevo, Erdut, Ilok) is famous for its white wines.

ESSENTIAL INGREDIENTS

Olive oil, wine vinegar, red peppers and various spices a all used to enhance the flavor of tl region's dishe

Architecture

Ancient architecture, *54*

Pre-Romanesque architecture, *58*

Romanesque architecture, *60*

Renaissance architecture, *62*

The villas of Dubrovnik, *64*

Baroque architecture, *66*

Rural architecture, *68*

From Neoclassicism to
  Modernism, *70*

● Ancient architecture

The first urban centers began to appear in the 4th century BC. Colonies such as Issa and Pharos were instrumental in the diffusion of Greek civilization throughout Croatia, as the population gradually adopted the innovations – writing, minted coins, trade, urban planning and fortifications – introduced by the Greeks. Architecture was at its height during the Roman period, with the construction of a dense road network, a great many public buildings (amphitheaters, triumphal arches, temples, baths) and the infrastructures required for urban living (fortifications, drainage, aqueducts). Villas and rural estates sprang up, especially along the Adriatic coast. Law and order was maintained by the legions, while military camps guarded the national frontiers.

PLAN OF ROMAN JADERA ▲ *190*
The Romanization of the regions that are now Croatia was at its height during the Empire. Some cities – for example Salona (Solin) ▲ *210*, capital of the Roman province – have an even older urban structure. In Zadar, traces of the Roman plan (*ager*) of Jadera (*right*) are still clearly visible. For example, the perpendicular network of centuries (voting divisions) that lay behind the Roman town today lie within the modern town of Zadar.

PLAN OF PHAROS ▲ *230*
The Syracusan colony of Issa ▲ *232* (on present-day Vis) and Pharos (*left*, on Hvar), a dependency of the Aegean island of Paros, were founded in the 4th century BC. They were the largest Greek settlements on the Croatian coast and fine examples of Greek urban development. The streets intersected at right angles and the city was protected by fortifications. Traces of the Greek plan can still be seen in the fields around Pharos, present-day Stari Grad.

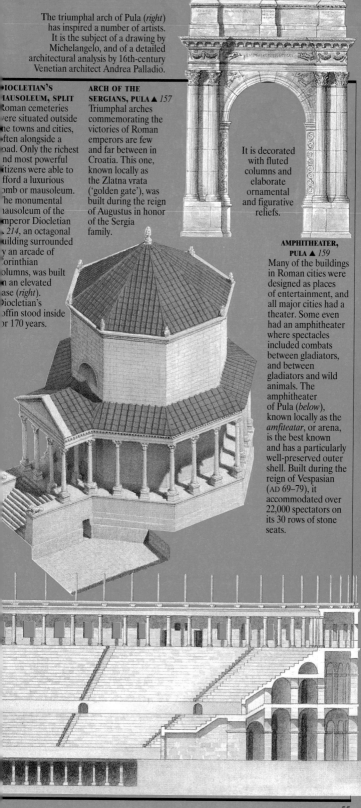

The triumphal arch of Pula (*right*) has inspired a number of artists. It is the subject of a drawing by Michelangelo, and of a detailed architectural analysis by 16th-century Venetian architect Andrea Palladio.

DIOCLETIAN'S MAUSOLEUM, SPLIT
Roman cemeteries were situated outside the towns and cities, often alongside a road. Only the richest and most powerful citizens were able to afford a luxurious tomb or mausoleum. The monumental mausoleum of the emperor Diocletian ▲ 214, an octagonal building surrounded by an arcade of Corinthian columns, was built on an elevated base (*right*). Diocletian's coffin stood inside for 170 years.

ARCH OF THE SERGIANS, PULA ▲ 157
Triumphal arches commemorating the victories of Roman emperors are few and far between in Croatia. This one, known locally as the Zlatna vrata ('golden gate'), was built during the reign of Augustus in honor of the Sergia family.

It is decorated with fluted columns and elaborate ornamental and figurative reliefs.

AMPHITHEATER, PULA ▲ 159
Many of the buildings in Roman cities were designed as places of entertainment, and all major cities had a theater. Some even had an amphitheater where spectacles included combats between gladiators, and between gladiators and wild animals. The amphitheater of Pula (*below*), known locally as the *amfiteatar*, or arena, is the best known and has a particularly well-preserved outer shell. Built during the reign of Vespasian (AD 69–79), it accommodated over 22,000 spectators on its 30 rows of stone seats.

● Ancient architecture

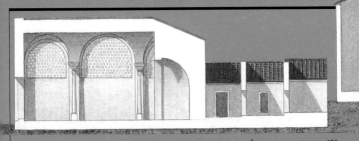

FORUM AND BATHS AT AQUAE JASAE, PRESENT-DAY VARAŽDINSKE TOPLICE ▲ 128

The development of towns and cities was based on the principles of Roman architecture. In the major urban centers, which were often fortified, all public events took place in the main square or forum. As the hub of the city's political, cultural and religious life, it was surrounded by such public buildings as temples, baths and markets. The road networks were carefully planned, as were the water and drainage systems. Most of the buildings on the Adriatic coast were constructed in stone, whereas brick was used in Pannonia. In the spa town of Aquae Jasae, the forum (*above*) was bounded by an arcaded portico, temples, baths and a basilica built during the reign of Constantine.

BRIJUNI, VERIGE ▲ 1(

The Romans built a great many villas, wit their adjoining outbuildings, througho Croatia. While most were modest, som were really luxurious – fo example, the villa built in the 1 century AD on the island Veli Brijun, and the palace bu during the late Classical period Polace, on the island of Mljet ▲ 25 The villa complex of Veliki Brijun has residential part, with temples, baths and palestra, and buildings devoted to econom and port activities (*see plan below*

METICULOUS CONSTRUCTION
The *cella* comprises a coffered barrel vault and projecting cornice. Its decorative reliefs influenced the sculptors of Split during the Middle Ages, and the Renaissance masters working in Trogir.

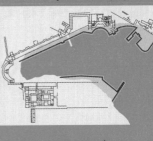

DIOCLETIAN'S SMALL TEMPLE, SPLIT ▲ 214
Temples dedicated to Roman gods and local deities were built both insid and outside the towns. This small, rectangular temple in Diocletian's Palace is both tetrastyle (it has four frontal columns) and prostyle (there is a row of freestanding columns at th rear) in design. It was built using large, freestone blocks and has a richly decorat *cella* and portal.

Diocletian's Small Temple, Split.

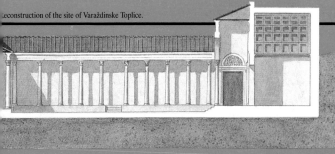

Reconstruction of the site of Varaždinske Toplice.

MILITARY CAMPS

The army played a key role in the Romanization of the region and in the construction of a high-quality road network linking the major towns and cities of Dalmatia and Pannonia. Military camps were rectangular, with entrances and roads set at right angles. Their fortifications were strengthened by towers and often surrounded by defensive earthworks and ditches. Inside were the military accommodation and outbuildings. If Diocletian's Palace ▲ 216 has some of these features, it is because this fortified villa was designed as an imperial residence and a venue for official ceremonies.

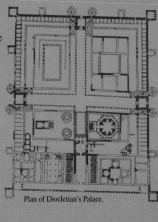

Plan of Diocletian's Palace.

Reconstruction of the site of Marusinac.

MARUSINAC, SALONA ▲ 210

The Paleochristian buildings of Marusinac, one of the necropolises of Salona (Solin), date from the 5th century AD. Two basilicas have been discovered, one of which appears to have had a central nave open to the sky. The architectural style of the mausoleum that housed the body of the Christian martyr, Saint Anastasius of Aquileia, influenced subsequent constructions in the region. However, the best-preserved religious building in Croatia is the famous Basilica of Euphrasius in Poreč ▲ 168.

Pre-Romanesque architecture

Because it lay on the borders of the Carolingian and Byzantine empires, Croatia has an extremely diverse body of pre-Romanesque architecture. The oriental influence, which dominates in the southern provinces and coastal towns, is reflected in centralized plans, sometimes combined with an axial plan and walls punctuated by lesenes. In Istria and the kingdom of Croatia, the Carolingian influence is expressed via the monumental, triple-apse churches, while rounded buttresses attest to the practice of large-span vaulting, which was rare in Europe during the early Middle Ages.

Above, plans of:
1. St Michael
2. St Cecilia
3. St Savior
4. Brnaze
5. St Donat

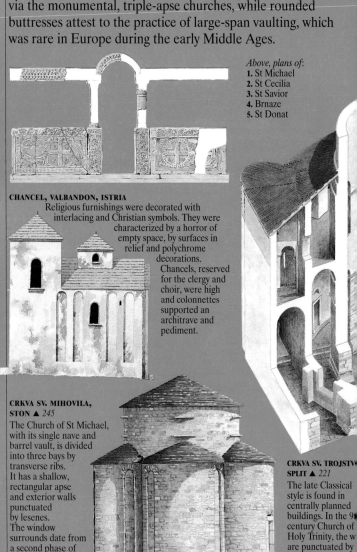

CHANCEL, VALBANDON, ISTRIA

Religious furnishings were decorated with interlacing and Christian symbols. They were characterized by a horror of empty space, by surfaces in relief and polychrome decorations. Chancels, reserved for the clergy and choir, were high and colonnettes supported an architrave and pediment.

CRKVA SV. MIHOVILA, STON ▲ 245

The Church of St Michael, with its single nave and barrel vault, is divided into three bays by transverse ribs. It has a shallow, rectangular apse and exterior walls punctuated by lesenes. The window surrounds date from a second phase of construction, as do the frescos of the interior (11th century).

CRKVA SV. TROJSTV● SPLIT ▲ 221

The late Classical style is found in centrally planned buildings. In the 9● century Church of Holy Trinity, the w● are punctuated by shallow niches and lesenes. At the eas● end, the chevet is formed by three a●

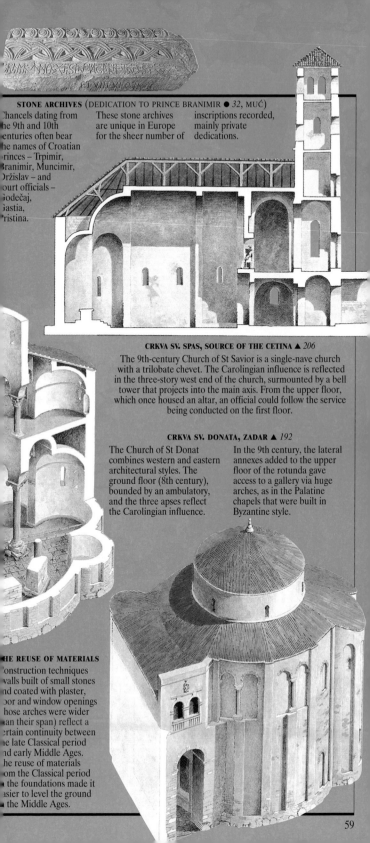

Chancels dating from the 9th and 10th centuries often bear the names of Croatian princes – Trpimir, Branimir, Muncimir, Držislav – and court officials – Godečaj, Gastia, Pristina.

These stone archives are unique in Europe for the sheer number of inscriptions recorded, mainly private dedications.

CRKVA SV. SPAS, SOURCE OF THE CETINA ▲ 206

The 9th-century Church of St Savior is a single-nave church with a trilobate chevet. The Carolingian influence is reflected in the three-story west end of the church, surmounted by a bell tower that projects into the main axis. From the upper floor, which once housed an altar, an official could follow the service being conducted on the first floor.

CRKVA SV. DONATA, ZADAR ▲ 192

The Church of St Donat combines western and eastern architectural styles. The ground floor (8th century), bounded by an ambulatory, and the three apses reflect the Carolingian influence.

In the 9th century, the lateral annexes added to the upper floor of the rotunda gave access to a gallery via huge arches, as in the Palatine chapels that were built in Byzantine style.

THE REUSE OF MATERIALS

Construction techniques – walls built of small stones and coated with plaster, door and window openings whose arches were wider than their span) reflect a certain continuity between the late Classical period and early Middle Ages. The reuse of materials from the Classical period in the foundations made it easier to level the ground in the Middle Ages.

● Romanesque architecture

Chancels in early Romanesque style are dominated by figurative scenes – the life of Christ, the Madonna in Glory, Croatian princes (*right*).

Croatia's Romanesque architecture is extremely diverse, subject to both new Italian influences and the local pre-Romanesque tradition. The 12th century was characterized by the reconstruction of the Paleochristian cathedrals along the Adriatic coast. Campaniles, churches with a single nave and façade bell tower, or a double apse, and triple-nave basilicas began to appear, all influenced by the architectural trends of Apulia, Lombardy, Tuscany and Venezia.

CRKVA SV. MARTIN, LOVREČ, ISTRIA
The 11th-century Church of St Martin is a triple-nave church in early Romanesque style, with smooth exterior walls and apses decorated with shallow niches. Columns with Corinthian capitals attest to the Venetian influence.

CRKVA SV. MARIJE, MLJET ▲ 250
The proportions of this single-nave Church of St Mary, with its three bays, are designed with great harmony. The central bay is surmounted by an oval dome, and the three-story chancel has a single apse. The triple-arched triumphal arch is reminiscent of the imperial palaces of the late Classical period and show Apulian influence.

KATEDRALA SV. STOŠIJE, ZADAR ▲ 192
In the 12th century, a triple-nave crypt and raised chancel were built in the Paleochristian Cathedral of St Anastasia. Columns and pillars with clusters of colonnettes punctuate the central nave and reflect the northern Italian (Tuscan) influence. In the 13th century, two bays were added and a new façade was constructed in the style of Pisan and Tuscan churches.

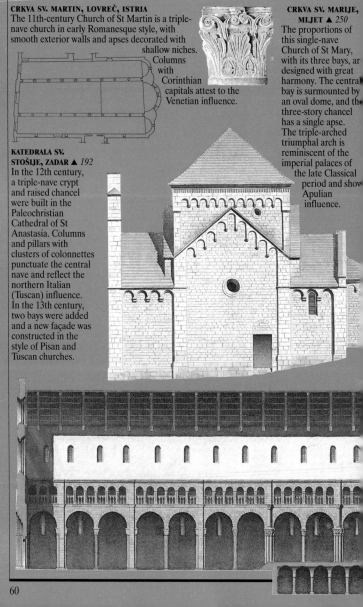

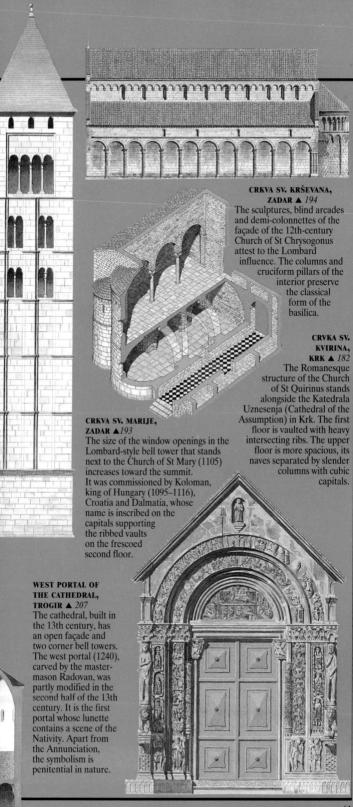

CRKVA SV. KRŠEVANA, ZADAR ▲ *194*
The sculptures, blind arcades and demi-colonnettes of the façade of the 12th-century Church of St Chrysogonus attest to the Lombard influence. The columns and cruciform pillars of the interior preserve the classical form of the basilica.

CRVKA SV. KVIRINA, KRK ▲ *182*
The Romanesque structure of the Church of St Quirinus stands alongside the Katedrala Uznesenja (Cathedral of the Assumption) in Krk. The first floor is vaulted with heavy intersecting ribs. The upper floor is more spacious, its naves separated by slender columns with cubic capitals.

CRKVA SV. MARIJE, ZADAR ▲ *193*
The size of the window openings in the Lombard-style bell tower that stands next to the Church of St Mary (1105) increases toward the summit. It was commissioned by Koloman, king of Hungary (1095–1116), Croatia and Dalmatia, whose name is inscribed on the capitals supporting the ribbed vaults on the frescoed second floor.

WEST PORTAL OF THE CATHEDRAL, TROGIR ▲ *207*
The cathedral, built in the 13th century, has an open façade and two corner bell towers. The west portal (1240), carved by the master-mason Radovan, was partly modified in the second half of the 13th century. It is the first portal whose lunette contains a scene of the Nativity. Apart from the Annunciation, the symbolism is penitential in nature.

● Renaissance architecture

KARLOVAC, THE IDEAL TOWN ▲ *137*
In 1579, Archduke Charles of Austria ordered the fortress of Karlovac to be built at the confluence of the Kupa and Korana rivers to guard against Ottoman attacks. The six-pointed-star layout was devised by theoreticians of Renaissance architecture as the plan for an ideal town.

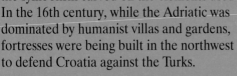

In the 15th century, the Renaissance in Croatia was characterized by the Dalmatian school of architecture. Its main principles were integrity of materials (the use of the same stone for the exterior and interior, the absence of polychrome), a method for assembling stone blocks without mortar, and unity of the architecture and the symbolism carved on the elements used in its construction. In the 16th century, while the Adriatic was dominated by humanist villas and gardens, fortresses were being built in the northwest to defend Croatia against the Turks.

KATEDRALA SV. JAKOVA, ŠIBENIK ▲ *202*
The Cathedral of St James was originally designed as a triple-nave Gothic Renaissance basilica. In 1441, a new architect, Juraj Dalmatinac, added the transept, the three polygonal apses decorated with recessed niches and the dome with its octagonal drum. He built the quatrefoil baptistery beneath the south apse and the adjoining sacristy set on pillars. He devised a new method, borrowed from carpentry, for assembling stone blocks without the use of mortar. It involved inserting pre-cut blocks into transverse ribs by means of tongue-and-groove joints. He created the copings of 72 sculpted human heads, in the manner of a portrait gallery. On his death (1475), his apprentice Nikola Firentinac ('Nicholas of Florence') finished the upper part of the cathedral (vaults, roof and dome).

KAPELA SV. IVANA TROGIRSKOG, TROGIR ▲ *207*
St John of Trogir's Chapel (1468–82) was built in stone using the Dalmatinac method, by Nikola Firentinac and Andrija Aleši. The niches with their life-size sculptures are reminiscent of Classical mausoleums. The symbolism of the reliefs is an integral part of the architecture and expressed the triumph of humanism during the first Renaissance.

SPONZA PALACE, DUBROVNIK ▲ 238
This regional style is not so much a pastiche as a creative synthesis of forms in which the façade is used to reflect function. Thus, the first floor of the former customs house and mint has broad Renaissance arcades to accommodate pedestrians, the windows of the second-floor reception rooms are in Flamboyant Gothic style, while the windows of the third floor offices are in simple Renaissance style.

The Cathedral of St James in Šibenik is the only stone building in Europe built without the use of mortar.

VELIKI TABOR ▲ 122
While villas ● 64 sprang up along the Adriatic coast, Renaissance architecture in the northwest took a more defensive form. In the 16th century, fortresses – predominately square with circular angle towers – were built between Cakovec and Senj to protect Croatia against Ottoman incursions. The fortress of Veliki Tabor (c.1505) has five monumental semicircular towers and three levels of well-proportioned Tuscan arcades overlooking an elliptical courtyard.

The villas of Dubrovnik

Decorated capitals of
the Villa Crijević-Pucić.

In the 14th century, elegant villas of modest dimensions began to appear along the coast and on the islands around Dubrovnik, at the time the only independent region in Dalmatia. The merchant classes were fascinated by the Classical image of the villa, the favorite retreat of educated Greeks and Romans. The style of these country residences became clearly defined in the 15th century – a walled garden, an L-shaped building and a blend of Gothic and Renaissance styles. The best examples are the villas built by the merchants of the then city-state of Ragusa, under the humanist influence of the late 15th and early 16th centuries.

AN ARCHITECTURAL GARDEN

Jasmine and vines scramble over the pergolas shading the intersecting pathways that divide this walled garden. The compartments thus formed are bounded by small freestone walls, filled with earth (often brought by sea) and planted with orange, lemon and other fruit trees. The pathways are paved or cobbled.

STONE FURNISHINGS

The degree of decoration was indicative of function, with basin-fountains, fireplaces and niches among the most richly decorated pieces. Basin-fountains were often placed next to a water cistern and the precious liquid was channeled directly through special conduits.

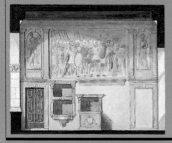

PORTICOS, LOGGIAS AND TERRACES

Porticos, loggias and terraces were the intermediate spaces between house and garden. The loggia was often used as a pleasant summer living area, as evidenced by the presence of stone tables, benches and basin-fountains. The roof-terrace overlooking the enclosure walls and pergolas offered a splendid view of the walled gardens and surrounding countryside.

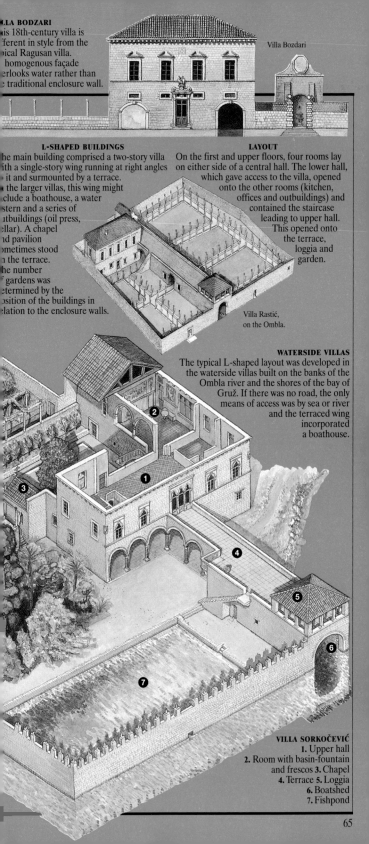

VILLA BODZARI

This 18th-century villa is different in style from the typical Ragusan villa. Its homogenous façade overlooks water rather than the traditional enclosure wall.

Villa Bozdari

L-SHAPED BUILDINGS

The main building comprised a two-story villa with a single-story wing running at right angles to it and surmounted by a terrace. In the larger villas, this wing might include a boathouse, a water cistern and a series of outbuildings (oil press, cellar). A chapel and pavilion sometimes stood on the terrace. The number of gardens was determined by the position of the buildings in relation to the enclosure walls.

LAYOUT

On the first and upper floors, four rooms lay on either side of a central hall. The lower hall, which gave access to the villa, opened onto the other rooms (kitchen, offices and outbuildings) and contained the staircase leading to upper hall. This opened onto the terrace, loggia and garden.

Villa Rastić, on the Ombla.

WATERSIDE VILLAS

The typical L-shaped layout was developed in the waterside villas built on the banks of the Ombla river and the shores of the bay of Gruž. If there was no road, the only means of access was by sea or river and the terraced wing incorporated a boathouse.

VILLA SORKOČEVIĆ
1. Upper hall
2. Room with basin-fountain and frescos 3. Chapel
4. Terrace 5. Loggia
6. Boatshed
7. Fishpond

Baroque architecture

A CLASSIC PLAN. The octagonal, centralized plan of the Church of St Vitus (Sv. Vid) in Rikeja was the first of its kind on Croatia's Adriatic coast. It was influenced by Baldassare Longhena and the Palladian tradition of Venice.

In the 17th century, baroque architecture asserted itself most strongly in northwestern Croatia – then in direct contact with the Austro-Hungarian culture – due to the influence of the dominant trend in central Europe. It did not begin to make inroads in Slavonia until after the departure of the Ottomans (1699), and permeated Istria and Dalmatia gradually from the Venetian capital. In the independer city-state of Dubrovnik, there was a marked Roman influence.

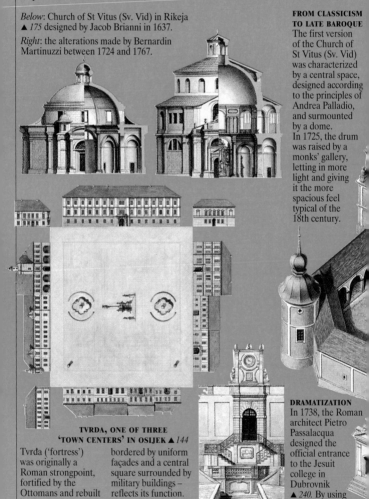

Below: Church of St Vitus (Sv. Vid) in Rikeja ▲ *175* designed by Jacob Brianni in 1637.

Right: the alterations made by Bernardin Martinuzzi between 1724 and 1767.

FROM CLASSICISM TO LATE BAROQUE
The first version of the Church of St Vitus (Sv. Vid) was characterized by a central space, designed according to the principles of Andrea Palladio, and surmounted by a dome. In 1725, the drum was raised by a monks' gallery, letting in more light and giving it the more spacious feel typical of the 18th century.

TVRDA, ONE OF THREE 'TOWN CENTERS' IN OSIJEK ▲ *144*

Tvrda ('fortress') was originally a Roman strongpoint, fortified by the Ottomans and rebuilt by the Austrians in the style of the great fortified towns constructed along the frontiers of the Austro-Hungarian Empire. Its design – broad streets bordered by uniform façades and a central square surrounded by military buildings – reflects its function. The military rigor of this vast square, which is also a parade ground, is attenuated by a Plague Column, two fountains and the arcaded baroque façades.

DRAMATIZATION
In 1738, the Roman architect Pietro Passalacqua designed the official entrance to the Jesuit college in Dubrovnik ▲ *240*. By using a series of concave and convex staircases aligned along a central axis, he brought the design of late Roman Baroque to Ragusa.

VOJKOVIĆ-ORŠIĆ PALACE, ZAGREB

nlike most urban palaces
the period, whose plans
ere usually
etermined
earlier
undations,
e Oršić
lace (1764),
bove) has a
U-shaped layout with the wings
to the back. The slightly projecting
part of the façade overlooking the
street is magnified by the pediment.
The bay windows are framed
by pilasters and have alternate
triangular and semicircular
pediments in a register of
typically baroque forms.

**CHURCH OF ST MARY
(SV. MARIJE) OF
JERUSALEM, TRŠKI
VRH ▲ *124* (*below left*)**
In line with a layout
typical of the golden
age of central
European baroque,
the way of the cross
starts in the valley
and climbs to the
last station at the foot
of a flight of steps
leading to a
portico
punctuated
by angle
towers. In the
center stands the
church with its
centralized plan.

A BAROQUE PALACE
he Krsto Oršić Palace
n Gornja Bistra ▲ *117*
(*right*), built in 1774,
as a U-shaped layout
d a second-story main
floor. It is constructed
around a central axis
unctuated by a façade
projection that houses
a vast split-level
reception room.

Rural architecture

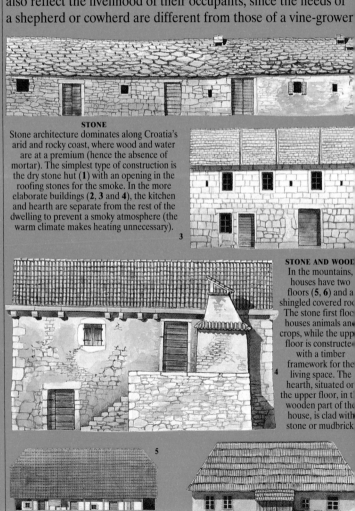

Rural architecture uses locally available materials – stone along the rocky coast, stone and wood in the mountains, wood on the banks of the Kupa and Sava rivers, clay and reeds on the plains of Pannonia. Thus, from east to west, Croatia's rural architecture blends organically with its natural environment. Although the materials reflect a concern for economy, the builders are unstinting in their ingenuity as they develop amazing construction techniques. The characteristics of rural dwellings also reflect the livelihood of their occupants, since the needs of a shepherd or cowherd are different from those of a vine-grower.

STONE

Stone architecture dominates along Croatia's arid and rocky coast, where wood and water are at a premium (hence the absence of mortar). The simplest type of construction is the dry stone hut (**1**) with an opening in the roofing stones for the smoke. In the more elaborate buildings (**2**, **3** and **4**), the kitchen and hearth are separate from the rest of the dwelling to prevent a smoky atmosphere (the warm climate makes heating unnecessary).

STONE AND WOOD

In the mountains, houses have two floors (**5**, **6**) and a shingled covered roof. The stone first floor houses animals and crops, while the upper floor is constructed with a timber framework for the living space. The hearth, situated on the upper floor, in the wooden part of the house, is clad with stone or mudbrick.

A wooden wall daubed with clay (**a**).

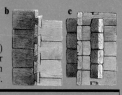

Corner joints – horn-work (**b**) and halved joint (**c**) – in which the timber framing with filling is replaced by wooden sections stacked one above the other.

WOOD

Houses on the borders of Pannonia (**9**, **10**), on the banks of the Kupa and Sava, and sometimes along the Lika (**7**, **8**) and Zagorje (**11**), are built of oak with shingle or thatched roofs. The layout of these houses reflects a certain wealth – they have a number of rooms with a clearly defined function (living room, kitchen, bedrooms and toilet). They are more elaborate than many rural dwellings and reflect a true art of living.

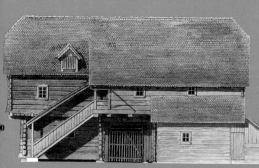

1. Stone hut (*bunja, kažun, čeramica*), near Šibenik ▲ 202
2. Bukovica, between the Velebit and the sea
3. Makarska ▲ 226
4. Veli Lošinj ▲ 181
5. Jarče Polje, near Karlovac ▲ 137
6. Kuti, in the Gorski kotar ▲ 140
7. Otočac, on the slopes of the Velebit ▲ 186
8. Lički Ribnik, Lika ▲ 140
9. Turopolje ▲ 132
10. Brest Pokupski, on the banks of the Krupa, near Petrinja ▲ 135
11. Near Belec, Hrvatsko Zagorje ▲ 120
12. Vuka, in Slavonia, between Đakovo and Osijek ▲ 148

COB AND MUDBRICK

The houses on the plains of Pannonia (**12**) are built of cob (a mixture of mud and straw) or dried mudbrick, and thatched with reeds or straw. In the villages, the gable end facing onto the street serves as a façade – it has windows with elaborate architraves and a door. Although the door makes the building look wider, it doesn't open into the house but onto a long exterior gallery leading to the various rooms.

From Neoclassicism to Modernism

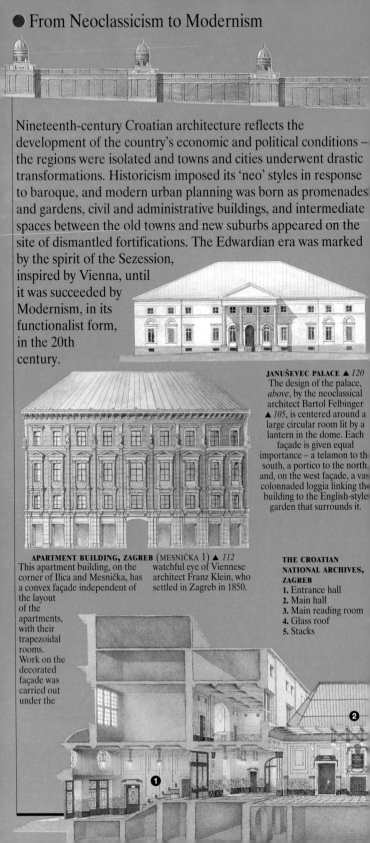

Nineteenth-century Croatian architecture reflects the development of the country's economic and political conditions – the regions were isolated and towns and cities underwent drastic transformations. Historicism imposed its 'neo' styles in response to baroque, and modern urban planning was born as promenades and gardens, civil and administrative buildings, and intermediate spaces between the old towns and new suburbs appeared on the site of dismantled fortifications. The Edwardian era was marked by the spirit of the Sezession, inspired by Vienna, until it was succeeded by Modernism, in its functionalist form, in the 20th century.

JANUŠEVEC PALACE ▲ *120*
The design of the palace, *above*, by the neoclassical architect Bartol Felbinger ▲ *105*, is centered around a large circular room lit by a lantern in the dome. Each façade is given equal importance – a telamon to th south, a portico to the north and, on the west façade, a vas colonnaded loggia linking th building to the English-style garden that surrounds it.

APARTMENT BUILDING, ZAGREB (MESNIČKA 1) ▲ *112*
This apartment building, on the corner of Ilica and Mesnička, has a convex façade independent of the layout of the apartments, with their trapezoidal rooms. Work on the decorated façade was carried out under the watchful eye of Viennese architect Franz Klein, who settled in Zagreb in 1850.

THE CROATIAN NATIONAL ARCHIVES, ZAGREB
1. Entrance hall
2. Main hall
3. Main reading room
4. Glass roof
5. Stacks

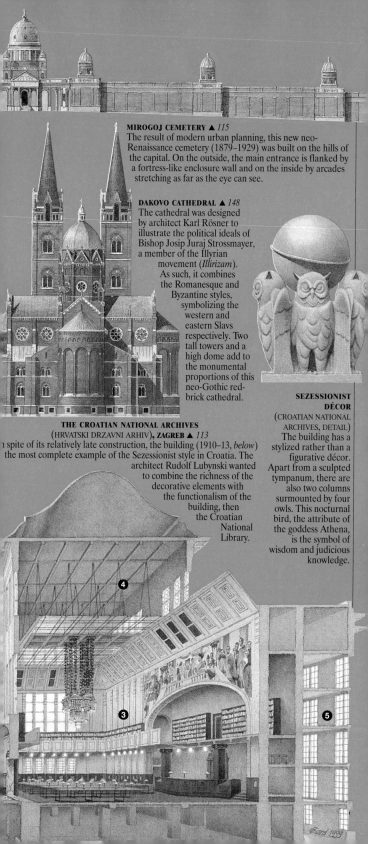

MIROGOJ CEMETERY ▲ 115
The result of modern urban planning, this new neo-Renaissance cemetery (1879–1929) was built on the hills of the capital. On the outside, the main entrance is flanked by a fortress-like enclosure wall and on the inside by arcades stretching as far as the eye can see.

DAKOVO CATHEDRAL ▲ 148
The cathedral was designed by architect Karl Rösner to illustrate the political ideals of Bishop Josip Juraj Strossmayer, a member of the Illyrian movement (*Illirizam*). As such, it combines the Romanesque and Byzantine styles, symbolizing the western and eastern Slavs respectively. Two tall towers and a high dome add to the monumental proportions of this neo-Gothic red-brick cathedral.

SEZESSIONIST DÉCOR
(CROATIAN NATIONAL ARCHIVES, DETAIL.)
The building has a stylized rather than a figurative décor. Apart from a sculpted tympanum, there are also two columns surmounted by four owls. This nocturnal bird, the attribute of the goddess Athena, is the symbol of wisdom and judicious knowledge.

THE CROATIAN NATIONAL ARCHIVES
(HRVATSKI DRZAVNI ARHIV), **ZAGREB ▲** *113*
In spite of its relatively late construction, the building (1910–13, *below*) the most complete example of the Sezessionist style in Croatia. The architect Rudolf Lubynski wanted to combine the richness of the decorative elements with the functionalism of the building, then the Croatian National Library.

From Neoclassicism to Modernism

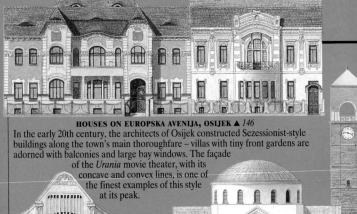

HOUSES ON EUROPSKA AVENIJA, OSIJEK ▲ 146
In the early 20th century, the architects of Osijek constructed Sezessionist-style buildings along the town's main thoroughfare – villas with tiny front gardens are adorned with balconies and large bay windows. The façade of the *Urania* movie theater, with its concave and convex lines, is one of the finest examples of this style at its peak.

'URANIA' MOVIE THEATER, OSIJEK ▲ 146

CRKVA SV. BLAŽ, ZAGREB ▲ 114
The Church of St Blaise, designed by Viktor Kovačić, combines Historicism and Modernism in a completely original way. The interior space is dominated by a neo-Byzantine dome in reinforced concrete, while the lower part of the exterior walls is built of rubble stone.

VILLA PFEFFERMANN, ZAGREB (JURJEVSKA, 27)
Modernism is characterized, as in the Villa Pfeffermann, by smooth surface flat roofs and a very rational layout based on extreme functionalism.

Above: Villa Pfeffermann, by Vidakovićo.
Below: apartment building on Gajeva, by Stjepan Planić.

VILLA KRAUSS, ZAGREB (NAZOROVA, 29)
This villa (*below*), built by Weissmann in 1936–7, was influenced by the work of Le Corbusier. It successfully combines comfort with a resolutely modern style. The slender pillars and high walls pierced by bay windows make the house appear as if it is suspended in mid-air.

APARTMENT BUILDING ON GAJEVA, ZAGREB
The social architecture of the 1930s gave rise to a new form of architectural design and an unusual form of planimetry. The resulting buildings are extremely comfortable and met very strict criteria in terms of materials, color, furnishings and original designs.

Croatia
as seen by painters

The history of Croatia, *74*

Between land and sea, *76*

Everyday life, *78*

Modern visions of Dalmatia, *80*

The history of Croatia

An allegorical figure of Victory over a battlefield littered with Turkish dead. Hans von Aachen depicted the Austrian eagle triumphantly repelling the Turkish crescent.

JACOPO TINTORETTO (1518–94) painted décors and several large canvases for the Doges' Palace in Venice, including *The Taking of Zadar* (**1**), celebrating the Venetian victory (1346) after a sixteen-month siege ▲ *191*. Although the depiction of the city is imaginary, the artist makes full use of Mannerist techniques – in his portrayal of the frenzied sinuosity of the figures and his use of light – to emphasize the dramatic nature of the event. On June 22, 1593, Croatian and German troops defeated the Turkish army at the Battle of Sisak. Their victory, which halted the Ottoman advance into central Europe, was celebrated throughout the Christian world ● *33*. HANS VON AACHEN (1552–1616), attached to the court of Rudolf II, painted *The Battle of Sisak* (**2**), a fine example of a style influenced by the artist's travels in Italy and encounters with Flemish Mannerists. During the Middle Ages, the city-state of Ragusa established firm ties with Naples, as evidenced by the many paintings by Neapolitan and southern Italian artists preserved in Dubrovnik. One of these, *The Madonna flanked by St Blaise and St Francis* (**3**) – an altarpiece by ANTONIO DE BELLIS (d. Naples c.1660) – is in fact a valuable historic document since the lower part of the painting shows Dubrovnik before the earthquake in 1667 ▲ *235*.

Al. Medović

When MATO CELESTIN MEDOVIĆ (1857–1920) entered the Franciscan monastery of Dubrovnik in 1868, his superiors recognized his talent and sent him to study art in Rome, Florence and Munich. He continued to paint after his ordination in Zagreb (1895), favoring historical and religious subjects. From 1898 onwards, he often stayed on his native Pelješac peninsula ▲ 245, where he painted Dalmatian landscapes, showing great sensitivity in his use of color. *Heathland* (1911) (**1**) illustrates the spontaneity of his work.

MENCI KLEMENT CRNČIĆ (1865–1930) was born at Bruck an der Mur in the Austrian Alps. He was fascinated by the sea and became famous for his seascapes. He skillfully represented the variations in atmosphere and the effects of light upon the water, as evidenced by *Rain* (1914–18) (**2**). LJUBO BABIĆ (1890–1974) ● 78 worked under the direction of Menci Klement Crnčić in 1910–11. Between 1913 and 1914, he attended the Académie de la Grande Chaumière in Paris and, on his return to Zagreb, taught at the Academy of Fine

Arts. In the 1930s, he painted his native region of Zagorje. His ideal landscapes are bucolic, with the rounded hills, clumps of trees, vineyards and plowed fields depicted in *Zagorje Landscape* (**3**). Trieste artist LORENZO BUTTI (1805–60) was one of the best seascape artists of his time. He traveled a great deal but was based in Rijeka, where he produced several views of the town, including *Rijeka* (**4**), painted in 1830 in the exaggeratedly realistic Biedermeierstil. In 1847, Butti became the official seascape artist at the court of Ferdinand I of Habsburg.

77

VJEKOSLAV KARAS (1821–58) perfected his art at the Nazarene school in Rome. On his return to Karlovac, he painted portraits of Ana Krešić – *Ana Krešić* (1853) (**3**) – in the then fashionable Biedermeierstil ● *77*. She and her husband symbolized the emerging Croatian bourgeoisie who, having made money through commerce, played a decisive political role in the mid-19th century. VLAHO BUKOVAC ▲ *249* (1855–1922), who studied with the French academic painter Alexandre Cabanel, traveled in Europe and taught at the Academy of Fine Arts in Prague before settling in Zagreb. He established a national reputation as a portraitist. During a stay in Split (1884–5), he painted *The Katalinic Children* (**2**), in which he summed up the social and artistic tendencies of late 19th-century Croatia. LJUBO BABIĆ ● *77* found that the Neue Sachlichkeit ('new objectivity') movement offered an ideal opportunity to paint according to his convictions, which were a far cry from modern artistic trends. His paintings, in which ideas often take precedence over emotions, were allied to the poetics of new realisms that were reflected in Croatian art of the inter-war years – *Croatian Peasant*, 1926 (**4**). KRSTO HEGEDUŠIĆ (1901–75) recorded the social trends that affected Croatian society in the 1930s and '40s. As the founder of Zemlja ('the union of artists of the land') and mentor of the first generation of naïve artists of the Hlebine school ▲ *131*, he believed that 'individual artists could not dissociate themselves from the artistic community', and so he evoked the hardships endured by the peasants and working classes of northern Croatia – *Hlebine* (**1**).

When the Slovenian painter ZORAN MUŠIĆ (Gorica, 1909) was studying in Zagreb (1930–5) with Ljudo Babić ● 77, he discovered the island of Korčula where he returned after World War Two. The bare, petrified Dalmatian landscape bore an obvious resemblance to the limestone plateaus of his native Karst, and its mineral expanses became a leitmotiv in his work. Mušić successfully captured the underlying strength of Dalmatia and its inhabitants, overwhelmed by hard work and the weight of a turbulent past. His *Motif in Dalmatia* (1) encapsulates the quintessential spirit of this region on the borders between East and West. FRANO ŠIMUNOVIĆ's (1908–1995) paintings of the Dalmatian landscape verge on the obsessive. He explores the arid, rocky terrain of the inland regions of his native Dalmatia and tries to express the true essence of this wilderness. *Deserted Landscape* (1987) (2) is one of his variations on the theme of the bareness of rock. By reducing his palette, he conveys the tectonic structure and undulations of fields bounded by stone walls, suggested in white.

Croatia
as seen by writers

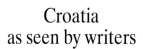

Just as one who, from Croatia perhaps,
has come to visit our Veronica –
one whose old hunger is not sated,
who, as long as it is shown,
repeats these words in thoughts:
"O my Lord Jesus Christ, true God, was then
Your image like the image I see now ?"

DANTE, PARADISO, CANTO XXXI,
translated by Allen Mandelbaum,
Alfred A Knopf & Everyman's Library, 1995

● Croatia as seen by writers

The seafaring Dalmatians

E rnst Jünger (1895–1998), who served as an officer in the Reichswehr (Nation Militia) between 1914 and 1923, also studied natural sciences and philosophy. 1926, he embarked upon an intensely active career in politics and journalism, making name for himself as one of the key figures of the neo-nationalist movement. H abandoned active politics when Hitler came to power but pursued his career as a write His work, which was greatly influenced by Nietzsche, included memoirs, essay accounts, aphorisms and utopian views, as well as his wartime experiences. During th summer of 1932, he traveled to Dalmatia and the Greek island of Rhodes with his po and essayist brother, Friedrich Georg. An account of his travels was published London, in 1947, in an edition destined for German prisoners held overseas.

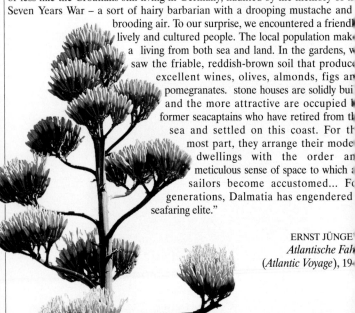

"In 1932, I spent the months of June and July with Friedrich Georg on th Dalmatian coast. According to the fantasy map the mind creates of the countrie you haven't yet visited, I had always imagined Dalmatia as a sort of extension Italy. During the course of a long day, as our white steamer sailed quietly pa jagged islands and the offshore bars of a deeply indented coastline, I had amp opportunity to rid myself of this misconception. I came very close to bein disappointed by my first impressions. The masses of fissured karstic rock that fa steeply to the sea, spreading like molten lead as they reach the breakers, seeme nothing more than a skeletal landscape whose lack of fleshy contours left totally devoid of pleasantly rounded features. In fact, I later realized that th country had its own secret strengths, resurfacing in your memory and soon givir rise to a feeling of nostalgia.... I had imagined the modern Croatian to be mo or less like the Croatians still living in Germany, haunted by the memory of th Seven Years War – a sort of hairy barbarian with a drooping mustache and brooding air. To our surprise, we encountered a friendl lively and cultured people. The local population mak a living from both sea and land. In the gardens, w saw the friable, reddish-brown soil that produc excellent wines, olives, almonds, figs an pomegranates. stone houses are solidly bui and the more attractive are occupied former seacaptains who have retired from th sea and settled on this coast. For th most part, they arrange their mode dwellings with the order an meticulous sense of space to which sailors become accustomed... Fc generations, Dalmatia has engendered seafaring elite."

ERNST JÜNGE
Atlantische Fah
(Atlantic Voyage), 19

Bird's-eye view of a town

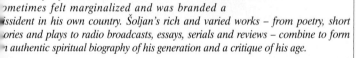

Antun Šoljan (1932–93) is the most interesting of the group of writers associated with the Zagreb magazine Krugovi (The Circles) (1952-8). His work was among the first of the era to expound freedom of expression and personal opinion, while his brilliant translations and anthologies of Croatian and foreign literature enabled his contemporaries to discover the main literary trends of the period. He wrote his first poems at the age of 16 and went on to found and edit a number of literary reviews. However, the reality of his time meant that he sometimes felt marginalized and was branded a dissident in his own country. Šoljan's rich and varied works – from poetry, short stories and plays to radio broadcasts, essays, serials and reviews – combine to form an authentic spiritual biography of his generation and a critique of his age.

"From above, the entire town of Murvica looked like a carefully constructed child's toy, faithfully reproduced down to the last detail. Even the narrow railway line that cut across the slopes of the mountain, high above the town, looked like a toy. The higher you go, the more certain you become that it's easy to fashion all this. The colors are all so pure, the scenography so kitsch, that it seems impossible that it's all real – tiny red roofs, the dark lines of the cypresses, paths winding through olive groves, hillsides covered with parallel rows of vines. A model landscape made out of Plasticine. Only the sea – even on this model – seems real, vast and unchanging. But the sea, too, is hard to believe.

Nor would you have thought that anyone would actually build a port here, in the shallow waters of the tiny gulf of Murvica, at a point where the sea, lolling out its tongue like a huge dog, had lapped away at the flat shoreline and hollowed out a broad, sandy bay, open to the south winds and no more than five or six meters deep.

The town of Murvica lay huddled on the narrow strip of flat land between the troubled waters of the sea and the steep rocks along which the north wind rolled wave upon wave of winter mists and cold, while the torrid summer heat beat down relentlessly, projecting its rays with the accuracy of a laser. A hundred or so houses, turning their backs to the tiny chapel and its cemetery on the slopes above them, looked onto a few acres of shore and a short, crooked jetty sheltering a harbor basin with a few fishing boats and schooners."

ANTUN ŠOLJAN,
Luka [The Port],
Grafički Zavod Hrvatske, 1974

Now there is war

Vesna Parun was born in 1922 on the Croatian island of Zlarin ▲ 204, and was to become one of the most widely read poets of the 20th century in her native land. She rejected Communist themes for more personal subjects like youth, beauty, eroticism, the joy of living, the pain of love gone wrong, and the glories of the Croatian landscape. This poem is about the chaos that was inflicted on everyday life by the outbreak of World War Two.

THE WAR
My grandfather sits in front of the house as leaves fall.
He looks at the figs that dry on the stone,
while the sun, very orange, vanishes behind the small vineyards
I remember from childhood.

The voice of my grandfather is golden, like the melody of an old clock,
and his dialect is rich, his words filled with restlessness.
The legend of 'Seven Lean Years' follows right after the 'Our Father',
short and eternal.

One day, there was no more fishing.
Now, there is war.
The enemy surrounds the port for miles around.
The whole tiny island trembles in eclipse.
All her sons disappeared in search of war wages
a long time ago.
Canada,
Australia...
They'll board them next for Japan.
It's possible they'll stay forever with their heads among the bamboo.
This is the second winter they've marched nonstop.
Even the fish sound gloomy in their chase.

One grandson is handsome and good, yet we'll find him in the snow one day
when the mountains are tired.

The girls sing as they prepare the picnic soup.
The children squat on the floor, very frightened
of the boots of the elegant old man.
One mother thinks of the sons and father who became a Malayan.

Strange, how this family has been scattered over four continents.
These big brawny people sound like children in their letters.

My grandfather stares at the red sun in the vineyard,
worn to silence, because death is near the old fisherman of the sea.
Foreign greed; strange hunger. Freedom is a bit of bread crust.

Ah, tell the earth that watermills should run faster!
A storm took away leaves; whatever's right shall be.
So, the young boys die, and the old men warm up their sorrows
staring at the horizon.

> From *Women in War: An Anthology of Women's Writings*
> *From Antiquity to the Present*
> edited by Daniela Gioseffi, and published by the Feminist Press
> Cuny Graduate Center, New York, March 2003

Guard duty

Samuel Pepys (1633–1703), England's most famous diarist, was working as 'clerk of the King's ships' in 1662 when this description of Dubrovnik's intricate security system was written.

Another account was told us, how in the Dukedome of Regusa in the Adriatique (a State which is little but more ancient they say then Venice, and is called the mother of Venice) and the Turkes lie round about it – that they change all the officers of their guard, for fear of conspiracy, every 24 houres, so that nobody knows who shall be Captains of the guard tonight; but two men come to a man, and lay hold of him as a prisoner and carry him to the place; and there he hath the keys of the garrison given him, and he presently issues his orders for the night's Watch; and so always from night to night."

> SAMUEL PEPYS,
> *Diary*, 11 January 1662

Walking round Dubrovnik

In 1932, Jules Romains (1885–1972) – founder of the literary movement known as 'unanimism', the 'expression of human and collective life' – began his major work, Les Hommes de Bonne Volonté (Men of Goodwill). It took him twelve years to complete this 27-volume chronicle of the events that drastically altered the face of Europe, from London to the Volga, between 1908 and 1933. He wrote the last volume, Le 7 Octobre (The Seventh of October), reflections on the identities and contradictions of Europe in 1933, in 1944. Romains discovered Dubrovnik in June 1933, when he attended the 11th international conference of the PEN (Poets, Essayists, Novelists) Club, a group of writers who championed the cause of peace and the unity

of nations. Captivated by the beauty of the city, one of the centers of Europea[n]
civilization, he decided to use it as the backdrop for the death of one of the character[s]
in Les Hommes de Bonne Volonté.

"The true wonder of this place, a source of inexhaustible charm, is the rampar[t]
walk that encircles the old town of Dubrovnik. It takes you a little above th[e]
town, defining, tracing and enveloping it. It's easy to imagine a man who like[s]
nothing better than to complete this circuit twice a day – once in the mornin[g]
(early in summer before the sun gets too hot) and once just before dusk (an[d]
once more, after dinner, when there's enough moonlight). That and a littl[e]
house in this town – what more could you possibly want, what other luxur[y]
wouldn't become rather superfluous? Strolling along this walk on a surface o[f]
hard stone. It's just wide enough to walk on without feeling constrained and ye[t]
it remains a rampart walk – compact, military, feudal. Beside you, the expanse o[f]
the town lies exposed, pouring out its feelings. A contained and solidifie[d]
outpouring in which each detail is pleasurably reassuring. This town is a work o[f]
human construction in exactly the same way as a palace or a castle. Chance an[d]
circumstances have been completely subsumed, with traces surviving only in th[e]
irregularities of shape and the unpredictability of the pleasure taken in walking[.]
You become attached to this town as if to a house. Everything encompassed b[y]
these ramparts belongs to you. There are these few steps to climb, this sentry bo[x]
and then this watchtower. Then there's a corner, and steps to go down, leadin[g]
to a narrow flight of steps that enters a fissure in the town and becomes
a narrow street. But you don't take the narrow flight of steps. You'll
play the rampart game to the end. A game for children, for
sleepwalkers and for men who have survived everything. Survived
to the point where you wonder whether the conundrum of life
wasn't a little simpler than you'd believed, believed on the
word of your contemporaries, those 'modern' men."

JULES ROMAINS, *Les Hommes de Bonne Volonté*
[Men of Goodwill], le 7 octobre, volume 27,
Editions Flammarion, Paris, 1958

A story by the sea

*M**arguerite Yourcenar (1903–87), the first woman to be*
elected to the Académie Française, in 1980, gained
international renown with her two major works, Mémoires
d'Hadrien *(Memoirs of Hadrian) (1951) and* L'Oeuvre au noir
(The Abyss) (1968). She was widely traveled, visiting England in
1914, returning a number of times to Italy and Austria, and
discovering Greece in 1932 and 1933. She began Nouvelles
orientales *(Oriental Tales) in 1935, while on a cruise with the*
Greek poet and psychoanalyst, Andhreas Embiríko, who no
doubt drew her attention to medieval Balkan ballads, Greek
superstitions and the history of tsarist Russia. The collection was
also inspired by the tales of the brothers Grimm and Hans
Christian Andersen.

"The long, dappled line of tourists stretched along Ragusa's
main street. Braided hats and opulent embroidered jackets
swimming in the wind at the entrance of the shops tempted

the eyes of travelers in search of inexpensive gifts or costumes for the masked balls held on board ship. It was as hot as only hell can be. The bald Herzegovinian mountains kept Ragusa under the fire of burning mirrors. Philip Mild entered a German alehouse where several fat flies were buzzing in the stifling gloom. Paradoxically, the restaurant's terrace opened onto the Adriatic, which sprang up suddenly in the heart of the city, there where one would least expect it, and yet that sudden burst of blue did nothing but add yet another color to the motley of the Market Square. A sickening stench rose from the pile of fish leftovers picked clean by almost unbearably white seagulls. There was not a breath of sea air. Philp's friend, the engineer Jules Boutrin, sat at a small zinc table, holding a drink in the shade of a fire-colored parasol that from afar seemed like a large orange floating on the waters.

'Tell me another story, old friend,' Philip said, dropping heavily into a chair. 'I need both a whiskey and a story told beside the sea – the most beautiful and the least true of all stories imaginable – to make me forget the contradictory and patriotic lies in the papers I just bought on the quay. The Italians insult the Slavs, the Slavs the Greeks, the Germans insult the Russians, the French insult England almost as much as they insult Germany. I imagine they are all in the right. Let's change the subject...' "

MARGUERITE YOURCENAR,
Oriental Tales, Translated by Alberto Manguel,
1983, pub. Aidan Ellis Publishing, UK, 1985

Living on the Edge

*F*ynes Morrison (1566–?) was well aware of the security problems experienced by the city of Dubrovnik (or Ragusa) when he visited it duringhis travels. He took law degrees at both Oxford and Cambridge before embarking in 1589 on a ten-year journey that would take him to the furthest reaches of Europe. He did this 'to gain experience by travelling into forraigne parts' and wrote about his impressions in Itinerary.

"Dubrovnik is the 'chiefe City of Sclauonia, built at the foot of an high mountaine, upon the Sea shoare, and hath great trafficke by those Seas, and huge ships, which the Kings of Spaine have often hired and joined to their Navy.... the City is very strongly fortified towards the sea, whence the Venetians can onlely assaile them: besides, that they pay great customes of their trafficke to the State of Venice, for which reason that State attempts nothing aginst the freedom of the City."

FYNES MORRISON,
Itinerary,
London 1617

● Croatia as seen by writers

The noble and free town of Zagreb

*A*ugust Šenoa was a leading figure in Croatian literature, so much so that the period i
which he wrote is sometimes referred to as the 'age of Šenoa'. He was a write,
journalist, translator and drama critic, artistic director of the Croatian National Theate
editor-in-chief of an arts magazine (The Crown) between 1874 and 1881, as well as
lawyer and senator. His work marks the beginning of a new era in Croatian literature. Th
native and eulogist of Zagreb, a city to which he dedicated his most remarkable work
contributed to the formation of both a literary and popular readership kept well-informe
by his daily newspaper columns. Historical novels such as Zlatarovo Zlat
(The Goldsmith's Gold) brought the issue of Croatian national identity to his reader.
attention. Thanks to Šenoa, the Croatian novel was able to take its place in the ranks c
European literature.

"In the 16th century, the old royal town of Zagreb – or, as the inhabitan
themselves called it, the 'noble and free town of Zagreb, on the heights of Gric'
looked very different from the city that it became over the next few hundred year
Sixteenth-century Zagreb was a fortified town and several fortresses stood withi
the city as we know it today. The royal town covered the entire tract of lan
between the Sava and its tributaries, the Crnomerec and Medvenica, and, in th
center of this vast fertile area, stood the natural bastion known as the hill of Gri
On this hill, surrounded by strong walls, stood the old town of Zagreb or 'Uppe
Town', inhabited by the citizens of Gric. Below, in what later became known as th
'Lower Town', there were virtually no houses – just fields, gardens and thicket
The only dwellings were grouped around the parish church of Svete Margerita [S
Margaret] at the place known as Ilica, a hamlet consisting of a few wretche
wooden houses. The low-lying Harmica ("square of the thirtieths" – so calle
because used as a collection point for local taxes – from the Hungarian harminca
– a thirtieth) was nothing but an area of marshy ground where a few white house
had been built near the source of the Manduševac. It was on this spot that witche
were once burned at the stake."

AUGUST ŠENOA, *Zlatarovo Zla*
[*The Goldsmith's Gold*], 187

The changing face of Split

Rebeccca West (1892–1983), an early feminist journalist, novelist and prose writer, born in London and brought up in Edinburgh, was never afraid of controversy. Her ten-year affair with H.G. Wells, which produced a son, Anthony, caused a scandal in its day. In 1937, she toured Yugoslavia as Europe was on the brink of World War Two, and her two-volume study of the nation, Black Lamb and Grey Falcon, *is the work for which she is perhaps best known today.*

"It recalls Naples because it also is a tragic and architecturally magnificent sausage-machine, where a harried people of mixed race have been forced by history to run for centuries through the walls and cellars and sewers of ruined palaces, and have now been evicted by a turn of events into the open day, neat, and slick, and uniform, taking to modern clothes and manners with the adaptability of oil, though at the same time they are set aside for ever from the rest of the world by the arcana of language and thoughts they learned to share while they scurried for generations close pressed through the darkness."

REBECCA WEST,
Black Lamb and Grey Falcon, 1942

The soft warm pillow of Zagreb

Antun Gustav Matoš (1873–1914) always remained loyal and unfaltering in his love for Croatia, even though he spent much of his life abroad. He was profoundly marked by his exile – in Belgrade (1894–8 and 1904–8), Paris (1898–1904) and Switzerland – and by his travels to Vienna, Munich and Italy. His own esthetic criteria and the European models he encountered led him to raise his literary aspirations. The aim of his virulent polemics was to encourage Croatian writers to match the high standards of European literature. Toward the end of a literary career marked by prose, essays and accounts of his travels, Matoš began to write poetry.

You have to have grown up in Zagreb, and been away from Zagreb for fifteen years, to feel, understand and love this strange city. Overwhelmed by misfortune, reeling under the terrible image conveyed by the newspaper reports of the

continually worsening disaster assailing m
homeland, it was in vain that I tried to sleep in
foreign land, in some cold dwelling or a garr
whose rent was sometimes still unpaid. Th
possibility of returning, healthy in body an
mind, to the city that, for a native of Zagre
has a human voice, whose very roofs and wa
speak the language of the homeland and t
past – all that seemed an impossible an
magical dream. Even now, I sometim
dream I am lying alone, ill and weak,
some garret in Paris or a damp hovel
Belgrade, my only prospect a hospice f
homeless vagabonds and an unmark
grave. And when I wake, the dead leaves
the walnut tree are rustling in the famili
garden, the reassuring sound of the facto
whistle is summoning the workers, t
Angelus bell is ringing out through t
balmy autumn air, like the ancien
unchanging prayer of the old town, to greet t
new day, the sun is rising in the same pla
above Salata, to the left of the wayside cro
and beneath my head is the only pillow on whi
you can truly rest, the pillow of the family home
the soft, warm pillow of Zagreb.

Oh, even if I were a foreigner, Zagreb would captivate my heart like few other
cities. Resplendent in the ways of life of an, as yet, embryonic city, it has all the
advantages of a healthy and picturesque resort. If Zagreb becomes the Croatia
equivalent of Paris and continues to develop in the same way, until its palaces
and factories reach the Sava and its vast buildings fill the beautiful open space
between the Crnomerec and Maksimir, our descendants – poetic souls thirsting
for nature - will long for the time when carts heavy with the scent of haymaking
passed along our streets, when Zagreb, our pure Zagreb, was a town of gardens
air and light."

ANTUN GUSTAV MATO
Kod Kuće [*At Home*], 19

The décor in Zagreb

R obert Kaplan (b. 1953) is an opinionated journalist, who writes for Atlan
Monthly, *as well as the author of several unconventional travel books. "Wha
try to do is to provide the experience of a backpacker with the disciplined analysis
a good journalist or policy specialist," he explains.*

"Zagreb is an urban landscape of volume and space arrangement, where color
secondary. The city requires no sunshine to show it off. Clouds are better, and
chilling drizzle is better still. I walked a hundred yards in the rain from the railw
station to the Esplanade Hotel: a massive, sea-green edifice that might easily
mistaken for a government ministry, manifesting the luxurious decadence – t
delicious gloom – of Edwardian England or fin-de-siècle Vienna. I entered

bbed, black-and-white marble lobby adorned with gold-framed mirrors, drawn
elvet curtains and valences, and purple carpets. The furniture was jet black, and
he lamp shades were golden yellow. The lobby and dining hall resembled a
uttered art gallery whose pictures recalled the universe of Sigmund Freud,
ustav Klimt, and Oskar Kokoschka: modernist iconography that indicates social
sintegration and the triumph of violence and sexual instinct over the rule of law.
avenka Draculic is a Zagreb journalist who writes in Croatian for Danas
Today), a local magazine, and in English for The New Republic and The
ation. Wearing designer black glasses and a bright red headband that perfectly
atched her red blouse and lipstick, she – and the other women in the hotel
stro – dressed with a panache that complemented the boldness of the hotel's
t. The overall message was unmistakable: despite Communist-inflicted poverty
d the damp, badly heated apartments and the sorry displays in the shop
ndows all around, we Croats are Roman Catholic, and Zagreb is the eastern
stion of the West; you, the visitor, are still in the orbit of Austria-Hungary, of
ienna – where the modern world was practically invented – and don't you
rget it!"

ROBERT KAPLAN, *Balkan Ghosts*,
St Martin's Press, 1993

● Croatia as seen by writers

Returning to Croatia

Dea Birkett is a distinguished travel writer and broadcaster, who tends to throw herself in at the deep end when researching her books. For her first, A Woman at Sea, she was a crew member on a West African cargo ship. For Serpent in Paradise, she lived on remote Pitcairn Island alongside the survivors of the mutiny on the Bounty, and she also spent time as a member of an Italian circus troupe. By comparison, her visit to Croatia was relatively tame.

"Dubrovnik is defiantly alive. It refused to die in the bombardment, and now refuses to become a moth-balled museum piece. No cars are allowed inside the walled city, so people walk all over it, reduced to the size of so many insects inside its mighty walls. The city manages to be majestic without being intimidating, and the inhabitants of even its most ancient allies feel free to hang their washing out of their windows, blowing above the trickle of tourists who wander through the light-less back streets....

The city itself is so embraced by its mighty walls, up to six metres thick, that it is cradled and utterly cut off from the unregulated urban sprawl beyond. It looks as if it has landed on the edge of town, a massive medieval space machine constructed in a Hollywood studio. It is so enclosed that after a couple of hours

aimless wandering the cobbled streets, round and round and round inside the circle of its walls, I began to bump into people I'd already seen, again and again, as if I had made friends....

Now I am dancing through the Dalmatian islands again, on a Jadrolinya ferry from Dubrovnik to the island of Korcula, which we had visited on day three of our cruise. Croatia is about water. This small country has a 1000-mile rocky coastline stretching from Slovenia in the north to Montenegro to the south. There are almost 2000 offshore islands, only 66 of them inhabited. Most men I met had, at some time, served at sea. Croatian cuisine consists almost entirely of sea delicacies - strange, tough but tasty Adriatic fish, squid and black seafood risotto....

On the way back from Korcula I stopped in Cavtat, a small town of red-hued buildings lining a small harbour. But on the hill behind, the monstrous Hotel Croatia shines down, all white, a fortress to Soviet-inspired 1970s ideals."

DEA BIRKETT,
Returning to Croatia,
article for the website
www.travelintelligence.net

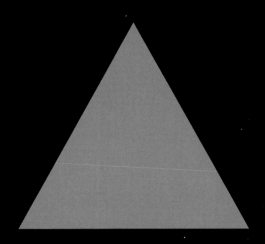

Itineraries in Croatia and the Dalmatian coast

Zagreb, *99*

Slavonia, *141*

Istria, *153*

Rijeka, *171*

Zadar, *189*

Split, *213*

Dubrovnik, *233*

▲ Cycling through the streets of Varaždin

The roofs of Kaptol, Zagreb

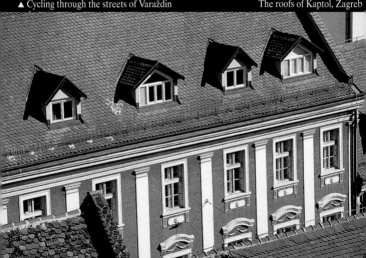

Trg Republike (Republic Square), Split

▼ Tourist office, Zagreb

▲ The Pakleni otoci (Islands of Hell), off the coast of Hvar

Brela

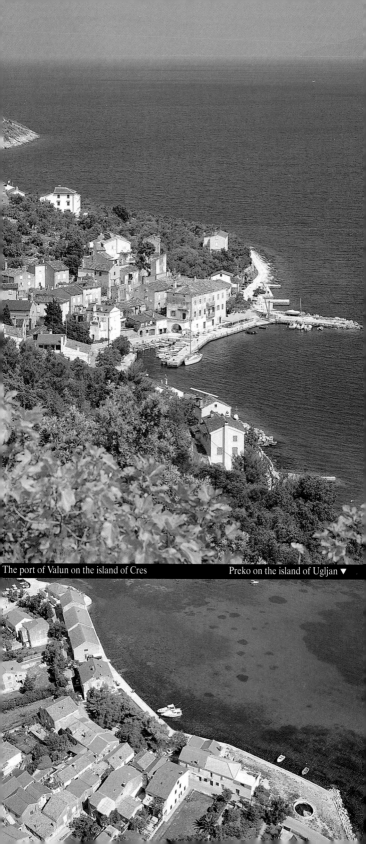

The port of Valun on the island of Cres

Preko on the island of Ugljan ▼

▲ Lacemakers in Pag

▲ Vineyard on the island of Korčula

Diocletian's Palace, Spli

Zagreb

Zagreb, *100*

The Upper Town, *102*

The Museum of Zagreb, 106

Kaptol, *108*

The Lower Town, *111*

Mount Medvednica, *116*

Western Zagorje, *120*

St Mary of Jerusalem,
Trški Vrh, 124

Northern Zagorje, *126*

Varaždin, *127*

The Međimurje, *130*

The Podravina, *131*

The Turopolje, *132*

Sisak and around, *134*

Banovina, *135*

From Zagreb to Karlovac, *136*

Toward the Adriatic coast, *137*

Plitvice National Park, 138

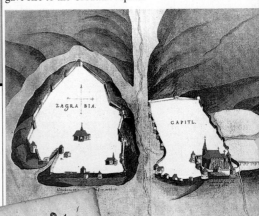

900 GODINA ZAGREBAČKE BISKUPIJE

REPUBLIKA HRVATSKA

4,00

◆ D

CENTRAL EUROPEAN CHARM ★
Trg Bana Jelačića, a huge square surrounded by cafés, is a good place to start a tour of Zagreb. The hills of Gradec and Kaptol are the medieval parts of the city. Donji Grad, the lower town built in the 19th century, is raved about by fans of neoclassical and modern architecture, while the city's parks and gardens offer a refreshing diversion.

The Bishop of Zagreb thanking Pope Pius II for his financial aid during the struggle against the Ottomans (15th-century illumination).

Zagreb, the capital of the Republic of Croatia, lies between the southern slopes of Mount Medvednica (Bear Mountain) to the north and the River Sava to the south. The city's main shopping street, Ilica, runs below the foothills of the mountain. The history of the capital is one of twin – or rather two rival – towns, Gradec or Grič (now the Upper Town), inhabited by the nobility and middle classes, and Kaptol, occupied by the ecclesiastical community. These two fortified, hilltop towns faced each other across the River Medveščak – which dried up in the 20th century and was converted into a street, Krvav most ('bloody bridge') – and Tkalčićeva ulica, then an open road leading into the town from the country, today a pedestrianized strip of cafés and restaurants popular with the younger generation. These two, sometimes hostile elements gave rise to the Croatian capital.

Birth of a city

According to the earliest record mentioning the city – a document dated 1094, the year in which a bishopric was established by Ladislas I of Hungary – Zagreb was officially founded 900 years ago. While some prehistoric remains have come to light, in particular the remains of Bronze Age dwellings found beneath the foundations of the Museum of Zagreb ▲ *10* there is much more evidence of the Classical period – sacrificial altars, funeral steles, statues and inscriptions. The site of present-day Zagreb was occupied by an Illyrian

**ZAGREB,
900 YEARS OLD**
Stamps issued in 1994
to commemorate the
city's 900th
anniversary.

BELA IV
In 1241–2, the
Mongols invaded
Hungary and Croatia
and captured Kaptol.
During this period,
Bela IV (1235–70)
(*above*) sought refuge
in Gradec. He
subsequently
embarked upon a vast
program for the
reconstruction of
Croatia in an attempt
to resolve internal
conflicts and guard
against invasions.
He built fortresses
and founded vassal
towns whose citizens
received economic
and administrative
privileges in return
for paying taxes.
Gradec, declared
a royal free town by
Bela, was fortified as
part of this program.
Under the royal aegis,
Gradec was obliged
to provide Bela with
food and shelter
whenever he stayed
in the region, and to
furnish ten soldiers
in the event of a war.
When the Ban
(governor) of Croatia
was appointed,
Gradec only had to
present him with an
ox, 100 loaves of
bread and a cask
of wine.

...be known as the Andautonians who, in the early 7th
...ntury, were overrun by Avars and Slavs. In the 8th and 9th
...nturies, there were Slav fortifications on the surrounding
...lls. A few valuable and functional objects – Slav jewelry and
...ramics unearthed in front of the cathedral and in the
...pper Town – have survived from this period.

...ortunes of a city

...the 12th century, four key elements of the city were there
...the school, the royal fair, performances on the parvis of the
...thedral and the 'street of foreigners' known variously as
...*us Latinorum*, Šoštarska ves and 'German street'.

...E MIDDLE AGES. In 1242, the Mongols destroyed Kaptol
...d converted the cathedral into a stable before being
...feated by the Croatian army. In the same year, King Bela
... of Hungary and Croatia issued a golden bull (charter)
...cording the status of a royal free town to Gradec, which by
...en had a school, hospital, public baths and royal mint.
...owever, there were constant conflicts of interest, disputes
...er property and dynastic struggles between Gradec and
...aptol, with the truces only lasting for the duration of such
...ajor annual events as the festivals of St Stephen the King
...d St Margaret. By the 14th century, around 60 crafts were
...ing practiced in Gradec, while Italian artists were painting
...escos in the episcopal buildings of Kaptol.

...VERSITY AND DEVELOPMENT. In the 16th century, the
...valry between the two factions subsided in the face of the
...ttoman threat. The Turks reached the foot of the fortified
...ll of the cathedral but their advance was halted in 1593,
...ar Sisak ▲ *134*. In spite of these crises, the cathedral
...easure, which was used to finance wars, remained one of
... richest in Europe. The 16th century also witnessed the
...ening of a seminary in Zagreb and the establishment of
...stal links with Vienna, Buda and the provinces. The first
...condary school was founded in 1607 and the university
...ened in 1669, closely followed by a girls' school and
...inting press. In the 17th and 18th centuries, the capital
...as devastated by outbreaks of plague and fire but, even
..., newspapers began to be printed and a permanent theater
...as opened.

...ODERN TIMES. In the early 19th century, the city was the
...nter of the movement for the national revival of Croatia,
...own as Illyrianism (*Illirizam*) ● *35*. In 1850, Gradec and
...aptol were brought under a single administration. The late
...th century witnessed the golden age of architecture and the
...y acquired a first-rate cultural infrastructure and a large
...condary school (now the Mimara Museum ▲*113*). Its urban
...velopment extended over a vast area to the south ▲ *111* and
...was also spreading north to the hills. During the first half
...the 20th century, it was an important center for modern
...chitecture. Today, Zagreb has one million inhabitants and
...s spread onto the right bank of the River Sava.

▲ Zagreb

Most of the buildings of the Upper Town – formerly Gradec and also known as Grič and *Mons Graecensis Zagrabiensis* – are of historical and architectural interest. But it's also a good place to take a stroll and explore the back alleys.

KULA LOTRŠČAK
Burglars' Tower, a remnant of the 13th-century fortifications, is named for the bell (*campana Latrunculorum*) rung from the tower each evening before the city gates were closed to keep out burglars. Today, the cannon fired at midday recalls the legend of a cannonball fired at the Turks that blew away the turkey about to be served to the pasha, precipitating the Ottoman retreat and saving Zagreb from destruction.

MATOŠ ON ZAGREB
Strossmayerovo Šetalište, opened in 1843, follows the line of Gradec's former south-facing fortifications. On it is the seated bronze statue of Antun Gustav Matoš (1873–1914) ● *90* cast by Ivan Kožrić in 1978. The writer's native city was never far from his thoughts during his exile: 'I carry within me the misty bitterness of your mountains, The despair of the stars sparkling above you. The darkness of your palaces sobs within me, ... my noble Grič!'

The Upper Town ◆ D A-C1-3

The Upper Town is home to the highest state authorities and the Sabor, the parliament to which Croatia owes the continuity of its institutions throughout its history. Since frequent wars and numerous fires have destroyed a considerable part of the original urban fabric, most of the remaining buildings date from the 17th, 18th and 19th centuries.

GETTING TO GRADEC. One way of getting to the Upper Town is by the FUNICULAR (*upsinjača*), which first came into service in 1889 and was converted from steam to electricity 1934. More energetic visitors can climb the steps that run parallel to the railway and emerge onto a promenade – STROSSMAYEROVO ŠETALIŠTE – offering a splendid view of the city, or the Zakmardi steps that existed in the 18th century. Alternatively, there is the picturesque and gently sloping RADIĆEVA ULICA or, to the east, the steep MESNIČKA ULICA (Butchers' Street) named for the Mesnička Gate, one of the city gates that, until 1836, stood on the spot now occupied by no. 14.

THE FORTIFICATIONS. The buildings along Strossmayerovo Šetalište and Opatička ulica, and those on the west side of Jezuitski trg (Jesuits' Square) follow the line of the fortifications, punctuated by five gates that once surrounded Gradec. The only surviving gate is the KAMENITA VRATA (Stone Gate), flanked by a square tower dating from 1266. It houses an

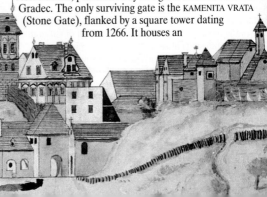

tar decorated with a painting of the Madonna, the patron
int of Zagreb. In 1731, the gate was badly damaged by
re but this image was found intact amongst the debris.
commemorate the miracle, a shrine was built into the
amenita vrata to preserve the painting, thought to be
e work of a 17th-century local artist. It is protected by a
rought-iron grille, a masterpiece of baroque art. A niche in
e west façade contains a more secular icon, Ivan Kerdić's
atue (1929) of Dora, the daughter of Petar Krupić, a
oldsmith and keeper of the gate in the 16th century. Krupić
as depicted in *Zlatarovo Zlato* (*The Goldsmith's Gold*),
novel by the 19th-century writer August Šenoa ● *88*.

RG SV. MARKA (ST MARK'S SQUARE). The church of
v. Marka (St Mark), built in the first half of the 13th century
d subsequently renovated several
mes, stands on the square of the same
ame. The church played a key role
Zagreb's history since the city's
gh-ranking officials and the Bans
overnors) of Croatia were sworn
before the altar of the Holy Cross.
he niches of the magnificent south
ortal house statues of Christ, the
irgin Mary, Saint Mark and the twelve
postles sculpted in the studio of Ivan
arler between 1364 and 1377 – three
ere replaced with wooden statues
uring the baroque period. The church's
ulticolored tiled roof, designed in
lectic style by Herman Bollé ▲ *108*,
as become one of the symbols of the
pital since it depicts the coats of arms
Zagreb and Croatia, whose emblems
present the three areas (Croatia, Dalmatia, Slavonia) that
ade up the medieval kingdom. On the west side of the
uare stands the late-baroque *banski dvori* (Ban's Palace)
iginally the seat of the Ban and today an official
overnment building (*above, right*). On the east side stands
e Sabor (parliament) building, constructed in 1910, from
whose balcony the separation of Croatia from the
Austro-Hungarian empire was declared
on October 29, 1918. The southwest
side of the square is occupied by the
former town hall, where Zagreb's first
permanent theater was
opened in 1834.

**FROM THE LOWER
TO THE UPPER TOWN**
Leave the busy Trg
bana Jelačić via the
Radićeva ulica, turn
left when you get to
the equestrian statue
of St George (Sv.
Juraj) and go through
the Kamenita vrata
(Stone Gate). You'll
pass a pharmacy,
opened in 1355, just
before you get to Trg
Sv. Marka.

CRKVA SV. MARKA
In spite of the 14th-
century vaults and
pillars, and the 20th-
century frescos by
Jozo Kljaković and
sculptures by Ivan
Meštrović, the
interior has retained
its Romanesque style.

▲ Zagreb

A GRAND MASTER
Sculptor Ivan Meštrović ▲ 222 influenced an entire generation of Croatian artists. The painter Ljubo Babić ● 77 said of him: 'His greatness, and his personal tragedy, lie in the fact that his entire work, and therefore his spiritual and intellectual life, with its positive and negative aspects, aspires to create a unique form of expression that is completely different from any other form of sculpture, past or present'.

A BAROQUE DÉCOR
The church of Sv. Katerine has a baroque interior, with stuccowork by Antonio Quadrio (1720), the medallions of the vault by Giulio Quaglio, the trompe l'oeil of the chancel by Slovenian artist Kristof Jelovšek (1762), paintings by Zagreb artist Barnard Bobić (d. 1695) and a statue of Saint Ignatius of Loyola to the right of the main altar, by Francesco Robba (1730) ▲ 130.

TOWARD KATARININ TRG (ST CATHERINE'S SQUARE) The MUSEJ NAIVNE UMJETNOSTI (Museum of Naïve Art) stands on Čirilometodska next to the Greek Catholic church renovated by Herman Bollé ▲ 108. Founded in 1994, the museum was based on the 'permanent exhibition of peasant artists', comprising more than 1,500 works by artists from Croatia and abroad, that had been in Zagreb since 1952. The street opens onto Katarinin trg (St Catherine's Square) where the Jesuits built the CHURCH OF SV. KATERINE (ST CATHERINE) between 1620 and 1632. The church, whose magnificent Baroque interior symbolizes the triumph of the Counter-Reformation, was modeled on the Gesù in Rome. The SEMINARY, converted into a boarding school, formed generations of Croatian intellectuals, while the CONVENT was transformed into a vast art gallery. Next to the secondary school built on the south side of the square (1607), and which formed the nucleus of the University of Zagreb, the DVERCE ('small gate') PALACE stands against the medieval enclosure wall. Some historians believe it was once a royal palace. It was converted in 1881 and bequeathed to the city in 1911 by the Countess Buratti and is today used to host official functions. For visitors interested in modern art, the baroque Kulmer Palace, on the north side of the square, houses the MUZEJ SUVREMENE UMJETNOSTI (Museum of Modern Art). Its temporary exhibitions – based on a collection of some 4,000 paintings by artists from Croatia and abroad, including works by Pablo Picasso, Fernand Léger and Victor Vasarely – retrace the artistic movements of the 20th century. Constructivism, conceptual art, kinetic art and letterism are particularly well represented.

THE WEST OF THE UPPER TOWN. The most beautiful
Baroque building in the Upper Town – the VOJKOVIĆ-ORŠIĆ
PALACE (1764) ● 67 – stands on Matoševa. It houses
impressive collections of sculpture, engravings, paintings,
ancient maps, photographs, religious artifacts, weapons and
everyday objects belonging to the HRVATSKI POVIJESNI MUZEJ
(Historical Museum of Croatia). If you retrace your steps
across Trg Sv. Marka and turn down Mletačka ulica, you can
visit the MEŠTROVIĆ ATELIER at no. 8, where sculptor Ivan
Meštrović lived and worked between 1922 and 1942 ▲ 222.
At the end of the picturesque Demetrova stands the
PRIRODOSLOVNI MUZEJ (Natural History Museum) with
its amazing mineralogical, botanical, zoological,
geological and paleontological collections.

OPATIČKA. The former 17th-century CONVENT OF THE
POOR CLARES today houses the MUZEJ GRADA ZAGREBA
(Museum of Zagreb) ▲ 106. Below the museum stands the
PREPORODNI DOM (Revival Center), a symbol of the Croatian
national Renaissance, designed in neoclassical style by Bartol
Felbinger (1838). The building, which was the seat of the
country's main cultural and educational institutions,
witnessed some important political events in the 1840s – it
was here that Josip Jelačić ▲ 110 was appointed Ban, and
the popular demands for national unity ● 35 were adopted.
A little further on, an elaborate wrought-iron grille,
produced according to the designs of Herman Bollé by the
Arts and Crafts School (Zagreb's school of applied art,

opened in 1882) ▲ 114, draws
the eye toward a palace that
once housed the MINISTRY OF
NATIONAL EDUCATION AND
RELIGIOUS AFFAIRS. In 1892,
its director, Isidor Kršnjavi,
entrusted its renovation to
Herman Bollé, who produced
one of the most successful
examples of Croatian
Historicism. This is illustrated
by the ZLATNA DVORANA
(Golden Room), whose
frescos by Vlaho Bukovac
▲ 249, Ferdo Kovačević,
Celestin Medović, Bela
Csikos-Sessia, Oton Iveković,
Ivan Tišov and sculptor
Robert Frangeš-Mihanović
give an overview of late 19th-
century Croatian painting.

**THE INVENTION OF
THE FOUNTAIN PEN,
CELEBRATED BY THE
MUSEUM OF ZAGREB**
Just as Waterman
had done in 1884,
the Zagreb engineer
Slavoljub Penkala
(1871–1922) patented
the mechanical pen in
1907. The pen, whose
empty barrel served
as a reservoir for ink,
proved a huge success
and, in 1911, Penkala
opened a fountain-
pen factory employing
300 workers. By 1913,
the number had
increased to 800 and
the factory was
exporting pens
worldwide, from Paris
to Tokyo, and Vienna
to London.

▲ Muzej grada Zagreba (The Museum of Zagreb)

Medal from the chain of the Mayor of Zagreb (1902).

The Museum of Zagreb was founded in 1907 by the Braæa hrvatskog zmaja (Brothers of the Croatian Dragon), a society formed in 1905 to promote the cultural heritage of Croatia. For more than 50 years, the museum has occupied the former Convent of the Poor Clares, built in the mid-17th century, which stands on Opatička (Street of the Abbesses) in the Upper Town. The façade is both striking and unusual; originally blind because it housed a cloistered order, it now has windows painted in trompe l'oeil. As the natural custodian of the city's architectural and urban heritage, the museum presents and exhibits each document, each objet d'art and each piece of craftsmanship in its historical and cultural setting.

1

MEDIEVAL TOWNS
The rooms devoted to the Middle Ages (**6**) are divided into two sections, each beginning with a model, just as Zagreb was then divided into two distinct political entities: Gradec and Kaptol ▲ *101*. Gradec was declared a royal free town in 1242 by the famous *golden bull* ▲ *101* issued by Bela IV (**3**).

2

CARTOONS
The museum celebrates the work of Dušan Vukotić (1927–98), one of the pioneers of the world famous Zagreb School of Animation. In 1962, he won an Oscar for *Ersatz* (**2**).

BENEATH THE MUSEUM
Archeological excavations carried out beneath the museum foundations unearthed several objects that confirmed the continuity of the site's occupation from prehistoric times through to the 17th century. These pieces are presented as part of the museum's permanent exhibition, with the collections displayed above the actual spot where they were discovered. Visitors can examine some fine pieces illustrating the life of Zagreb's earliest inhabitants – and there are also *in situ* reconstructions offering an insight into the way of life during the Hallstatt (7th century BC) and La Tène (1st century BC) periods –, or find out about the techniques used to build the medieval fortifications (**7**).

3

The interior courtyard of
the Museum of Zagreb.

SCENOGRAPHY

The arrangement of exhibits in the museum recreates the atmospheres that prevailed during the various periods of the city's history. Documents and objects are not simply displayed in showcases but situated within their historical period and presented within context to create a relationship that shows their historical and/or artistic value off to advantage. This is demonstrated in the room devoted to the cathedral (**6**), where the eye is drawn to an impressive sculpted stone portal dating from 1643. It was dismantled after the earthquake of 1880 and recently restored to its original size and former glory.

The showcases devoted to the 19th century (**1**) trace the development of the city's urban fabric during that period. These changes are explained to visitors via a large-scale model of the Lower Town (**5**) which shows the buildings devoted to the arts, sciences and politics. The last rooms, designed according to the scenographic principles that are one of the great strengths of the museum, are given over to the 20th century (**4**) and provide an objective presentation of the modern history of Croatia and its capital. After World War Two and the Communist era, the visit ends with the struggle for Independence (1991–5).

Kaptol ♦ **D** D1-3

THE SECOND HILL. The Kaptol ('cathedral chapter') district grew up on a hill that was slightly lower than that of the Upper Town (Gradec). This is the old part of Zagreb, with its episcopal district (cathedral and fortified palace on Vlaška) and chapter district, where the canons lived on Kaptol, the funnel-shaped street to the north of the cathedral. In 1570, Canon Franjo Filipović, who lived at what is now no. 29, was captured by the Turks and converted to Islam. The citizens of Zagreb responded by covering his house with black paint. Some time later, the residence of the renegade canon, replaced by a new building in 1827, housed the seminary and faculty of theology that has since been known as the 'black school'. Like the Upper Town, the Kaptol was surrounded by fortifications – now incorporated into more recent buildings – punctuated with towers. The 16th-century PRIŠLIN TOWER, the only one to survive, stands to the northwest at the end of the OPATOVINA PARK.

THE EARLY CATHEDRAL. The existence of the cathedral – mentioned for the first time in a document dated 1094, the year in which a bishopric was established by Ladislas I of Hungary – undoubtedly attests to the presence of an earlier church. However, the only evidence of any continuity of occupation on the site was the discovery of Roman funerary steles incorporated into the north tower. A pre-Romanesque capital (9th–11th century) was also discovered nearby. An early cathedral completed and consecrated under Bishop Stjepan I (1215–25) was badly damaged by the Mongols in 1242. It was restored by Bishop Timotej (1263–84); at a time when the city had only 3,000 inhabitants, the cathedral had three naves and was almost 100 feet (30 meters) wide, with a 43-foot (13-meter) nave.

THE FORTIFIED CATHEDRAL. In the 14th and 15th centuries, the basilical plan of the early cathedral was gradually transformed into a hall church (three naves of the same height), whose style was similar to the High-Gothic Rayonnant style

KAPTOL
FROM THE AIR
From the Trg bana Jelačića (Governor Jelačić Square), Bakačeva runs north to the cathedral and Archbishop's Palace, on the right, and the Dolac market and the church of Sv. Marija on the left. Further on is the Franciscan monastery.

RESTORER
OF THE CATHEDRAL
Many architects have left their mark on Zagreb, but none more so than Herman Bollé (1845–1926), the brilliant disciple of Viennese architect Friedrich von Schmidt. His major work is undoubtedly the restoration of the cathedral, between 1879 and 1905.

St Urbain (1262) in the French town of oyes, and the Cathedral of Ratisbon (now egensburg, Germany). Then fortifications ere built to guard against the increasing rkish threat – Zagreb Cathedral was the most iental church in the Christian world – with bishops ka Baratin (1500–10) and Šimun Erdödy (1518–43) ding the lateral towers. In the early 17th century, Ivan lbertal constructed a 230-foot (70-meter) Renaissance wer that stood on Romanesque foundations. In the d-17th century, a pentagonal bell tower was built that rved as a watchtower. Overall, the cathedral now had e appearance, and fulfilled the function, of a fortress.

E NEO-GOTHIC CATHEDRAL. The great earthquake at devastated Zagreb in 1880 coincided with the desire the ecclesiastical authorities to carry out renovations in the style of French Gothic Revival architect Eugène-Emmanuel Viollet-le-Duc, and Herman Bollé was commissioned to restore the damaged cathedral. He constructed a neo-Gothic pediment and two 345-foot (105-meter) bell towers without destroying the basic structure of the cathedral, which retained its medieval character. A fragment of a 13th-century fresco, a rare apocryphal scene from the life of the Virgin Mary – *Aqua probationis* – has survived on the wall of the south nave, while the sacristy is decorated with frescos by the 13th-century Italian school. However, many of the cathedral's centuries-old works of art have been divided between other churches, museums and even the cathedral treasure.

THE ARCHBISHOP'S PALACE. For centuries, the stone *kaštel* that stood in the garden to the south of the cathedral shared its fortunes and fell victim to wars and fires. Gradually, as the Turkish threat receded, the stone fortress became a palace. In 1692, Bishop Aleksander Mikulić realized the cultural ambitions of the ecclesiastical community by adding a wing with a LIBRARY to house the books and etched engravings that the bishop had bought from the Slovenian historian, Janez Vajkard Valvasor. The building was demolished in 1906 and the collection preserved

THE CATHEDRAL TREASURE Constantly under threat, the cathedral treasure was often hidden, sometimes as far afield as Dalmatia. The treasure is of exceptional quality and contains hundreds of works of art – gold- and silverware, illuminated manuscripts, embroidered fabrics, priests' garments, jewelry – dating from the 11th century to the present day.

A CATHEDRAL-PANTHEON A number of prominent Croatians are buried in the cathedral, including Ban (governor) Toma Bakać Erdödy, who halted the Turkish advance at the battle of Sisak ▲ *134*, counts Petar Zrinski (1621–71) and Fran Krsto Frankopan (1643–71) ● *34* and Cardinal Alojzije Stepinac (1898–1960) (*above*).

in the Croatian Academy of Arts and Sciences. In the 18th century, Bishop Juraj Branjug converted his residence into the largest baroque palace in Croatia and, in the early 19th century, Bishop Aleksander Alagović landscaped the episcopal garden, adding a verandah and the main flight of steps. In the late 19th century (1887–92), Herman Bollé refurbished the building in Historicist style. The 13th-century CHAPEL dedicated to Svetog Stjepan (Saint Stephen), which stands on the site of the city's first cathedral, has undergone numerous modifications and is now part of the Archbishop's Palace. The interior has some beautiful 14th-century frescos by the successors of Giotto from the Rimini school.

DOLAC. Only a stone's throw from the cathedral is Zagreb's main market (*below*), a riot of colors, scents and flavors that vary with the season. It was built between 1925 and 1930 on the site of the medieval district of Kaptol, of which only the CHURCH OF SV. MARIJA (St Mary) has survived. Extensively renovated in 1740, the church houses baroque works by Slovenian artists, including altars by Rottman, frescos by Jelovšek and a painting by Cebej.

BAN JOSIP JELAČIĆ (1811–59) ● 35
The Ban's equestrian statue (1866), by Viennese sculptor Anton Fernkorn, stands in Zagreb's main square. Originally, his drawn saber pointed north toward Hungary, where the Ban's army crushed a rebellion in 1848. Consigned to the scrap heap by the Communists in 1945, the statue was reinstated on the square in 1991 – with the saber pointing to the south.

REGRETTABLE DESTRUCTION
Due to the general disregard for Historicism and the functionalism of Secessionist architecture, only two buildings on the Trg bana Jelačića reflect these styles – an 18th-century one on the corner of Ilica and a neoclassical building by Felbinger on the square's south side.

THE FRANCISCAN CHURCH AND MONASTERY.
According to legend, Saint Francis stayed in the convent's early 13th-century buildings, which were renovated in the 17th century. The baroque interior of the tiny CHAPEL dedicated to Svetog Franjo, which used to be the saint's cell, was completed in 1683. It is decorated with stuccowork and paintings representing the traditional regional costumes of Croatia.

The Lower Town ♦ D A-C4-6

Modern Donji grad (Lower Town) grew up around old Zagreb, along roads traced since time immemorial across the plain that now lies within the 19th-century grid layout.

TRG BANA JELAČIĆA (GOVERNOR JELAČIĆ SQUARE). The inhabitants of Zagreb are extremely attached to their capital's busy main square, which lies at the junction of the city's old districts. Its position at the crossroads of the main communication routes with Vienna (Vlaška), the Adriatic (Ilica and Savska) and Bosnia (Petrinjska) also made it a major market place from the 13th century. In the past, activity was centered around a stream, the Manduševac, that used to run through the area. Today, this has been replaced by a modern fountain.

AN URBAN DEVELOPMENT PLAN. In the 19th century, many Croatian towns felt constrained by their fortifications. They therefore dismantled and replaced them with broad, often circular thoroughfares like the Ringstrasse (1865) in Vienna. Zagreb was an exception since the outline of its more recently constructed districts is not the result of the destruction of earlier structures but the calculated configuration of a grid layout. Thus Zagreb, a small town on the borders of a great empire, implemented a specific model that combines the constituent elements of modern urban planning – streets, squares, main thoroughfares, parks and walkways – in which Romantic inspiration governs the creation of green spaces within the urban fabric, and urban planning highlights the city's public buildings.

LENUCI'S HORSESHOE. Based on the urban development plan of 1857 and the first regulatory plan of 1865, the idea for the city center was defined in a new regulatory plan, in 1882–7. Although the buildings constructed before the early 20th century were collective undertakings, one name stands out from the rest – Milan Lenuci (1849–1924) who devised

ŠENOA,
A LIFE-SIZE STATUE
On Vlaška, a statue of August Šenoa ● 88, sculpted by Marija Ujević (1986), leans against a column. The poet is also commemorated by a plaque on Mesnička, a bust by Bohutinski on Opatička, and one by Rendić on Zrinjevac.

The *Liber linteus Zagrabiensis* ('the shroud of the Zagreb mummy') is thought to date from the 3rd century BC but could be even older.

ILICA
(*above*, in 1930) The city's main shopping street is undoubtedly also its oldest and longest, stretching for almost 3½ miles (6 km) from the Trg bana Jelačića.

TOMISLAV, THE FIRST KING OF CROATIA
Between the neoclassical train station (1890) and the Umjetnički paviljon (Art Pavilion, *above*) stands the equestrian statue of Tomislav, by Robert Frangeš-Mihanović (1872–1940). In 1901, the sculptor studied with Rodin.

the plan for the city center's parks and promenades, which formed what is known as Lenucijeva podkova (Lenuci Horseshoe). Although the original idea has not been entirely respected and the quality of the spaces varies, the architect's plan was implemented. You can see for yourself by following the 'horseshoe' from Trg bana Jelačića to Trg Nikole Šubić Zrinskog, usually referred to as Zrinjevac, and the train station, and then west to the Croatian National Library and north to the National Theater.

FROM ZRINJEVAC TO THE TRAIN STATION. Zrinjevac is the first and probably the most delightful of the green space in Lenuci's Horseshoe. The square is planted with huge plane trees and adorned with fountains, a bandstand and busts of famous Croatians. It is surrounded by buildings whose quality is comparable to those of the Viennese Ringstrassse and visitors can feast their eyes on the Historicist and the Secessionist architecture before entering the ARHEOLOŠKI MUZEJ (Archeological Museum). The museum, founded in 1846, brings together more than 450,000 objects dating from prehistoric times to the Middle Ages, including a number of Egyptian mummies, and has one of the most beautiful coin collections in Europe. On the south side of the square stands the CROATIAN ACADEMY OF ARTS AND SCIENCES. The building was designed in 1877 in rigorous neo-Renaissance style by Friedrich von Schmidt, one of Vienna's finest architects, and built by Herman Bollé. On the third floor, the STROSSMAYEROVA GALERIJA STARIH MAJSTORA (Strossmayer Gallery of Old Masters) was donated by Bishop Josip Juraj Strossmayer ▲ *148*, a prominent 19th-century figure and patron of the arts. A life-size statue of the bishop by Ivan Meštrović stands behind the academy. The gallery has a wealth of paintings representing the major European school (Italian, Flemish, French) and Croatian works from various periods, from the Middle Ages to the 19th century. In the row of buildings stretching toward the station are the Chemistry Laboratory, by Herman Bollé, and the UMJETNIČ PAVILJON (Art Pavilion), brought to Zagreb from Budapest, where it was designed for the 1896 World Fair. The pavilion whose metal framework was added by Viennese architects Helmer and Fellner, is today an exhibition center.

ROM THE STATION TO THE LIBRARY. The Horseshoe,
iterrupted by two 1920s buildings – the Esplanade Hotel
id the Social Security building – continues with the
)TANIČKI VRT (Botanical Gardens, 1890), an oasis of
eenery in the urban landscape. Founded in 1606, the
rmer NACIONALNA I SVEUČILIŠNA KNJIŽNICA (National and
niversity Library) ● 70 housed almost two and a half million
ilumes that have been transferred to the new Croatian
ational and University Library ▲ 115. This masterpiece of
cessionist architecture – rational, elegant, symmetrical,
ht and airy – by Rudolf Lubynski (1911) houses the
rvatski državni arhiv (Croatian National Archives). Inside
e sculptures, frescos, stained-glass
indows and furnishings by the best late
th-century and early 20th-century
roatian artists – sculptors Frangeš-
ihanović, Valdec and Vod, and
inters Crnčić, Iveković, Auer, Rački,
šov, Kovačević and Jurkić.

ROM THE LIBRARY TO ILICA. From
e library, Vukotinovićeva brings you to
e Muzej Mimara (Mimara Museum),
th more than 3,700 works of art from
periods, the lifetime collection of Ante Topić Mimara.
1972, Mimara presented his collection to the nation on
ndition that it was exhibited in the Donji Grad secondary
hool. The authorities complied and transformed the vast
hool into a museum. The building, designed by Isidor
ršnjavi and completed in 1895 by the German specialists
scholastic architecture, Ludwig and Hülsner, reflected the
tion's educational and cultural ambitions. Retrace your
eps to Trg bracé Mažuranića, where a Secessionist palace
903) surmounted by a dome houses the collections of the
NOGRAFSKI MUZEJ (Ethnographic Museum) from Croatia
id other countries, especially traditional Croatian costumes.
ie HRVATSKO NARODNO KAZALIŠTE (Croatian National
ieater), one of the centers of Croatian culture, was built in
pastiche of neo-baroque and Rococo styles by Helmer and
llner in 1894–5. In the course of their careers, these

▲ Zagreb

TWO FAMOUS SOPRANOS
The voices of Milka Trnina (1863–1914) and Zinka Kunc (1906–89) delighted music lovers throughout Europe and the United States.

INTERIOR DÉCOR OF THE NATIONAL THEATER
The theater was decorated by Croatian and Austrian artists. The five stage curtains, including the famous *Croatian National Revival* ● *35*, by Vlaho Bukovac, alone constitute a résumé of 19th-century Croatian art.

VIKTOR KOVAČIĆ (1874–1924)
In 1900, this disciple of Otto Wagner published a program for the inclusion of Croatian architecture in progressive European trends. In it, he rejected Historicism in favor of an 'individual and contemporary', and supposedly practical, form of architecture. Among the monuments he bequeathed to Zagreb are the church of Sv. Blaž (St Blaise) ● *72*, on Primorska (1912), the Frank House on Mažuranićev Trg, and the Zagrebačka Burza (Stock Exchange) on the Trg Burze.

architects constructed 53 theaters throughout Europe, including those of Rijeka ▲ *174* and Varaždin ▲ *128*. The National Theater in Zagreb is the result of a bold vision of urban development given the modest size of the town and position of the theater in the late 19th century – at the time, going to the theater from the Upper Town involved crossing a field of maize. Opposite the theater, in front of the building that houses the University education offices, stands a sculpture – the *History of the Croats* ● *29* – by Ivan Meštrović. The building, originally a hospital, was renovated to fulfill its present function after the earthquake of 1880. The northwest side of the square is bounded by one of Herman Bollé's finest achievements, the MUZEJ ZA UMJETNOST I OBRT (Museum of Arts and Crafts), flanked by the OBRTNIČKA ŠKOLA (Arts and Crafts School) of which the architect was the first director. As well as a rich collection of religious sculpture, the museum houses a wealth of Croatian and European works of art, including gold- and silverware, glassware (*below*), clocks and bells dating from the Middle Ages to the present day.

Other places of interest

Among the many places of interest located outside the city center, four in particular are well worth a visit – Maksimir park, to the east, Mirogoj cemetery and the suburb of Remete, to the north, and Novi Zagreb (New Zagreb), to the south.

MAKSIMIR. You can reach the park from the city center via the TRG HRVATSKIH VELIKANA (Square of Great Croatians), with its rotunda (1939) by Ivan Meštrović ▲ *222*, now the House of Croatian Artists. This vast, green space was donated to the city by its bishopric. In 1787, Bishop Maksimilijan Vrhovec started work on the Classical-style park that was named for him. His work was continued by his successors, Aleksandr Alagović and Juraj Haulik, who completed it, in the style of an English landscaped country park, in 1838. When it was opened, in 1843, the park covered an area greater than that

MIDDLE-CLASS INTERIORS
Zagreb's school of applied art has recreated interiors from the 18th to the early 20th centuries based on the styles then in vogue.

Detail of the *Source of Life* (1905), which stands in front of the National Theater.

'SOURCE OF LIFE'
In this bronze by a youthful Meštrović ▲ 222, the influence of Rodin's lyricism is noticeable in the treatment of the figures as they try to quench an eternal thirst. Meštrović first met Rodin and discovered his work in Vienna, in 1902. They became friends in 1907 during Meštrović's stay in Paris and re-established contact in Rome during World War One.

he capital. Today, it forms an integral part of the city and sts an authentic oak forest, many exotic species, themed ver beds, a lake and a number of buildings, including the nop's summer residence, a belvedere (*vidikovac*), a vilion of echoes', a mock Swiss chalet (Švicarska kuca) a chapel dedicated to Svetog Juraj (Saint George). 925, a ZOO was built at the southern end of the park.

ROGOJ CEMETERY. On Medvedgradska, to the north of ptol, the GLIPTOTEKA HAZU (Sculpture Museum) presents s of ancient and medieval works, as well as sculptures najor 19th- and 20th-century Croatian artists. Mirogoj, onumental neo-Renaissance cemetery (1883–1914) by man Bollé, is one of the most beautiful in Europe. It is nded to the west by domed arcades (*below*) which, as a of religious tolerance, exist alongside the Catholic and hodox crosses and the Jewish Star of David. Midway ng the arcades stands the church of Christ the King. Many Zagreb's and Croatia's prominent artistic, political and nomic figures are buried in this multi-faith cemetery and theon of Croatian history.

1ETE. This former village is today a suburb he Croatian capital. The Pauline Crkva Marija (Church of St Mary) was damaged he Turks in the 16th century, renovated ing the baroque period and restored by man Bollé after the earthquake of 1880. de are trompe l'oeils by Ivan Ranger ▲ *119*, othic altarpiece, a baroque altar by Jurjević Belina, and a 15th-century wooden statue he Madonna. Outside the church stands tue of Saint Simeon the Stylite (1739) ring the coat of arms of Bishop Branjug, roque relief of Saint Paul the Hermit, the remains of a baroque convent.

WEEN THE RAILROAD AND THE RIVER
. For decades, the city did not spread thward beyond the railroad but expanded to the east west. Today, the southern district of Novi Zagreb (New reb) has a number of ambitious modern architectural ctures – Zagrebački velesajam (Zagreb Fair Grounds), City Hall by Ostrogović, the new Croatian National and versity Library by Neidhart, Hržić, Krznarić and Mance, the Lisinski Concert Hall by Haberle, named for oslav Lisinski (1819–54), who composed the first atian opera *Ljubav i Zloba* (*Love and Malice*) (1846).

MIROGOJ CEMETERY
In this open-air museum of Croatian art, the architects Hržić, Krznarić and Mance reinterpreted the work of Herman Bollé and incorporated a crematorium in 1985.

The new Croatian National and University Library.

▲ From the Zagorje to the Podravina

1. ZAGREB ★   2. MOUNT MEDVEDNICA   3. MEDVEDGRAD   4. GORNJA BISTRA   5. STUBIČKE TOPLICE   6. DONJA STUBICA   7. GORNJA STUBICA   8. MARIJA BISTRICA   9. BELEC   10. ZAPREŠIĆ   11. BRDOVEC   12. KLANJEC   13. KUMROVEC   14. MILJANA   15. VE

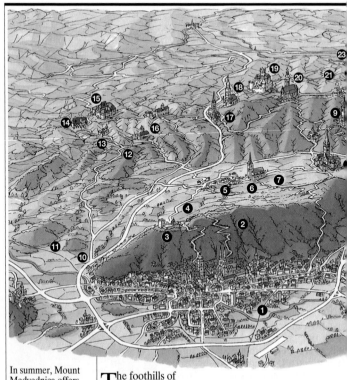

In summer, Mount Medvednica offers an escape from the oppressive heat of the city. In winter, 'Bear Mountain' is transformed into one of the country's largest areas of ski slopes.

The foothills of the 'Slovenian Alps' lie to the north of Zagreb. Throughout history, this part of the country has always be known as 'Croatia'. Together with the plain to the south o the capital, it escaped Ottoman domination and, like the of Christian Europe, experienced an age of feudalism tha bequeathed many chateaux, most of which had been renovated by the 18th century. This is also a region of baroque churches which, like the rest the former Habsburg empire, was de marked by the Counter-Reformation This itinerary starts from Mount Medvednica (Bear Mountain) to the north of Zagreb, and passes through western Zagorje, to the west of the capital, and then northern Zagorje, to the magnificent baroque town of Varaždin. After a brief visit to the Međimurje, Croatia's northernmost region, it returns to Zagreb via the Podravina or 'Drava Valley'.

Mount Medvednica ♦ A A2-3

Mount Medvednica, to the north of Zagreb, has been a nature reserve sir 1981 and is the city's ultimate green space. Marked woodland paths lead

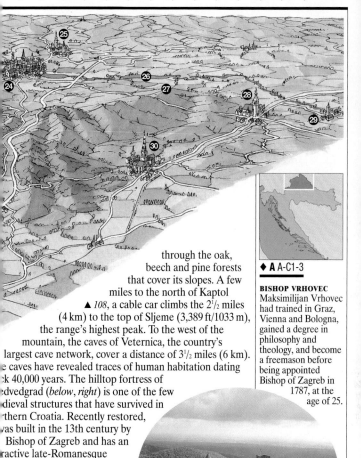

through the oak, beech and pine forests that cover its slopes. A few miles to the north of Kaptol ▲ *108*, a cable car climbs the 2½ miles (4 km) to the top of Sljeme (3,389 ft/1033 m), the range's highest peak. To the west of the mountain, the caves of Veternica, the country's largest cave network, cover a distance of 3½ miles (6 km). e caves have revealed traces of human habitation dating ck 40,000 years. The hilltop fortress of dvedgrad (*below, right*) is one of the few dieval structures that have survived in thern Croatia. Recently restored, as built in the 13th century by Bishop of Zagreb and has an ractive late-Romanesque pel. The bishop and humanist t, Ivan Česmički (1434–72), o wrote his famous epigrams d elegies under the name Janus nonius, died in the fortress.

RNJA BISTRA. Several baroque tles stand at the foot of the western pes of the mountain. Gornja Bistra 70–5) has the U-shaped layout typical of the e-baroque period. The great oval hall is decorated th trompe-l'oeil frescos.

UBIČKE TOPLICE. In the early 19th century, Maksimilijan novec, Bishop of Zagreb, began to build a spa around se famous springs (*toplice* means 'baths'). The architect H. Vesteburg successfully incorporated neo-Gothic, ssical and Biedermeier elements into the buildings.

NJA STUBICA. The Gothic church of Sv. Trojstva (the ly Trinity), renovated during the baroque period, houses ulpit in late-Gothic style and the tomb of Franjo Tahi, overlord whose cruelty helped to trigger the Peasants' volt of 1573.

♦ **A** A-C1-3

BISHOP VRHOVEC
Maksimilijan Vrhovec had trained in Graz, Vienna and Bologna, gained a degree in philosophy and theology, and become a freemason before being appointed Bishop of Zagreb in 1787, at the age of 25.

He was well-versed in philology and founded a printing press. His social preoccupations led him to build a hospital in Zagreb and the thermal baths at Stubičke Toplice. He began landscaping the main park, named Maksimir in his honor ▲ *114*, and contributed to the region's economic development.

117

Gubčeva Lip ('Gubec's lime tree') in Gornja Stubica, which also has a monument to the Peasants' Revolt of 1573 by Antun Augustinčić ▲ 120.

SAMOSTAN SNJEŽNE GOSPE (Our Lady of the Snow) According to a 13th-century legend, the Virgin Mary appeared to Pope Liberius in 352 and asked

him to build a church on a spot that would be covered with snow the next night. This 'spot' was the Esquiline Hill and the Pope built the Basilica of Santa Maria Maggiore. The legend is illustrated in many paintings and frescos in Croatia. The Virgin Mary is depicted with angels carrying snowballs on a platter.

Church of Marija Bistrica (*right*).

STUBIČKE GOLUBOVEC. Situated between Dona Stubica and Gornja Stubica, this manor house was transformed into a castle by Bishop Maksimilijan Vrhovec in the early 19th century. The Classical avant-corps and English-style garden added by the bishop can still be seen today.

GORNJA STUBICA. In the arcaded Orsić Palace (1756), the Muzej seljačkih buna (Museum of Peasant Uprisings) presents reconstructions of the everyday life of the nobility and common people, an exhibition on the Croatian national revival – Illyrianism (*Illirizam*) – and major collections devoted to the Peasants' Revolt of 1573. This was triggered by the hardships suffered by the local inhabitants as a result of the war with the Turks – tens of thousands of dead, plundering, heavy taxes, famine and epidemics. The revolt broke out in 1572, on the estate of Franjo Tahi, an extremely cruel overlord. Led by a local man, Matija Gubec, it spread throughout northwest Croatia and into Slovenia and the Venetian possessions. The peasant army was routed near Stubičke Toplice on February 1573. Six thousand peasants were hanged and dozens of villages burnt to the ground. Matija Gubec was tortured to death in Zagreb. The famous Gubčeva Lip ('Gubec's lime tree') under which the peasants supposedly met on the eve of the uprising, stands in the center of the village

The baroque interior of Sv. Marija Snježna (Our Lady of the Snow) in Belec, with frescos by Ivan Ranger.

ARIJA BISTRICA. This small, stic town became the most portant Marian shrine in oatia when a statue of the *ack Madonna* was discovered, 1648, bricked into a wall in e Hodočasnička crkva Marija stričke (pilgrimage church of Mary of Bistrica) at the time the Ottoman advance. This rk-wood statue, which dates om around 1500 and is supposed have miraculous properties, presents a Virgin and Child nding on a crescent moon with man features. In the 18th ntury, the church was rrounded by a covered gallery ilt against the outer wall to ovide shelter for pilgrims and rious kinds of merchants. These lleries were a characteristic feature of the pilgrimage urches built in northern Croatia during this period. The lery of Marija Bistričke (St Mary of Bistrica) is decorated th scenes representing the miracles performed by the Holy rgin. The church was renovated in 1879 by Herman Bollé *08*, who created a remarkable pastiche of several chitectural styles. Near Marija Bistrica, the delightful assical-style manor house of the Hellenbach family is in a beautiful park.

LEC. The village of Belec lies about 12½ miles (20 km) rth of Marija Bistrica, as you leave Mount Medvednica d head north into the Zagorje. On the main street, the urch of Sv. Marija Snježna (Our Lady of the Snow) has a ly remarkable trompe-l'oeil baroque interior in which veral altars laden with sculptures transform the rectangular ve (which predates the refurbishment of 1741) into an oval ace filled with the movement typical of this style. The namism of the interior created by painting and sculpture lies the modest dimensions of the building, which is the rm in northern Croatia. The church, which received merous donations from the Croatian nobility, was pendent on the Pauline order to which the painter, n Ranger – a master of Italian trompe l'oeil – belonged. re, the Pauline monk has represented scenes from the life the Virgin Mary in richly decorated medallions and ated a painted scenography of pilasters, niches, vs and draperies. The pulpit and the altars of int Joseph and Saint Barbara are by Josip hokotnig of Graz whose presence ests to the cultural links between oatia and central Europe, which re particularly strong at the time. contrast to its rich interior, e church's enclosure wall s an arcaded gallery and is nctuated by small towers.

IVAN RANGER, A PAULINE ARTIST
Ivan Ranger, a member of the Pauline order ▲ *126*, was born in the Austrian Tyrol. Between 1731 and 1752, he executed a major body of work in the small churches of northern Croatia, where he introduced monumental trompe l'oeils as well as the grace and serenity of Rococo by using fresh colors and light spaces. He also provided original solutions to complex iconographic problems, including the first independent landscape in Croatian art. His disciples made extensive use of the forms of expression employed in the painted décors of northwest Croatia during the late-baroque period.

Gingerbread hearts are a traditional decoration on Christmas trees.

Western Zagorje ♦ A A2

Hrvatsko Zagorje or 'transmontane Croatia' is bounded by Mount Medvednica to the south, a imaginary line between Zagreb and Varaždin to the west, and the Slovenian border to the east and northeast. Varaždin marks its northernmost point. It is a hilly region that rarely exceeds 1,600 feet (500 meters), plante with vines and orchards, and scattered with villages and hamlets. Above 1,300 feet (400 meters), the forest tends to be the preserve of ramblers. The Zagorje is famous for its castle built or renovated in baroque style in the 18t century, and for its 19th-century manor houses. The region is also renowned for its thermal springs

ZAPREŠIĆ. Western Zagorje begins just outside Zagreb, a few miles west of the capital. Near Zaprešić stands the cast of Novi Dvori, acquired in 1852 by Ban Josip Jelačić ● *35* who refurbished it in neo-Gothic style. An amazing, cusped façade forms a sort of central avant-corps in the long building. Visitors can still see the circular building where horses were used to do the threshing, and the old grain silo where 50 or so paintings by Matija Skurenji are on display. French writer André Breton described the work of this naïv painter, born in the late 19th-century, as 'enchanted'.

LUŽNICA. Situated to the west of Zaprešić, the palace of Lužnica, with its three wings and U-shaped layout, is typica of the late baroque period (second half of the 18th century It is flanked by two small, round towers and has sculpted reliefs above the windows.

JANUŠEVEC. This castle near Brdovec is regarded as the most beautiful Classical-style building in Croatia ● *70*. It was built in c.1825 on plans by Bartol Felbinger ▲ *105*, the Zagreb architect whose neoclassical style marked the capital and surrounding area during the first half of the 19th century. Based on the Palladian model, the square building conceals a circular central hall surmounted by a coffered dome that opens onto the other rooms. In this instance, the dome is concealed beneath the roof. Today, the castle houses the National Archives.

KLANJEC. Beyond the modern spa town of Krapinske Toplice, the village of Klanjec stands on the banks of the River Sutla near the Slovenian border. In the 17th century, it acquired a Franciscan monastery, courtesy of Ban Sigismund and Nikola Erdödy. The adjoining church house a pewter baroque sarcophagus. A museum presents the works of local sculptor Antun Augustinčić (1900–79), a pup of Ivan Meštrović ▲ *222* and Robert Frangeš-Mihanović, wl studied in Paris in the mid-1920s. Augustinčić sculpted the statues of several heads of state and the *Peace Monument* that stands in front of the United Nations building in New York. He also sculpted Klanjec's war memorial. The sculpture dedicated to Antun Mihanović (1872–1940), who wrote the Croatian national anthem, is the work of Robert Frangeš-Mihanović ▲ *112*, the poet's great-grand-nephew a one of the champions of the Secessionist style in Croatia.

WAYSIDE SHRINES
Small wayside shrines, decorated with flowers and sometimes ribbons, are a common sight throughout northern Croatia. They contain a painting, photograph or a small statue of the patron saint of the village. The shrines – the oldest are made of wood – were often erected when a catastrophe befell the village. Until the 19th century, they also served as markers for traveling merchants.

ANTUN AUGUSTINČIĆ
Augustinčić was a naturalist sculptor who worked mainly on the human figure. In 1929, he co-founded Zemlja ('Earth'), a group of socialist artists from Zagreb. The detail (*above*) is from his monument to the 1573 Peasants' Revolt in Gornja Stubica.

THE FRESCOS OF MILJANA

When the Ratkaj family refurbished their palace (*below*) in Miljana, in the 18th century, they decorated it with Rococo frescos. Scenes such as the one featuring the horn player (*bottom left*) evoke the age of gallantry and combine traditional imagery of the seasons, the zodiac and human characters.

KUMROVEC. As you head northwest along the Sutla, you come to the village of Kumrovec, the birthplace of Josip Broz (Tito) ● *36* (1892–1980). The house where Tito lived as a child is now part of the vast ecomuseum that is the village's main attraction. It comprises 18 traditional houses dating from th late 19th and early 20th centuries (*above*) based on various themes – the production and weaving of hemp and linen, basketry, the manufacture of wooden toys, the marriage ceremony and the life of a young couple – all reconstructed in minute detail.

MILJANA. Built in the 17th century, modified and extended until the 19th century, and renovated in the early 1980s, the palace of Miljana is a fine blend of baroque and Rococo styles. A single-story building, with a central tower and a sculpted portal, precedes the main part of the palace, relegating it to the background and creating a typically baroque sense of depth. Inside, the Rococo frescos (1772) are mostly the work of Anton Lerchinger, an eminent late-baroque artist ▲ *124*.

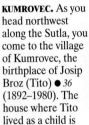

VELIKI TABOR. During the 16th century, a great many Renaissance castles, influenced by Italian models, were built in inland Croatia. Their circular towers and bastions meant that these unprecedented structures were ideally suited to the introduction of firearms and defensive artillery. Veliki Tabor is one of the most original of these castles ● *63*. The medieval castle was modified in the 16th century by the Ratk family, who had been local overlords for 300 years. It has a distinctive projecting upper story supported by consoles, and four prominent, semicircular towers which, as well as fulfilling a defensive function, were

so designed to give the impression of power. Inside, the typically Renaissance courtyard has three tiers of galleries, supported by Tuscan columns on the two upper levels. The ramparts, which no longer exist, made this truly formidable fortress.

VINAGORA. At the top of the village of Vinagora, about 4 1/2 miles (7 km) west of Pregrada, stands the pilgrimage church of Sv. Marija od Pohoda (St Mary of the Visitation), where a Gothic wood statue of the Madonna has been worshipped for centuries. It is surrounded by a traditional enclosure wall with an arcaded gallery to shelter pilgrims, and dominated by a bell tower with an onion-shaped dome. The main entrance is flanked by two round towers that serve as chapels. Perched on a hillock in a picturesque landscape, this baroque church (1657) looks more like a small fortress.

KRAPINA. This busy little town is famous for *Homo krapinensis* or 'Krapina Man' (*krapinski čovjek*), at least amongst paleontologists. In 1899, the Zagreb paleontologist, Dragutin Gorjanović Kramberger, discovered around 50 fossilized human bones in the caves of Hušnjakovo Hill. These were the remains of twenty or so Neanderthals, between the ages of two and forty, who had lived here during the Middle Paleolithic, between 80,000 and 50,000 years ago. A number of Mousterian-type flint tools and weapons, made by *Homo krapinensis*, as well as bear, elk and rhinoceros bones were also discovered on the site. The human bones are preserved in Zagreb, but other remains are on display *in situ* within the context of life-size reconstructions of scenes from this distant past. Other places of interest include the birthplace of Ljudevit Gaj, a key figure in the Croatian national revival, and a 17th-century Franciscan monastery whose richly decorated baroque church has frescos by Ivan Ranger. Only one of the town's three castles can still be seen. The extraordinary baroque church of Trški Vrh, about half a mile (1 km) northeast of Krapina, is well worth a visit ▲ *124*.

THE PRISONER OF VELIKI TABOR
Legend has it that a rich young duke fell in love with a beautiful but penniless girl named Veronika from the village of Desinić. The duke's family did everything in their power to destroy this liaison. They had the girl imprisoned in the castle of Veliki Tabor (*left*), accused her of witchcraft and finally had her strangled, in 1428.

▲ Crkva Sv. Marija Jerusalemske (St Mary of Jerusalem), Trški Vrh

Its architectural and decorative unity probably mak[es] the church of Sv. Marija Jerusalemske (St Mary of Jerusalem) the most beautiful baroque church in Croatia. Begun in 1750 and completed in 1761, the church received donations from the inhabitants and merchants of the free town o[f] Krapina. The beauty of its interior structu[re] in which space seems to expand like a bubb[le] is enhanced by the illusionist paintings that cover the walls from floor to vaulted ceiling. Surrounded by an arcaded gallery, the building is the epitome of the pilgrimage churches of northern Croatia.

THE BELL TOWER
The façade of St Mary of Jerusalem reflects the resolutely baroque part of the church, with the many set-backs of its pediment and the motive sculpture of its onion-shaped dome.

AN UNUSUAL DÉCOR
The paintings that completely cover the walls and vaulted ceiling of St Mary of Jerusalem combine architectural illusionism and allegorical scenes. The church's curved lines are transposed into two dimensions by false cornices and scrolled cartouches framing subjects drawn from the Old and New Testaments and the life of the Virgin Mary. These murals are the work of Anton Lerchinger (1720–92), a champion of the Styrian baroque style that adorned many Croatian and Slovenian churches. The high altar, a sort of tectonic retable housing a tiny statue of the Madonna brought back from Jerusalem in 1669, is by Filip Jacob Straub (1706–74) of Graz, who hailed from a family of Würtemberg sculptors. The church's pulpit and three other altars were created by wood sculptor and gilder Anton Mersi.

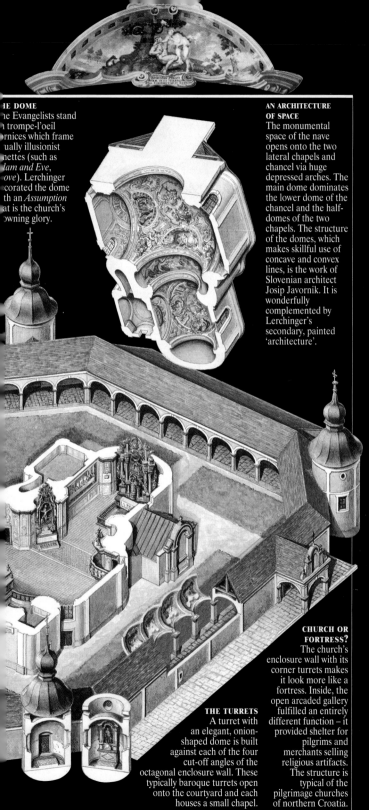

THE DOME
The Evangelists stand in trompe-l'oeil cornices which frame equally illusionist vignettes (such as *Adam and Eve*, above). Lerchinger decorated the dome with an *Assumption* that is the church's crowning glory.

AN ARCHITECTURE OF SPACE
The monumental space of the nave opens onto the two lateral chapels and chancel via huge depressed arches. The main dome dominates the lower dome of the chancel and the half-domes of the two chapels. The structure of the domes, which makes skillful use of concave and convex lines, is the work of Slovenian architect Josip Javornik. It is wonderfully complemented by Lerchinger's secondary, painted 'architecture'.

CHURCH OR FORTRESS?
The church's enclosure wall with its corner turrets makes it look more like a fortress. Inside, the open arcaded gallery fulfilled an entirely different function – it provided shelter for pilgrims and merchants selling religious artifacts. The structure is typical of the pilgrimage churches of northern Croatia.

THE TURRETS
A turret with an elegant, onion-shaped dome is built against each of the four cut-off angles of the octagonal enclosure wall. These typically baroque turrets open onto the courtyard and each houses a small chapel.

Suit of armor in the Trakošćan castle collection.

THE PAULINE ORDER
From the late 13th century to 1786 (the date of its dissolution), the Pauline order played a key role due to its wealth, its support of the Counter-Reformation and its defense of a national identity. The monastery of Lepoglava was extremely influential, founding the first secondary school in inland Croatia in 1503, and a university, in 1700. When the Pauline establishments of Croatia and Slavonia gained independence from the Hungarian branch of the order in the late 17th century, Lepoglava became their main monastery. The Paulines were ardent defenders of Catholicism and their buildings – practically all destroyed by the Turks – were built in baroque style, a symbol of the Counter-Reformation. It was this style that the studio of Pauline artist Ivan Ranger expressed with such strength and vitality. The stances of the order partly explain its dissolution by Joseph II, the Austrian Habsburg emperor inspired by the spirit of the Enlightenment.

Northern Zagorje ◆ A A1-2

TRAKOŠĆAN. To reach Varaždin from Krapina, a detour to the north will take you via the delightful castle of Trakošćan (*above*). The original building, dating from the 12th to the 13th century, was one of the smallest structures in the Zagorjes's fortification system. It became the property of the Drašković family in 1568, remaining in their possession until World War Two, and was enlarged several times. However, its transformation dates from the mid-19th century when Count Juraj Drašković converted the abandoned fortress into a Romantic castle. The count spared no expense, to the point of near bankruptcy, as he added neo-Gothic elements in the taste of the time, and created an artificial lake, a wooded park and gardens. Since 1953, 25 of the castle's rooms, complete with furnishings, have been open to the public. Among other things, visitors can see ancient weapons and a collection of family portraits dating from the 14th to the 19th century, a relatively rare phenomenon since most collections of this type have been divided between museums.

LEPOGLAVA. The long history of the Pauline monastery is reflected in the merging of Gothic and baroque styles that make it so charming. For several centuries, the establishment (founded in 1400) was a cultural center frequented by scholars, linguists, artists and sculptors. The vast complex is dominated by the Gothic church of Sv. Marija (St Mary) with its single nave and polygonal chancel. In the late 17th century, the church was refurbished in baroque style as part of a process characteristic of northern Croatia, with lateral chapels transforming the axial plan into a cruciform layout that emphasized the dynamic nature of the space. The façade, renovated in 1710, is a fine example of many façades created at the time in a distinctively

roque style, with pilasters and
rnices, statues in niches and
vish stucco décors. The interior
as frescos, including *Apocalypse*
the chancel, painted by Ivan
anger in 1742. The pulpit and
e altar dedicated to Svete Ana
aint Anne) (detail, *below left*)
e by Aleksije Köninger, a
uline sculptor from Graz who,
tween 1762 and 1782, executed
considerable body of work in the
der's establishments (Lepoglava,
orica, Križevci and Olimje).
ENOVNIK. About 6 miles
0 km) north of Lepoglava is
e castle built by the Drašković
mily (1616) which, with its
bedrooms and 365 windows, is
e largest in Croatia. In 1927, the
chitect H. Ehrlich transformed it
to a sanitarium, a function that
still fulfills today.
PEKA. You can reach Varaždin
a Maruševec or by making a
tour to Vinica and the nearby castle of Opeka, built in
e 18th century and renovated during the Romantic period.
ae castle's magnificent park, planted with exotic trees,
as created in the 1850s by the Bombelles family, nobles
French and Italian descent.

**THE FAÇADE OF
SV. MARIJA,
LEPOGLAVA**
The façade of the
church of Sv. Marija
(St Mary) is a rare but
extremely successful
combination of early
18th-century baroque
decoration and
Gothic verticality.

araždin ◆ A B1-2

araždin still has the architecture and décors for which
t became known as the 'capital of baroque'. The town
njoyed its golden age during the 17th and 18th centuries,
ue to the arrival of the Jesuits, who built baroque churches
d monasteries, and the presence of many noble families,
no built magnificent palaces. From 1756 to 1776, Varaždin
as the political center of Croatia, the seat of the Ban
governor) and council of governors. The terrible fire of
776 halted the town's expansion but did not destroy its
historic center. It was subsequently restored and is today
one of the region's main economic and cultural centers.
   A good starting point for a visit is the Palača Klegević,
opposite the north corner of the castle. Rebuilt in
Rococo style in 1775, it is one of the town's most
beautiful palaces. By following the fortifications
toward the west, you come the CHURCH OF
SV. FLORIJANA (St Florian) which houses a
tabernacle and stalls by Matija Saurer, a local
wood sculptor during the first half of the 18th
century, and a painting depicting the great fire
of 1776. The CASTLE (*stari grad*) or 'Old Town', with its
distinctive Italian-Renaissance-style buildings (*left*),
was designed in the mid-16th century by Domenico
dell'Allio, the Italian architect who supervised the

A BAROQUE JEWEL ★
It's advisable to leave
cars around the Trg
Ban Jelačića because
the streets of Varaždin
are pedestrian only.
Trg kralija Tomislava,
with its palaces with
ornate façades, is like
an encyclopedia of
Baroque architecture.
Autumn is the best
season for visiting the
city, when the colors
of the leaves match
those of the façades.
There are Baroque
soirées in Varaždin at
this time of year, as
part of Croatia's most
important music
festival ▲ *129*.

THE BATHS OF VARAŽDIN
Varaždinske Toplice has some impressive Roman
baths ● 56, restored in neoclassical style by Bartol
Felbinger (1820). The modern spa continues to
exploit the sulfur springs that emerge at a
temperature of 136°F (58°C).

Old Varaždin (*above*).
Trg kralija Tomislava
(*below*) with the Town
Hall on the right, and
the arcaded town
house of
the Ritz
family on
the left.

vast undertaking of the fortification of the Military Frontier
of Croatia and Slovenia. It houses an interesting museum
with reconstructions of aristocratic interiors. To the southea
of the Castle, on Trg Miljenka Stančića, the 18th-century
PALAČA SERMAGE is richly decorated in Rococo style. Today,
the palace houses an art gallery that brings together works
by Croatian, Italian and Scandinavian artists (15th–20th
century). Trg kralija Tomislava (Tomislav Square) and the
neighboring Franjevački trg (Franciscan Square) are
bordered by some remarkable buildings. The TOWN HALL
dates from the Gothic period, as evidenced by an arch of its
tower, although its present exterior – the work of Taxner an
Lossnert, two famous stonemasons working in Varaždin –
dates from 1793. On the east side of Trg kralija Tomislava
stands the PALAČA DRAŠKOVIĆ, whose Rococo façade dates
from the second half of the 18th century. Opposite the Tow
Hall, the former JESUIT MONASTERY (1671–91) stands
alongside the CRKVA MARIJINOG UZNESENJA (Church of the
Ascension) (1642–6), with its 18th-century façade, which
belonged for a time to the Pauline order. Inside are stalls
painted with scenes by Ivan Ranger, and a high altar in gilt
wood dating from 1737 (*right*). The frescos of the vault are
the work of local artist Blaž Grueber. The adjoining church
and college (reserved for the nobility) illustrate a type of
architecture that appeared in the baroque period, when the
Jesuits undertook to spread the faith by forming elites,
whereas the religious orders had hitherto tried to educate t
ordinary people. The huge seminary building, also known as
the PALAČA ZAKMARDI, stands a little further to the south.
The 16th-century town house owned by the Ritz family, on
the corner of Trg kralija Tomislava and Franjevački trg, is o
of the oldest in Varaždin. On the south side of Franjevački
trg stands the magnificent Rococo PALAČA PATAČIĆ and the
monumental PALACE OF THE COUNTS OF VARAŽDIN, complet
in 1769. The north side of the square is bounded by the
PALAČA PATAČIĆ-BUŽAN (c. 1785) and CHURCH OF SV. IVANA
KRSTITELJA (St John the Baptist), a baroque Franciscan
church built in c. 1650 by an architect from Graz. The churc
houses statues of Saint Francis of

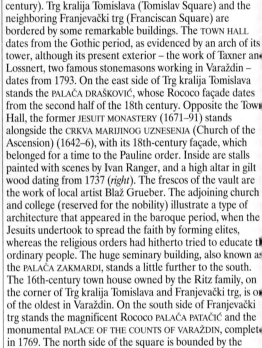

...ssi and Saint Anthony of Padua by the Varaždin sculptor
...ltenbach, and stuccowork by Quadrio, who also decorated
...e church of Sv. Katerine (St Catherine) in Zagreb ▲ *104*.
...he former pharmacy of the adjacent monastery has frescos
... Ivan Ranger. The PALAČA HERCZER at Franjevački trg 6,
...blend of baroque and neoclassical styles, houses
...e Entomološki muzej (Entomology Museum)
...th its collection of more than 10,000 insects.
... n the west side of Uršulinska, the street
...at runs from the museum up to the
...astle, are the URSULINE CONVENT
...749) and church (Uršulinska crkva)
...729) with statues by the famous
...aribor sculptor Jožef Straub.
... n Trg slobode (Freedom Square),
... the south of Franjevački trg,
...and the CHURCH OF SV. NIKOLA
...t Nicholas) and its 15th-century
...wer. The triple-nave Gothic church
...as given a baroque layout in the mid
...8th century by the addition of lateral
...apels. A fresco above the high altar
...ows the town during this period. Not
...r from the church is the neo-Renaissance
...roatian National Theater (1873) designed
... the Austrian architect Helmer. With Fellner,
...elmer specialized in the construction of theaters which,
... the time, were the ultimate form of entertainment for the
...w middle classes created by the industrial age. Opposite
...e theater, the PALAČA PATAČIĆ-PUTTAR (1745) combines
...roque and neoclassical styles.
... the west of Kapucinski trg stands the KAPUCINSKA CRKVA
...ETOG TROJSTVA (Capuchine church of the Holy Trinity)
...705) and its monastery and, to the north of the monastery,
...e PALAČA ERDÖDY, an impressive Rococo palace dating
...om the mid-18th century. Finally, Varaždin's MUNICIPAL
...EMETERY, a few hundred yards to the west of the Castle, is
...ell worth a visit. Laid out in 1905 by chief cemetery-keeper
...ermann Haller, it combines sculptures and kiosks in the
...edermeier, Historicist and Secessionist styles, while
...sculpted shrubs and trees add
to its charm.

MUSIC
Varaždin's long
musical tradition
dates from 1828 when
a school of music was
founded in the town.
Even earlier, in the
mid-18th century,
Ivan Franjo
Čikulin
bequeathed
3,000 florins to
the Ursuline nuns so
that they could teach
music to local girls.
Since 1971, Varaždin's
annual Festival of
Baroque Music,
held in
September,
features
concerts in
the theater
and the
town's
historic
churches
and
palaces.

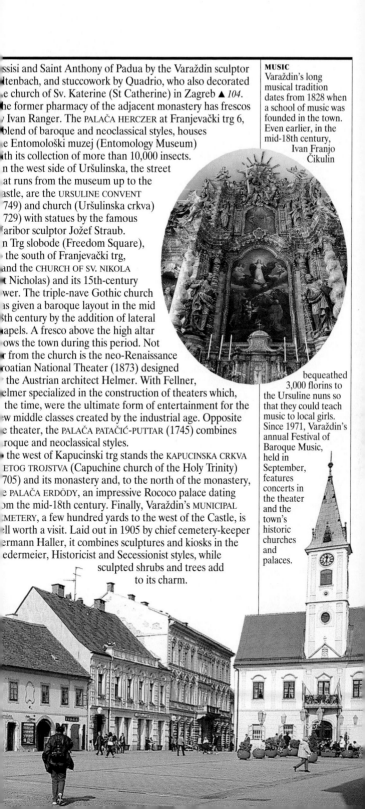

▲ From the Zagorje to the Podravina

The Međimurje ◆ A B1

The Međimurje lies on the borders of Slovenia and Hungary, between the Drava and Mur rivers. Western Međimurje is an undulating region renowned for its wines, while the fertile eastern plain produces cereals and early vegetables. For a long time a bone of contention between Hungary and Croatia, the Međimurje was ceded to Croatia after World War One. The region has a lively popular culture, especially when it comes to traditional songs.

ČAKOVEC. The old Renaissance and new baroque castles, which stand opposite each other within the town's originally medieval fortification, are the main attraction of the capital of the Međimurje. The town passed into the hands of the Zrinski family in the mid-16th century. In the 17th century, they strengthened the fortifications with polygonal bastions, thus adding one more rampart against the Turks in the vast system known as the *antemurale christianitatis* ('outpost of Christianity'). Today only the first story of the old castle – a long, curved building above the fortification – remains. The second castle, higher and rectangular in shape, contains several baroque elements, such as colossal pilasters (two stories high) and a portal set off by a balcony. It was built by P. Lucchese and rebuilt by Anton Erhard Martinelli, in 1743, after the great earthquake of 1738. Both architects came from Vienna – whose School of Architecture had gained international renown – during a period when the Croatian nobility was turning to architects from central Europe to build or renovate castles that were to be more residential than defensive. Perched on one of the bastions, the bell tower that announced the castle's presence far and wide dates from the 18th century. The wooden Franciscan monastery, built outside the castle's fortifications in 1659, was replaced by a baroque building (begun in 1702) which today houses portraits of the Zrinski family. The Museum of the Međimurje has an exhibition devoted to local composer Josip Slavenski (1896–1955) who drew his inspiration from the region's rich musical tradition.

The Podravina ♦ A B-C2

The Podravina or 'Drava Valley' occupies a broad sweep of the River Drava. This flat region criss-crossed by fast-flowing rivers and streams is popular with fishermen, while the Bilogora Mountain that forms its southeastern boundary is famous for its game, vast forests and timber industry.

LUDBREG. This former Roman town – the baths can still be seen – has been a major place of pilgrimage for 600 years. Legend has it that in 1411 a local priest saw the communion

wine change into blood. The chalice that contained the wine is preserved in the church of Sv. Trojstva (Holy Trinity), a Gothic building renovated in 1829. The Chapel of the Precious Blood of Jesus, which the diet of Croatia promised to build in 1739, was finally consecrated in 1994.

KRIŽEVCI. As the region's administrative center since the 14th century, Križevci was the seat of the 'bloody diet' of 1397, during which King Sigismund of Hungary and Croatia ordered the assassination of Stjepan Lacković, the pretender to the Hungarian throne. Outside the city walls, the 14th-century church of Sv. Križ (the Holy Cross), renovated repeatedly until the early 20th century, has a beautiful altar (1756) by Francesco Robba. The 17th-century Fransican monastery in the lower town was gifted to the Uniate Church in 1791. It was restored by Bartol Felbinger ▲ *105* in 1817 and the portico added in 1845 by the neoclassical architect Aleksandar Brdarić. Herman Bollé ▲ *108* undertook the restoration of the church in neo-Gothic style between 1892 and 1897. The chapel dedicated to Sv. Majike Božje Koruške (Our Lady of Carinthia), which stands apart from the church, contains a statue by the Varaždin sculptor Altenbach. Ivan Ranger ▲ *119* created the altarpieces for this chapel and for the church of Sv. Floijana (St Florian) in Varaždin.

▲ Central Croatia

1. ZAGREB ★ 2. SAVE 3. VUKOMERIČKE GORICE 4. VELIKA MLAKA 5. VELIKA GORICA 6. LUKAVEC 7. BREZOVICA 8. SELA 9. SISAK 10. KUPA 11. LONJSKO POLJE 12. ČIGOČ 13. JASENOVAC 14. PETRINJA 15. HRVATSKA KOSTAJNIC 16.

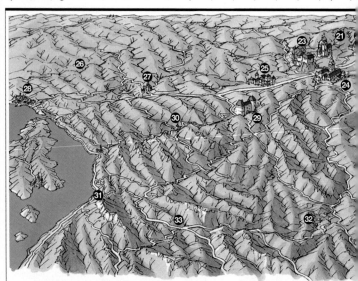

◆ **A** A-B1-4 **B** C-F2-6

ROMAN ANDAUTONIA
The Romans made Andautonia, the town of the Illyrian tribe known as the Andautonians, the capital of Upper Pannonia. From the 1st to the 4th centuries, it was a major administrative and economic center, as evidenced by the remains of the baths, public buildings and streets in present-day Šćitarjevo.

Central Croatia has a range of different landscapes, from the plains of the Sava, Kupa, Korana and Mrežnica rive to the hills and valleys of Banovina, the Samobor hills and the Žumberak. It has two major towns – Sisak in the east and, in the west, Karlovac, the main gateway town between inland Croatia and the coast. In the 12th century, as the center of power shifted to Zagreb, central Croatia enjoyed a revival, and market towns sprang up near the junctions of major trade routes. This period of relative peace and prosperity was brought to an end in the late 15th century by the Ottoman invasions and the establishment, by Austria, of the Military Frontier. Like the rest of inland Croatia, the central regions did not prosper again until the 18th century. These regions have suffered throughout the course of history, up to and including the recent conflict of 1991–2, and the conservation of buildings leaves much to be desired The first itinerary runs through the Posavina or 'Sava Valley' to the Lonjsko Polje nature park (*park prirode*) and the Banovina region to the south. The second, from Zagreb to Karlovac, makes a detour via the Samobor hills and the steep hills and wooded valleys of the Žumberak, while the third offers a choice of three different routes running from Karlovac to the Adriatic coast.

The Turopolje ◆ **A** A-B3

The Turopolje stretches from southeast of Zagreb to Sisak, incorporating the eastern slopes of the Vukomeričke Gorice and the plain of the River Sava to the east. In the 13th century, Bela IV ▲ *101*, King of Hungary and Croatia, accorded free status to the region's inhabitants, who established a royal free province with its own legislative assemb

18. TOPUSKO 19. SAMOBOR 20. JASTREBARSKO 21. THE ŽUMBERAK 22. PISAROVINA 23. OZALJ 24. KARLOVAC 25. BOSILJEVO 26. THE GORSKI KOTAR 27. DELNICE 28. RIJEKA 29. OGULIN 30. JASENAK 31. SENJ 32. PLITVICE LAKES 33. OTOČAC

and elected leader. Although this gave them a certain autonomy, it was subject to the payment of a heavy tribute. Even so, they defended their very particular status and, until the 19th century, the Turopolje remained an [au]tonomous province, with its own administrative [an]d legal institutions, represented at the parliament [in] Zagreb.

[VE]LIKA GORICA. Velika Gorica has been inhabited [fo]r thousands of years, as evidenced by the remains [of] prehistoric burial urns, Roman tombs dating from [th]e early empire and Slav tombs [da]ting from the early Middle [Ag]es (c. 800), discovered on [th]e site and now on display [in] the fortress. The town [ex]panded considerably during [th]e 17th century, after it was [gr]anted commercial [pr]ivileges, while the [co]nstruction of the railroad [to] Sisak and the development [of] trade with Zagreb made it a busy little town. The fortress [of] the Turopolje (c. 1765), so called because it housed the [se]at of the royal free province, today houses a museum [of] local crafts and Roman remains from Šćitarjevo.

[LU]KAVEC. This austere 18th-century castle surrounded by [m]oats was built on the site of a 15th-century timber fortress. [O]ne of its five towers dominates the baroque porch and [ar]mories built in 1752. The legislative assembly of the royal [fr]ee province of the Turopolje met in different towns, [in]cluding Lukavec.

[B]REZOVICA. Freed from Turkish occupation in the 18th [ce]ntury, western Croatia experienced a period of [re]generation. New towns developed, timber architecture [wa]s replaced by masonry, and the nobility brought architects [fr]om central Europe to build castles that were residential as [we]ll as defensive. The castle of Brezovica, flanked by two [el]egant, round towers, was built for the Drašković family by [an] Austrian architect. Today it has been converted into a [ho]tel whose main entrance hall is decorated with murals [(1]776) depicting the Seven Years' War (1756–63).

THE TIMBER ARCHITECTURE OF THE TUROPOLJE The Turopolje is famous for its religious and secular timber architecture ● 69. Today, you can still see peasant houses built of timber with carved decorative elements. Donja Lomnica is a fine example of the country residences built in timber by the local nobility – simple buildings with high, steeply pitched roofs. Some villages, such as Velika Mlaka, Pleso and Buševec, still have their timber churches. The walls and ceiling of the church of Velika Mlaka (*above*) are covered with paintings.

133

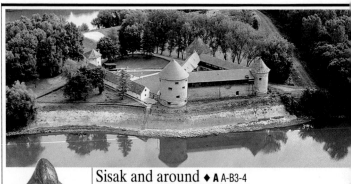

Sisak and around ◆ A A-B3-4

SELA. About 4½ miles (7 km) from Sisak, Sela's church of Sv. Marija Magdalena (St Mary Magdalen), completed in 1765, reflects the influence of the Viennese architectural school. The church, with its oval nave, is regarded as one of the most beautiful late-baroque buildings in Croatia.

SISAK. In the 2nd century AD, the town, which lies at the confluence of the rivers Kupa and Sava, was the capital of the Roman province of Upper Pannonia. As a major river port, commerce and crafts flourished and it also had an imperial mint. Among the many remains from this period of prosperity are a basilica and baths. Sisak was overrun by the Avars in the 5th and 6th centuries and finally superseded by Zagreb in the 11th century. The town re-emerged from obscurity in 1593 when the Turks were defeated below its fortress – a defeat that brought 300 years of Ottoman expansion to an end. The battle fired many imaginations and engravings of the event were soon circulating throughout Europe. As the major town in the region, Sisak has a number of late-baroque and Classical buildings, including the baroque church of Sv. Križ (the Holy Cross) which houses two marble statues by Francesco Robba ▲130.

LONJSKO POLJE. The wetland known as Lonjsko polje lies to the east of the River Sava and stretches from Ivanić Grad to the Bosnian border. Since 1990, the area – which covers 463 square miles (1,200 km²) and is flooded for six months of the year – has been the largest wetland nature park (*park pirode*) in Europe. Its ash, willow and oak forests and vast expanses of water offer an exceptional habitat to some relatively rare species – otters, beavers and wild cats. In summer, the swamplands are transformed into pastures grazed by the Posavlje horse (*Posavski konj*), a semi-wild, protected breed, while some 239 species of birds also frequent the park. The Krapke dol bird sanctuary, which covers an area of 62 acres (25 hectares) to the west of Jasenovac, is home to such rare species as the white-tailed sea eagle, the spoonbill and the black stork. In Čigoč, a village situated 18½ miles (30 km) to the southeast of Sisak, storks have colonized the roofs of timber houses.

Roman bronze statuette, discovered in Sisak.

THE CASTLE OF SISAK
The castle (*above*), situated about 1½ miles (3 km) south of the town, was modified at the instigation of the Zagreb cathedral chapter in order to defend the *reliquiae reliquiarum* – 'the remains of the remains' of the glorious kingdom of Croatia ● *33* – against the Turks. The three massive, barrel-shaped bastions were added to the 13th-century triangular citadel between 1544 and 1550 by Pietro da Milano. The Turks were defeated here in 1593.

anovina ◆ A A-B4

is green, undulating region lies to the south of Sisak,
tween the Sava and Glina rivers. Petrinja and Glina,
e two main towns, were the headquarters of the two
giments stationed in the region at the time of the Military
ontier ● *33*. Today, ruins are all that remain of the medieval
ber fortifications that were used to form a defensive
rrier against the Turks in the 16th century.

TRINJA. In the late 16th century, the Turks rebuilt the
wn at the confluence of the Petrinjčica and Kupa rivers.
wever, they were driven out in 1596 and Petrinja became
e starting point for the re-conquest of the Banovina region.
e main square is bounded by baroque and Classical
ildings, while the 18th-century park has trees planted
1810 under the French occupation. Gavrilović, the famous
rk butcher's that once supplied Napoleon I, was founded
Petrinja in 1744.

RVATSKA KOSTAJNICA. This beautiful 15th-century fortress
nds on an island in the River Una. Until the 17th century,
was a Turkish outpost against the Austro-Hungarian empire.
INA. Like Petrinja, Glina has a beautiful park and
assical buildings. A Croatian Catholic church and a
rbian Orthodox church once stood on the same square,
uxtaposition typical of the Military Frontier. Like so
ny of the religious buildings in Banovina and Slavonia,
e Catholic church was destroyed in 1991–2.

PUSKO. The springs of this spa town have been in use
ce Roman times. They became famous in the second half
the 19th century when Francis Joseph, emperor of Austria
d king of Hungary, came to take the waters. The baths and
ars (several dedicated to Silvanus, god of countryside, and
e to Mithra, god of light) found on the site can be seen in
e local museum. An impressive portal, built c.1300, is all
at remains of the Cistercian abbey founded in the early
th century by King Andrew II of Hungary, who had monks
me to Topusko from Clairvaux Abbey in northeast France.

**FROM
ZRIN TO ZRINSKI**
In 1347, the fortress
of Zrin, whose ruins
can be seen 7¹/₂ miles
(12 km) west of
Hrvatska Kostajnica,
fell into the hands of
the Šubić family ▲ *205*
The family adopted
its name and became
famous under the
Zrinski patronymic.

**JASENOVAC
CONCENTRATION
CAMP**
During World War
Two, Jasenovac, on
the Bosnian border,
was the largest
concentration camp
established by the
pro-Nazi Ustaše
authorities. Tens of
thousands of Serbs,
Jews, gypsies and
Croatian anti-Fascists
were exterminated
here. Today, the site
has a memorial park
(*spomen-park*),
centered around a
monument to the
victims by the Serbian
architect, sculptor and
politician Bogdan
Bogdanović.

♦ B E-F1-2

PISAROVINA, AN OPEN-AIR MUSEUM

Pisarovina, about 5½ miles (9 km) west of the Crna Mlaka (Black Marsh), has an unusual museum. It comprises several timber houses, over 200 years old, set in gardens filled with local plants. Inside, objects and costumes evoke the everyday life, traditional crafts and ceremonies of bygone days.

THE UNIATES OF THE ŽUMBERAK

The Uskoks who settled in the Žumberak in the 16th century were either Catholic or Orthodox Slavs. In the early 17th century, the Orthodox Slavs joined the Greek Catholic or Uniate Church, which had resulted from the rapprochement of the Orthodox and Roman Catholic Churches. In so doing, they became Byzantine Catholics.

Today, the Žumberak has a large Uniate community whose largest church, the Crkva Sv. Petar i Pavao (Church of St Peter and St Paul, 1756), is in Sošice.

Samobor. Stari grad god. 1775.

From Zagreb to Karlovac

The road from Zagreb to Karlovac, a major gateway town between north and south Croatia, follows the line of the Samobor hills which rise to a height of 2,887 feet (880 meters). They are extended to the west by the Žumberak, a range of hills that reaches its highest point – 3,865 feet (1,178 meters) – at Sveta Gera and marks the border with Slovenia.

SAMOBOR. The delightful town of Samobor, to the west of Zagreb, is famous for its glassware, mustard, sausages, cakes (try the *samborska kremšnita*, layers of flaky pastry filled with vanilla custard) and its carnival. Present-day Samobor is dominated by the ruins of the early town, built in the 13th century and abandoned 600 years later. The central square, Trg Kralja Tomislava, is bordered by elegant 18th- and 19th-century town houses. Among the town's religious buildings, the CHURCH OF ST ANASTASIA was inspired by the church of Sv. Katerine (St Catherine) in Zagreb, whose model was also replicated in Varaždin. The 18th-century Franciscan church of Sv. Marija (St Mary, 1722) is decorated with major work by Valentin Metzinger, in particular *Saint John Nepomucen* in one of the dramatic poses favored by the artist.

THE SAMOBOR HILLS AND THE ŽUMBERAK. To the west of Samobor and Jastrebarsko lies a range of karstic hills whose rocky peaks, gorges and caves were popular with 19th-century climbers. The lower slopes are planted with vines, while the higher pastures and forests harbor rare plants, including 35 species of orchid in the Žumberak alone. The Samobor hills are a popular place for walks and outings among the inhabitants of Zagreb, and the summits of Japetić, Oštrc and Plešivica are well provided with footpaths and mountain huts (weekends only). Further west the hills of the Žumberak stretch to the Slovenian border. They used to be known as the 'mountain of the Uskoks', after the people of Senj who were displaced by the Habsburgs in 1617 ▲ 185.

JASTREBARSKO. Declared a royal free town by Bela IV in 1257, this small town between Samobor and Karlovac was an important commercial center. A fortified castle was built in the early 16th century and later modified. The baroque-style church of Sv. Marija (St Mary) has an altar by Giovan Rossi and a painting by Valentin Metzinger (1735).

OZALJ. Built on a cliff overlooking the picturesque valley of the River Kupa, the medieval fortress of Krupa was transformed into a castle in the 18th century, although the 16th-century *palas* (corn exchange) and a Gothic chapel can still be seen. Today, the castle houses the local museum and s collection of ancient weapons. Don't miss the Munjara ('lightning factory'), the country's oldest hydro-electric power station (1908). Its architecture makes it look more like a Gothic-Romantic folly than an industrial building.

KARLOVAC. The town was founded in 1579, when a military outpost designed to strengthen Austria's southern defenses against the Turks was built at the confluence of the Korana and Kupa rivers. This huge undertaking was financed by contributions from several crowned heads of Europe. The fortress – an 'ideal town' contained within a perfect hexagon that formed a six-pointed star – reflects the urban layout inspired by the Italian Renaissance *62*. Karlovac's bastions were demolished in the late 19th century, when ramparts and fortifications were being demolished throughout Croatia. They were later transformed into gardens and today only their outline can be seen on the ground. Once the Ottoman threat had been removed, the construction (18th century) of several roads linking inland Croatia with the coast made Karlovac the country's principal commercial center. Its timber houses were replaced by baroque town houses. On the main square stand the Catholic Crkva presvetog Trojstva (Church of the Holy Trinity), built in the 17th and renovated in the 18th century, and the Orthodox Church of Sv. Nikola (St Nicholas), built in 1784–6.

Toward the Adriatic coast ◆ B C-F2-6

Three major routes link inland Croatia with the Adriatic coast. From Karlovac they climb the coastal mountains, which rise to heights of over 4,920 feet (1,500 meters), before plunging toward the sea, offering some spectacular views.

KARLOVAC TO RIJEKA. Beyond Bosiljevo, the road enters the GORSKI KOTAR ('wooded district'), the most densely wooded mountain region in Croatia. This route crosses landscapes reminiscent of the Alps.

'Only one town [in western Croatia] – Karlovac, for a long time known as Karlstadt – combined traditional, industrial and commercial activities until the late 19th century. The town has a truly remarkable history. In the 17th century, it was a simple, fortified town that, in the space of 100 years, became one of the largest business centers in the South Slav states of the Austro-Hungarian empire. Like Glina, Ogulin and Petrinja, it was built from scratch by the military. Like Rijeka, Bakar and Zagreb, it was the merchants who ensured its development.'
La Croatie occidentale, étude de géographie
André Blanc, 1957

Bosiljevo (*left*) was almost given the strategic role that fell to Karlovac. Its medieval castle was refurbished in Romantic style in the early 19th century.

137

▲ The Plitvice Lakes National Park

Many species of fish, including trout (*right*), live in the pure waters of the lakes.

The Plitvice Lakes are hollowed out of the karstic plateau separating the Mala Kapela from the Lička Plješivica mountains, on the edge of the Croatian highlands. In a fairytale setting, 16 lakes are linked, over a distance of 5 miles (8 km), by a string of foaming waterfalls and cataracts. The upper lakes, nestling among densely forested hills, have formed in dolomite rock whose erosion has given rise to broad, open valleys. Some 330 feet (100 meters) below, the four lower lakes have formed in limestone, hollowing out the vertiginous Korana gorge with its network of caves.

HOW THE LAKES WERE FORMED

The lakes were created by the erosion of the substrata (limestone and dolomite) and the formation of tufa barriers. The climate and high oxygen content of the turbulent water favor the proliferation of mosses which, with the help of algae and bacteria, retain the calcium carbonate that saturates the water. These deposits build up and produce tufa or light travertine. Over millions of years, a series of rocky barriers was created, behind which the lakes formed.

THE UPPER LAKES

The first of the upper lakes, Lake Prošćansko, which has a surface area of 169 acres (68.2 hectares), acts a sort of filter for the detritus (loose stones and silt) carried down by the River Matica, its principal source of water. Below the lake, the water flows via a series of lakes and falls into Lake Kozjak, the last but also the largest – 201 acres (81.5 hectares) – and deepest – 152 feet (46.4 meters) – of the upper lakes.

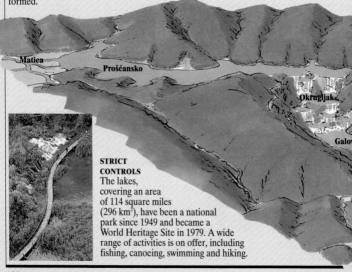

Matica
Prošćansko
Okrugljak
Galov

STRICT CONTROLS

The lakes, covering an area of 114 square miles (296 km²), have been a national park since 1949 and became a World Heritage Site in 1979. A wide range of activities is on offer, including fishing, canoeing, swimming and hiking.

TRIUMPHANT NATURE ★
All year round, the park offers spectacular displays. In winter, the snow and ice adorn lakes and waterfalls. In spring and fall, the water takes on the colors of the reflected trees. In summer, the approach routes to Veliki Sklap, the largest of the waterfalls that falls into Kaluderovac, one of the lower lakes, are thronged from morning to evening. In order to appreciate the surroundings fully, take the paths, bridges and footbridges as early as possible. The boat trip across Lake Kozjak, the biggest body of water in Plitvice, is magical in the morning light (there are departures every half hour in summer).

FLORA AND FAUNA
The park's forested hills, which are covered with common beech, white pines, Scots pines and European maples, are home to more than 150 species of birds. Mammals such as bears and wolves, which are quite rare in Croatia, also find refuge here.

sko

Kozjak

Korana

ANTE STARČEVIĆ
The democrat and liberal Ante Starčević (1823–96) created the ideology of the Croatian Party of Rights that favored the formation of an independent Croatian state and regarded the Croatian people as a sovereign subject within their territory. In spite of its limits in historical terms, Starčević's ideology played a key role in the creation of the modern sense of Croatian national identity. A house in his native village of Veliki Zitnik, about 3 miles (5 km) from Gospić, houses a museum that traces his life and work.

Landscapes of the Gorski kotar (*below*).

After Delnice, the region's main town, the road branches off to Crni Lug, starting point for a visit to the RISNJAK NATIONAL PARK which lies at the foot of Risnjak, the highest mountain – 5,190 feet (1,582 meters) – in the Gorski kotar. The park is home to a few brown bears, wild cats and wolves. Driven out in the 19th century, the lynx (*ris*) that gave its name to the mountain is gradually returning from the neighboring mountains of Slovenia.

KARLOVAC TO SENJ. This route follows the old *Voie Joséphine*, built by the French between 1772 and 1779. It winds its way through the delightful Mrežnica Valley, with its waterfalls and clear lakes, before crossing the Kapela mountains and then the northern Velebit via the Vratnik pass, which offers a spectacular view of the sea. From Josipdol, you can make a detour to Ogulin and the beautiful 15th-century castle of the Frankopan family. About 12½ miles (20 km) west of Ogulin, beyond Jasenak, the BIJELE STIJENE NATURE RESERVE rises to 4,377 feet (1,334 meters) – a labyrinth of bare summits above thick forests and deep valleys. Back on the main road, a few miles south of Josipdol stands the ruined fortress of Modruš which, until the Ottoman invasion, was the main residence of the Frankopan family ▲ *182* and the seat of a bishopric. Just before the Vratnik pass, a road turns off to Otočac which still has a number of two-story buildings from the time of the Military Frontier. The nearby River Gacka is famous for its trout.

KARLOVAC TO ZADAR. This is the longest and most scenic of the three routes since it passes through the Plitvice Lakes National Park ▲ *138*. From Karlovac, the road crosses the KORDUN, the high karstic plateau overlooking the Korana River that flows through Slunj before entering the Plitvice Lakes. Southwest of the lakes, the LIKA is an isolated region bounded by the Velebit along the coast, and the Lička Plejšević and Mala Kapela inland. During the early Iron Age (1000–500 BC), this was home of the Illyri-Celtic tribe known as the Japodes (or Iaopodes). From Gospić, a detour to Smiljan will take you to the birthplace of Nikola Tesla (1856–1943), the engineer who developed the first hydroelectric power station at Niagara Falls. Back in Gospić, the road to Zadar takes you via Gračac from where you can visit the underground cave network of Cerovac ■ *28*, which runs for over 2 miles (3.5 km). Some chambers are as much as 98 feet (30 meters) high, with spectacular mineral décors

Slavonia

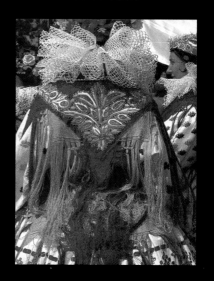

Osijek, *142*
The Baranja Region, *146*
The Podravina Region, *147*
Southeastern Slavonia, *148*
Central Slavonia, *150*
Western Slavonia, *151*

▲ Slavonia

1. OSIJEK 2. DRAVA RIVER 3. DANUBE RIVER 4. BILJE 5. DARDA 6. KOPAČKI RIT 7. ALJMAŠ 8. ERDUT 9. DALJ 10. VALPOVO 11. DONJI MIHOLJAC 12. ĐAKOVO 13. VINKOVCI 14. BOSUT RIVER

♦ A C-F3-4

**SLAVONIA, THE
GRANARY OF CROATIA**
Despite its
predominant
flatlands, this region
boasts many different
landscapes. Extensive
wheat fields,
particularly in eastern
Slavonia, alternate
with hills, ideally
suited to wine-
growing, and forests
of ancient oaks ■ 16.
There are also
pasturelands dotted
with *djerams*, a type
of well operating on
a balanced counter-
poise system, once
a common sight in
Slavonia.

In the Middle Ages, Slavonia was an umbrella term for all Slavic countries. As part of the Hungaro-Croatian kingdo (1102–1527), it described the area bounded by the Sava and Drava basins, now the entire Croatian plain, including the Zagreb region. In the 16th and 17th centuries, the term Slavonia was used exclusively to refer to the region captured by the Ottomans, the northeastern part of the present Republic of Croatia. After Turkish rule was finally overthrown in 1691, Slavonia became part of the kingdom of Croatia, Slavonia and Dalmatia. Bordered to the north by Hungary, to the south by Bosnia-Herzegovina and to the east by the Federal Republic of Yugoslavia, Slavonia now numbers about one million inhabitants. Despite the ravages of the recent War of Independence, Slavonia still possesses enough treasures to make it a fascinating tourist destination

The history of Osijek ♦ A F3

Osijek, Slavonia's largest city (around 105,000 inhabitants) and its traditional capital, is a dynamic, lively center, despite its legacy of Pannonian melancholy and its Central Europea trappings. Its historic districts extend along the right bank o the Drava, while the marshy left bank has never been developed.

ANCIENT TIMES. The Roman city of Mursa originally stoo on the site of Osijek's present Donji Grad (Lower Town). Mursa was founded by the Andizetes, a Pannonian tribe wh came under the yoke of the Roman Empire during the reig

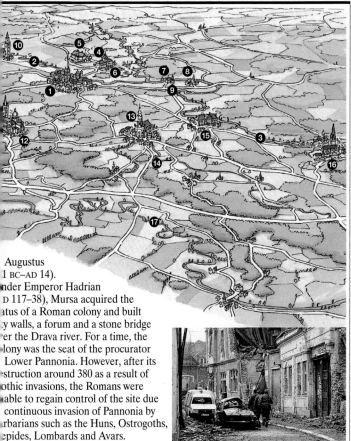

Augustus
(1 BC–AD 14).

...nder Emperor Hadrian
(AD 117–38), Mursa acquired the
...atus of a Roman colony and built
...y walls, a forum and a stone bridge
...er the Drava river. For a time, the
...lony was the seat of the procurator
...Lower Pannonia. However, after its
...struction around 380 as a result of
...othic invasions, the Romans were
...able to regain control of the site due
...continuous invasion of Pannonia by
...rbarians such as the Huns, Ostrogoths,
...epides, Lombards and Avars.

...IE MIDDLE AGES. The market town
...d river port of Osijek first appeared in 1196. This Magyar
...d Slavic village, whose name was usually found in its
...ungarian spelling, Eszék, occupied the site of what was
...be Tvrđa.

...IE OTTOMAN OCCUPATION. Osijek consolidated its
...portance during this period (1526–1687), becoming a
...saba (small town) which was home to a Cadi (Turkish
...dge). In 1566, the Turks built a floating wooden bridge
...er the Drava, extended by a stilted structure above the
...arshland of the left bank as far as Darda, a distance of
...out 4 miles (7 km). Osijek was a major trading and
...ansportation center. The explorer Atanazije Georgiceo
...ted that the town had eight mosques in 1626. Outside the
...lls lay the suburbs and the fairground, the site of a market
...at was vividly described by many travel writers.

...IE MODERN PERIOD. After the Ottomans left Osijek
...587), the inner town was fortified in line with modern
...litary principles. A large area was cleared around the site
...the new fortress (Tvrđa) and, in 1691, the people living in
...e suburbs were relocated a mile (1.5 km) further west
...ng the Drava river.

SCARRED BY THE CROATIAN WAR OF INDEPENDENCE
During the years of conflict (1991–5), some of the bloodiest battles were fought in eastern or western Slavonia. Vukovar – a symbol of Croatian resistance – was almost totally destroyed while towns like Osijek, Vinkovci, Slavonski Brod, Nova Gradiška and Pakrac still bear the scars of war. It will take years, if not decades, to repair the damage.

Kuhačeva

Markovića

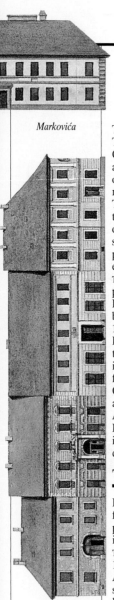

Boškovića

This led to the foundation of the Gornji Grad (Upper Town) which, like Tvrđa, excluded 'heretics and non-Catholics'. The Donji Grad (Lower Town) sprang up a few years later, just over a mile (2 km) east of Tvrđa, on the eastern boundary of ancient Mursa. As right of residence was not restricted to Catholics here, the Lower Town swiftly became the most densely populated of the two. Although Tvrđa ceased to serve as the headquarters of the General Command in 1783, it continued to house a substantial garrison. In 1809, Emperor Francis I of Austria proclaimed Osijek a Royal Free Town, thereby putting an end to Hungarian feudal power over this territory.

THE 19TH CENTURY. Osijek wavered between the politic poles of Zagreb and Budapest throughout this century. During the Hungarian revolution, Tvrđa surrendered briefly to the Hungarian army (October 1848–February 1849), but was brought back under the rule of the Croatia Ban (ruler), Josip Graf Jelačić (1801–59) ● 35. Osijek was the largest city in continental Croatia in the 1850s. Its industrial sector included silk mills, an oil-mill, a match factory, a brewery and a flour-mill and its Chamber of Commerce, founded in 1853, eventually extended its authority across the whole of Slavonia and Srijem. After the demilitarization of the Vojna Krajina (Military Frontier) in 1873, the fortress continued to diminish in importance and the ramparts and bastions were demolished in 1922.

Tvrđa, Osijek's fortress

Formerly impregnable and defended on all sides by fortifications, Tvrđa now opens onto three beautiful parks. Most of its buildings house academic or cultural institutions.

THE FORTIFICATIONS. These were built between 1709 a 1721 to plans by Colonel Maximilian Gosseau d'Heneff. After completion, Tvrđa was protected by a star-shaped system of ramparts, a moat with five bastions – three adde later – and by the Crown Fort on the other bank of the Drava. Four gates, one at each cardinal point, provided access. All that survives today is the massive bastion facin

Kuhačeva

TVRĐA, OSIJEK'S FORTRESS: façades around Holy Trinity Squar

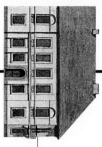

Katančića

e Drava, a section of wall including the Vodena
rata (Water Gate) and part of the fort that remains
the left bank.

RG SVETOG TROJSTVA (HOLY TRINITY
UARE) ● *66*. Since 1946, the Muzej Slavonije
Museum of Slavonia), founded in 1877, has been
used in the town's former Magistrate Building,
ich was built between 1700 and 1702. On the
rthern side of this vast square stands the
eneralate Palace, now the University Rectorate,
ich served as the Command Headquarters of
avonia's Military Frontier until 1783. From the mid
th century, it staged performances by touring
erman theater companies. The western side of the
uare is occupied by the Main Guard building
728) and, on the northeastern side, next to the Law
urts, stands the Jesuit college, founded in 1765,
ere lessons were taught first in Latin then, from
49, in Croatian. Slavonia's greatest encyclopedist,
atija Petar Katančić (1750–1825), taught poetry
re for a time. At the center of the square stands
e *Kužni Pil* (Plague Column) erected by the widow
General Maximilian Petraš in 1729.

ROUND THE SQUARE. The narrow winding roads
the Turkish *kasaba* were replaced by straight
enues and it became mandatory to use brick or
one for construction, because a fire would have
en disastrous so close to an ammunitions
rehouse. On the site of the medieval church, the
anciscans built the church of the Sv. Križ (Holy
oss, 1709–c. 1720), next to their monastery, which
s constructed in several stages between 1699 and
67. Slavonia's first printing house was established
this monastery in 1735 and was bought by Martin
vald in 1775. The famous business printed nearly
0 titles in Latin, Croatian and German, before it
s forced to close in 1856. On the site of the Kasim
sha Mosque, the Jesuits built their monastery
d the great church of Sv. Mihovil (St Michael,
25–42), whose two bell towers soar above the
ofs of Tvrđa.

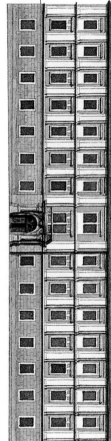

Boškovića

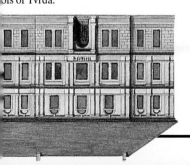

Bösendorfera

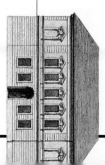

Osijek's Gornji Grad (Upper Town)

The town's architecture reflects its rapid economic expansion in the second half of the 19th century and the early 20th century.

AROUND TRG ANTE STARČEVIČA. This square is the site of the City Hall (1894). Further east, in Kapucinska (Capuchins' Street), the Hotel Royal, dating from the 1900s stands opposite the church of Sv. Jakov (St James, 1723–7). The sacristy of this church, built in the early 18th century by Capuchins from Buda to service the needs of their monastery, contains a valuable cycle of paintings about the life of St Francis, dating from 1752. Županijska ulica, the 19th-century street running through the town center, is hom to the neoclassical Virovitica County (*županija*) building (1834–46), the Croatian National Theater with its lavish interior, completed in neo-Moorish style in 1866, and the neo-Gothic church of Sv. Petar i Pavao (St Peter and St Paul, 1894–8).

EUROPSKA AVENIJA ● 72. Europe Avenue is a particularly attractive street, especially heading west, where two rows of eclectic Secession-style (Art Nouveau) buildings house, among other institutions, the central post office, the Urania movie theater, the university library and the Galerija Likov Umjetnosti (Gallery of Fine Arts). This museum, founded i 1954, has a particularly interesting collection of the works o two artists from Osijek, Hugo Conrad von Hötzendorf (1807–69) and Adolf Waldinger (1843–1904).

The Baranja Region ◆ **A** F3

This historic region, bounded by the Drava and Danube rivers and the Hungarian border, belonged to the fief Belje which was, until World War One, private Habsburg property and one of best managed and most extensive estat in Hungary. Its first owner, Prince Eugene of Savoy (1663–1736), built a baroque hunting lodge (1705–12) near the village of BILJE. Nearby DARDA boa

Gornji Grad was inhabited by civil servants and noble families, while Donji Grad was the home of craftsmen and tradespeople.

OSIJEK'S KEY AUTHORS
The leading figures in Osijek's literary past are two women: Jagoda Truhelka (1864–1957), a sensitive prose-writer fascinated by childhood, and Vilma Vukelić (1880–1956), a Jewish novelist who wrote in German.

COOKING SEASONED WITH PAPRIKA
This mild spice is used to pep up traditional Slavonian dishes, such as *fiš paprikaš*, a type of fish stew.

sijek's Upper Town is dominated by
e red-brick outline of the church of
. Peter and St Paul.

mansion built by the Esterházy barons
econd half of the 18th century) and two
aroque churches, the Catholic church
f Sv. Ivan Krstitelj (St John the Baptist,
715), which was seriously damaged in
e 1991–5 conflict, and the orthodox
urch of Sv. Mihovil (Saint Michael,
777).

OPAČKI RIT ■ 20. In the loop formed by
e confluence of the Drava and Danube
vers, the Kopački Rit nature park
ight) stretches over more than 44,478
res (18,000 hectares) of wooded
arshland and was designated a
otected area in 1967. The twists and
rns of the Danube provide spawning
tes for fish and thousands of migrating
rds flock here in the fall. The
undance of game (stags, deer, boar)
ade it a popular hunting ground for the aristocracy, from
ugene of Savoy to Archduke Frederick of Habsburg, who
tertained the German Kaiser Wilhelm II here.

he Podravina Region ♦ A D3-F3

JMAŠ. This village, close to the confluence of the Drava
d Danube rivers, has a castle with an impressive neoclassical
rtico, built by the Adamovic family. These progressive
ndowners, active in the 18th and 19th centuries, drained and
anted the marshlands between the Vuka and Drava rivers.
ospa od Utočišta (Our Lady of Refuge) has been a
lgrimage center since the mid 19th century.

RDUT. In the 19th century, the Cseh family built a mansion
th wine cellars, surrounded by extensive grounds, on a bend
the Danube river.

ALJ. This town is situated a little further down the Danube
this wine-growing region. Since the end of the 17th century,
alj has been largely inhabited by Orthodox Serbs. They
ilt a baroque church here (1715) and the Patriarchal
lace (c. 1830).

LPOVO. Next to the 15th-century Gothic castral chapel
ands a circular tower which survives from the town's
edieval fortifications. The barons of Prandau built the castle,
rrounded by an English-style landscaped park, in the 19th
ntury. This building now houses the Muzej Valpovštine
Iuseum of Valpovo). The church of the Začeće Marijino
nmaculate Conception) dates from 1722.
modern thermal spa resort, BIZOVAČKE
OPLICE, lies to the east of Valpovo.
is spa was built over deep, hot springs
04.8°F/96°C), rich in minerals, which
re discovered in 1970.

ONJI MIHOLJAC. This small town on
e Hungarian border has a picturesque
glish-style manor house set
vast grounds, built by the
jlath family (1905–14).

**KOPAČKI RIT, A
BIRD-WATCHER'S
PARADISE**
Abundant plankton
and insects and lush
vegetation explain the
presence of 275
species of birds, about
100 of which nest in
the park. Some
waterbirds, like the
black stork or the
great white heron, are
very rare in Europe.
During the War of
Independence, the
area was mined, so
visitors should
exercise extreme
caution and follow
the signs.

The view from the
ruins of the fortress
and the circular
Renaissance tower at
Erdut takes in the
tranquil waters of the
Danube as far as its
left bank in
Vojvodina.

Southeastern Slavonia ♦ A E4-F4

The Dakovo and Vinkovci region immediately springs to mind as the epitome of the quintessential Slavonic landscape.

DAKOVO. The red-brick bell towers of Dakovo's cathedral, which can be seen from several miles away, make this town especially easy to find. The cathedral was commissioned by Bishop Strossmayer and built in 1882 to plans by Karl Rösner and Baron Frederick Schmidt ● *71*. It contains frescos by Alexander and Ludwig Seitz, among others, and sculptures by Vatroslav Donegani. The immense wine cellars in the Bishop's Palace are stocked with the bishop's famous wines, made in the hillside vineyards to the west of Dakovo. Strossmayer also modernized the vast episcopal estate, one of the ten largest in Croatia, in the early 20th century. In 1854, he founded a Lippizaner stud farm ▲ *152* and laid out a large park to the south of the cathedral. The church of Svi. Sveti (All Saints) was actually a Turkish mosque which acquired a façade and bell tower in the 18th century.

VINKOVCI. This town stands on the site of the Roman town of Aurelia Cibalae, where Bishop Eusebius (in AD 258) and Lector Pollio (AD 304) were martyred for their Christian beliefs. This was also the birthplace of the two brothers and joint emperors, Valentinian I and Valens (4th century). Many archaeological finds, kept in the Gradski Muzej (Town Museum), bear witness to this period. Vinkovci entered the modern era in the 18th century when it became the base of the Command of Slavonia's Cavalry Regiment and the 7th Infantry Regiment of the Military Frontier. The baroque church of Sv. Euzebije i Polion (St Eusebius and St Pollio) dates from 1777. The college, the largest educational institution in the history of Slavonia, was founded in the late 18th century. Lessons were initially taught in German but Croatian was gradually introduced from 1850 onward.

MGR JOSIP JURAJ STROSSMAYER
(Osijek, 1815– Dakovo, 1905) Strossmayer was the Bishop of Dakovo and greatly influenced the political and cultural life of Croatia in the second half of the 19th century. A supporter of the Illyrian movement from his youth, he advocated Slavic unity, Church unity and the federalization of the Austro-Hungarian monarchy. He was the main founder of the Croatian Academy of Sciences and Arts in 1866 ▲ *112*, and established the Gallery of Old Masters in Zagreb in 1884.

AGE-OLD FORESTS ■ *18*
To the southeast of Vinkovci, around the Bosut river and its tributaries, lie vast forests of pedunculate oaks and hornbeams, the largest of which is the Spačva forest. In the late 19th century, forestry intensified and oak was exported in the form of untreated logs and curved planks for barrels. The writings of author Josip Kozarac (1858–1906) on this subject are tinged with melancholy.

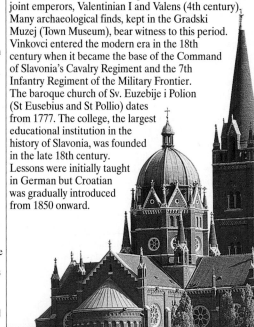

1730, Maximilian Gosseau d'Heneff, the architect of
…sijek's Tvrđa ▲ *144*, built a fortress with a chapel in NUŠTAR,
…st under 4 miles (6 km) from Vinkovci.

…**KOVAR.** At the confluence of the Vuka and Danube rivers,
…e town and river port of Vukovar was the third largest town
…Slavonia (45,000 inhabitants) until the recent war. From
…'36 onward, it came under the rule of the Eltz counts,
…German origin, who built a baroque palace here in
…'51. Other baroque gems include the County
…lace of Srijem, a historic county which covered
…e easternmost stretches of modern Slavonia
…d whose center was Vukovar; the
…anciscan monastery; the church of
…. Filip i Jakov (St Philip and
…James), which houses the
…dy of Saint Bon, transferred
…m Rome in 1754; and the Orthodox
…urch of Sv. Nikola (St Nicholas, 1732–7).
…e Gradski Muzej (Town Museum) and the
…alerija Umjetnina (Gallery of Fine Arts) were
…unded with donations from the archeologist
…d museologist Antun Bauer, who was born in Vukovar
…in 1911. Another famous figure who came from the area
… was Lavoslav (Leopold) Ružička (1887–1976),
…a brilliant chemist who received the 1939 Nobel Prize
…for Chemistry. In late 1991, after bombing raids and a
…siege lasting several months, the Serb militia captured
…and sacked Vukovar, which remained under Serb
…occupation until 1995.

ILOK. This is the easternmost town in the republic
…of Croatia. It flourished in the 15th century under the
…rule of the counts of Ilok, whose most famous
…representative was Nikola (who died in 1477),
…Vojvod (governor) of Transylvania and King of
…Bosnia. For this reason, Ilok had several churches
…and two monasteries, one Augustan, the other
…Franciscan. The Italian saint, John Capistrano,
…died in the latter, making the town a pilgrimage
…center. During the Ottoman period, Ilok was
…capital of the district (*sandjak*) of Srijem: a
…hammam and a *turbe* (mausoleum) survive from
…this period. Livio Odescalchi inherited the fief in
…1697. His descendants, who used to stay here
…during the hunting and wine-harvest season in
…particular, built a mansion on the site of the
…Iločki manor house in 1793. It is now home
…to the Town Museum. The Franciscan
…monastery and the church
…of Sv. Ivan Kapistran
…(St John Capistrano),
…which contains the
…tombstones of Nikola
…and Lovro Iločki,
…were enlarged in the
…18th century and
…restored in neo-Gothic
…style in 1907.

VUČEDOL
Discovered in the
early 20th century,
3 miles (5 km)
downstream from
Vukovar on the
Danube, this
archeological site
gave its name to the
Eneolithic civilization
which developed in
southeastern Europe
between 3,000 and
2,200 BC. Kept at the
Archeological
Museum in Zagreb
▲ *112*, the Vučedol
Dove (*above*), whose
tail is pierced by two
small holes, was a cult
object, although its
function is not yet
known.

For centuries, Ilok
has been the center of
the wine-growing
industry in Srijem; its
most renowned wine
is the dry white
Traminac.

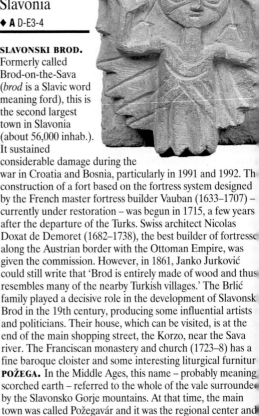

Central Slavonia
♦ **A** D-E3-4

SLAVONSKI BROD.
Formerly called
Brod-on-the-Sava
(*brod* is a Slavic word
meaning ford), this is
the second largest
town in Slavonia
(about 56,000 inhab.).
It sustained
considerable damage during the
war in Croatia and Bosnia, particularly in 1991 and 1992. The
construction of a fort based on the fortress system designed
by the French master fortress builder Vauban (1633–1707) –
currently under restoration – was begun in 1715, a few years
after the departure of the Turks. Swiss architect Nicolas
Doxat de Demoret (1682–1738), the best builder of fortresses
along the Austrian border with the Ottoman Empire, was
given the commission. However, in 1861, Janko Jurković
could still write that 'Brod is entirely made of wood and thus
resembles many of the nearby Turkish villages.' The Brlić
family played a decisive role in the development of Slavonski
Brod in the 19th century, producing some influential artists
and politicians. Their house, which can be visited, is at the
end of the main shopping street, the Korzo, near the Sava
river. The Franciscan monastery and church (1723–8) has a
fine baroque cloister and some interesting liturgical furniture.
POŽEGA. In the Middle Ages, this name – probably meaning
scorched earth – referred to the whole of the vale surrounded
by the Slavonsko Gorje mountains. At that time, the main
town was called Požegavár and it was the regional center and
metropolis of Slavonia. Požega remained the capital of a
sandjak during the Turkish period. During a visit, the famous
historian Mustafa Ali (1541–99) made a portrait of Governor
Hadji Mehmed Aga, who owed his fortune to the chestnut
groves on the Požega mountains. The Turks were chased out
of Požega by the legendary Franciscan friar, Luka Ibrišimović,
who led the uprising between 1687 and 1691. In the 18th
century, Požega enjoyed a period of rapid cultural
development. The Jesuits founded a college and a gymnasium,
which was attended by Slavonia's
great baroque poet, Antun

…anižlić (1699–1777). The principal area of interest is the …ain square, with its Plague Column, two medieval churches …modeled during the baroque period and its rows of arcaded …uses. The baroque church of Sv. Terezija Avilska (St …eresa of Avila) became a cathedral in 1997. The Požeški …uzej (Požega Museum) houses a fine collection of …omanesque sculptures (*left*), discovered in the ruins of the …onastery of Sv. Mihovil na Rudini (St Michael of Rudina) … the western slope of Mount Psunj. There are many …edieval churches and fortresses in the Požega Valley and …rrounding mountains. The best preserved fort in this area …he one overlooking the village of Kapitol. This residence, …abited by the canons of St Peter of Požega, was fortified …ortly before the Turkish conquest.

…TJEVO. Situated on the southern slopes of Krndija …ountain (2,599 feet/792 meters), this town is at the heart of … region famous for its vineyards (*right*). Its mansion (*bottom,* …) possesses vast underground wine-cellars and a round …ne table around which, according to …gend, Baron von Trenk and Empress …aria Theresa would carouse. The Serb …rthodox monastery of Sv. Nikola zvan …emeta (St Nicholas of Remeta) was …ilt in the late 16th century in a peaceful …ountain setting on the northern slope … Krndija, near Orahovica.

…ŠICE. In 1736, this fief, at the foot of … Slavonsko Gorje mountains on the …rava plain, came under the control of … Pejačević family, which produced …veral Bans and Župans, as well as the …mposer Dora Pejačević (1885–1923), …o wrote some fine symphonies and …ano concertos. In 1812, this family built …e of the best neoclassical manor …uses in Slavonia, set in an English-style …dscaped park. Their neo-Gothic …usoleum in the cemetery was designed … French architect, Herman Bollé ▲ *108.*

…estern Slavonia ◆ A C3-4

…odern western Slavonia has closer links …h central Croatia than with the rest of … region. The second largest mountain … the Slavonsko Gorje range, Papuk …ountain (3,130 feet/954 meters), stands … the center of western Slavonia.

…ROVITICA. This Slavonian town only …mained under Ottoman rule from 1552 …1684. The vast neoclassical palace, built by the Pejačević …mily in 1804, now houses the Town Museum. The mid-18th-…ntury church of Sv. Rok (St Roch) contains a wonderful …roque pulpit, sacristy and side altars. Most of the liturgical …rniture was made by Franciscan friars from the adjoining …onastery, who numbered some skillful craftsmen: painters, …ver and goldsmiths, sculptors and carpenters.

'In Slavonia, with the exception of Srijem, the largest wine harvests are those on the mountains of Požega, Aljmaš, Erdut and Trnava. However, it is my opinion that nowhere are they merrier than in Brod. Most people here have vineyards, albeit formed of a single span; and many have built themselves a home which is more beautiful and more comfortable than their house in town.'
Janko Jurković, 1861

JANKOVAC FOREST
The beeches, oaks and maples of this forest park on the slopes of Papuk Mountain (*above*) are the perfect place for a stroll.

151

ROMAN SCULPTURES
A sarcophagus decorated with panthers drinking from a handled vessel (*right*) and a slab bearing a funerary inscription have been discovered at Veliki Bastaji, a village near Daruvar.

The baroque church of Sv. Terezija (St Theresa, *below*) in Nova Gradiska dates from 1756.

LIPPIZANER HORSES
These appeared in the late 16th century, from crossbreeding between Andalusian thoroughbred stallions and Neapolitan mares at the stud farm in Lippiza (Slovenia), which was founded in 1562 by Archduke Charles II. They are used exclusively at the famous Spanish Riding School in Vienna.

DARUVAR. This town occupies the Roman site of Aquae Balissae, named for the healing properties of its hot spring (115.9°F/ 46.6°C). Daruvar, formed by the joining of three medieval villages, owes its name to the Hungarian Janković counts: *daruvár* means 'city of the crane' and refers to the bird featured on the family's coat of arms.

PAKRAC. After the Ottoman invasion, the deserted region was partly colonized by the Serbs and the Valachians, which is why it is sometimes called Little Valachia. An eparchy was founded here in 1705. The Bishop's Palace (1732) and the Orthodox church of the Sv. Trojstvo (Holy Trinity, 1768) were built in baroque style, as was the Catholic church of Marijino Uznesenje (Our Lady of the Assumption, 1763). In the town center, the palace belonging to Baron von Trenk ▲ *150* and that built by Count Janković are worth a visit.

LIPIK. This village is renowned for its hot spring (136.8°F/ 58.2°C), which provides relief for various ailments. The Count of Daruvar, Izidor Janković built thermal baths and a hotel here in the first half of the 19th century. Surrounded by a park, the current neoclassical buildings, including the superb treatment room, were built at the end of the century when a French company became joint-owner of the spa. Bottled mineral water is sold under the name of Lipički Studenac. Lipik also has a Lippizaner stud farm. In the east, PSUNJ MOUNTAIN rises to an altitude of 3,229 feet (984 meters) at Brezovo Polje. The beeches and oaks of Muški Bunar forest park are almost 300 years old.

NOVA GRADIŠKA. Built of wood in 1750 as a base for the Command of the Gradiška Infantry Regiment, the town was originally named Friedrichsdorf after its first colonel. The construction of the neoclassical church of Sv. Stjepan Kralj (St Stephen of Hungary) was aided by Emperor Francis I of Austria who, during a visit in 1828, donated money and allowed five cannons to be melted down to make the bells. The church was partially destroyed during the 1991–5 conflict. In the north lies CERNIK, whose rulers, the Marković family, converted the fortress into a baroque palace, which accounts for its square floor plan flanked by corner towers.

Istria

The History of Istria, *155*
Pula, *157*
From Pula to Pazin via Labin, *160*
Pazin, *162*
From Pazin to Pula, *163*
From Pula to Rovinj, *164*
From Rovinj to Poreč, *165*
Poreč, *166*
The Northern coastline, *167*
The Basilica of Poreč, *168*
Northern Istria, *170*

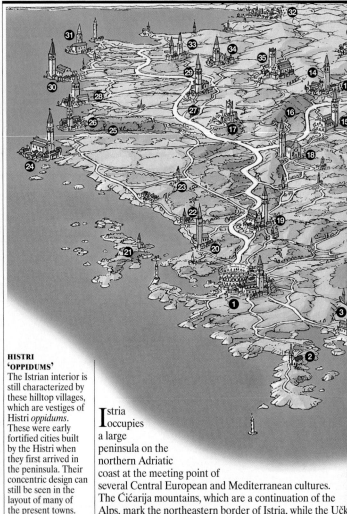

1. PULA ★
2. PREMANTURA
3. MEDULIN
4. LIŽNJAN
5. NESACTIUM
6. MARČANA
7. RAKALJ
8. BARBAN
9. RAČA RIVER
10. LABIN
11. PLOMIN
12. GRAČIŠĆE
13. PAZIN
14. BERAM
15. ŽMINJ
16. SVETI PETAR U ŠUMI
17. DVIGRAD
18. SVETVINČENA
19. VODNJ
20.

HISTRI 'OPPIDUMS'

The Istrian interior is still characterized by these hilltop villages, which are vestiges of Histri *oppidums*. These were early fortified cities built by the Histri when they first arrived in the peninsula. Their concentric design can still be seen in the layout of many of the present towns. There are over 400, including that of Motovun, *below*, which is situated at an altitude of 909 feet (277 meters).

Istria occupies a large peninsula on the northern Adriatic coast at the meeting point of several Central European and Mediterranean cultures. The Ćićarija mountains, which are a continuation of the Alps, mark the northeastern border of Istria, while the Učk mountains, which reach their highest point of 4,580 feet (1,396 meters) with Vojak Peak, protect the region to the ea Istria is divided into three distinct areas: White Istria in the northeast, stretching across a limestone or karst plateau of the Ćićarija mountains, which is the home of cattle breedin Gray Istria, with rolling farmland; and Red Istria, o the southern and western coasts of the peninsula, wi its plains of reddi brown soil. With exception of Pazi the region's main towns are on the

22. PEROJ   **23.** BALE   **24.** ROVINJ   **25.** FIORD DE LIM   **26.** VRSAR   **27.** SVETI LOVREČ   **28.** POREČ ★   **29.** VIŠNJAN   **30.** NOVIGRAD   **31.** UMAG   **32.** TRIESTE   **33.** BUJE   **34.** GROŽNJAN   **35.** MOTOVUN   **36.** BUZET   **37.** ROČ   **38.** HUM   **39.** RIJEKA   **40.** BELI

JUNI ISLANDS

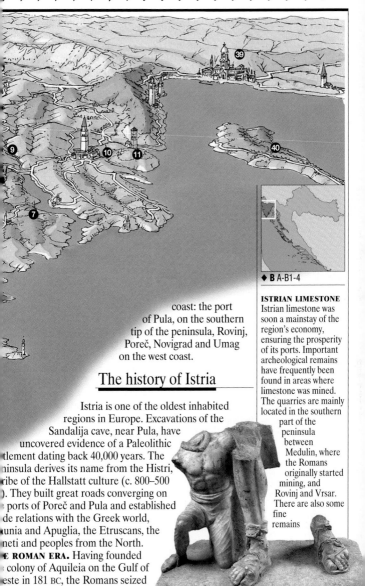

♦ **B** A-B1-4

ISTRIAN LIMESTONE
Istrian limestone was soon a mainstay of the region's economy, ensuring the prosperity of its ports. Important archeological remains have frequently been found in areas where limestone was mined. The quarries are mainly located in the southern part of the peninsula between Medulin, where the Romans originally started mining, and Rovinj and Vrsar. There are also some fine remains

coast: the port of Pula, on the southern tip of the peninsula, Rovinj, Poreč, Novigrad and Umag on the west coast.

The history of Istria

Istria is one of the oldest inhabited regions in Europe. Excavations of the Sandalija cave, near Pula, have uncovered evidence of a Paleolithic ﬆlement dating back 40,000 years. The ﬁinsula derives its name from the Histri, ﬃibe of the Hallstatt culture (c. 800–500). They built great roads converging on ﬆ ports of Poreč and Pula and established ﬄe relations with the Greek world, ﬆunia and Apuglia, the Etruscans, the ﬅeti and peoples from the North.
﹢E ROMAN ERA. Having founded ﹢ colony of Aquileia on the Gulf of ﹢ste in 181 BC, the Romans seized ﹢trol of Istria after a long siege of ﹢ Histri capital, Nesactium (178–7 BC) ▲ 160. The ﹢querors rebuilt Nesactium and constructed fortified ﹢nps, while *villae rusticae* were built along the western coast ﹢d on the Brijuni islands. After several Histri uprisings, ﹢peror Augustus (31 BC–AD 14) recognized the citizenship ﹢ll the inhabitants of Istria. Parentium (Poreč) and Pola ﹢la), linked to Tergesta (Trieste) by the Via Flavia, were ﹢ge administrative centers and ports for a flourishing trade ﹢live oil, wine and Istrian limestone with Italy, Gaul, ﹢aetia (Switzerland) and Pannonia.

of ancient quarries at the Punta Barbariga between Pula and Rovinj. The crystalline limestone found on the Brijuni Islands was mined intensively until the Middle Ages, which accounts for the large number of ruins on the archipelago.

▲ Istria

LARGE-SCALE INVASIONS. Istria became part of the Weste Roman Empire in 395, then was invaded by the Visigoths (399), the Huns, who destroyed Aquileia in 452, and the Ostrogoths in the late 5th century, before the region came under Byzantine rule. It was largely colonized by Slavic and Avar tribes at the turn of the 6th and 7th centuries.
LOMBARDS AND FRANKS. In the 8th century Istria was occupied by Lombards, who seized control of coastal cities and transformed Novigrad into a major administrative center. In 788, the Franks exerted their dominance over the Lombard kingdom and Istria and established a feudal syste In the 10th century, Istria became part o the Germanic Holy Roman Empire. Subjected to new taxes, the coastal citie lost their autonomy and economic influence, while Slavic colonies were ordered to clear the countryside.
BETWEEN VENICE AND THE HABSBURG DYNASTY. In the 13th century, power struggles between the kingdom of Croatia, the Holy Roman Empire and Venice, and clashes between secular and religio powers (the Pope gave Istria to the Patriarch of Aquileia in 1074) ended with the formation of two entitie Central Istria and a small eastern enclave came under the power of the Habsburgs, while the surrounding coastal area and several inland towns accepted the authority of Venice. Pazin became the administrative center of continental Istri while, after initially being based in Poreč in 1267, the headquarters of the Venetian Captaincy were moved to Sveti Lovreč, Grožnjan, Rašpor and finally Buzet. This period resulted in an extraordinary legacy of architectural and artistic works. Ceded to Austria by the Treaty of Campoformio (1797), Istria came under French rule in 1805, then once more under Habsburg authority in 1815.
THE 20TH CENTURY. Annexed by Italy in 1921, Istria became part of Croatia as a result of Italo-Yugoslavian agreements signed in February 1947, based on a vote taken by the People's Deputies in Pazin in September 1943. Istria became a *županija* (region) of Independent Croatia in 1991

ula ♦ B A4

ula is one of the oldest cities on the eastern Adriatic coast.
occupied since the Neolithic period and fortified by the
listri, the site was mentioned in the 3rd century BC by
allimachus and Lycophron, two Greek authors who
tributed its foundation to the Argonauts. The port
ourished under Roman occupation. An important military
ase as well as a thriving cultural and commercial center
etween Aquileia and the Near East, Pula became an
iscopal see in 425. Decimated by the Goths at the end of
e 5th century, the city rallied under protection of the
yzantines, acquiring a Benedictine monastery and an
nposing basilica. The Franks, who captured the city around
88, made it a prosperous trading center with a large fleet.
s a result, Pula aroused Venetian interest from the 11th
entury and was forced to become a protectorate of the
erenissima Republic in 1331. Ravaged by epidemics and
urther battles, the city began to decline in the 14th century.
s population plummeted from 5,000 inhabitants in the 15th
entury to 300 in 1631. Many monuments were dismantled
nd sent to Venice to enrich the republic's artistic heritage.
was only after 1848, with the construction of an Austrian
rsenal, that Pula recovered to become the Austro-
ungarian monarchy's main port. Ceded to Italy soon after
orld War One and liberated in May 1945, Pula fell under
e control of the Allies before becoming part of Croatia in
947. It quickly became a thriving center of industry and
urism and regained its status as Istria's main city.
HE ROMAN TOWN. Pula's Roman remains, described by
ante in his *Divine Comedy*, inspired some of the great
enaissance artists, like Palladio. Istarska Street leads from
e amphitheater toward the old town. On the left are
stiges of the ancient and medieval ramparts, the 2nd-
ntury DVOJNA VRATA (Twin Gate), Istria's ARHEOLOŠKI
UZEJ ISTRE (Archeological Museum), which charts the
story of the peninsula from prehistoric times to the Middle
ges, and the HERKULOVA VRATA (Gate of Hercules), the
dest Roman structure in Pula (1st century BC). The street
ads finally to the PORTA AUREA or SLAVOLUK OBITELJI
RGIJEVACA (Arch of the Sergians) ● 55, often taken as a
odel by Palladian architecture.

ROMAN HERITAGE ★
All morning there
are tourist coaches
parked in front of
the Roman sites.
It's better to visit the
majestic amphitheater
in the afternoon, when
it's calmer and the
light falling across
the arches provides
some great photo
opportunities. On the
ancient Roman forum,
café terraces take
advantage of the view
of the temple of
Augustus. The sites
are imbued with a
special charm in the
morning, as the city
awakes.

JAMES JOYCE
A plaque near the
Porta Aurea recalls
that this famous Irish
writer was professor
of English in Pula
between 1904 and
1905.

The *Traditio Legis* kept at the Istrian Archeological Museum ▲ *157*.

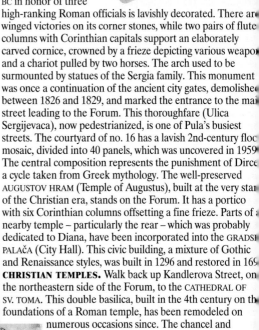

THE CHAPEL OF SV. MARIJA FORMOZA (Chapel of St Mary of Formoza) This chapel in the shape of a Greek cross with frescoed walls is situated at the corner of Maksimijanova and Flacijusova streets (to the southwest of the old town). It was once part of a large proto-Byzantine basilica built in the 6th century by Archbishop Maximian of Ravenna, a native Istrian. The basilica's decoration was similar to that of the Euphrasian basilica in Poreč ▲ *168*. It was demolished by the Venetians, who took its columns and mosaics to Venice, with the exception of a carved fragment depicting the *Traditio Legis* (*above*).

ALONG THE STREETS Pula extends over the slopes of eight low hills, overlooking a sheltered natural harbor. Its steep streets are lined with the brightly colored façades of houses, as can be seen on the pedestrianized Ulica Prvog Maja (*above*) and Ulica Giardini.

This small triumphal arch erected between 29 and 27 BC in honor of three high-ranking Roman officials is lavishly decorated. There are winged victories on its corner stones, while two pairs of fluted columns with Corinthian capitals support an elaborately carved cornice, crowned by a frieze depicting various weapons and a chariot pulled by two horses. The arch used to be surmounted by statues of the Sergia family. This monument was once a continuation of the ancient city gates, demolished between 1826 and 1829, and marked the entrance to the main street leading to the Forum. This thoroughfare (Ulica Sergijevaca), now pedestrianized, is one of Pula's busiest streets. The courtyard of no. 16 has a lavish 2nd-century floor mosaic, divided into 40 panels, which was uncovered in 1959. The central composition represents the punishment of Dirce, a cycle taken from Greek mythology. The well-preserved AUGUSTOV HRAM (Temple of Augustus), built at the very start of the Christian era, stands on the Forum. It has a portico with six Corinthian columns offsetting a fine frieze. Parts of a nearby temple – particularly the rear – which was probably dedicated to Diana, have been incorporated into the GRADSKA PALAČA (City Hall). This civic building, a mixture of Gothic and Renaissance styles, was built in 1296 and restored in 1695.

CHRISTIAN TEMPLES. Walk back up Kandlerova Street, on the northeastern side of the Forum, to the CATHEDRAL OF SV. TOMA. This double basilica, built in the 4th century on the foundations of a Roman temple, has been remodeled on numerous occasions since. The chancel and fragments of the floor mosaic preserved behind the choir date from the 5th–6th centuries. The gable of the southern doorway dates from the 9th century, the sacristy from the 13th, the façade from the 16th, and the bell tower was built between 1671 and 1707 with materials taken from the amphitheater. To the southeast of the cathedral, in Castropola Street, stands the CHURCH OF SV. NIKOLA (St Nicholas), founded in the 6th century. Dedicated to the Orthodox faith since the 16th century, it has a beautiful iconostasis from the 17th and 18th centuries. The same street leads to the FRANCISCAN MONASTERY built in the 14th century at the foot of the fortress on its western side. The cloister, remodeled in the 16th century, has been converted into a lapidary museum which contains the tombstone of Salamon, deposed King of Hungary (1063–74), who ended his days as a hermit. The adjoining church, in late Romanesque style with Gothic decorative elements, has a polychromatic wood polyptych by the Vivarini studio (15th century).

FORTRESS. The Histri hilltop village was replaced by a Roman Capitol, then a small medieval fort. The Venetians built this star-shaped fortress composed of four spur bastions linked by a curtain (1629–38). The wall-walk affords a breathtaking view. The fortress houses the POVIJESNI MUZEJ ISTRE (Museum of Istrian History) which charts the history of the peninsula in the first half of the 20th century.

**PULA'S
AMFITEATAR ●** *55*
This amphitheater
was built in the reign
of Augustus and
enlarged in the reign
of Vespasian (69–79).
It is one of the six
largest surviving
Roman amphitheaters
in the world. Elliptical
in shape (436 feet/
133 meters x 345 feet/
105 meters with a
maximum height of
107 feet/32.5 meters),
this amphitheater was
built to accommodate
the different gradients
of a hill. The façade,
with its two main
entrances and four
towers, is well
preserved with two
rows of 72 arches
topped by
67 quadrangular
windows. The
auditorium, which
could seat an
audience of 23,000
people, was used to
host gladiatorial
contests until 404 and
then a market, before
being used as a quarry
in the Middle Ages.
In 1583, the Venetian
Senate was keen to
demolish the
amphitheater and
rebuild it in Venice.
Fortunately the
project was
abandoned owing to
intervention by
Gabriele Emo, the
Venetian senator
honored by a plaque
on the northeastern
tower. Various shows
and festivals are now
held in the
amphitheater. The
tribunes have been
restored and the
vaulted basements
house an exhibition
devoted to the
production of wine
and olives during the
Roman period.

From Pula to Pazin via Labin ◆ **B** A4-**B** B2

ANCIENT NESACTIUM
Nesactium is one of the most important archeological sites in Istria. It not only has prehistoric remains, but also vestiges from the Roman period and the early Middle Ages. Inside the ring of Roman and Illyrian walls, archeologists have unearthed many finds: thermal baths, a forum, Roman temples, an end-of-Empire house, two Paleochristian basilicas and a palace which was the seat of the Histri rulers.

Labin (*below*).

THE PENINSULA'S TWO SOUTHERNMOST POINTS.
Heading south out of Pula will bring you first to CAPE KAMENJAK and the village of PREMANTURA, famous for its crab fishing, and then to Cape Karga, covered in pine groves, whose main town, MEDULIN, was built on the site of a Histri village conquered by the Romans. There are numerous Roman remains in the vicinity. Near LIŽNJAN, there is a small church (Gospa od Kuja) with a floor mosaic dating back to Late Antiquity.

NORTHEAST OF PULA. Founded by Histri tribes, besieged by the Romans in 177 BC, rebuilt by Emperor Augustus and then sacked by the Slavs in the 7th century, NESACTIUM is a remarkable site. The FORTRESS OF MUTVORAN, to the north of Marčana, which bears the stamp of various different periods, is also worth visiting. Its ramparts, built reusing Roman materials, conceal a church with ancient foundations which is a fusion of Gothic and baroque styles.

RAKALJ. This town produces a rustic type of pottery, similar to objects made by the prehistoric Liburnians. Its ramparts are overlooked by the bell tower of the church of Rađenije Blažer Djevice Marije (the Nativity of the Virgin), which contains some Roman sculptures.

BARBAN. Venice conquered this village in 1474 then granted it to the powerful Loredan family in 1535. In 1555, a loggia, whose upper floor served as a grain warehouse, was built on the main square, a baroque gate, the Vela Vrata (Great Gate, 1718), was fashioned in the ramparts and the church of Sv. Nikola (St Nicholas, 1700), whose bell tower was built on the foundations of a former medieval defense tower, was built against the walls.

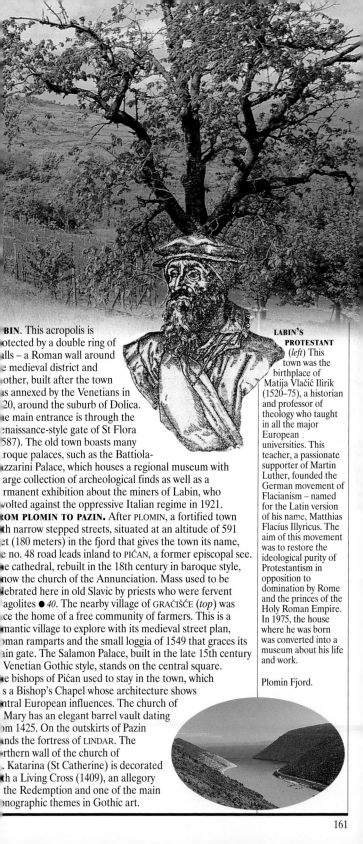

BIN. This acropolis is
...otected by a double ring of
...alls – a Roman wall around
...e medieval district and
...other, built after the town
...as annexed by the Venetians in
...20, around the suburb of Dolica.
...e main entrance is through the
...enaissance-style gate of St Flora
...587). The old town boasts many
...roque palaces, such as the Battiola-
...azzarini Palace, which houses a regional museum with
...large collection of archeological finds as well as a
...rmanent exhibition about the miners of Labin, who
...volted against the oppressive Italian regime in 1921.

ROM PLOMIN TO PAZIN. After PLOMIN, a fortified town
...th narrow stepped streets, situated at an altitude of 591
...et (180 meters) in the fjord that gives the town its name,
...e no. 48 road leads inland to PIĆAN, a former episcopal see.
...e cathedral, rebuilt in the 18th century in baroque style,
...now the church of the Annunciation. Mass used to be
...lebrated here in old Slavic by priests who were fervent
...agolites ● *40*. The nearby village of GRAČIŠĆE (*top*) was
...ce the home of a free community of farmers. This is a
...mantic village to explore with its medieval street plan,
...oman ramparts and the small loggia of 1549 that graces its
...ain gate. The Salamon Palace, built in the late 15th century
...Venetian Gothic style, stands on the central square.
...e bishops of Pićan used to stay in the town, which
...s a Bishop's Chapel whose architecture shows
...ntral European influences. The church of
... Mary has an elegant barrel vault dating
...om 1425. On the outskirts of Pazin
...ands the fortress of LINDAR. The
...rthern wall of the church of
...Katarina (St Catherine) is decorated
...th a Living Cross (1409), an allegory
...the Redemption and one of the main
...onographic themes in Gothic art.

**LABIN'S
PROTESTANT**
(*left*) This
town was the
birthplace of
Matija Vlačić Ilirik
(1520–75), a historian
and professor of
theology who taught
in all the major
European
universities. This
teacher, a passionate
supporter of Martin
Luther, founded the
German movement of
Flacianism – named
for the Latin version
of his name, Matthias
Flacius Illyricus. The
aim of this movement
was to restore the
ideological purity of
Protestantism in
opposition to
domination by Rome
and the princes of the
Holy Roman Empire.
In 1975, the house
where he was born
was converted into a
museum about his life
and work.

Plomin Fjord.

Pazin ♦ B B2

Pazin is at the heart of Istria. Mentione for the first time in a document signed by Otto II in 983, the town was an important strategic center at the juncti of the roads to Trieste and Poreč. Pazin became a powerful Germanic Margravate in the 12th century and came under the control of the Habsbur in 1374. The town, which governed the region, helped to form the border separating Venetian lands from Habsburg territory, as recorded in a document called the Istarski Razvod. After the fall of the Habsburgs, Pazin remained the center of Istria until its annexation by Italy, when it became a center of resistance to Fascism.

THE CASTLE. Overhanging the gorges of the Fojba river, this castle was built in the 9th century and completed between the 13th and 16th centuries. Its walls date from the 15th century, except for the northern section which wa built a century later. Jules Verne (1828–1905) imprisoned th hero of his novel *Mathias Sandorf* (1885) in the castle and had him taking refuge after his escape in the gorges at the foot of the fortress. Verne has become very popular in the city and, since 1998, a tribute has been paid to him every ye in the month of June. The castle houses an Ethnographic Museum with a rich collection of jewelry, costumes and furniture. Nearby, there are some 15th- to 17th-century noblemen's houses.

THE CHURCH OF SV. NIKOLA (ST NICHOLAS). This Gothi church, mentioned as early as 1266, was given a ribbed vault in 1441 which served as a model for many of Istria's rural churches. In the 15th century, the vault and its walls were frescoed by an unknown Tyrolean artist. During the 18th century, the church was enlarged and remodeled in a baroque style.

DVIGRAD
With its roofless basilica and crumbling towers, the abandoned walled town (*above*) was bound to appeal to the Romantics who rescued it in the 19th century. There used to be two castles here protecting the Venetian border and keeping watch over the Draga Valley. Parentino, in the north, was soon deserted, but Moncastello, in the southwest, survived until 1630; it was then hit by the plague and its residents forced to take refuge in neighboring villages, especially Kanfanar.

View from the citadel at Pazin (*below*).

ROUND PAZIN. Ancient BERAM is situated to the west of [Pa]zin. This fortified village was built in the Middle Ages over [th]e remains of a Histri burial mound, from which 172 urns [su]rvive. The church of Sv. Martin (St Martin) boasts some [It]alian frescos, a Gothic bas-relief dating from the late 14th [ce]ntury, a baptistery carved with Glagolitic inscriptions in [1]493 and some extensive liturgical collections. In a quiet [w]ood just over half a mile (1 km) away, stands the 15th-[ce]ntury chapel of Sv. Marija na Škrilijinah (Our Lady of the [R]ocks). It was modeled on the church at Beram and has the [b]est-preserved fresco cycle in Istria.

[F]rom Pazin to Pula ♦ B B2-B A3

[GRA]MINJ. This medieval citadel overlooks the fertile, wooded [hi]lltops of Red Istria. Inhabited since the Paleolithic Era, the [si]te is full of architectural finds, including remains from the [B]ronze Age and a Paleocroatian necropolis from between [th]e 9th and 11th centuries. From the 14th century, the city [m]arked the border between the Habsburg kingdom and [V]enetian territory. This border had no effect on artists: the [ch]apel of Sv. Antun (St Anthony) contains frescos painted [in] 1381 by Armigirius in typical Italian Trecento style, while [th]e paintings decorating the chapel of the Sv. Trojstvo (Holy [Tr]inity), which date from 1471, depict the life of Christ in the ['s]ophisticated style' brought over from the Alps.

[S]VETVI VINČENAT. This elegant city only gained peace [in] 1389 when it came under the rule of the Morosini, an [im]portant Venetian family. It boasts Renaissance houses with [ar]ched windows, the Grimani Palace and an 18th-century

loggia, but its most interesting attraction is the ancient abbey-church of Sv. Vinčenat (St Vincent), which contains murals painted by Ognobenus of Treviso in the late 13th century. This artist, deeply influenced by Byzantine art and theology, produced the most complete and accessible cycle of frescos in Istria.

VODNJAN. Cobbled streets (*right*) lead to the church of Sv. Blaž (St Blaise, 1760), whose walls were built with stones from the Pre-Romanesque structure which once stood here. The church has an extensive collection of sacred art, including a Renaissance custodial from 1451, a *Madonna* painted by Jacobello del Fiore in Venetian Quattrocento style and some Byzantine icons. Regional costumes can be admired at the museum in the Bettica Palace or during the Festival of the Bumbari, held in August.

THE BERAM CYCLE
The frescos covering the walls and vaults of the church of St Mary were painted in late Gothic style by Vincent of Kastav in 1474. They relate the life of Christ and the Virgin Mary in 46 panels which depict scenes from the Old Testament using traditional medieval iconography. The west wall shows *Adam and Eve*, *The Wheel of Fortune* and a *Dance of Death* (*above*). The north wall is covered by a fresco stretching for 26 feet (8 meters), which depicts the Three Kings in an Istrian landscape.

Vodnjan.

SVETI PETAR U ŠUMI
This village was the spiritual center of inland Istria in the 16th century. In 1459, its monastery was remodeled by the Pauline monks ▲ *126* who restored it in their characteristic baroque style. The unusual monastery roof is worth a look, as it is tiled with shingles, like the Istrian *kazuni* or beehive-shaped dry-stone huts ● *68*.

163

NONALIGNED ISLAND
Egypt's Gamal Abdel
Nasser, Indian Prime
Minister Jawaharal
Nehru and Maršal
Tito (*right*) signed the
famous declaration
defining the principles
of nonalignment on
July 19, 1956 on Veli
Brijun. The Cold War
was still raging and
the world was divided
between the United
States and the USSR.
In this declaration,
the three men refused
to take sides and
urged the Developing
World to follow suit in
refusing to 'align'
themselves with the
major powers.

From Pula to Rovinj ◆ **B** A4-**B** A3

THE BRIJUNI ISLANDS. A ferry from Fažana takes visitors
to the archipelago that was one of Maršal Tito's favorite
resorts and was designated a National Park in 1983. These
islands boast a mild climate and lush vegetation. On VELI
BRIJUN, 600 endemic plants flourish alongside cedar trees,
bamboos and other exotic species presented to Tito by
foreign statesmen. There are around 200 species of bird, an
moufflons, deer and even an elephant wander freely around
the safari park. The architecture reveals the same diversity.
The island has a Roman villa ● *56*,
a Byzantine fortress, a Romanesque
tower, a baroque *kaštel* and the former
president's White Villa.
PEROJ. This small island, decimated by
the plague, was repopulated in 1648 by
15 Orthodox families from Montenegro
The medieval basilica of Sveta Foška
(St Foska) has a triple nave, a projectin
open loggia and 12th-century frescos.
BALE. This village, on a karst plateau, has narrow streets
shaded by a fortress, whose galleries and balconies are a
testament to its Venetian rulers. The crypt of the church
contains some carved fragments from the 11th-century
basilica, as well as one of the finest Roman
crucifixes in the region.

'The land overlooking
the bay in the Ionian
sea is covered with
olive trees, strewn
with the fruits of the
earth and rich in
vineyards; it is
regarded with good
cause as a place
full of pleasure
and happiness.'
Cassiodorus,
6th century

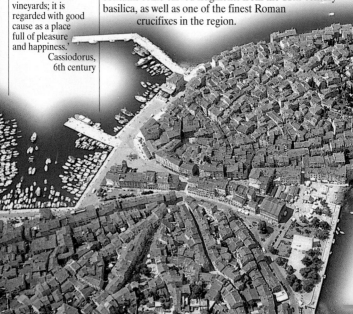

ROVINJ. The old town is almost entirely contained within a rocky island, which was linked to the mainland in 1763 (*below*). Its narrow streets (*right*) are crisscrossed by passageways and surmounted with archways decorated with ancient frescos. The houses are tall and fairly narrow. At the highest point of the island stands the church of Sv. Eufemija or Fumija (St Euphemia), whose bell tower, modeled on St Mark's in Venice, is the tallest in Istria at 200 feet (61 meters). This baroque church, built in the 18th century to plans by Venetian architect Giovanni Dizzi, is an important place of pilgrimage. The Venetian influence is particularly visible in the port. Rovinj was one of the first cities in Istria to come under the control of the Serenissima Republic in 1283.

From Rovinj to Poreč ◆ B A3-B A2

LIMSKI KANAL. This fjord, 1,969 feet (600 meters) wide and 7 miles (11 km) long, cuts a deep channel inland between Rovinj and Poreč. The clay soil of the valley and the low salt content of the water make it ideal for many species of plants and fish, and oyster-farming thrives here. The cliffs are dotted with caves, some of which have been occupied since the Stone Age. One was inhabited in the 11th century by Saint Romualdo, who founded the monastery of Sv. Mihovil (St Michael) near Kloštar (meaning 'cloister' in Croatian). The monastery church contains frescos painted around 1040 in the so-called Ottonian style, named for the descendants of the bishops of Poreč.

VRSAR. This Histri oppidum (whose name derives from *ursaria*, the Latin for 'bear') became the summer residence of the bishops of Poreč in the early Middle Ages. The old town dates from this period. There are the remains of an early Christian church with a floor mosaic decorated with floral motifs. The 12th-century church of Sv. Marija (St Mary) is one of the most beautiful Romanesque churches in Istria.

SVETI LOVREČ. On the main road between Pula and Trieste, this village was the headquarters of Venice's Military Command in Istria in the Middle Ages. The 11th-century church of Sv. Martin (St Martin) is modeled on the early Istrian churches with a single nave and three semicircular apses. The 15th-century loggia houses a lapidary museum which displays sculptures from the monastery of Sv. Mihovil (St Michael) in the Limski Kanal.

BIRDS IN THE BRIJUNI ISLANDS
The Sardinian warbler, the Orphean warbler, the yellow-legged gull and the Cory's Shearwater are among the many species of bird that winter on these islands.

THE SARCOPHAGUS IN ST EUPHEMIA
This is one of the treasures of the church at Rovinj, with carvings from the 4th or 5th century. It contains the saint's remains, according to the legend that is illustrated by a mural near the sarcophagus. Euphemia was tortured in 304 in Chalcedonia. Her body was taken to Constantinople, but disappeared during the iconoclastic uprisings in 800 and was miraculously found washed up on the beach at Rovinj, on July 13 that year.

ISTRIAN WINES
With 24,710 acres (10,000 hectares) of vineyards, its renowned wine-producing centers of Poreč, Buje, Buzet, Motovun and Novigrad, and its AOC labels, Istria is a leading wine producer. Reds include a Merlot, a Teran and the famous Cabernet Sauvignon from Poreč. Whites include the yellow Malvazija. There is also the Hrvatica rosé, the golden Malmsey from Buzet, the sparkling wine made by two persistent producers from the tiny village of Vrh, and the Momjanski Muscat from the region of Buje, which is a very drinkable wine.

BYZANTINE TREASURE AND PERFECT BEACHES ★
The Roman road that crosses the peninsula from the old forum to Marafor Square has become the town's principal artery. Halfway along, a narrow street leads to the Basilica of Euphrasius. Activity is focused around the port, where there are plenty of cafés with terraces. Fishing boats and water taxis bob on the water, and there is a shuttle to the beaches of Sveti Nicola every half-hour in summer.

Poreč ◆ B A2

Poreč has been inhabited since the Neolithic Period, when a port was built to trade with the Etruscans. It was conquered by the Romans in 129 BC and became an important military base. In the 7th century, the unbeaten Slavs tried in vain to capture Poreč, then under Ostrogoth control. The city was ruled by Byzantines, Lombards and Franks before the bishop began to exert their power, becoming the effective rulers of the city. During the Middle Ages, Poreč was an influential city in Istria, laying down the law as far as Pazin. In 1267, it was the first city in Istria to yield to the Venetians. Attacked by the Genoese in 1354 and decimated by plague epidemics, the city's population had plummeted to around 100 inhabitants in the 18th century, forcing Venice to call on Balkan immigrants to repopulate Poreč. Severely damaged during World War Two, but skillfully restored, Poreč has become the most popular tourist destination in the Upper Adriatic, particularly because of its beautiful Paleochristian Basilica ▲ *168*.

THE OLD TOWN. Contained within a narrow peninsula and surrounded by walls, the town's layout reflects the Roman geometric design. It retains a 1st-century pentagonal tower, restored in the 11th century, and a round Gothic tower dating from 1474. Trg Marafor (Marafor Square) occupies the site of the ancient Roman forum. The ruins of a temple dedicated to the Capitoline triad (Jupiter, Juno and Minerva) still stands here, surrounded by small temples dedicated to Neptune and Diana. On the northern side of the square is a 13th-century

ranciscan church with a stucco interior dating
om 1751, which was used to host the regional
arliament in the 19th century. In the center of town, there
re some fine Romanesque and Gothic houses as well as
ome Renaissance and baroque palaces. The Council House
ith its wooden balcony at the entrance to Trg Marafor is
orthy of mention, as are the Canons' House (1251), the
ouse of Two Saints, the Lion Palace (1473), the Zuccato,
anzin and Polesini Palaces. Since 1950, the 17th-century
nčić Palace, at the eastern end of the Decumanus, has
oused the collections of the oldest museum in Istria.
HE POREŠTINA. There are many Histri and Roman ruins
ong the coast and further inland. The hilly landscape of
ray Istria is dotted with woods, well-tended fields of crops
d flourishing vineyards. In NOVA VAS, the Baredine Cave,
hich is 459 feet (140 meters) deep, provides a fascinating
sight into karst geology. Although the town of VIŠNJAN
rther east is 6 miles (10 km) from the coast as the crow
es, the loggia in its vast square has a spectacular bird's eye
ew of the sea. The parish church contains a *Madonna* by
orzi (Juraj) Ventura (1598), a painter from Zadar.

he Northern coastline ♦ B A2

OVIGRAD. This 'new town' (*below*, *right*) was built in the
h century alongside the ramparts of a Roman *castrum*
lled Aemona. Ruled by the Greeks, Romans,
yzantines, then the Venetians from 1270, Novigrad
as an influential episcopal see between the early
iddle Ages and 1828. Its church of Sv. Pelagije
t Pelagius), with its typically Venetian campanile,
as built in the 15th century over the foundations of
basilica whose 11th-century Romanesque crypt still
rvives. There is a collection of antiphonaries with ornate
othic initials on display in the sacristy. The Serenissima
epublic erected various palaces, which were rebuilt
ter the Turkish attack of 1687. The Rigo Palace,
th its Rococo façade, houses a modern art gallery.
MAG. This town (*below*, *left*) outgrew its medieval
mparts long ago. The leading port in Istria for the
port of wine and an international sports center, Umag
famous for its vast bays. An 118-foot (36-meter) tall
ghthouse at Cape Savudrija, near the Slovenian
rder, marks its northernmost shore. The Venetians
feated the fleet of Frederick Barbarossa and Pope
lexander III off this cape in 1177.

▲ The Basilica of Poreč

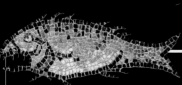

The ornamental tiling in the oratory of St Ma (4th century) features the fish (*ikhthus*), the symbol of Christ most frequently used after th cross. *Ikthus* forms the Lord's initials in Greek

The Basilica of Poreč, a super testament to the first golden age of Byzantine art, was built in the 6th century by Bishop Euphrasius. Taking in some pre-existing buildings, the complex includes a baptistery, an atrium and the basilica itself, buildings that traditionally stood alone in older groups. Decorated by beautiful mosaics with gold backgrounds, the basilica was classified a World Heritage Site by Unesco in 1997.

FROM HOUSE TO BASILICA
Originally a simple oratory in a private house where, in the 3rd century, St Maur used to gather the early Christians in secret, the building doubled in size in the 4th century, after the Edict of Milan proclaimed freedom of worship. The building, converted into a double basilica (a temple with two buildings) in the 5th century, was completed by Euphrasius in 539.

Right, Euphrasiu draped in dark clo holds a model of h basilic

THE MOSAICS
The apse contains mosaics with gold backgrounds that would have sparkled in the light of the thousands of candles that once illuminated the building. The *Annunciation* (*above*) and the *Visitation* on the side walls, have a background of colored bands which represent the green vegetation, blue sky and red horizon. There are portraits of saints on the intrados of the arch.

STUCCO WORK
Resting on Corinthian and Byzantine capitals, the arches separating the nave from the left aisle are decorated with 6th-century stuccos.

THE CHOIR
There is a wide inlaid frieze around the choir, which is bordered by a stone bench and the Bishop's cathedra, in a typically Byzantine layout (*above*). The 1277 ciborium is decorated with Venetian mosaics and supported by marble columns.

THREE-NAVE BASILICA
The earliest churches had only one altar in the apse. When a second religion was to be celebrated, another church was built beside it. Three-nave basilicas, like the one at Poreč, were an architectural innovation. They had three altars and were used for as many different forms of worship.

THE MARIAN CULT

The Cult of Mary spread after the Council of Constantinople (1552) proclaimed that she was the Mother of God and the Immaculate Virgin. The 16th-century mosaic decorating the arched ceiling of the apse, with its typically Byzantine symmetry, shows Mary at the center in the place usually reserved for Christ.

1. Baptistery
2. Atrium
3. Basilica
4. Choir and ciborium
5. Oratory of St Maur
6. Commemorative chapel
7. Campanile
8. Episcopal palace

THE BAPTISTERY

Built in the 5th century, this is octagonal in shape, like the baptismal fonts at its center where, until the Middle Ages, adults would receive baptism by immersion.

The vil
of Buje

Northern Istria ◆ B A2-B B2

Northern Istria is dotted with hilltop villages surrounded by sturdy walls built by the farmers in the Middle Ages to protect Venetian property. This is a region where age-old customs endure and where it is not unusual to hear different dialects spoken. The cuisine is superb: delicious *pršut* (ham) and exquisite white truffles washed down by fragrant red wines. BUJE is the first place to explore, with its circular square in provincial Venetian style, its frescoed façades and a campanile decorated with the lion of St Mark. GROŽNJAN, at an altitude of 945 feet (288 meters), is next, with its sensational view of the Alps and Mount Učka. At Oprtalj, winding streets lead through archways to the church of Sv.

Juraj (St George), with its rich altars and paintings by the school of Carpaccio (c. 1460–c. 1525). Nearby, the churches of Sv. Marija (St Mary), Sv. Jelena (St Helen), Sv. Leonard (St Leonard) and Sv. Rok (St Roch) contain some remarkable frescos by Clerigin of Kopar (15th century), Anthony of Padua or Zorzi Ventura (17th century). Motovun has the remarkable church of Sv. Stjepan (St Stephen), modeled on the design made popular by Palladio, the master of Classicism. Buzet, the headquarters of the Venetian Captaincy, has a museum charting the history of the region. Near Draguć, the church of Sv. Rok has frescos by Anthony of Padua (1529), a brilliant local artist.
FROM ROČ TO HUM. The Glagolitic Alley, a winding road lined with strange monuments shaped like letters, slabs and arches, stretches for 4 miles (7 km). Key events and figures from Glagolitic culture are commemorated here ● 40, with a homage to Cyril and Methodius, to the Lucidar, the famous medieval encyclopedia, and the Istarski Razvod, the collection of laws that were in force until the 18th century. Roc boasted many studios producing Glagolitic script, whose illuminated gospels take pride of place in museums in Zagreb, Copenhagen and Vienna. The church of Sv. Antun (St Anthony) has an *abecedarium* on one wall which was engraved in 1200. In Hum, a small hamlet with 12 intact houses, the church of Sv. Jerolim (St Jerome) has some Byzantine-style frescos dating from the 12th century, which are similar to those decorating the crypt of the Aquileian Basilica.

Rijeka

Rijeka, *172*
Trsat, *176*
The Opatija Riviera, *177*
From Rijeka to Senj, *177*
Opatija and early
tourism in Croatia, 178
The Cres and Lošinj
Archipelago, *180*
Krk island, *182*
Rab Island, *184*
Senj, *185*
At the foot of the Velebit, *185*
The Velebit, 186
Pag Island, *188*

1. RIJEKA
2. OPATIJA
3. LOVRAN
4. KRALJEVICA
5. CRIKVENICA
6. NOVI VINODOLSKI
7. BELI
8. CRES
9. OSOR
10. MALI LOŠINJ
11. VELI LOŠINJ
12. UNIJE
13. SUSAK
14. KRK
15. VRBNI

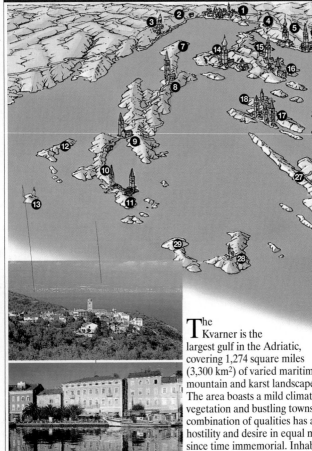

MARE QUATERNARIUM
This is the Latin derivation of the name Kvarner. The gulf, which sweeps in an arc from Istria (*top*: Brseč, at its southwestern tip) to the steep shores of Dalmatia, is fringed with a dense system of islands that forms approximately four groups: the Cres and Lošinj archipelago (*above*: Mali Lošinj, the island's main town) and the islands of Krk, Rab and Pag.

The Kvarner is the largest gulf in the Adriatic, covering 1,274 square miles (3,300 km^2) of varied maritime, mountain and karst landscapes. The area boasts a mild climate, lush vegetation and bustling towns, and this combination of qualities has aroused hostility and desire in equal measure since time immemorial. Inhabited by the Illyrian tribes, conquered by the Romans, invaded by the Croats, and fought over by the Franks and Byzantines, the Kvarner area enjoyed a short period of respite in the Middle Ages with the birth of the kingdom of Croatia which, in 1102, entered a personal union with the king of Hungary. This was a gold age for the region. However, it was not long before such prosperity made the region a target for Venice. The Kvarner area next came under threat from the Ottomans and the fortified region became an arena for many sieges, privateering and battles. Peace was briefly restored under the Habsburgs in the late 17th century but, from 1809 onward, the Kvarner again fell prey to friction between France, Hungary, Austria and Italy. The site of continual fighting and a melting pot of races, the region is dotted with Latin ramparts, Romanesque churches and Venetian palaces. Nevertheless, despite being so open to foreign influences, this narrow crescent of land, with its oft-invaded string of islands and islets, continued for many centuries to use the Glagolitic alphabet ● *40*, which is at the root of Croatian culture.

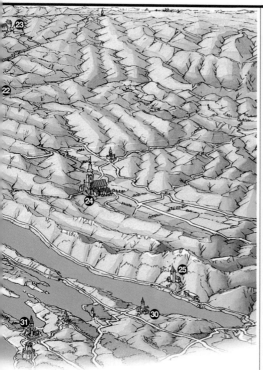

♦ **B** C-D2-6

THE BURA ■ *17*
Italian writer
Giovanni Comisso
described the Bura
thus: 'And, in the
midst of a beautiful
summer, you should
always expect the
sudden onset of the
Bura. Under cover
of a night storm, the
Bura blows down
from the high
mountains of Segna
and remains for
several days, whipping
the sea into a frenzy.'

MORČIĆI
These earrings, which
are only found in
Rijeka, are famous
throughout the world.
Their motif, the head
of a Moorish woman
wearing an enamel
turban and trimmed
with gold, recalls
victory over the Turks
in the 17th century.
The latter were on the
point of winning when
their leader was felled
by an arrow through
the temple. The
whole army fled,
leaving nothing but
turbans on the
battlefield.

Rijeka ♦ G

Straddling both banks of the Rječina river, Rijeka is a busy
modern town with a vast, sprawling port and suburbs
encroaching into the surrounding hills. However, despite
its industrial character, it also has a rich heritage of Gothic
and baroque treasures.

A DIVIDED TOWN. In the Iron Age, Rijeka Bay was under
dual occupation: the Illyrian Liburnian tribes inhabited the
coastal areas and the Iapodes lived in the hills. With the
arrival of the Romans in the 2nd century BC, the rebellious
Iapodes were driven out while the Liburnians remained. A
town called Tarsatica was constructed at the mouth of
the Rječina river. Initially a simple trading post on the road
from Senj to Trieste, it was enclosed by high walls in the 4th
century and became the main town on the military border
of the Eastern and Western Roman Empires, the famous
limes liburnicus (Liburnian frontier), opposing the Barbarian
world which began in the north. In the 7th century, the
defense system crumbled before the Slavic invasions. The
town thrived as part of the kingdom of Croatia but, after
the Germanic offensive that began in 799, it was split in two
at the end of the 11th century. Ancient Tarsatica on the
right bank of the Rječina came under the control of the
Holy Roman Empire while, on the left bank, the Croatians
founded Trsat, which was governed by the Frankopan
dukes ▲ *182* throughout the Middle Ages.

LOVRO MATAČIĆ
Born in Sušak, Rijeka's eastern district on the left bank of the Rječina, this talented conductor (1899–1985) was renowned for his interpretations of Mozart, Wagner, Verdi and Bruckner.

RIJEKA'S RAPID GROWTH
In the 19th century, the city acquired large-scale industries, shipyards and rail links. It was here that the torpedo was invented in 1866.

THE BAROMETER OF EUROPE. Acquired by the Habsburgs in 1466 and made a Free Town in 1530, Tarsatica, renamed Fiume, was coveted by the Venetians and fought off raids by the Turks, continuing to play its role as a military border until the early 18th century. Fiume, now called Rijeka, became a free port in 1719 and expanded its merchant fleet. Linked by road to Zagreb and central Europe, Rijeka expanded rapidly with the construction of numerous baroque houses and broad classical avenues, like the famous Korzo. Between 1873 and 1914, it was the eighth largest port in Europe. New districts sprang up, monumental mansions were built by the business community and Art Nouveau buildings were constructed for administrative offices. This boom was brought to a sudden halt by World War One. Initially part of the Kingdom of Serbs, Croats and Slovenes, Rijeka was taken hostage for 16 months from September 1919 by Gabriele d'Annunzio (1863–1938), an Italian poet, dramatis and high-ranking solider, who played a part in the rise of Fascism in Italy. Rijeka became an independent republic in 1920, before the right bank of the Rječina river was annexed by Mussolini's Italy in 1924, although Trsat and the neighboring village of Sušak remained Croatian. This situation lasted until the peace treaty between Italy and Yugoslavia, signed in 1947, when the city was reunified and became part of Croatia.

Exploring Rijeka ♦ **G** A-B3

'GRADSKI TORANJ'
The City Tower with its clocks and baroque dome overlooks the Korzo. After 1750, when the ramparts were demolished, it was built on the site of an ancient gate, and became a landmark of the modern city.

ALONG THE RIVA. The Riva is a seafron boulevard lined with magnificent mansions, built between 1870 and 1914 during the city's heyday. Many Croatian Viennese and Italian architects were experimenting with Art Nouveau at thi time and their innovative work can be seen in the glass and metal halls of the covered market, built in 1881 by Izidor Vauchnig, and the groundbreaking design of the fish market by Carlo Pergoli, which drew inspiration from both neo-Romantic and Secession style Nearby, the imposing Palladian façade of the IVAN ZAJC CROATIAN NATIONAL THEATER stands beside the former mou of the Rječina River, which was made into a canal. Named for the famous composer and conductor who was its directo between 1855 and 1862, this theater was built by Austrian architects Fellner and Helmer in 1883 ▲ *113*. Its pediment is decorated with an elegant carved group in neo-Renaissance style by Augusto Benvenuti and its attractive neo-baroque auditorium has three tiers of boxes, ornate lamps and a ceiling painted with allegorical figures by Franz Matsch and the Klimt brothers.

The Riva in Rijeka.

ONG
E KORZO.
st the small
THODOX CHURCH
dicated to St
cholas, which contains
me valuable 16th-century
ns, you will come to the Korzo, a
destrianized street that is the hub of
e city. The MODERNA GALERIJA (Modern
t Gallery) shares a building with the
iversity Library with its display of manuscripts in
agolitic script ● *40*. There are works by illuminators
m the 14th and 15th centuries and the first books printed
Croatian, the fruit of Bishop Kožičić's work in the late
th century. The baroque façade of the 1315 CHURCH OF SV.
RONIM conceals two Gothic chapels, with remarkable
scos. The AUGUSTAN MONASTERY next to the church, built
1408 and restored in 1835 in neoclassical style, was the
cus of spiritual life, particularly during the 16th century
der the aegis of its Father Superior, Ivan Klobučarić, the
nous cartographer. The CHURCH OF SV. VID (St Vitus) ● *66*,
med for the city's patron saint, is worth visiting for its
tagonal design, African marble altars, and its reputedly
raculous Gothic crucifix. This opulent church was begun in
27 by Jesuits, with the aid of donations from the Baroness
nnhausen. The CHURCH OF THE ASSUMPTION, which dates
ck to the 5th century, has a 10th-century bell tower, known
ally as Kosi Toranj (Leaning Tower).

E MUSEUM DISTRICT. Vladimir-Nazor park provides a
h setting for the palace which was once the home of
chduke Josef of Habsburg – now the City Museum – and
e former Governor's Palace, rebuilt in the neo-baroque
le by Hungarian architect Alajos Hauszmann in 1896.
iefly occupied by Gabriele d'Annunzio, this building now
uses the HISTORY AND MARITIME MUSEUM.

RIJEKA CARNIVAL
Since the Middle
Ages, the last Sunday
before Lent has been
a day of celebration: a
procession of several
hundred masked
revellers dances along
the Korzo ● *49*.

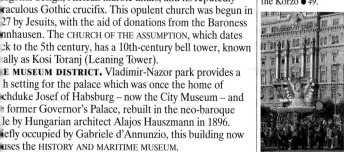

This is the other name of Our Lady of Trsat. According to legend, the House of the Virgin Mary and Joseph was brought to Rijeka by angels in 1291, before being rebuilt in Loreto in Italy three years later. In exchange, in 1367 Pope Urban V gave the basilica an icon reputedly painted by St Luke (*below*).

THE GARDENS OF OPATIJA
Planted with precious flowers from China, Australia and South America, tall plane trees and trees from Judea, the park of the Villa Angiolina is the most famous of Opatija's gardens. Iginio Scarpa ▲ *178*, the owner of the house between 1844 and 1873, laid out these gardens which boast a luxuriant bed of Japanese camellias that bloom in February when the surrounding mountains are still covered with snow. Other gardens were built later, like the Margerita Park in 1900, and the many seafront promenades, planted with Mediterranean or subtropical species like cypress trees, white or green oaks and palm trees.

Trsat ♦ B C2

On the opposite bank of the Rječina river, you come to the foot of the famous Trsat stairway with its 561 steps. This steep hillside ascent of 453 feet (138 meters) leads to the fortress built at the turn of the 13th century by the Frankopan Dukes, the rulers of Krk island ▲ *182*, who were charged with the administration of Trsat by Andrew, the Hungarian-Croatian king. In 1826, the fortress was in a stat of disrepair when Vice-Marshal Laval Nugent bought it and commissioned Venetian architect Paronuzzi to restore it. Nugent is buried in the unusual Doric mausoleum that was added to the medieval buildings. Near the fortress, one of the first Frankopan Dukes, Nikola I, built the church of Our Lady of Trsat to house the relics of the Virgin Mary. The current building, restored in 1453 by Martin Frankopan is an important Marian pilgrimage center. A Franciscan monastery stands beside the church.

KASTAV. A visit to this medieval hilltop city, 7 miles (11 km) to the west of Rijeka, provides a panoramic view of the who gently curving bay, from the crowded beaches of the Kvarn Gulf to the fishing villages of Istria. Kastav has a delightful timeless atmosphere with its winding lanes, its loggia dating from 1571 and its Lokvina square, shaded by the baroque church of Sv. Jelene (St Helena) and a few olive trees.

he Opatija Riviera ◆ B B2

ne white stone walls and slate roofs of
xury hotels like the Kvarner, Imperial
d Palace ▲ 178 make an attractive
ght among the laurels, magnolias and
lm trees at the foot of the hill. The
chitecture of Opatija clearly shows
e influence of 19th-century Austrian
ste. With its stately buildings, mild
mate and the contrast between sea
ews and the snow-capped peaks of
ount Učka (4,580 feet/1,396 meters),
is resort rapidly became one of the
ost popular aristocratic resorts in
urope. The Lungomare (promenade)

as built in 1900 and stretches 7 miles (12 km) to the village
Volosko and then Lovran, with its elaborate Gothic church
St George and its fine 18th-century Patrician mansions.

rom Rijeka to Senj ◆ B C2-B D3

ne 'Magistrala', which tacks from resort to resort along the
ast, and the winding road running through the Vinodol
lley, present the two dramatically different faces of this
gion with its stunning sea views and mountainscapes.
IE COAST. Once through the industrial suburbs of Rijeka,
e first coastal town of any interest is KRALJEVICA with its
o Zrinski fortresses. The road then runs past a maze of
tle bays to arrive in CRIKVENICA, the largest resort before
nj. This town owes its name to a church – *crkva* in Croatian
uilt in the early 15th century. The Frankopans built a
rtress adjacent to it in 1412, then granted it to the Pauline
onks ▲ 126. In 1786, the monastery passed into the hands
Archduke Josef, who converted part of it into an officers'
natorium. The city became a renowned spa resort in the
th century. The monastery is now the Hotel Kaštel,
though the monks' cells have been preserved intact. A little
rther south lies the historic capital of the Vinodol valley,
OVI VINODOLSKI, the birthplace of Ivan Mažuranić. Most of
e town is on a hill, dominated by the bell tower of Sv. Filip i
kov (St Philip and St James), which slopes down to the sea.
NODOL, THE 'WINE VALLEY'. The earliest Croatian
ocument in Glagolitic script, the 'Vinodol Codex' was
oduced here in the late 13th century, during the reign of
e powerful Frankopan Dukes (1225–1544) ▲ 182, who built
merous churches and fortresses. They were succeeded by
e Zrinski family ▲ 205, who also built Renaissance and
roque fortresses. About a mile (2 km) from the coast, the
all villages of DRIVENIK, TRIBALJ, GRIŽANE and BRIBIR
elter in the lee of a mountain range reaching an altitude
984 feet (300 meters). Visitors can enjoy the cool shade
the forests with their nearby lakes and waterfalls, before
mbing to Grižane, at the foot of the Velika Kapela massif,
the more urbanized Bribir, whose lavishly decorated
urch of Sv Petar i Pavao (St Peter and St Paul) contains a
ashing of the Feet, painted by Palma Giovane (1544–1628).

IVAN MAŽURANIĆ
A fervent supporter
of Illyrianism,
Mažuranić (1814–90)
was the first Croatian
Ban (ruler) of the
people. He
modernized the
government and gave
new impetus to
national culture. One
of the most brilliant
exponents of Croatian
literature, he wrote an
epic poem, *The Death
of Smail – Aga Cengić*
(1846), that has
become a classic in
Croatia.

**THE MASTER
MINIATURIST**
A monument to the
memory of Julije
Klović or Giulio
Clovio (1498–1578),
who was born in
Grižane, stands at the
center of Drivenik.
This miniaturist, a
pupil of Giulio
Romano in Mantua,
painted for the pope
in Rome and for
Cosimo I de Medici
in Florence. He was
a friend of Vasari,
Michelangelo,
Bruegel The Elder
and El Greco.

▲ Opatija and early tourism in Croatia

Villa Angiolina.

Abbazia von S

Fr. Schiller Strand weg.

Abbazia vom Südstrand.

Brunnen im Park

Foreign scientists, attracted by the mild
weather, fascinating fauna and hospitality of the
Croatians, were the first to discover many of the vacation resort
along the Adriatic coast and in continental Croatia. Doctors,
meteorologists and geographers as well as mountaineers spread
the word about Croatia's qualities as a tourist destination from
the 1860s onward. Its ideal location – on the shores of the
Adriatic and at the foot of Mount Učka – and the construction
of railroad links to Vienna, Budapest and Zagreb from 1873,
meant that Opatija was the first health spa in Croatia to
welcome the European elite in the 19th century.

THE EARLY DAYS IN OPATIJA

Although the construction of the Villa Angiolina in 1844 by Iginio Scarpa, a nobleman from Rijeka ▲ 176, might have paved the way for Opatija's glittering new development, it was

four scientists – Feliks-Jačić, a member of the Marseilles Academy of Medicine, Šporer, a physician and writer, Billroth (*left*) and Glax, two brilliant doctors – who were responsible for making the health spa

and seaside resort famous beyond the borders of the Dou Monarchy. Before World War One, a host of practitioner specializing in balneotherapy (the therapeutic use of mineral baths) worked in twelve sp

ABBAZIA, SÜDL STRANDWEG

TOWN PLANNING IN OPATIJA

As a seaside resort, Optaija extends mainly along the seafront. Hotels, boarding houses, villas, sanatoriums and public baths, built in eclectic or Secession styles, are surrounded by the lush vegetation of parks and gardens. The most striking architectural achievements are the Dom Zdravlja (Health Center), the Villa Schwegel by Max Fabiani, the buildings designed for Austria's Southern Railways and those by Viennese architect, Karl Seidl.

E 'AUSTRIAN NICE'
ore 1914, crowned
ds (Francis
eph of Austria,
helm II of
rmany and
arles I of
mania), politicians,
lionaires, famous
sts and bon viveurs
d to vacation in
atija, a popular
ter resort. This
a prosperous
when the leading
ts of Europe
ald flock to stay in
ury hotels – the
t to be built along
Croatian Adriatic
re were the
arner (1884) and
Imperial (1885) –
visit the casinos,
nnese coffee
ses and beautifully
dscaped parks.

TOURISM IN CROATIA

Other towns along the coast (Hvar, Dubrovnik, Rab, Krk, Crikvenica) and in continental Croatia (in the Hrvatsko Zagorje and the Gorski kotar) experienced a similar kind of boom to that of Opatija in the days before the tourist industry took off. As people became increasingly interested in tourism, lifestyles changed drastically and traditional activities such as farming, fishing and shipping stagnated.

Beach fun in the 1920s in Opatija, the 'pearl of the Kvarner', known as Abbazia by the Italians.

Abbazia - Bagno Lido.

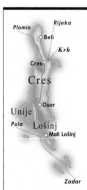

Plomin
Rijeka
Beli
Krk
Cres
Cres
Osor
Unije
Pula
Lošinj
Mali Lošinj
Zadar

The Cres Archipelago ◆ B B-C3-5

With an area of 198 square miles (513 km²), this is the larg
archipelago in the Adriatic. It includes the islands of Cres,
with its quiet coves; Lošinj, with old-fashioned ports; sandy
Sušak, with its women in embroidered skirts; Ilovik, the
island of flowers; and Unije, a traffic-free haven of peace.
Although in Beli, in the north, the wind blows down from
the Istrian mountains and the landscape is planted with
vineyards, olive groves and beeches and sessile oaks, the
south is predominantly scrubland. This is the place to eat
sheep's milk cheese, cured ham and freshly caught fish.

Cres Island ◆ B B-C3-4

FAITHFUL VULTURES
The archipelago is
home to some 60
pairs of white-headed
griffon vultures, a
rare species whose
closest relation lives
in South Africa.
These birds mate for
life and a center has
been set up to protect
and monitor them in
Beli. The small village
of Orlec, on the
eastern shores of the
island, was named for
these vultures, known
locally as *orel*.

Occupied by the Liburnians, ruled by the Greeks then the
Romans, and governed by Venice between 1000 and 1797,
the island remains a haven of peace, despite its military pas
BELI. The Romans named this town perched on its
promontory '*caput insulae*' (head of the island), and cut it o
from the rest of the island by a ravine stretching for 7½ mil
(12 km). The Roman bridge still straddles the gully and the
town continues to look down on the cove.
CRES. Nestling in a bay, the island's main town has some fi
churches and palaces behind its fortifications. From the
harbor, where women sell fruit, you can wander through
cobbled lanes to the Renaissance church of Sv. Marija
Snježna (St Mary of the Snow) ▲ *118* with its rich collection
paintings. The ornate Gothic church of Sv. Sidar (St Isidor
and the Roman amphorae in the Municipal Museum, hous
in the Petrić (or Arsan) Palace, are worth seeing.
A SUCCESSION OF COVES. VALUN's church has one of the
oldest examples of a Croatian inscription, the Valun Tablet
(11th century), which bears a combination of Glagolitic an
Latin scripts; their symbolism has yet to be deconstructed.
LUBENICE, which can only be reached by boat or on foot, is
little gem. Perched on a cliff, enclosed by walls to the east,
has three churches for just 43 inhabitants. MARTINŠĆICA, wi
its shingle coves, is the last village before the wild, unspoile
shoreline of Cape Kijac.
OSOR. Situated at the end of the channel which divides Cre
from Lošinj, this port, originally Greek, enjoyed a position
some importance for many years. It fell into decline in the
15th and 16th centuries, however, and its role was taken by
Cres, which had a larger harbor. The town has retained the
layout of an ancient city, as well as the remains of the
town walls and, in the cemetery, the ruins of a

**FRANJO PETRIĆ
OR PATRICIUS
FRANCISCUS**
This Gnostic,
Neoplatonic
philosopher (1529–97)
was born in Cres. A
brilliant Hellenist, he
translated many texts
including hermetic
writings. He also
published treatises
in which he criticized
the philosophy of
Aristotle and
introduced Platonic
cosmogony.

THE VALLE D'AUGUSTO
The natural harbor of Mali Lošinj
owes its name to Emperor Augustus:
his fleet found a much-needed refuge here
during a battle with Mark Antony in 31 BC.

leochristian church. Osor, which was
ll prosperous in the Renaissance, has
athedral (1463–97) of the Assumption
d a Bishop's Palace decorated with
ats-of-arms.

ošinj Island ◆ B B-C4-5

latively untouched by Roman
nquest, Lošinj was the poor relation
Cres for centuries. However, in the
th century, the Venetians arrived in
ali Lošinj. Ports were built, shipyards
ened, and a brisk trade began with
e Black Sea. The island's mild climate
racted wealthy Austro-Hungarians
d many villas were built. Lošinj is
w one of the most popular tourist
stinations in the Adriatic.

ALI LOŠINJ. Founded about 1398, the
wn only began to expand in the 17th
ntury when it became the archipelago's largest town as a
sult of its perfectly situated port, one of the most beautiful
the Adriatic. The town has a 1490 church of Sv. Martin
t Martin), and the baroque church of the Rođenje Marijino
lativity of the Virgin Mary), and the Čikat peninsula has
ajestic villas amidst pine forests.

The harbor of Cres
Town and that of Veli
Lošinj.

LI LOŠINJ. This town is characterized by its 19th-century
oclassical Austrian houses, including the *Seewarte*, built in
85 for the Archduke of Austria, Charles of Habsburg. It is
rrounded by a park planted with 200 species of trees
ipped from all over the world. The church of Sv. Antun
nthony) also takes its theme from the sea: as well as some
lian paintings and seven marble altars,
ich were presented by sea-captains,
e church and its small square are
corated with motifs of carved
ips.

MYTHICAL ORIGINS
In Antiquity, when
the archipelago was
home to a Greek
colony, the islands
were called the
Absyrtides. This is
because, according to
an episode in the
legend of the
Argonauts, Jason and
Medea were said to
have taken refuge
here to escape pursuit
by Absyrtus, the
sorceress's brother,
after they had stolen
the golden fleece.
Medea's brother
found them, however,
and fell into a trap
she had laid: he was
chopped into pieces
and thrown into the
sea where his body
parts formed the
many islets
surrounding Cres and
Losinj. The small
village of Nerezine, in
the northern part of
Losinj, was founded
on the remains of a
temple of Artemis,
which is said to be the
exact spot where the
crime was committed.

THE DUKES OF KRK
When Dujam (d. 1163) became the first Duke of Krk, he and his successors were vassals of Venice. The family extended their power over the sea and then to the mainland. They threw off the Venetian yoke in 1358 after their victory alongside Hungaro-Croatian king Louis I of Anjou ● *32* and became the most powerful family in Croatia, particularly under Duke Nikola IV (1352–1432). He united all the family estates and was Ban between 1426 and 1432. The Dukes of Krk adopted the name of Frankopan. The family died out with the execution of Fran Krsto Frankopan in 1671 for taking part in a conspiracy against the Habsburgs ● *34*.

Silver reredos made by Koler in 1477 for Krk cathedral.

Krk Island ◆ B C3

A popular tourist destination in the Kvarner Gulf, Krk is now more a peninsula than an island, due to the constructi of the Krčki Most bridge (4,295 feet/1,309 meters) in 1981, which links it to the mainland. With an area of 158 square miles (408 km²), Krk is the largest island in the eastern Adriatic. Its barren, mountainous eastern shoreline forms a stark contrast to the sun-drenched hills in the west and the fertile flatlands of the interior, their fields bounded by picturesque dry-stone walls called *gromače*.

THE HISTORY OF KRK. The seat of an independent town under the Roman Empire, the island also enjoyed its independence in the Middle Ages. The Dukes of Krk, who were keen to preserve Croatian traditions, threw off the Venetian yoke in 1358 and their power soon extended acro the entire Kvarner Gulf. The Serenissima Republic regaine control over Krk from 1480 until its fall in 1797. The island then came under the authority of the Habsburgs. It was occupied for a short time by Italy between 1918 and 1920, before becoming part of Croatia.

KRK'S NORTHERN COASTLINE. OMIŠALJ, the northernmos city on Krk, is a circular acropolis, 269 feet (82 meters) above sea level. Although nothing remains of the *castrum musculum* founded by the Romans, the town preserves trac of its patronage by the Frankopan dukes, particularly in the decoration of the interior of the church of the Assumption whose three-nave plan is modeled on Romanesque basilica In the neighboring bay of Sepen, the site of another ancien city, there are remains of a 5th-century Paleochristian temple. From here, the road runs inland, branching west toward the seaside complexes of Haludovo and Malinska, and east toward DOBRINJ, the oldest village on Krk, nestling in the shade of chestnut and fig trees. A town from 1100 onward, Dobrinj prospered due to the Soline salt marshes. Its strategic hilltop position meant that there was no need to build any walls around it: the high walls of the houses on the outskirts provided ample defense. There is a fine polychromatic wood reredos dating from 1602 above the high altar of the church of St Stephen.

THE WESTERN SHORE. The small fishing village of
ǦLAVOTOK lies on Krk's westernmost shore. In 1473,
ǁuke Ivan Frankopan ceded the peninsula to the
ǅanciscans. The monastery and church built
ǅre in 1507 by the monks display the simple style
ǆaracteristic of the mendicant orders. There are
ǆctures by Venetian masters and a large
ǆllection of Glagolitic texts.

KRK. A peaceful port (*above*), the main
ǁwn on the island is dominated by the
ǅion-domed bell tower of its Romanesque
ǆthedral ● *61*. Originally a Roman town
ǅled Curicum, and the site of many battles,
ǅk boasts an impressive defensive system
ǆting from the 12th century. With its
ǅund-tiled roofs and the walls of the white
ǅankopan fortress, Krk Town could be
ǅstaken for a Provençal city. The cathedral,
ǆlt over the ruins of a Roman bath,
ǆmbines elements of different styles
ǆomanesque capitals, Gothic Frankopan
ǅapel, baroque furniture and fine wood
ǅrvings, done by Mihovil Zierer in the late
ǆh century). The Bishop's Palace houses
ǅ extensive collection of paintings,
ǆluding an early 14th-century work
ǆ the Venetian artist, Paolo Veneziano.

THE SOUTHEASTERN SHORE. To the east
ǆ Krk Town, the port of Punat, renowned as
ǆ safest harbor in the Adriatic, boasts the
ǅall Pre-Romanesque chapel of Sv. Dunat
ǆp), a testament to early Croatian art. In
ǆush setting on the small island of Košljun,
ǆ church of a Franciscan monastery
ǆssesses a polyptych by Girolamo da
ǆntacroce (16th century). From Krk, you
ǅ take a detour to VRBNIK (*center*), the only
ǆside resort on the eastern shore, whose
ǆall houses, narrow streets and church of St Mary with its
ǆnaissance tower are celebrated in folksongs. The road to
ǆŠKA, on the southeastern tip of the island, runs through the
ǆeyards that produce *žlahtina*, a golden wine tasting of
ǆney. In JURANDVOR in 1851 the Baška tablet ● *40* was found
ǆ the church of Sv. Lucije (St Lucy). This 'precious stone of
ǆoatian literacy' is written in Glagolitic script and records
ǆift to the Benedictines by King Zvonimir.

POPULAR BAŠKA
Ringed by barren
karst peaks, Baška
(*above*) is the island's
favorite tourist
destination with its
narrow lanes,
balconies and fine
sandy beach.

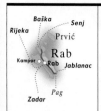

Rab Island ◆ B C4

This small island, with an area of 35 square miles (91 km²) and three mountainous ridges running its length, enjoys a mild climate. Its barren eastern coast is overlooked by the peaks of the Kamenjak range, while its interior, devoted to olive farming and wine-making, and its western side, with forests of cork-oak and little coves, make it perfect for walking. Populated first by the Illyrian tribes and then by the Romans, the island still bears traces of its domination by the Croatian princes and, from 1409 onward, of the presence of the Venetians. From the Middle Ages onward, the island has numerous working quarries, which mined a red-veined stone widely used in Rab Town and also along the Adriatic coast, particularly in the cathedrals of Zadar and Šibenik.

RAB. Encircled by four Romanesque bell towers, three of which are original, and enclosed by walls, Rab's terraced lanes spread over a narrow spit of land. The layout of the medieval city that resisted attacks by the Uskoks and the Saracens is still intact. The cathedral of Sv. Marija Velika (St Mary the Great), built in the 11th century, was restored in the 15th century. A Romanesque masterpiece with its basilical three-nave plan and interior richly decorated with knotwork and symbolic motifs, it has some typically Renaissance elements such as the Pietà on the portal, the baptismal fonts (1497) by Petar Trogiranin, the intricately carved choirstalls and the tombstones. Its Romanesque campanile, which stands 82 feet (25 meters) high and has numerous arched windows, recalls the bell tower of the abbey of Pomposa, near Ferrara. The precious reliquary of the island's patron saint, St Christopher, made in the 13th century, holds pride of place in the collection of sacred art in the church of Sv. Justine (St Justine). The church of Sv. Ivan (St John), the Benedictine monastery, the stately houses from the 15th and 16th centuries and Komrčar Park are all worth a visit.

HEADING NORTH. Kampor Bay is the site of the Franciscan convent of St Euphemia with its Romanesque church adorned with braided motifs and its Gothic chapel. The convent's most important piece is the 15th-century polyptych by the Venetian Vivarini brothers. SUPETARSKA DRAGA has the best preserved 11th-century Benedictine monument in Dalmatia: the ancient abbey church of St Peter

‍enj ◆ B D3

‍istling with walls and towers and buffeted by the chilly
‍ra wind, Senj has the coldest weather in the Adriatic and
‍n seem rather austere. Situated at the foot of the Vratnik
‍ss (2,261 feet/689 meters), the lowest pass through the
‍lebit mountains, Senj was strategically placed between
‍ntinental Europe and the sea. Attacked first by the Turks
‍d then by Venice, the town was the linchpin of the Military
‍ontier established by Matthias Corvinus (1458–90). It
‍sisted invasion and offered asylum to the warlike Uskoks.
‍ wealthy merchant town, Senj has palaces built round its
‍rtress and encouraged the spread of Croatian literature.
‍**ITHIN THE WALLS.** Winding lanes lead to the cathedral of
‍. Marija (St Mary), whose simple façade with brick arches
‍veal its Romanesque origins. In the next street, the
‍kasović Palace, with its fusion of Gothic and Renaissance
‍ements, houses the Town Museum, whose archeological
‍d botanical collections offer a good introduction to the
‍gion. Not far from here lies the baroque Trg Cilnica.
‍ beautiful neoclassical fountain stands at the center of
‍s main square, which is bordered by tall buildings and
‍closed on its eastern side by the palace of the Frankopans,
‍o governed the town until 1469.
‍**TSIDE THE WALLS.** The Art headland is the province of
‍lors and poets. Near Writers' Square, lined with statues of
‍n of letters, stands the church of St Mary, the 'Sailors'
‍urch', which is filled with votive offerings. At the far end
‍ the bay, the mighty fortress of Nehaj stands on Trbušnjak
‍l. Built in 1558, it symbolizes the fierce resistance of the
‍skok pirates against the Turks, who had joined forces with
‍e Venetians.

‍o the Velebit ◆ D D-E3-5

‍aving Senj, the 'Magistrala' runs
‍ng the coast toward Dalmatia,
‍ween the flat Adriatic
‍oreline and the rocky slopes of
‍e Velebit. This is an area worth
‍ploring and visitors are spoiled
‍r choice with a variety of
‍eathtaking landscapes, interesting
‍cursions, little coves and stylish ports. Karlobag is the point
‍ departure for crossing the Velebit through the Ostarije
‍ss (3,045 feet/928 meters). The road zigzags as it climbs,
‍ering some fine panoramic views of Pag and the sea.

THE USKOKS
In the second half of
the 15th century,
armed fighters left the
areas conquered by
the Ottomans to
improve their chances
of opposing them.
After the loss of Klis
▲ 212 in 1537, the
Uskoks settled in Senj,
which served as a base
for their attacks on the
Turks by sea and by
land. According to the
terms of the treaty of
1540, Venice
undertook to protect
the Turkish fleet, so
the Uskoks also began
targeting Venetian
ships. These attacks
contributed to the
outbreak of the war
between Venice and
Austria in 1615. After
the peace treaty of
1617, the Habsburgs
ousted the Uskoks
from Senj, resettling
them in Zumberak
▲ 136 and Pazin ▲ 162.

GOLDEN AGES
The little town of Sveti
Juraj, to the south of
Senj, owes its name to
a Benedictine
monastery built in
1242. It was razed to
the ground not long
after by the
Tartars.
Karlobag,
which was
destroyed
and rebuilt
many times,
takes its
name from its
successive
benefactors: Archduke
of Austria, Charles of
Habsburg in 1579 and
the Hungaro-Croatian
King, Charles VI, in
the 18th century.

▲ The Velebit

The Velebit is the longest, most majestic mountain range in Croatia. It runs parallel to the coast, following an arc of 90 miles (145 km) from the Vratnik pass, above Senj, to the banks of the Zrmanja River. It offers a variety of striking landscapes. The rocky side facing the coast sweeps almost straight down to the sea, while its eastern slopes overlook the mountainous, wooded region of the Lika. The highest part of the range is an irregular succession of peaks and valleys overlooked by the Velebit's most prominent mountains: Mali Rajinac (5,574 feet/1,699 meters) in the north and Vaganska Vrh (5,765 feet/1,757 meters) and Sveto Brdo (5,745 feet/1,751 meters) in the south.

The griffon vulture is found in the Paklenica region.

THE ZAVIŽAN MOUNTAIN HUT
The mountain trail that starts at the coast near Sveti Juraj leads into the center of the northern Velebit mountains and ascends as far as the Zavižan group. The mountain hut of the same name (5,230 feet/1,594 meters) is situated next to a meteorological station (*left*). The Premužić hiking trail is nearby, while the Velebit Botanical Garden, founded in 1966 by Croatian botanist Fran Kušan, is 15 minutes' walk away. This garden has a number of endemic plants, as well as some rare species from other areas in the Velebit.

THE PAKLENICA NATIONAL PARK
The magnificent gorges of Velika Paklenica and Mala Paklenica were eroded by two mountain rivers winding their way across the coastal karst slopes of the Velebit. The cliffs of Velika Paklenica are very popular with mountaineers: the most famous rock face is the Anića Kuk (about 1,312 feet/400 meters).

A PROTECTED NATURAL HERITAGE SITE
In 1978, the Velebit mountain range was designated an International Biosphere Reserve by Unesco. Since 1981, the entire massif has enjoyed the status of a Nature Park. Certain areas are under special protection: the Paklenica National Park and the Northern Velebit National Park, the Hajdučki and Rožanski Kukovi Nature Reserve, the Cerovačke caves and the Special Forest Vegetation Reserve of Štirovača.

A CHALLENGE FOR HIKERS
There are many mountain trails in the Velebit, but the most remarkable is that of Premužič, built by forestry expert Ante Premužić across the Rožanski Kukovi in about 1930. It covers a distance of 31 miles (50 km) at an almost constant altitude of 4,922 feet (1,500 meters).

KARST LANDSCAPES
Situated in the Northern Velebit, the Rožanski Kukovi Nature Reserve comprises about 50 peaks: oddly shaped limestone formations that are divided by deep fissures. The Tulove Grede are jagged, barren peaks overlooking the lush valleys of the Southern Velebit.

▲ From Rijeka to Zadar

Pag (*below*) and the town's collegiate church (*right*), whose rose window reproduces motifs similar to the patterns found in the lace made by the island's women.

Pag Island ♦ **B** D5

The island can be reached by ferry or, since 1970, by a bridge.

PAG LACE
Pag's needlework or *roželica* is equal in quality to Brussels embroidery or Venetian *reticella*. The rosettes, stars and geometric shapes of its interwoven patterns have been developed over the centuries by the women who live on the island. Pag lace was so famous that, under the Habsburgs, two lacemakers from the island lived at court in Vienna, where they worked for the emperor and his retinue. The headdress and blouse of traditional women's costumes are decorated with this lace (*right*).

Pag is a large island, with an area of 110 square miles (285 km²), buffeted by the Bura wind blowing down from the Velebit. The landscape is a combination of vast stretches of rocky land grazed by sheep, whose milk is used to make the famous *paški sir* ● *52*, and small fertile hollows planted with vineyards. Inhabited by th Illyrians, then colonized by Rome, the island and its salt par were bitterly fought over by Rab and Zadar in the Middle Ages. In 1409, Pag, like the rest of Dalmatia, came under th economic control of Venice, which made an annual revenue of 80,000 ducats from salt mining in the 15th century.
PAG TOWN. The old town was destroyed by forces from Zadar. The famous architect, Juraj Dalmatinac ▲ *202*, was commissioned to produce a design for the new town, which was built, half a mile (500 meters) further east, in 1443. The town was modeled on the layout of ancient cities, supplemented with Renaissance notions of perspective. Two main streets intersected at the central square and were flanked by a tight grid of narrower streets. The collegiate church of Blažena Djevica Marija (St Mary) was built at the same time as the city. Its façade is adorned with statues and a stone rose window. On the tympanum, a *Madonna* by Petar Berčić, a pupil of Dalmatinac, protectively spreads her mantle over the town and her people.
FROM NOVALJA TO LUN. Founded in Late Antiquity, Novalja, now a large tourist resort, has various Roman ruins, including an aqueduct and three Paleochristian basilicas. Just over a mile (2 km) from the town lies the archeological site of Caska, which has the foundations of Cissa, the island's main town until the 15th century. The Lun peninsula is covered with olive groves full of centuries-old trees standing on the loos pebbles of a limestone plateau, and forming an unsettling lunar landscape.

Zadar

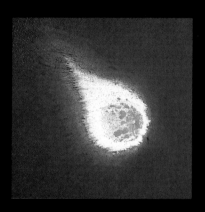

Zadar, *190*
Inland from Zadar, *196*
The Zadar Archipelago, *198*
The Kornati Islands, 200
Šibenik, *202*
Around Šibenik, *204*
The Krka National Park, *204*
Along the Krka, *205*
Trogir, *206*
Kaštela (The Castle Trail), *209*
Salona, Capital of Roman
   Dalmatia, 210
Toward Sinj, *212*

◆ H

Jadera (the Roman name for Zadar) was enclosed by walls built with the aid of subsidies from Emperor Augustus. This statue of the emperor is kept at the Archeological Museum ▲*192*.

With 76,000 inhabitants, Zadar is the largest city in northern Dalmatia. Protected by one of the longest archipelagos in the Mediterranean, the city is situated on the northeastern shores of the Ravni Kotari region ▲*196*, and bordered by a vast fertile plain. Zadar has been a key center on the eastern Adriatic coast for centuries due to this excellent geographical location.

The history of Zadar

ANCIENT TIMES. Zadar's historic center was built on a peninsula which runs parallel to the coast, forming a natural harbor. Its earliest mention dates back to the 4th century BC when its inhabitants, the Jadasinoi, were fighting the Greek colonies in the Adriatic. At this time Idassa, as the Greeks called it, was the main settlement of the Illyrian Liburnian tribe. In the 1st century BC, it became a *municipium* and an imperial colony under the name of Jadera.

THE MIDDLE AGES. After the destruction of Salona in the early 7th century, Zadar became the capital of Byzantine Dalmatia and, in the 10th century, the city forged links with the kingdom of Croatia while retaining its municipal independence. An important port on the trade route along the eastern Adriatic, Zadar posed a threat to the expansion of the Republic of Venice, which strove hard to subjugate it between the 12th and 15th centuries. After a short period under Venetian rule in the late 11th century, the inhabitants of Zadar accepted the Hungaro-Croatian King Koloman's suzerainty in 1105, enabling them to withstand attempts by the Serenissima Republic to take over the city. However, following political unrest and despite fervent opposition by the Zadarans, the Venetians regained control of the city from 1116. After three abortive uprisings, Zadar recovered its independence in 1181. However, Venice was not defeated: in 1202, Doge Enrico Dandolo called on French knight who were preparing for the 4th crusade and,

with their help, captured the city. The Zadarans won a few short-lived victories in their struggle for independence during the centuries that followed, culminating in the famous Venetian siege of the city in 1345–6. After holding out for 16 months, the Hungaro-Croatian King Louis I of Anjou was defeated and the city again came under Venetian control. Barely ten years later, a skillful military campaign by Louis I forced the Venetians to give up any claim to Zadar once and for all in 1358. This was followed by 50 years of prosperity during which Zadar once more became one of the most important cities in the Adriatic. However, in 1409, Venice took advantage of the rebellion by the aristocracy against the absolutism of the Anjou dynasty to buy the sovereignty of Dalmatia from Ladislas, King of Naples, for the sum of 100,000 ducats.

VENETIAN FORTIFICATION. Zadar, then called Zara, began to decline, after the loss of its political and economic independence and the subsequent arrival of the Turks, who decimated its hinterland in the 15th century. In later centuries, the city became a Venetian stronghold and the Republic's administrative center in the Adriatic.

THE MODERN CITY. Zadar came under the rule of the French, then the Austrians with the fall of the Republic of Venice in 1797. When the Austro-Hungarian kingdom was dissolved, Zadar and its surroundings were ceded to Italy in 1920 under the Treaty of Rapallo. After World War Two, during which the city was almost completely destroyed, Zadar once again became part of Croatia within the framework of the Yugoslav Federation. During the Croatian War of Independence, Zadar was attacked frequently by the Yugoslav army between 1990 and 1995 due to its strategic position.

THE TURKO-VENETIAN WARS
These wars threatened Zadar for nearly two centuries. Most of its hinterland came under Turkish rule, while the rest of the region, which was frequently sacked and abandoned, was no longer able to support a prosperous economy.

PETAR ZORANIĆ
This poet and lawyer from Zadar (1508–69) described the region's lost beauty with patriotic fervor in his pastoral novel *Mountains* (1536), which is liberally sprinkled with myths and legends. 'Over there, where the blossoming tree would soon be weighed down by fruit, we no longer hear the girls sing or the shepherds pretend to be bowmen and play their pipes; the rivers running past mills have been filled in and the flowing water no longer turns the wheel; everyone is abandoning the castles, villages and towns in haste, fleeing enemy attacks; we see palaces and villages burned, the mountain gods and the fairies have left their sanctuary; nothing worse, in my opinion, can befall us; we must head down to the sea, or remain in chains. Happy are those who have had the good fortune to die before seeing their heritage in such deep mourning.'

Like Tintoretto ● 74, Andrea dei Michieli (1539–1614) painted the Venetians capturing Zadar.

Exhibits in the
Archeological Museum.

**ST ANASTASIA'S
FAÇADE**
There are two rose
windows above the
triple portal: a large
Romanesque window
surmounted by a
smaller Gothic one.
The tympanum over
the main entrance is
decorated with a
group carved in the
14th century depicting
the Virgin Mary with
Zadar's patron saints,
Chrysogonus and
Anastasia.

**A WELL-PRESERVED
LAYOUT**
Jadera's Forum is at
the center of the
town. The regular
layout of streets
separating
blocks of houses
recalls the design
of the ancient
insulae.

Roman Forum
♦ H B2

Construction of Jadera's main square
(312 feet/95 meters by 149 feet /
45.5 meters) lasted from the 1st century BC to the 3rd century
AD. Three of the sides were bordered by monumental arches
supported by marble colonnades. Visitors can still admire
most of the original paving, the foundations of the *tabernae*
(stores) in the southeast and northwest, as well as the ruins
of a civic basilica or meeting hall in the southwest, where
the town council used to meet. Numerous fragments of
ornamental carvings still survive, as does one of the Forum's
two colossal columns which was used as a 'shame post'
in the Middle Ages. The chains, the plaque decorated with
knotwork and the statue of the griffin on top date from this
period. The ruins of a temple built in the 1st century BC and
the Capitol, whose walls were decorated with masks of
Jupiter-Amun and Medusa, stand southwest of the Forum.
ARHEOLOŠKI MUZEJ. Founded in 1830, this museum is
now housed in a modern building to the east of the Forum.
The second floor is devoted to the prehistoric era, from the
Paleolithic period to the Iron Age. Objects illustrating daily
life in northern Dalmatia in Roman times are exhibited on
the second floor. The first floor, devoted to the early Middle
Ages (7th–11th centuries), has a particularly interesting
display of liturgical stonework carved with interwoven
ornamental motifs (*above*) and early representations of
human figures in Croatian art.

The Cathedral complex ♦ H A-B1-2

This group of buildings was constructed in the northern part
of the ancient Forum. A three-nave Paleochristian basilica
with a baptistery, then a Bishop's Palace, were soon built
alongside the early 4th-century oratory. Today, the cathedral
of Sv. Stošije (St Anastasia), the baptistery, the church of
Sv. Donata (St Donat) and the Bishop's Palace, which has
been regularly remodeled since the Paleochristian era, form
harmonious complex built around
inner courtyards.

CATHEDRAL OF SV. STOŠIJE (ST ANASTASIA) ● 60. This Romanesque church was built to a basilical plan in the 12th century over the foundations of the Paleochristian structure. It was extended westward in the 13th century with the construction of an arcaded façade in Tuscan style which reused elements of the former façade. The monumental interior is punctuated by baroque altars lining the side walls. The chancel, raised above a crypt, contains wooden choir stalls carved in the early 15th century by the Venetian artist, Matteo Moronzoni. The sacristy is on the site of the early oratory and has a Paleochristian mosaic depicting stags drinking from a cantharus, as well as vestiges of early 14th-century frescos. The 5th-century baptistery, destroyed during World War Two, was restored in 1990. It houses a fine Romanesque baptismal font. The campanile was constructed in neo-Romanesque style by the British architect, Sir Thomas G. Jackson (1835–1924) in the late 19th century.

CHURCH OF SV. DONATA (ST DONAT) ● 58. Donat, the bishop of Zadar in the early 9th century, built this church (right), probably modeled on the Palatine Chapel of Charlemagne in Aix-la-Chapelle. Its foundations reused stones and carvings taken from the ruins of the Forum. The impressive dimensions of this church, which is 89 feet (27 meters) high, make it an exceptional example of pre-Romanesque European religious architecture. It now hosts summer concerts put on as part of the *Zadarske glazbene Večeri* (Zadar Musical Evenings).

The Convent of St Mary ♦ H B2

THE CHURCH OF SV. MARIJA (ST MARY). This abbey church belonging to a Benedictine convent was founded in 1066 by the Abbess Čika, a patrician of Zadar, who obtained the support of the Croatian King Petar Krešimir IV. It was remodeled and given a new façade in the 16th century (*below right*). The interior was lavishly decorated with stucco work in 1744. The bell tower was built in 1105 with a donation from the first Hungaro-Croatian sovereign, King Koloman. This

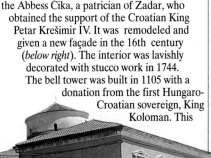

BISHOP DONAT
This shrewd diplomat acted as an arbitrator between East and West on missions to

Charlemagne's palace and to the Imperial Palace in Constantinople, from where he brought back relics of St Anastasia the Martyr. He built the city's symbol, the church of the Holy Trinity, later renamed in his honor.

RELIQUARY OF ST SIMEON
The large silver-gilt sarcophagus containing the body of elderly St Simeon was a gift from Queen Elizabeth, daughter of the Ban (governor) of Bosnia, Stjepan Kotromanić, and wife of the Hungaro-Croatian King, Louis I of Anjou, probably as a means of assuring the city's wholehearted support. It was made in Zadar between 1377 and 1381 by silversmith Francesco da Milano, who used around 550 lb (250 kg) of silver and a large quantity of precious metal for the gilding. It is decorated with reliefs depicting various scenes, including Louis I of Anjou's entry into Zadar with his wife and the Croatian Ban, Pavao Šubić, and the death of Stjepan Kotromanić.

RELIQUARY OF ST ANASTASIA
On display in the Permanent Exhibition of Church Art, this was commissioned in Venice in 1622 by Luca Stella, Archbishop of Zadar. The halo is engraved with the words *Sanctae Anastasiae martyris*.

historical event is documented by an inscription on the tower's outer wall at the same height as the second-floor capitals, which are engraved with the ruler's name. In the 15th century, the Zadaran architect, Nikola Bilšić, demolished it to the height of the second floor, then rebuilt it in original Romanesque style, thereby implementing one of the first restoration projects in Europe.

STALNA IZLOŽBA CRKVENE UMJETNOSTI (PERMANENT EXHIBITION OF CHURCH ART). This collection occupies two wings of St Mary's Convent and displays most of the famous 'Silver and Gold of Zadar' – reliquaries, chalices, crosses, monstrances, pyxes and fabrics embroidered with gold thread – made by skilled Zadaran gold- and silversmiths. Exhibits include medieval sculptures, a series of Romanesque-Byzantine icons, works by local Gothic painters and paintings by great Venetian masters such as Paolo Veneziano (14th century), Catarino (second half of the 14th century), Vittore Carpacc (c. 1460–c. 1525) and Lorenzo Luzzo (16th century).

CHURCH OF SV. KRŠEVAN (ST CHRYSOGONUS). Poljana Pape Aleksandra III (Pope Alexander III Esplanade) leads to a Romanesque building consecrated in 1175. This was once the abbey church of a Benedictine monastery with a famous *scriptorium*. The interior contains vestiges of frescos dating from the late 12th century. Above the baroque main altar are statues of the city's patron saints, Chrysogonus, Zoilus, Simeon and Anastasia, carved by the Venetian sculptor Alvise Tagliapietra.

The Franciscan Monastery ◆ H A1

The church of Sv. Frane (St Francis), completed in 1280 is the oldest Gothic church in Dalmatia. The simple interior is decorated with numerous altars, the most remarkable of which is the high altar, built in 1672 to a design by the Venetian architect, Baldassare Longhena (1598–1682). The finely carved wooden choirstalls were the work of Ivan Jakovljev of Borgo San Sepolcro (1394). Among other things, the monastery's Treasury contains a large carved crucifix from the 12th century (*center*), some precious illuminated manuscripts and a superb polyptych in late Gothic style by Ivan Petrov of Milan. The cloister, built in 1556 to the south of the church, is surrounded by monastery buildings.

arodni Trg (People's Square) ◆ H B2

e Town Hall was built in 1934 along the northern side of
at has been Zadar's main square since the Renaissance.

On the western side stand the remains
of the 9th-century church of Sv. Lovro
(St Lawrence), sandwiched between a
café of the same name and the superb
Guard House, built in 1562 and crowned
with a clock tower in 1798. Opposite,
the Gradska Loža (City Loggia), the
former city courts – now used to mount
exhibitions – was rebuilt in 1565 by
Michele Sanmicheli of Verona.

CHURCH OF SV. ŠIME (ST SIMEON). The
narrow street of Kotromanić leads to this
white and ocher church. The 5th-century

Paleochristian building was initially
remodeled in the Gothic period, then
again in the baroque period. Inside, the
north wall still has some Gothic frescos
attributed to the artist Antonio Veneziano.
There is a 13th-century Byzantine statue
of the Virgin Mary as Theotokos (bearer
of god) made of gilded marble in the north
side aisle, and the reliquary of St Simeon
rests on the high altar.

The fortifications

Although some of
the ramparts were
demolished in the
19th century to
construct the pleasant
omenade known as the Riva, stretches
wall dating from ancient, medieval
d Renaissance times still stand in the
utheastern and northeastern parts of
e city. Most of the surviving sections
wall date from the 16th century:
rtifications strengthened by sturdy bastions were built
ound Zadar in response to the Ottoman threat.

LOZOFSKI FAKULTET (FACULTY OF LETTERS AND
CIAL SCIENCES). The oldest Croatian university was
unded in 1396 in Zadar by the Dominicans. The faculty,
ich has been housed in a 20th-century building since
56, is now the hub of the city's scientific and cultural life.

195

Church of
St Nicholas, between
Zadar and Nin.

From remote islands
to the white waters of the
Krka River, from Adriatic coastline
to mountainous hinterland, from medieval
fortresses to gems of Gothic and Renaissance
architecture, like Trogir and Šibenik: taking a
leisurely drive from Zadar toward Split provides
ample opportunity to enjoy the wide diversity of landscape
in northern and central Dalmatia.

Inland from Zadar ◆ B D6-E6

The area between Zadar and the Velebit is composed of tw
regions: Ravni Kotari (literally 'flat districts') and Bukovic
beyond Novigrad's lagoon. Various *oppidums* appeared in t
Illyrian period, several of which became large towns after t
Roman conquest. This area formed the initial nucleus of th
Croatian state ● *32* in the early Middle Ages, after the Got
and Avar invasions. From the end of the 15th century, the
Ravni Kotari region was the scene of numerous battles
against the Turks, while the Bukovica region, whose main
town is Obrovac, fell into the hands of the Ottoman Empir
in 1527. After this, the area's fate was linked closely to tha
of Zadar ▲ *190*. The people are now largely farmers,
even though tourism is a growth industry along the coast.

NIN. The remarkable little 12th-century CHURCH OF
SV. NIKOLA U PRAHULJIMA (St Nicholas of
Prahulje), which lies along the main road
between Zadar and Nin in Prahulje, acquire
a central watchtower in the 17th century.
Nin, located on an islet in the center of a
shallow lagoon, was urbanized in Roman
times (*Aenona*) and became one of the
capitals of the Croat rulers in the early
Middle Ages. The town found it very har
to recover from the destruction inflicted
the Ottomans. Marble statues of Roman

**COMBATING
THE TURKS**
The Zadar hinterland
is dotted with the
ruins of medieval
fortresses remodeled
from the 15th century
onward to drive back
the Turks. The
fortress of Ražanac
(1507), whose square
central keep still
stands, enabled the
Croatians to
withstand an attack by
the Ottomans in 1645.
Conversely, the
fortresses of Obrovac
and Benkovac were
captured by the Turks
in the 16th century.

**10TH-CENTURY
RELIQUARIES IN NIN**
Their purse-like
shape, characteristic
of Carolingian
reliquaries, reveals
the close links
between Croatia and
the Frankish
kingdom, at that time
the most powerful
kingdom in Europe.

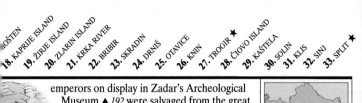

emperors on display in Zadar's Archeological Museum ▲ *192* were salvaged from the great ancient temple. Medieval buildings include the 10th-century church of the Sv. Križ (Holy Cross) and the late Romanesque church of Sv. Ambroz (St Ambrose).

◆ **C** A-D1-3

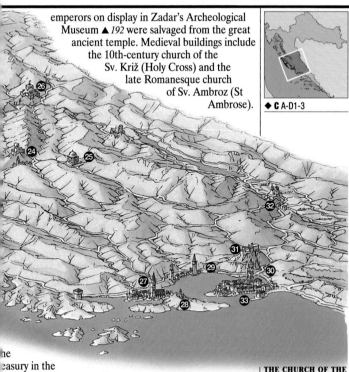

...he ...easury in the ...URCH OF SV. ANZELMO (St Anselm) has some precious ...ver and gold reliquaries that were made between the ...h and 15th centuries.

...VIGRAD. On a hilltop stands the ruined 13th-century castle ...here local lords opposing royal authority imprisoned Queen ...lizabeth ▲ *194*, King Louis I of Anjou's widow (whom they ...urdered here in 1386) and her daughter Marie, wife of the ...ungaro-Croatian ruler, King Sigmund of Luxembourg. In ...e 16th century, Novigrad was one of the fortresses which ...ayed a vital role in resisting the Ottomans. The partially ...eserved ramparts, which at that time extended as ...r as the sea, enclose a dense network of ...reets winding between stone houses.

...OGRAD. In the 11th century, this town ...came a Royal Town and the site of ...ng Koloman's coronation in 1102 ...*32*. The Venetians razed Biograd ...the ground in 1125, then later settled ...re between 1409 and 1797. Biograd ...ffered again during the Turko-...enetian wars. About half a mile (1km) ...om VRANA, a medieval Templar ...wn, stands the best-preserved ...onument of Islamic ...chitecture in the region: the ...aravanserai built in 1645 by ...zir Yusuf Mašković, who ...s born in Vrana.

THE CHURCH OF THE HOLY CROSS IN NIN
This is one of the most significant examples of Pre-Romanesque Croatian architecture. Its irregular plan was the result of its builders' desire to create a type of sundial marking the most important dates of the year.

TRAVELING TO THE ISLANDS
All can be reached by ferry from Zadar, except Murter, which has been linked to the mainland by a swing bridge since 1832.

DUGI OTOK OR 'LONG ISLAND'
This is the biggest island in the Zadar archipelago with an area of 44 square miles (115 km²) and a rugged, indented coastline. Its eleven villages straggle along the northeastern coast, while its southwestern shore, facing the Adriatic sea, is characterized by sheer cliffs plunging into the sea ▲201. In the north, the often deserted Sakarun Bay is fringed with a magnificent beach. The island's heyday was in the Middle Ages. Several places of worship date from this period, such as the churches of Sv. Marija (St Mary) in Sali, Sv. Pelegrin (St Peregrine) in Savar and Sv. Mihovil (St Michael) in Zaglav. Its largest hamlet, Sali, is a renowned fishing port. The oldest surviving written document on fishing along the Adriatic coast dates from 995 and describes catching mackerel and sardines in Telašćica Bay.

THE ISLAND OF IŽ
The only Dalmatian island where the inhabitants were once potters, Iž still boasts several examples of traditional buildings ● 68.

Father Simon, the Irish pilgrim who visited Zadar in 1323, reported that the city overlooked as many islands as there were days in the year. Although it is tempting to believe he was embellishing the facts, this statement is actually not far from the truth. With over 300 islands and islets, the Zadar Archipelago is one of the most deeply indented coastlines in the Mediterranean. Since prehistoric times, the islanders have lived on farming, stock breeding and fishing ● 48, although tourism is now becoming a boom industry since the islands represent such an attractive destination with their Mediterranean vegetation, picturesque villages, sheltered coves and many crystalline bays.

UGLJAN. The landscape on this island is predominantly scrubland, pine woods and Mediterranean crops with expanses of rocky limestone in the southwest. The island has been inhabited since prehistoric times and its seven villages are dotted along the northeastern coastline. There are remains of a *villa rustica* ● 56 dating from Late Antiquity and a Paleochristian basilica in MULINE, as well as some fragments of Roman sculpture and several sarcophaguses in PREKO. The carved capitals of the Romanesque cloister in the monastery of Sv. Jerolim (St Jerome) in UGLJAN VILLAGE attest to the high standard of the island's cultural achievements in the Middle Ages, as do the precious examples of sculpture, silverwork and painting from Ugljan now on display as part of the Permanent Exhibition of Church Art in Zadar ▲ 194. Also worthy of note are the Fortress of Sv. Mihovil (St Michael) on the hill above Preko and several medieval churches. During the Renaissance and baroque periods, many patrician families from Zadar built villas in the area.

PAŠMAN. This is an island of contrasts, where areas of bare rock, intensively cultivated farmland and scrubland are found in relatively close proximity. The island underwent a period of rapid cultural and economic development in the Middle Ages and most of its monuments date from this period. The only permanently occupied Benedictine monastery in Croatia, Sv. Kuzma i Damjan (SS Cosmas and Damian), is enclosed by medieval fortified walls on a hilltop near TKON. Its late medieval abbey church contains a painted Gothic crucifix by Menegelo Ivanov de Canali, the son of Giovanni de Canali. The Franciscan monastery in KRAJ and several churches with richly decorated interiors are also worth a visit.

VRGADA. Mentioned in the 10th century by the Byzantine Emperor Constantine VII under the name of Lumbrikaton, this small island lies to the southeast of Pašman. Its church of Sv. Andrija (St Andrew), dating from the early Middle Ages, stands in the village cemetery, overlooked by a hill which is the site of an ancient and medieval ruined *castrum*.

IŽ. This island was inhabited in prehistoric and protohistoric times. The vestiges of four *oppidums* date from this period. The Roman settlement occupied the site of present VELI IŽ. The small rotunda church of Sv. Marija (St Mary), with its semicircular chevet, is unique in Pre-Romanesque Croatian architecture.

THE DUGI OTOK NATIONAL PARK
Telašćica Bay, which stretches for 6 miles (10 km), is sheltered from sea winds by steep cliffs topped with lush Mediterranean vegetation. The Nature Park has become a major tourist attraction for its diverse fauna and beautiful landscapes. It also takes in the saltwater lake of Jezero Mir, bordered by the Grpašćak cliff, the longest in the Adriatic at 6 miles (10 km). In summer, the waters of the lake are 43°F (6°C) warmer than the sea. Its level varies depending on the tides, which occur slightly later than those at sea.

MURTER ISLAND
In Antiquity, this island, traditionally part of the Šibenik archipelago ▲ *202*, was called Colentum. It was then named Srimaz or Srimać between the 13th and 18th centuries, before acquiring its present name.

From top to bottom:
Jezero Mir Lake, Sakarun Bay, Vrgada, Murter, and its port.

199

After a visit to the archipelago,
George Bernard Shaw wrote that
'On the last day of Creation, God desired to crown His work, and
thus created the Kornati islands out of tears, stars and breath.'
A popular saying claims there are as many Kornati Islands as
there are days in the year. In fact, there are around 150 islands
but it's unusual to find so many gathered over an area of 116
square miles (300 km²) in the Mediterranean. Originally tectonic
and composed of limestone (karst), these islands are the peaks of
a mountain chain from the last ice age: what were deep valleys
are now straits and what were high mountaintops are now islands.

PROTECTING NATURE
Most of this
archipelago is
protected as the
Kornati National Park
which covers 27 square
miles (70 km²) of land
and 77 square miles
(200 km²) of sea.

FLORA AND FAUNA
Excessive sheep
farming has decimated
the flora. The islands
are bare or covered
with sparse maquis.
There are a few rare
species growing on
the sheer slopes of
the cliffs, such as the
Centaurea ragusina
(Dubrovnik
cornflower) and the
arborescent
Euphorbia. The sea
■ 26, however, is
exceptionally rich in
flora and fauna: 350
species of plant and
300 species of animal
which represents
most of the fish and
cephalopods in the
Mediterranean.
Fishing is not allowed

HUMAN OCCUPATION
Although there are no villages on the Kornati islands, there are about 300 houses, inhabited sporadically by shepherds and farmers who cultivate the small fields (vines and olive trees). Low walls pen in the sheep.

THE CLIFFS
Occasionally soaring to over 262 feet (80 meters), the cliffs on the islands off the coast and on Dugi Otok ▲ *198*, scored with crevices and fissures, plunge steeply into the sea. The islanders call them *krune* (crowns), which is the original derivation of the archipelago's name. They are also responsible for some of the more colorful place names: visitors can sail round an islet called Babina Guzica (Grandmother's Bum) or the Prduša Vela i Mala islands (Little Fart and Big Fart).

ARCHITECTURAL HERITAGE
The island of Kornat is the site of a remarkable example of Byzantine military architecture: the fortress of Toreta (6th century), which protected the Adriatic's eastern sea route. The church of St Mary dates from the same period, although it was remodeled in the 14th century. The Visitation is celebrated here on the first Sunday in July.

STONE PORTRAITS. This realist frieze of 72 carved stone portraits (*opposite*), running around the external walls of the apses is, along with the baptistery, the best example of Juraj Dalmatinac's expertise: an individual fusion of *Gotico Fiorito* and Renaissance style.

GEORGE THE DALMATIAN
Jurac Dalmatinac (c. 1400–73) was the most brilliant Croatian architect of the mid-15th century. He worked in Venice and Ancona, designed many religious, civic and military buildings in Šibenik, Split, Dubrovnik and Zadar, and built Pag Town. His style made him forefather of the Adriatic Renaissance. His pupils, Pribislavić and Aleši, continued his work.

Šibenik ♦ I

Unlike the other towns along the coast with their rich Greek Roman or Byzantine heritage, Šibenik is a new town, founded by the Croatian princes at the mouth of the Krka River between the 9th and 10th centuries. It was mentioned for the first time in 1066, in a charter by King Petar Krešimir IV; already fortified, it helped to counterbalance Byzantine influence in Dalmatia. In 1102, the town came under the control of Hungaro-Croatian rulers, like the rest of the coastal area. However, this hegemony was interrupted by numerous Venetian incursions and, by 1412, the Serenissima Republic was the only power passing legislation in the city. Between 1463 and 1683, the town resisted the Turks, who were occupying inland areas. Šibenik's conciliatory strategy proved very profitable: the town became a wealthy trading center, doing business with the enemy while keeping them at a safe distance. At the same time, Venice sent architects to the town, whose buildings reveal the influence of the Christian West. Šibenik's cathedral, churches and palaces, all Renaissance masterpieces, symbolize the city's victory over the East far more than the vestiges of its fortresses.

CATHEDRAL OF SV. JAKOV (ST JAMES) ● 62. Designated a Unesco World Heritage Site in 2000, St James' Cathedral is the Croatian monument that best illustrates the transition from

amboyant Gothic to Renaissance style. It was built in ree stages. Between 1433 and 1441, local artists assisted Italian masters such as Francesco di Giacomo, Pier olo Bussato and, particularly, Bonino da Milano, began nstructing a single-nave church. They built the main orway and the Door of Lions to the north, but their stere style, inherited from Late Lombard Gothic, was a sappointment for their patrons who, in 1444, turned to raj Dalmatinac. The latter added a transept, some apses, underground baptistery and, most importantly, introduced e more recent Flamboyant Venetian Gothic style into the sign, mingling it with early Renaissance elements. In 1477, er his death, Nikola Firentinac (Nicholas of Florence) ntinued his work. He crowned the building with galleries, ulted ceilings and a dome. Built of stone and marble using original construction technique, richly furnished th objects fashioned by the best artists in the th century, like Juraj Petrović, who made the oden crucifix, the cathedral prefigures the new irit of Humanism with its realistic iconography, namic carving and focus on profane themes.

ROUND THE CATHEDRAL. The Town Loggia, pposite the cathedral, was built between 1533 and 42. Its harmonious proportions, portico and lion otifs make it one of the most beautiful examples its type in Dalmatia. To the south of St James' athedral stands the Bishop's Palace, whose mboyant doorway, by Dalmatian architects, ves onto a 15th-century Gothic courtyard.

XPLORING THE STEEP STREETS. Šibenik is built to the mountainside like an amphitheater. From e cathedral, its lanes and staircases lead to urches in a variety of styles, including Gothic, Renaissance d baroque. The town boasts many beautiful sights: the oscolo Palace has a fine Gothic-Renaissance façade; the th-century baroque church of Sv. Nikola contains a richly inted coffered ceiling made of wood; the 14th-century urch of Sv. Frane (St Francis) has an organ made by the mous organ maker Petar Nakić (1694–1760), while the onastery next to the church boasts a wonderful library medieval manuscripts and early printed books); the bell wer of the Orthodox church of Uznesenje Bogorodičino f the Assumption) is typical of Adriatic baroque style.

E FORTRESSES. Tvrđava Sv. Ana (St Anne's Fortress) as built to the north of the medieval town center in 1000, though its present appearance dates back to the 18th ntury. The star-shaped Fort of Sv. Ivan (St John), built 1646, and the Šubićevac Fort were constructed to protect e town from Ottoman invasions launched from the nterland, while the Fort of Sv. Nikola (St Nicholas), built tween 1540 and 1547 by Gian Girolamo Sanmicheli, phew of the master builder from Verona, prevented cess to the city via the Krka River.

THE CATHEDRAL BAPTISTERY
Although the vaulted ceiling is decorated with intricate Late Venetian Gothic motifs, the fluted alcoves, Corinthian columns, inlaid scallop-shells and supple lines of the cherubs supporting the elegant basin of the baptismal font were the first Renaissance elements to appear in Dalmatia.

VIEW POINT ★
The tortuous alleyways of the Gradina district climb to the summit of the hill on which Tvrđava Sv. Ana, the town's only surviving fortress, is situated. Each step brings more visual treats of the majestic city, including its aristocratic homes with coats-of-arms on the façades, sculpted stone brackets and carved portals. At the highest level of the fortress, there is a striking view over the tiled roofs of the city, the dome of the cathedral and the islands in the distance.

The vineyards of the fertile Šibenik archipelago are renowned.

SKRADINSKI BUK
This is regarded as one of the most beautiful sequences of karst waterfalls in Europe. From a breathtaking height of 151 feet (46 meters), the water spills over a series of 17 travertine ledges

for a short distance of about 1,312 feet (400 meters). The tranquil banks are dotted with watermills and wash houses.

Around Šibenik ◆ C B2

The coastline around Šibenik, which was a center of resistance to the Turkish invasion, is dotted with ancient fortified villages nestling in sheltered coves. There are fortresses scattered around the hinterland. Only the islands facing the Croatian town were spared by war: they were home to the elegant villas built by local noble families who, in the 16th century, could enjoy an ideal Renaissance lifestyle at a safe distance from the battlefields. Small villages surrounded by plots of land planted with vines and olive trees, like VODICE and its Ćorić tower, TRIBUNJ and PIROVAC, lie to the west of Šibenik. Pirovac cemetery is the resting place for the Draganić-Vrančić family who are buried in the Gothic tomb carved by Andrija Budičić in 1477. To the east, PRIMOŠTEN, formerly cut off from the mainland by the sea, is characterized by plain stone buildings, typical of the area. The islands are more fertile: Kaprije ('caper bush') where they grow the famous capers; Žirje ('acorn') formerly planted with sessile oaks; and Prvić, where olive trees and vines thrive. Prvić was the home of the Draganić-Vrančić family. Faust Vrančić (1551–1617), father of Croatian lexicography and a famous physician, is buried here. Nearby Zlarin was the fief of the bishops of Šibenik between 1298 and 1843. Krapanj, a tiny flat island, occupied from 1446 by the Franciscans, once owed its fame to the sale of sponges and coral.

The Krka National Park ◆ C B-C1-2

The Krka River flows over 47 miles (75 km) from its spectacular source near Knin to the Adriatic at Šibenik. Forming a natural border between northern and central

Dalmatia, the river has scored its way through the karstic plateau of the foothills of the Dinara mountain range in a series of gorges, lakes and rapids. The river first passes through a limestone gorge round Roški Slapovi, where twelve waterfalls cascade over a drop of 89 feet (27 meters) between banks which are still the site of working watermills. The Krka widens for 8 miles (35 km) to form Lake Visovac, then narrows again at Skradinski Buk. It flows into an estuary 12 miles (20 km) long, where the combination of saltwater and freshwater has resulted in some unusual flora. You can take a boat trip upstream from Šibenik or drive along riverside roads. This is an ideal opportunity to visit the historic sites of Skradin and Bribir, ancient towns and powerful medieval centers. Bribir still has the remains of Roman ramparts while its buildings demonstrate the feudal power of the Šubić family who governed the entire region from here. Skradin, an episcopal town, was conquered by the infidels in 1522. Its cathedral, decorated with many silver votive offerings, was not rebuilt until the 18th century, along with the rest of the town. Further upstream on the Krka, you can take a trip to the tiny island of Visovac (2½ acres/1 hectare) at the center of the lake (*above*). Resembling a botanical garden with its lush vegetation, the island is the site of a Franciscan monastery dating from 1445, whose church was built in 1576 by monks driven out of Bosnia by the Turks. The last ports of call are the fortresses of Nečven and Trošenj on opposite banks of the river. They belonged to the Nelipić family in Nečven and the Šubić family in Trošenj. They were captured by the Turks in 1522 and used as a base until 1684.

Along the Krka ◆ C C1-2

The no. 33 road climbs from Šibenik to Knin. This area, dotted with fortresses, has a rich heritage, but unfortunately it also bears the scars of more recent battles (1991–5).
DRNIŠ. At an altitude of 984 feet (300 meters), this town still has its fortress, whose high medieval towers overlook the Petrovo Polje Valley and the gorges of the Čikola River. Occupied for two centuries by the Turks, its firepower posed a constant threat to Šibenik. The few surviving traces of Eastern influence can be seen in the remains of a minaret and a mosque incorporated into the church of Sv. Antun (St Anthony).

THE TREASURES OF VISOVAC
The Franciscan monastery contains a superb collection of canvases painted between the 16th and 19th centuries, including a work by the artist Bernardo Strozzi, some fascinating archives with an incunabulum of *Aesop's Fables* printed in 1487 by Dobrić Dobričević (Boninus de Boninis) ▲ *252*, and a precious collection of objects charting the history of the region. These include the saber of Vuk Mandušić, one of the most popular heroes from the ancient epics.

THE COUNTS OF BRIBIR
They were a branch of the Šubić family, the most important Croatian feudal lords from the late 13th century onward. The Šubić family extended their authority over a large number of towns in Dalmatia and Paul I Šubić (d. 1312), Ban (governor) in 1273, gained control of Bosnia in 1299. When the Hungaro-Croatian king consolidated his authority, the Šubić family were forced to swap their Dalmatian estates for the town of Zrin whose name they adopted ▲ *135* (1347). This fortress was one of the largest pockets of resistance against the Turks.

Knin, seat of the
Croatian kings in
the 11th century,
overlooked by the
huge fortress of
St Savior.

ČIOVO
This island, which
was largely populated
by undesirables
(dissidents, lepers,
etc.) throughout
Antiquity and for part
of the Middle Ages,
is now the site of
monasteries and
accommodation
for tourists.

**TROGIR'S CINEMA
BENEATH THE
STARS ★**
During summer the
tourist influx is in full
swing in this
medieval city, but
most visitors hardly
venture beyond the
square in front of the
cathedral. The
winding streets of
Trogir, lined with
pretty freestone
houses (below),
preserve all their
romantic charm.
On summer evenings
there is an open-air
cinema in the
courtyard of the
impressive
Kamerlengo fortress,
which overlooks
the sea.

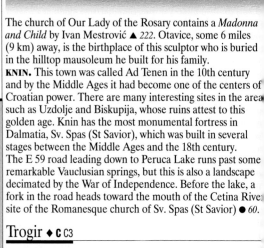

The church of Our Lady of the Rosary contains a *Madonna
and Child* by Ivan Mestrović ▲ *222*. Otavice, some 6 miles
(9 km) away, is the birthplace of this sculptor who is buried
in the hilltop mausoleum he built for his family.
KNIN. This town was called Ad Tenen in the 10th century
and by the Middle Ages it had become one of the centers of
Croatian power. There are many interesting sites in the area
such as Uzdolje and Biskupija, whose ruins attest to this
golden age. Knin has the most monumental fortress in
Dalmatia, Sv. Spas (St Savior), which was built in several
stages between the Middle Ages and the 18th century.
The E 59 road leading down to Peruca Lake runs past some
remarkable Vauclusian springs, but this is also a landscape
decimated by the War of Independence. Before the lake, a
fork in the road heads toward the mouth of the Cetina River,
site of the Romanesque church of Sv. Spas (St Savior) ● *60*.

Trogir ♦ c C3

The exceptionally well-placed site of Trogir was inhabited
very early. The town, founded toward the end of the 3rd
century BC by the Greeks of Issa ▲ *232*, still has remains from
this period, which is extremely unusual. Occupied by the
Romans, it was called Tragyrion, 'the island of goats', and
celebrated by Pliny the Elder for its yellowish-brown stone.
In the 7th century, Trogir was lucky enough to escape
destruction by the Slavs and remained under Byzantine rule
until the 11th century. After this, Trogir entered a more

turbulent period: the town, governed by local
nobles like the Šubić family ▲ *205*, was in continual
conflict with the hinterland, ruled by Croatians,
Venetians or Ottomans. Nonetheless, the 13th
century was a golden age for Trogir, marked by the
construction of numerous Romanesque buildings.
Venice gained control of the town in 1429 and
introduced new artistic trends. After it fell into the
hands of the Austrians after 1797, the town began
to decline and suffered the same fate as the towns
along the Adriatic coast.
A LISTED TOWN. The historic center of Trogir is
on a small island in the strait separating the coast
from the island of Čiovo. Further west, the suburb

f Pasike also forms part of Trogir. This delightful town, designated a World Heritage Site by Unesco in 1997, has cher-hued buildings, a tangle of streets, many of them aulted, Romanesque and Gothic houses and numerous quares, old churches, palaces and monasteries.

ATHEDRAL OF SV. LOVRO (ST LAWRENCE). This is one f the most important buildings in Croatia. Built in the arly 13th century to a three-nave basilical plan, it is largely Romanesque in style. Only its Gothic vaults date from the 5th century, while the bell tower demonstrates various tages in artistic development between the 15th and 16th enturies, moving from Venetian Gothic at its base to enaissance style and Mannerism at its spire. The main ntrance is the amous west portal, arved by the roatian master- ason Radovan om 1240. Its rches and columns reflect e iconographic conventions f the early Gothic period: they arrate the life of Christ, epict the Labors of the lonths and are decorated ith exotic and fantastic reatures. The interior is no ss elaborate. The baptistery y Andrija Aleši (1467), with its b vault, coffered ceiling and iezes of putti, is a perfect example f the fusion of Gothic and Renaissance ements employed in Šibenik by Juraj almatinac ▲ 202. The choir furniture includes finely carved stone lectern dating from the 3th century, a Romanesque ciborium and othic choirstalls carved by Ivan Budislavić in 39. Finally, St John of Trogir's ● 62, which as added along the north aisle by Nikola irentinac, Andrija Aleši and Ivan Duknović etween 1468 and 1489, is one of the most markable sculptural groups in Croatia.

GROUND-BREAKING WORK
The west portal by Radovan ● 61 is usually regarded as a masterpiece of Romanesque art. However, the artist seems to have been aware of designs being used at the time in French and Italian cathedrals, because he replaced the theme of the Last Judgement, characteristic of Romanesque dogmatism, which usually adorned the tympanum above portals, by that of the Redemption, creating a radiant image of the Nativity. The Virgin Mary, a new mother, is lying on a bed and tenderly uncovering the face of the Holy Child to show him to the world. Energy, realism and a close attention to the details of human life are the hallmarks of Radovan's work, in keeping with the great tradition of European Gothic.

THE CHAPEL'S 160 FACES
Heads of angels, stern apostles, saints and the blessed (for example, the statue of St John the Evangelist by Ivan Duknović, *right*) look down on visitors to the chapel of St John from the vault and niches. Whether happy or sad, male or female, they embody the new Renaissance spirit that was a source of inspiration for artists such as Nikola Firentinac (Nicholas of Florence). This brilliant architect introduced a pioneering construction technique in the chapel which involved placing chamfered cornerstones in such a way as to support the vault without a wooden frame, a technique which he reused later in Šibenik Cathedral ▲ *203*.

TRG IVANA PVALA II.
All the different architectural styles found in Trogir can be seen in this central square. The 13th-century Rector's Palace, now the Town Hall, has a Renaissance façade dating from the late 16th century, with a Gothic staircase in the courtyard. Above the table of judges on the 14th-century Loggia, once a court building, there are bas-reliefs by Firentinac and a relief by Mestrović ▲ *222*, depicting one of the heroes from the Croatian saga, Petar Berislavić. Both large and small Cipiko Palaces were the work of the famous trio of architects responsible for the chapel of St John of Trogir. Built around vast Renaissance courtyards, these palaces have arcaded façades that show the influence of Venetian Gothic. A wooden cockerel, brought back as a trophy from the Battle of Lepanto in 1571, can be seen perched beneath the porch of the larger palace.

CHURCHES AND MANSIONS. The church of Sv. Ivan Kriste (St John the Baptist) is just one of the many churches worth visiting in the town. This 13th-century building houses the Pinakoteka (Art Gallery) which has some prestigious paintings, particularly by Gentile Bellini (15th century), as well as illuminated medieval manuscripts and a treasury with several works by Blaž Jurjev Trogiranin (Blaise of Trogir). The Benedictine Monastery of Sv. Nikola (St Nicholas),

...ating from the 11th century, contains
...bas-relief from the Hellenist period
...*right*), depicting Kairos, the Greek god
...opportunity. The Dominican Monastery
...as many works of art, including the precious
...mb of the Sobota family, sculpted by Nikola
...rentinac, and a polyptych by Blaž Jurjev.
...he Garagnin Fanfogna Palace, which houses
...e Civic Museum, and the Lučić Palace, the
...rthplace of Ivan Lučić (1604–79), the forefather
...modern Croatian historiography, are both
...orth visiting.

...E RAMPARTS. These walls are well preserved.
...alking clockwise from south to north will bring you past
...e Južna Vrata (Sea Gate), built in 1593 in Mannerist style,
...e Kamerlengo Fortress built after 1420 by the Venetians
...prevent Turkish attacks, St Mark's Tower and the baroque
...opnena Vrata (Land Gate), constructed in the 17th century
...d dedicated to St John of Trogir, which leads inland.

...aštela (The Castle Trail) ♦ C C-D3

...etween Trogir and Split, the coastal road running parallel
...the 'Magistrala' travels through the seven fortified villages
...at form the so-called 'bay of castles'. These hamlets, which
...rang up in the 15th and 16th centuries around forts built
...local nobles and church dignitaries to protect their lands
...om the Ottoman threat, are still picturesque, despite the
...ctories that have been constructed around them.
...e first of these villages is Kaštel Štafilić (*bottom right*),
...hich owes its name to Stjepan Štafilić, a patrician from
...ogir who, in 1508, built his *kaštel* (castle) on an islet
...ked to the mainland by a drawbridge. The village church,
...ilt in the 18th century by Ignacije Macanović, is an elegant
...e baroque building. Kaštel Novi is the site of the fortress
...Pavao Ćipiko, built in 1512, while the castle at Kaštel
...ari is the oldest in the bay, built in 1476 for
...oriolan Ćipiko, a humanist and soldier; its south
...çade is residential in style. The finest building is
...Kaštel Lukšić. This summer palace was built in
...87 by the Vitturi brothers in a transitional
...naissance-baroque style. The village church,
...hich was rebuilt in the late 18th century, is
...onumental baroque in style. Its elaborate
...rniture includes the sarcophagus of the blessed
...nir sculpted by Juraj Dalmatinac in 1448. All
...at remains of the fortifications around Kaštel
...mbelovac is the tower, built in 1566. Situated
...the small island of Gomile, linked to the coast
...a bridge, Kaštel Gomilica (*above right*) was
...ilt in 1529 by the Benedictines. Its walls enclose
...monastery, 30 houses and two churches, one
...which, lavishly decorated, is dedicated to
...Jerome. At the far end of the bay, the ramparts
...Kaštel Sućurac, built in the late 14th century
...Andrija Gualdo, enclose a fine Gothic villa
...ting from 1483.

MASTERS OF TROGIR
Two names crop up
time and time again in
the town's churches
and museums: Blaž
Jurjev (d. 1450), and
Ivan Duknović
(c.1440–1505). The
former was a great
early 15th-century
Dalmatian painter
who drew his
harmonious style from
European Late
Gothic. The latter
worked extensively in
Rome on the tombs of
prelates as well as in
Ancona and Hungary,
which he visited on
the request of King
Matthias Corvinus.
His work bears
similarities to that of
painters from the
Italian Quattrocento.

Salona, Capital of Roman Dalmatia

Salona's expansion can be traced back to its exceptional location at the convergence of various sea and land routes. Its name appeared for the first time in documents in 119 BC when the Roman Consul Lucius Cecilius Metellus and his army wintered here. In the early years of the 1st century BC, Salona, described by the Greek geographer Strabo (64/63 BC–AD 23) in his *Geographica* as being the port used by the Dalmatians, was already the seat of a *conventus civium Romanorum*. After his victory over Pompey in 48 BC, Julius Caesar sent Italic settlers to live here. The lands around the town were divided into plots and distributed to the new arrivals. *Colonia Martia Julia Salona* then became the capital of the Roman province of Dalmatia.

1. Forum
2. Theater
3. Amphitheater
4. Caesarea Gate
5. Bishop's Complex
6. Baths
7. Necropolis of Manastirine
8. Necropolis of Kapljuć
9. Necropolis of Marusinac ● 57
10. Island of Our Lady

THE HELLENIST PERIOD
Salona was originally an Illyrian settlement founded by the Dalmatians and then colonized by the Greeks of Issa (Vis) ▲ 232. Its early center was in the Kaštela bay on the Jadro River. Its trapezoidal plan was bounded by a wall and the roads intersected at right angles. The theater stood to the west of the Forum which was situated at the center of the town, overlooking the harbor.

THE ROMAN EMPIRE
From the Augustan period, the town began to expand eastward and westward, although not as a result of any set urbanization program. It extended along the main road lined with metropolises. A monumental gate, the Porta Caesarea, was built into what used to be the easter[n] wall. The largest building in the west was the amphitheater (*top*), built around 170, which could sea[t] about 15,000 people

...RISTIANITY

...Domnius and ...Anastasius, who ...e martyred in ...ona, along with ...ny other disciples, ...ured the early ...ead of Christianity. ...e village then ...ame an episcopal ... and, in the early ...t of the 5th ...tury, the seat of an ...hbishopric. The ...istian necropolises ...ead around the ...bs of the martyrs. ...ne large funerary ...ilicas were built ...ard the end of the ... century or in the ...ly 5th century. The ...ny epitaphs and ...cophaguses which ...peared in these ...y places show how ...n the deceased ...e to be buried as ...se to the martyrs ...ossible. The ...cophagus of the ...od Shepherd ...ove).

THE BISHOP'S COMPLEX

The main district to the east of Salona, this complex sprang up round an early oratory and comprised two basilicas, a baptistery, a Bishop's Palace, an audience hall and adjoining rooms.

FRANE BULIĆ

(1846–1934)
The former director of the Archeological Museum of Split ▲ 220 is buried in the western part of the Manastirine, alongside the Tusculum. This small museum, was built to enable him to complete his research into Salona.

THE EARLY MIDDLE AGES

After Salona was destroyed in the early 6th century by Slav and Avar invasions and abandoned, life continued at the eastern end of the ancient village. Several Croatian rulers were buried in the church of Gospin Otok (Island of Our Lady) and an 11th-century church, built over the ruins of the Paleochristian basilica in the eastern necropolis, stands to the northeast. Dimitar Zvonimir was crowned here in 1075.

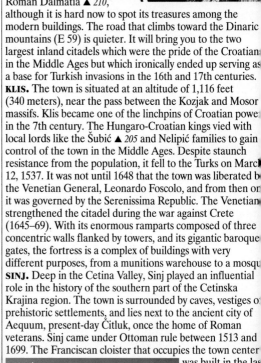

THE SINJSKA ALKA
JOUSTING
TOURNAMENT
Since 1715, when a company of 600 horsemen from Sinj drove back a Turkish attack, the town has held the Sinjska Alka (Ring of Sinj) jousting tournament on the first Sunday of August. Some 15 of the region's best horsemen attempt to hurl a lance through an iron ring suspended 10 feet (3 meters) above the ground while riding at full gallop. The ring is composed of two concentric circles, the largest of which is divided into three sections. Contestants earn one point by putting the lance through the two lower sections, two points through the top and three points through the central ring. The *alkaris* are dressed in the type of colorful costumes that would have been worn by ancient Croatian warriors. The tournament is accompanied by music and cannon fire. The most skillful lancer wins the symbolic shield which has served as a trophy for three centuries.

THE FORTRESS OF KLIS
This fortress, which protected the coast, was the scene for some bloody battles during the Turkish invasions.

Toward Sinj
◆ C D2

Shortly before Split, the Kaštela road runs through Solin. This town in the suburbs of Split occupies the site of Salona, the capital of Roman Dalmatia ▲ 210, although it is hard now to spot its treasures among the modern buildings. The road that climbs toward the Dinaric mountains (E 59) is quieter. It will bring you to the two largest inland citadels which were the pride of the Croatians in the Middle Ages but which ironically ended up serving as a base for Turkish invasions in the 16th and 17th centuries.

KLIS. The town is situated at an altitude of 1,116 feet (340 meters), near the pass between the Kozjak and Mosor massifs. Klis became one of the linchpins of Croatian power in the 7th century. The Hungaro-Croatian kings vied with local lords like the Šubić ▲ 205 and Nelipić families to gain control of the town in the Middle Ages. Despite staunch resistance from the population, it fell to the Turks on March 12, 1537. It was not until 1648 that the town was liberated by the Venetian General, Leonardo Foscolo, and from then on it was governed by the Serenissima Republic. The Venetians strengthened the citadel during the war against Crete (1645–69). With its enormous ramparts composed of three concentric walls flanked by towers, and its gigantic baroque gates, the fortress is a complex of buildings with very different purposes, from a munitions warehouse to a mosque.

SINJ. Deep in the Cetina Valley, Sinj played an influential role in the history of the southern part of the Cetinska Krajina region. The town is surrounded by caves, vestiges of prehistoric settlements, and lies next to the ancient city of Aequum, present-day Čitluk, once the home of Roman veterans. Sinj came under Ottoman rule between 1513 and 1699. The Franciscan cloister that occupies the town center

was built in the last years of the Turkish occupation by monks from Rama in Bosnia. They brought a precious painting called *Our Lady of Sinj* (*left*), said to have miraculous powers. The church, destroyed twice in the 17th century, was restored to protect this image which still draws a large number of pilgrims.

Split

Split, *214*

Diocletian's Palace, *216*

Ivan Meštrović, *222*

Crossing the Mosor
   Mountains, *224*

Omiš, *224*

Toward the Imotski Border
   Region, *225*

The Makarska Riviera, *226*

The Neretva Delta, *227*

Brač Island, *228*

Šolta Island, *229*

Hvar Island, *230*

Vis Island, *232*

◆ E

A MOSAIC TOWN ★
Along the eastern
side of Diocletian's
Palace is Split's
marketplace.
Strolling along its
passageways is a
good way to begin a
visit to the city. Next,
take in the Obala
promenade. Between
the café terraces
there is a door that
leads to the Peristyle.
The Louxor café sets
its tables opposite
the cathedral and a
few steps from a
thousand-year-old
sphinx. The façade
of the building is a
mixture of every
architectural style.
You can find Venetian
influence, as well as
Viennese, and a
touch of Roman in
the columns. This is
just a brief taste of
the delights Split has
to offer.

**THE CATHEDRAL'S
CAMPANILE**
This symbol of Split,
built between the 13th
and 16th centuries,
was restored in the
1990s.

Nestling at the foot of the Marjan Hill and sheltered
by the Kozjak and Mosor mountains, Split is fringed by
islands and surrounded by a fertile plain that extends toward
Omiš and Trogir. The most densely populated Croatian town
on the Adriatic coast, Split is the capital of Dalmatia as well
as a vibrant artistic center and university town.

History

An *oppidum* built by the Illyrian tribe of the Delmata, for
whom Dalmatia was named, probably stood on top of Gripe
Hill and on the southern slopes of Marjan Hill. The name
Aspalathos suggests that a small Greek settlement once
occupied the territory around Split, as the colony was named
for the plant of the same name (Spanish broom). The
present-day name of the town is thought to derive from this
Greek name: Aspalathos, then Spalatum which gave rise to
Spalato, in Italian, and Spaletum, Speleti, resulting in Split,
in Croatian. In Roman times, Split was situated less than

miles (10 km) from Salona ▲ 210, the capital of the Roman province of Dalmatia. Emperor Diocletian (245–313) selected this large, sheltered bay as an ideal spot for his palace ▲ 216, built at the end of the 3rd and in the early 4th century. In the late 5th century, the former imperial residence began to grow into a town and this accelerated in the 7th century. When Salona was destroyed by the Avars and Slavs around AD 630, the palace served as a refuge for fleeing inhabitants and, with the foundation of the archiepiscopal see, Split became the rightful heir of Salona. In the early Middle Ages, the town was governed by Constantinople, but the Croatian state, which had formed nearby ● 32, exerted considerable influence over the Byzantine towns. In the 12th century, the independent town of Split was part of the Hungaro-Croatian kingdom, but it fell into the hands of the Republic of Venice between 1420 and 1797. The centuries of Venetian rule have left their mark on the city's layout and artistic heritage. Split strengthened its fortifications to fend off Ottoman raids in the 16th and 17th centuries. After a short period of French government 34 in the early 19th century, the town became part of the Austro-Hungarian monarchy until 1918. During this period, Split was the cultural and political center of Dalmatia and a center of Croatian nationalism. Until the independence of the Republic of Croatia in 1990, Split was part of the Socialist Republic of Croatia. Today, visitors to Split's pedestrianized historic center will find a remarkable palimpsest of different periods: this medieval city with its classical past has narrow winding streets lined with the magnificent façades of Gothic and Renaissance mansions.

Inside the Palace ♦ E B-C2-3

The approach to the palace ▲ 216 is through the Mjedina Vrata (*Porta Aenea* or Bronze Gate) on the Obala, commonly known as the Riva, which once overlooked the seafront. This leads into the Subterranean Halls beneath the south wing that used to house Diocletian's apartments. Their structure indicates the majesty of the emperor's reception halls and private rooms. A staircase leads from the corridor into the Peristyle. This courtyard, with colonnades on three sides, marks the center of the palace and is crossed by the *cardo* and *decumanus* (called respectively Dioklecijanova, and Krešimirova and Poljana Kraljice Jelene).

THE CATHEDRAL OF SV. DUJMA (ST DOMNIUS). Split became a city in its own right when the archiepiscopal see was transferred from Salona. According to medieval sources, Archbishop John of Ravenna cleansed the mausoleum by removing its idols around AD 650 and founded the cathedral. He replaced them with relics of the holy martyrs St Domnius (Dujma) and Anastasius (Staš) ▲ 211.

INSIDE THE CATHEDRAL. The steps below the campanile are flanked by carved lions ridden by the statues of figures including the Hungaro-Croatian King Bela IV (1235–70) and his wife Maria Lascaris. Their daughters, who died in Split in 1242, are interred in the sarcophagus above the doorway.

CAIUS AURELIUS VALERIUS DIOCLES DIOCLETIANUS
Born into a Dalmatian family in 245, he served in a legion then became consul under Aurelian. He was proclaimed emperor by the soldiers after the death of Numerian in 284 and he appointed Maximian as joint emperor in 286. Diocletian governed the eastern part of the Empire and Egypt. He founded a tetrarchy in 293 – Galerius and Constantius I Chlorus were appointed caesars – to better protect the Empire. He then instituted a large-scale program of reform, which included reorganizing the provinces. At the end of his reign, Diocletian persecuted the Christians. He abdicated in 305 and lived in his palace in Split until his death in 313 ▲ 216.

THE SPHINXES
Twelve sphinxes were found in the palace and two can still be seen: one in front of the Baptistery and the other in the Peristyle (*above*). The latter, which dates from the reign of Pharaoh Thutmose III (1479–26 BC) is holding a sacrificial urn between its paws. A frieze depicting a procession of captive soldiers runs along the base.

▲ Diocletian's Palace

The Roman Emperor Diocletian built a palace not far from Salona, the capital of the province of Dalmatia. He lived here from his abdication, in 305, until his death. The residence, with an area of around 414,260 square feet (38,500 square meters), was built to a rectangular plan dictated by the site and doubled as a fortified military camp with a strong garrison and an imperial palace enabling Diocletian to maintain his rank.

THE MILITARY CAMP (A) ● *57.* The northern half of the palace was occupied by workshops, warehouses and the barracks of the imperial guard.

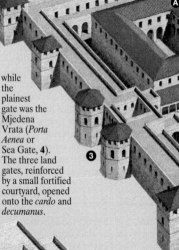

THE FORTIFICATIONS
The lower walls, supplemented by 16 towers, are solid with no openings although there are windows in the top part. The Zlatna Vrata (*Porta Aurea* or Golden Gate, **1**), which used to lead to Salona, is in the center of the north façade. Flanked by two octagonal towers, it was richly decorated with niches, columns and sculptures. The east and west gates were called the Srebrna Vrata and the Željezna Vrata (*Porta Argentea* or Silver Gate, **2**, and *Porta Ferrea* or Iron Gate, **3**), while the plainest gate was the Mjedena Vrata (*Porta Aenea* or Sea Gate, **4**). The three land gates, reinforced by a small fortified courtyard, opened onto the *cardo* and *decumanus*.

③

THE PORTICO
A long portico (the Cryptoporticus or Great Gallery, **10**), where the emperor used to promenade, ran along the south side of the palace, with 42 openings and three loggias facing out to sea.

THE SUBTERRANEAN HALLS (C)
These halls were built in the southern sector of the palace to compensate for the sloping terrain. Their plan mirrored that of the upper floor. Their formal complexity and exceptional state of preservation make this one of the most interesting rchitectural complexes of Late Antiquity.

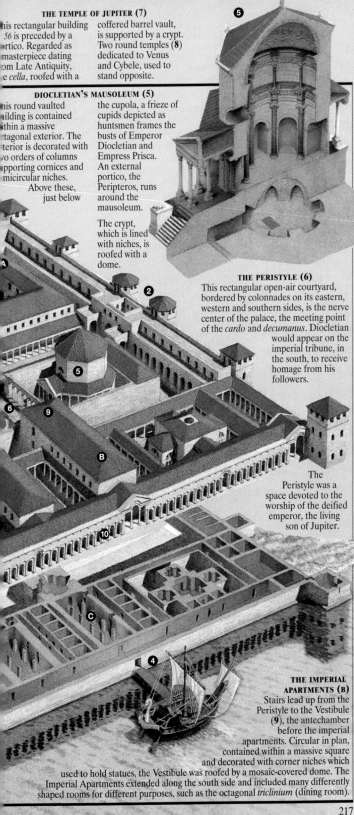

THE TEMPLE OF JUPITER (7)

This rectangular building [...] 56 is preceded by a [...] rtico. Regarded as [...] masterpiece dating [...]om Late Antiquity, [...]e *cella*, roofed with a coffered barrel vault, is supported by a crypt. Two round temples (**8**) dedicated to Venus and Cybele, used to stand opposite.

DIOCLETIAN'S MAUSOLEUM (5)

[...]his round vaulted [...]ilding is contained [...]ithin a massive [...]ctagonal exterior. The [...]terior is decorated with [...]o orders of columns [...]pporting cornices and [...]micircular niches.

Above these, just below the cupola, a frieze of cupids depicted as huntsmen frames the busts of Emperor Diocletian and Empress Prisca. An external portico, the Peripteros, runs around the mausoleum.

The crypt, which is lined with niches, is roofed with a dome.

THE PERISTYLE (6)

This rectangular open-air courtyard, bordered by colonnades on its eastern, western and southern sides, is the nerve center of the palace, the meeting point of the *cardo* and *decumanus*. Diocletian would appear on the imperial tribune, in the south, to receive homage from his followers.

The Peristyle was a space devoted to the worship of the deified emperor, the living son of Jupiter.

THE IMPERIAL APARTMENTS (B)

Stairs lead up from the Peristyle to the Vestibule (**9**), the antechamber before the imperial apartments. Circular in plan, contained within a massive square and decorated with corner niches which used to hold statues, the Vestibule was roofed by a mosaic-covered dome. The Imperial Apartments extended along the south side and included many differently shaped rooms for different purposes, such as the octagonal *triclinium* (dining room).

CATHEDRAL INTERIOR
1. Double doors carved by Buvina.
2. Paintings by Matteo Ponzoni.
3. High altar (1685–9).
4. *The Life of St Domnius* by Pietro Ferrari.
5. 13th-century choirstalls.
6. 13th-century pulpit (detail, *below right*).

The double doors leading into Split's richly decorated cathedral were carved by Andrija Buvina in 1214. Situated in the sacristy, which was added in the 17th century, the treasury contains a fine collection of sacred artworks rangin from the early Middle Ages to the 19th century. The most precious manuscripts are the 8th-century *Gospel of Split* an the 13th-century *Historia Saloniana* by Archdeacon Toma. There are also three Romanesque icons depicting the Madonna and Child, numerous objects in gold and silver and various sacerdotal vestments.

THE CATHEDRAL DOORS
In 1214, Andrija Buvina, a local sculptor, skillfully carved 28 chestnut panels framed with plant motifs and knotwork. They illustrate scenes from the life of Christ, with the right-hand door devoted to the Passion.

BAPTISTERY OF SV. IVAN (ST JOHN
The narrow alley of Kraj Sv. Ivana leads to the temple of Jupiter ▲ *217*, converted into a baptistery in the early Middle Ages. In the 11th century, the cruciform baptismal font was covered with a stone facing decorated with a pleated pattern known as *plutej*.
NEAR THE GOLDEN GATE. The gateway and inner courtyard of the 15th-century Augubio Palace on the *cardo* were strongly influenced by the art of Juraj Dalmatinac ▲ *202*. Split's finest late Gothic mansion – the Papalić Palace, on Papalićeva – was designed by Dalmatinac. He linked the buildings behind it to form a complex with an elegant façade and an enclosed courtyard. This palace now houses the GRADSKI MUZEJ (Town Museum) which offers a useful insight into the history of Split. The small CHAPEL OF SV. MARTIN (St Martin) resulted from an 11th-century conversion of the covered way which enabled guards to kee an eye on the Golden Gate. The chancel is preserved *in situ* A Benedictine monastery used to stand on the site of the

Altar dedicated to St Domnius,
y Bonino da Milano (1427).
rescos by Pietro da Milano
nd Dujam Vušković.
Altar dedicated to

St Anastasius, by Juraj Dalmatinac
(1448). Note the high relief of the
Flagellation of Christ.
9. Chapel of St Domnius, altar by
   Giovanni Maria Morlaiter in 1767.

rden opposite
e *Porta Aurea* and
u can still see
e remains of a
e-Romanesque
urch, which was
corporated into
e monastery in
69, and a chapel
Flamboyant
othic style added
 Dalmatinac in
44. The statue
 Ivan Meštrović

222 represents Grgur Ninski (Gregory of Nin), Bishop
Nin under Tomislav, who was King of Croatia (910–28).
gend has it that stroking his big toe brings good luck.
AR THE SILVER GATE. The Dominican Monastery
uated opposite the *Porta Argentea* was founded in 1217.
e church, which has been completely restored, contains
me fine wooden altars and paintings by Venetian masters.
AR THE IRON GATE. The CINDRO PALACE, one of the most
autiful secular baroque buildings in Dalmatia, stands to
e east of the *decumanus*.

he historic center to the west of the Palace ♦ E A1

ARODNI TRG (PEOPLE'S SQUARE). Split started extending
yond the city walls in the early Middle Ages. The first
ildings stood against the western ramparts and a wall was
ilt to protect the district formed in this way in the 14th
ntury. The People's Square is lined by the former Town
all, next to the Renaissance Karepić Palace, by the Pavlović
lace and a Romanesque tower house, which acquired the
y clock at its summit in the 15th century. The house of the
bleman Ciprijan de Ciprianis (1394), decorated with
omanesque bays and a statue of St Anthony, stands
posite the Cambi Palace and the synagogue at the top of
sanska Street. The Romanesque-Gothic Papalić Palace
and the baroque Tartaglia Palace
are in Subiceva Street. Trg Braće
Radića was built in the Middle
Ages at the southwest corner
of Diocletian's Palace. The
baroque Milesi Palace stands
on the north side of this square,
while the huge Marina Tower
of the 15th-century *kaštel* (castle)
stands on the south side.
TRG REPUBLIKE (REPUBLIC SQUARE).
This square stretches to the west of
Marmontova Street, which was named
for the Marshal of France, Marmont
(1774–1852), Duc de Raguse, commander in
chief of the Dalmatian army from 1806, then
Governor General of the Illyrian Provinces
(1809–11). The neo-Renaissance Prokurative

MARKO MARULIĆ
(1450–1524)
Born to a patrician
family in Split,
Marulić wrote
numerous works of
theology, history and
politics, including the
Institutio, from 1477
onward. In the 16th
century, these were
translated from the
original Latin into
five languages. His
Croatian poetry
ushered in the golden
age of Dalmatian
literature. He wrote
the first Croatian epic
poem, *Istorija Svete
Udovice Judit u Versih
Hrvacki Slozena* (*The
History of the Holy
Widow Judith*) in
1521. His output bore
the stamp of his
Humanist education,
his Christian morality
and his fear of seeing
his homeland
disappear. His bronze
statue, by Ivan
Meštrović, on Braće
Radića Square, is
adorned with lines by
the poet Tin Ujević
(1891–1955).

219

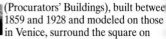

(Procurators' Buildings), built between 1859 and 1928 and modeled on those in Venice, surround the square on three sides. A Franciscan monastery was built along the quay on the southwestern side of the square. Although the medieval complex was radically restored in the early 20th century, the 14th-century cloister has been preserved. The monastery church has a 15th-century crucifix painted by Blaž Jurjev Trogiranin ▲ 209. This building has also been nicknamed the Split pantheon as it contains the tombs of various key figures from Split, such as Archdeacon Toma (1201–68), Marko Marulić ▲ 219, the composer Ivan Lukačč (1584–1648), the poet Jerolim Kavanjin (1641–1714) and the Croatian nationalist Ante Trumbić (1864–1938). Heading north along the pedestrianized Marmontova Street will bring you to the Trg Gaje Bulata, the site of the neo-Renaissance building that houses the Croatian National Theater, built in 1893.

The suburbs

From the Middle Ages onward, and particularly between the 17th and 18th centuries, working-class suburbs, which were often attractive clusters of stone houses lining narrow streets spread beyond the city walls: Lučac in the east, Manuš, Dobri and Lovret in the north, and Veli Varoš in the west. A trapezoidal FORTRESS strengthened with bastions was built to plans by the Venetian fortress-builder Domenico Maglia between 1648 and 1657 on top of Gripe Hill in the district of Lučac. The ARHEOLOŠKI MUZEJ (Archeological Museum) founded in 1820, has rich collections of artifacts excavated in Dalmatia, particularly Salona, which document life on the Adriatic coast during prehistoric times, the Greek colonization and Roman, Paleochristian and medieval periods. The 15th-century Franciscan monastery and church OF GOSPA OD POLJUDA (Our Lady of Grace in Poljud), has some interesting Renaissance paintings, including a polyptych depicting St Domnius, the patron saint of Split,

THE MYTH OF PHAEDRA
Found in Salona and on display at the Archeological Museum in Split, this sarcophagus (4th century, *above*) stands monument to the art of ancient Dalmatia. Three scenes are depicted: Phaedra and her maids, Hippolytus reading her love letter, Theseus's grief at the death of his son and wife.

SPLIT STADIUM
The home stadium of Hajduk Split football club, built in 1979 in Poljud to a design by Boris Magaš, can seat 50,000 spectators. Croatia's sensational performance at the 1998 World Cup showed that its footballers were a force to be reckoned with.

olding a model of the city. The Renaissance cloister
ontains tombs of nobles from Split and the small monastery
useum has a portrait of the Humanist Bishop Tommaso
igris, painted in 1527 by Lorenzo Lotto (1480–1556).
he Pre-Romanesque church of Sv. Trojstvo (Holy Trinity)
58, near Poljud, is also worth a visit. Time seems to have
ood still in Veli Varoš, Split's largest suburb. Its parish
nurch is flanked by a baroque bell tower. The church
f Sv. Nikola na Stagnji (St Nicholas), from the
arly Romanesque period, is built to
cruciform plan with a dome and
protruding western portal.

he Marjan Peninsula

he Marjan Hill, one of the symbols
f Split, was transformed into a park
n the early 20th century. There are
ome breathtaking views from its
ummit (574 feet/175 meters) over
ne city (*below*), and out to the islands
f Kaštela and Brač .

**UZEJ HRVATSKIH ARHEOLOŠKIH
POMENIKA** (MUSEUM OF CROATIAN
RCHEOLOGICAL MONUMENTS). The works
f art and archeological artifacts in this museum attest
o the high level of culture in the Croatian kingdom
Oth–11th centuries). It also possesses interesting
ollections of currency, Carolingian weapons and
nedieval jewelry.

ALERIJA MEŠTROVIĆ (MEŠTROVIĆ GALLERY) ▲ *222*.
he house built by this sculptor in the 1930s has about
00 works on display, charting his artistic development.
he nearby chapel of the Holy Cross in the KAŠTELET,
verlooking the Adriatic, has a completely different
tmosphere. This 17th-century residence contains some
agnificent wooden panels carved by Meštrović, depicting
enes from the New Testament.

**COLLECTIONS
IN THE MUSEUM
OF CROATIAN
ARCHEOLOGICAL
MONUMENTS**
Founded in 1893, this
museum houses the
finest works of art
produced during the
reign of the Croatian
kings. Prince
Višeslav's hexagonal
baptismal font in
marble (*above*), large
enough to be used
for adult baptism,
was carved in the
9th century and
commissioned by a
priest named Father
John. The epitaph of
the Croatian Queen
Jelena was carved on
the rear of her
sarcophagus in 976.
It cites her name
before mentioning
the Croatian kings
Petar Krešimir IV
and Držislav. This
sarcophagus was
discovered in the
ruins of the church
of Sv. Stjepan
(St Stephen) in Solin.
The museum also
has the chancel and
pediment from
Biskupija ▲ *206*
which depicts the
Virgin Mary.

▲ Ivan Meštrović

Ivan Meštrović
(1883–1962)
grew up in
Otavice, near Drniš, where he was already
carving wood and stone while working as a shepherd. After
a year's stone-cutting apprenticeship in Split, he traveled to
Vienna, where he studied at the Academy of Fine Arts between
1901 and 1905. Inspired by the creative climate in Vienna, where
the Sezession movement was at its height, he forged a personal
style under the influence of his professors, who included Austrian
architect Otto Wagner (1841–1918) and French sculptor Auguste
Rodin (1840–1917). His fervent patriotism and devout
Catholicism find full expression in his works.

EARLY WORKS
In 1908, Meštrović, who was working in Paris,
finished the *Kosovo Temple* which, in keeping
with his political ideas, reveals an attempt to
breathe new life into Balkan mythology. Some
parts of this cycle are true masterpieces
combining monumental forms with
Secessionist stylization. Some of the
sculptures from this work, which was
to remain unfinished, brought
him immediate recognition at
the Rome International
Exhibition of 1911.

THE MEDITERRANEAN
Some of the artist's
marble sculptures, like
Contemplation (*left*) or
Psyche, reveal his need
to wipe out the
harrowing memory of
World War One by
focusing on the vitality
and verve of life in the
southern Adriatic. The
emphasis here is placed
on rounded volumes,
harmonious shapes and
simple lines.

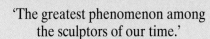

MYSTICISM

In the interwar period, Meštrović's work showed a desire for Humanism and spirituality. Sculptures like *The Madonna and Child* and his mausoleums in Cavtat or Odavice illustrate this process of artistic renewal. His propensity toward mysticism prevailed over bombastic Croatian patriotism.

THE BUILDER

Between 1921 and 1924, while living in Zagreb, Meštrović converted a house whose studio now contains a permanent exhibition of his works ▲ *105*. Between 1931 and 1939, he designed and built the Meštrović Palace ▲ *221*, a classical-style villa surrounded by a garden. About half a mile (300 meters) from here, he added a portico and chapel to the summer house of the Capogrosso Kavanjin family. The chapel of the Holy Cross contains his *Crucifixion* (*left*) and a series of wooden reliefs depicting scenes from the life of Christ, which occupied him for over 40 years.

ARCHITECTURAL SETTINGS FOR SCULPTURES

Influenced by the masters of the Secession movement, Meštrović became interested in creating an architectural framework for pieces of sculpture, realizing that the right backdrop could throw new light on a work. His entire output – buildings, bas-reliefs, fountains and monuments (*Gregory of Nin, above*) – shows his desire to combine these two arts in such a way as to complement each other.

THE IMMIGRANT

In 1947, Meštrović emigrated to the United States, where he continued to produce religious sculptures and portraits of key figures until his death.

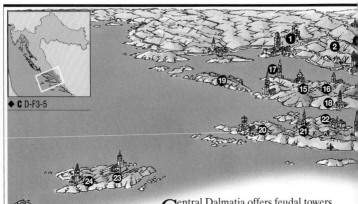

◆ **C** D-F3-5

DALMATIAN PIRATES
Between the 7th and 14th centuries, the territories between the Cetina and Neretva rivers were ruled by powerful Croatian lords who were pirates and sometimes heretics. They formed an independent political entity, the Principality of Neretva, which opposed Venetian, Hungarian and Bosnian rule and resisted the influence of Split and Ragusa. In 887, these pirates killed Doge Pietro Candiano during a naval battle and Venice was forced to pay a tribute to sail the Adriatic until 1000.

Central Dalmatia offers feudal towers, modern coastal towns, mountain villages, ancient villas, pirate hideouts and the fertile fields of the Neretva delta. The Biokovo mountain ridge, which reaches an altitude of 5,781 feet (1,762 meters) and plunges steeply into the sea, runs along the Makarska Riviera for about 22 miles (36 km). Its slopes are planted with cherry trees and vines, its high plateaus are scarred with ravines while the islands are covered with lavender and cypress trees.

Crossing the Mosor Mountains ◆ C D3

The ten villages of the former Republic of Poljica, founded in the 14th century and dissolved by Napoleon in 1807, are scattered on the slopes of this isolated mountain ridge. Despite their allegiance to the ruling powers, whether Venetian or Turkish, the inhabitants of the Republic of Poljica enjoyed a great deal of independence and elected their leader, the *Veliki Knez*, on St George's Day (April 23) every year. This small democracy may have been used as a model by the English Humanist, Sir Thomas More (1477–1535) for his *Utopia*. This period is well documented in the History Museum in GATA, and in the church of Sv. Kliment (St Clement) in SITNO, where the Statute of Poljica was written in Bosniak (Bosančica) script in the 15th century ● *39*. Hamlets, like SUMPETAR, possess Pre-Romanesque churches and Byzantine ruins, as in Gata, and farmhouses dating from the 18th and 19th centuries.

Omiš ◆ C D3

Omiš, which came under Venetian rule between 1444 and 1797, is situated at the mouth of the Cetina River, on the bare slopes of the Mala Dinara, a foothill of the

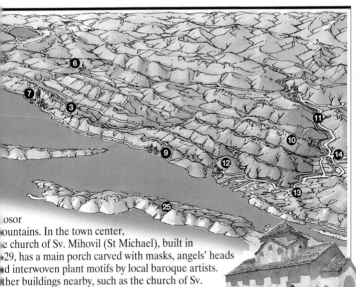

...osor

...ountains. In the town center,

...e church of Sv. Mihovil (St Michael), built in ...29, has a main porch carved with masks, angels' heads ...d interwoven plant motifs by local baroque artists. ...ther buildings nearby, such as the church of Sv. ...ok (St Roch) and the Oratory of Sv. Duh (Holy ...pirit), the clock tower, the Renaissance House ... the Happy Man and, further away, the Poljica ...uare with its baroque palaces and elegant column ... 1617, blend in with their surroundings, creating a ...armonious whole. Omiš was not always such a peaceful ...wn, as can be seen by the fortresses of Peovica (Mirabela) ...d Starigrad on the rocks above: in the Middle Ages, Omiš ...as a base for pirates from the Principality of Neretva.

...ward the Imotski Border Region ♦ **C** E3

...eading northeast from Omiš, you will come to the ...re-Romanesque church of Sv. Petar (St Peter) with its single ...ave and domed apse (*above right*).

...he road heads down through the ...etina Valley Nature Park, following ...e course of the river, which is a great ...vorite with swimmers and rafters. ...he Radmanove Mlinice is a good ...ace to enjoy the region's famous ...illed trout. Further downstream, at ...ADVARJE, the Gubavica waterfall, with ...drop of 161 feet (49 meters), marks the abrupt transition ...o flatlands. The road continues toward the vast Imotski ...ain, planted with tobacco and vineyards.

...**IOTSKI.** Mentioned as early as the 10th century, this town ...es in terraces between a Lower Town with its 18th-century ...ouses and an Upper Town dominated by a fortress. ...he town is surrounded by the ruins of Roman towns, ...aleochristian temples and *stećci* (medieval gravestones). ...he main attractions, however, are Imotski's two lakes to ...e west of the town: the Crveno Jezero (Red Lake) and the ...odro Jezero (Blue Lake), fed by waterfalls which tend to ...n dry during the hot summer months.

CRVENO JEZERO OR THE RED LAKE
This is one of the deepest lakes in Europe. It stands at the bottom of a breathtaking karst chasm, about 656 feet (200 meters) in diameter and up to 1,641 feet (500 meters) deep. It is ringed by tall cliffs whose reddish-brown rock is reflected in the clear waters. No scientific explanation has yet been found to account for its appearance and formation which was, some say, caused by earthquakes.

THE 'STEĆCI'
These funerary stelae decorated with symbolic reliefs are sometimes attributed to the influence of heretical Christians who belonged to the Bosnian church in the Middle Ages.

225

▲ From Split to Dubrovnik

THE SEASHELLS OF MAKARSKA
The Franciscan monastery on the Mala Obala quay has an unusual collection of seashells.

ANCIENT NARONA
Narona was, with Salona ▲ *210*, the largest ancient town on the Adriatic coast. Founded by the Greeks around the 4th century BC, it thrived through trade with the towns of Vis, Hvar and Korčula. It continued to expand under the Romans. Sacked by the Avars in the 7th century, its site is now occupied by the village of Vid, just over 2 miles (4 km) northwest of Metković, where there are numerous remains of ramparts, temples and baths, sarcophaguses in the cemetery, inscriptions and decorative motifs on the walls of houses.

The Makarska Riviera ♦ C E3

Inhabited early, sacked by the army of the Ostrogoth King Totila in the 5th century, this region was called Pagania in the 10th century by the Byzantine Emperor, Constantine VII Porphyrogenitus. Hostile to Venice, Pagania accepted the sovereignty of the Hungaro-Croatian kings, then came under the rule of the feudal lords of Bosnia from the 14th century onward. Conquered by the Turks in 1498, it was the first region in Central Dalmatia to belong to the Ottoman empire. In 1684, it passed to the Venetians but it was not until the Napoleonic occupation (1806–13), that the region experienced its heyday. After it was devastated by a severe earthquake in 1962, the Riviera turned its sights to tourism.

MAKARSKA. This town has narrow streets, steep steps leading up to little churches, pretty squares and picturesque quays. The main Velika Riva quay is the site of the church of Sv. Filip Neri (St Philip Neri), built in 1757, while the Mala Obala quay has terraces facing the sea and a Franciscan cloister, destroyed in 1496 by the Turks and rebuilt in 1540. Kačić Square honors the memory of Andrija Kačić Miošić (1704–69), poet, philosopher, theologian and the author of *Pleasant Talk of Slavic Folk*, which appeared in 60 editions and remains the most widely read book in Croatian. The cathedral of Sv. Marko (St Mark), built in 1776, stands at the top of this strangely sloping square.

THE COASTLINE. Stretching from Brela in the north to Gradac in the south, the Riviera has lots of sheltered coves and beaches. The villages in the Biokovo mountain range have been deserted since the 1962 earthquake. The seaside towns retain prehistoric and classical elements as in Baš Voda or Gradac, dominated by the ruins of the ancient Villa Labineca. There are churches in a range of styles – Pre-Romanesque in Igrane, Gothic or Romanesque at Tučepi and Rococo in Podgora. Zaostrog has a Franciscan cloister, which contains the tomb of Andrija Kačić Miošić, who was a friar here.

THE BIOKOVO MOUNTAINS. This mountain range, 22 miles (36 km) long and 4 miles (7 km) wide, was designated a nature park in 1981. The botanical garden of Kotišna, above Makarska, is planted with a number of native species. There are three types of habitat in the Biokovo massif. Above the

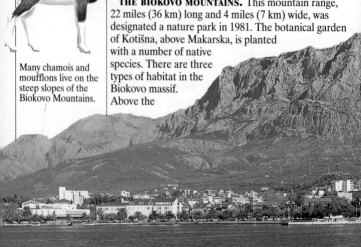

Many chamois and moufflons live on the steep slopes of the Biokovo Mountains.

The waters of the Neretva are renowned for exceptional trout and abundant eels. These are born off the coast of the Bermudas in the Atlantic, and come to die at the river mouth.

tile sea-facing slopes is a barren karst rrier which culminates in a high teau whose many caves are among the epest in Croatia. The *kašteli* (castles) ilt to fend off the Turks are still dotted und this quasi-alpine landscape.

e Neretva Delta ◆ C F4

e Neretva rises in Herzegovina and ds its way over 135 miles (218 km) fore branching into about 12 butaries. Its delta, covering an area of square miles (196 km²), is nicknamed e 'Croatian California'. The marshes, ich were once a breeding ground for laria-carrying mosquitos, have now en drained to become fertile fields igated by canals. The newest town on e Dalmatian coast is PLOČE, whose port was built in 1937. ar Ploče, the six Baćinska Jezera lakes form an attractive ht, their emerald waters fringed with poplars and pine es. Mullet find their way into these lakes from the sea ough underground channels and are fished here. OPUZEN, nded in the late 17th century behind the walls of the rtis Opus Fortress, built by the Venetians, demonstrates e region's military past. To the east of the town, another t, that of Brštanik, was used by the Turks for the slave de. The round tower of Kula Norinska in the north was ilt around 1500 by the Turks. METKOVIĆ is the last town in e Croatian part of the estuary. This town, with its cobbled eets and rustic houses, boasts a fascinating Ornithological useum. The 'Magistrala' rejoins the coastline at the village Slivno Ravno and the Klek peninsula, which once rked the border between the Ottoman Empire d the Venetian Republic. This stretch of coast is w Bosnia-Herzegovina's corridor the sea.

A NATURE PARK THAT WAS ONCE A SWAMP
The delta is home to non-migrant birds and a favorite stopover for birds migrating between Africa and Northern Europe. The Metković Museum possesses 360 specimens of the 236 species found in the delta.

▲ From Split to Dubrovnik

PALEOCHRISTIAN AND ROMANESQUE CHURCHES ● *58, 60*
Brač Island boasts numerous Paleochristian churches built to various plans, and an even greater number of churches were erected here between the 9th and 12th centuries. Unlike Pre-Romanesque churches, which were built around sheltered bays on the north side of the island, the latter were often constructed further inland on hilltops and in valleys. Almost all these Romanesque churches have a single nave and a distinctive structure.

MILNA
This deep bay is the site of the largest marina on the island.

Brač Island ♦ **c** D3

Fringed with delightful bays, this hilly island is dotted with forests of cypress trees and pastureland where goats feed c herbs that give their cheese a delicious flavor. The vineyard produce renowned wines, such as the *bolski plavac*, a red from the area around Bol. Brač is also famous for its quarr situated near Pučišća in the northern part of the island. Sin ancient times, millions of tons of white stone have been mined from the chalky soil and used to construct buildings the island, as well as elsewhere in Croatia (Diocletian's Palace ▲ *216*) and abroad (the Viennese Parliament buildin
ŠKRIP. Some 6 miles (10 km) to the east of SUPETAR, Brač's main port, Škrip is the oldest town on the island. It still has the ramparts of the Illyrian *oppidum* from the 3rd century The main buildings in the village are the Renaissance fortified house of the Cerinić family and the church of Sv. Jelena (St Helen) which contains an altar painting by Palm Giovane. This church was named for Helen, the mother of Emperor Constantine I (d. 337), who is thought to have be born in Škrip. The Kaštel Radojković, an Illyrian and Rom building fortified in the 16th century, houses the Museum of Brač, which has interesting lapidary and ethnographic collections. The small port of POSTIRA was the birthplace of Vladimir Nazor (1876–1949), a poet who sang the praises of Brač and the Mediterranean.
SUTIVAN. This village on the north coast still has the feel o a vacation resort. The Latin inscription *Ostium non hostium*

Morning the entrance to the summer house of the poet and
lawyer Jerolim Kavanjin (1641–1714) suggests that friends
would always have been welcome in his home. One of the
windmills built on the island to grind wheat in the early 19th
century still stands on the seafront to the east of Sutivan.

NEREŽIŠĆA. This was Brač's main town until Supetar was
designated chief town by Austria in 1828. Its baroque church
of Sv. Marija (St Mary) is the most monumental on the
island. There are several medieval churches worth visiting
in the vicinity, like Sv. Petar (St Peter), which has a pine tree
growing through the shingle-tiled roof of its apse.

BOL. The Branislav-Dešković Modern Art Gallery illustrates
the fondness felt by 20th-century Croatian artists for Brač's
landscapes. The sculptor Ivan Rendić (1849–1932), for
example, lived in Supetar for many years and produced
highly expressive works which transcended mere stone.
Vidova Gora (Mount St Vitus), the highest point on the
island at 2,553 feet (778 meters), affords a panoramic view of
the Adriatic, and the Mosor and Biokovo mountains ▲ 226.

BLACA. Situated in a steep-sided valley on the southern side
of Brač, two hours' walk from MURVICA, the hermitage of
Blaca was founded in 1551 by Glagolitic priests ● 40 from
the Poljica Republic who were fleeing the Ottomans. The
monastery, rebuilt around caves in 1757 after a devastating
fire, displays great architectural unity. After the death, in
1963, of the last Father Superior, Nikola Milićević, a leading
astrophysicist who brought the most powerful telescope of
the period (1,985 lb/900 kg) to Blaca, the hermitage was
converted into a research center and museum documenting
the religious community (*below*).

Šolta Island ♦ C C3

This island, with an area of 20 square
miles (52 km²), lies opposite Split, so
many of the city's inhabitants have
second homes here. Šolta's largest
bays, Rogač and Nečujam, are on the
northeast coast, which is covered with
dense scrub and buffeted by the Bura.
The cove at Maslinica, protected
by a group of islets, provides sheltered
mooring for boats.

BOL'S BEACHES
Its fine shingle
beaches and steady
breeze ideal for
windsurfing make this
a popular vacation
resort. The best beach
is the Zlatni Rat
(Golden Horn), a
small cape which
moves depending on
the currents (*above*).

**THE MYSTERY OF
THE DRAGON'S CAVE**
Situated 656 feet
(200 meters) above
Murvica, this cave,
which was hollowed
out in the 15th
century by Glagolitic
friars, is decorated
with strange carvings
whose meaning
remains unknown.

▲ From Split to Dubrovnik

SPLIT
Vlaka · Hvar · Starigrad · Jelsa · Hvar
Šćedro · Sućuraj
Korčula

Hvar Island ◆ **C** C-E4

In 385 BC, Greeks from the island of Paros, in the Aegean sea, founded Pharos (Starigrad) and Dimos (Hvar Town) on sites once occupied by the Illyrians. The island came under the rule of the Romans in 219 BC and was then governed respectively by Constantinople, the Hungaro-Croatian sovereigns and Venice. Despite Ottoman attacks in the 15th and 16th centuries, the island thrived under the government of the Venetian Republic (1420–1797) owing to its Arsenal and the cultivation of vines, olive trees, fig trees, almond trees and lavender. Its mild, sunny climate (over 2,700 hours of sunshine per year) and its typically Mediterranean landscapes have made it a popular tourist destination since the 19th century and its earliest luxury hotel dates from 1868. The island is almost 43 miles (70 km) long. A chain of limestone hills runs its entire length, plunging steeply into the sea on the southern side. Most of the villages are located in the north, along its indented coast.

HVAR TOWN. The town well, dating from 1529, stands in the center of the Pjaca (*below*), which is surrounded on three sides by noteworthy buildings. At the eastern end of this square is the CATHEDRAL OF SV. STJEPAN (St Stephen), a fusion of Renaissance and baroque styles. Its campanile with elegant arched windows was built in the 17th century. The interior contains many altars by Venetian masters (Longhena, Tremignon) and paintings (Palma Giovane, Celesti). Several stone sculptures and a precious Romanesque icon of the *Madonna and Child* came from the cathedral that originally stood on this site. The south side of the Pjaca is the site of the Fontiko (salt and grain warehouse) and the arsenal, completed in the 17th century. The elegant Civic Loggia, rebuilt in the late 16th century, stands on the north side of the Pjaca. The medieval church of Sv. Kozme i Damjana (SS Cosmas and Damian) and the Late Venetian Gothic Hektorović Palace are nearby.

BEYOND THE WALLS OF HVAR TOWN. The Franciscan monastery and church on the Križa headland date from the 15th century. The bas-relief of the *Madonna and Child* on the tympanum over the main door

HVAR'S PJACA ★
A campanile, a well and a loggia make this square feel like Venice as it comes into sight across the lagoon. The façade of the Palace Hotel is part of the old Civic Loggia, and it has a pleasant terrace looking out over the port. In season, water-taxis make regular trips to the isolated coves of Pakleni. Take your pick of the beautiful islets: Palmizana, Jerolim, Marinkovac, and many others.

AGAVE LACE
The nuns in the Benedictine convent on Hvar gather agave leaves that are at least three years old. They skillfully extract 3-feet (1-meter) long fibers which are woven according to three traditional techniques that have been used for over 100 years.

WINE-MAKING
Velo Polje, which lies to the east of Starigrad, is the most fertile plain on the island. One of the best red wines in Croatia, *Plavac*, as well as some fine whites, such as *Bogdanuša* and *Zlatan Otok*, have been produced here since ancient times. These wines are the perfect accompaniment for *gregada*, a fish specialty.

HVAR THEATER
The town theater was inaugurated in 1612 in the
Arsenal. Organized by the patrician council and the
people's assembly, performances were open to all,
regardless of class, which was very rare for the period.
The interior design (*below*) is from the 19th century.

by Nikola Firentinac. The interior
ontains many works of art, including
Last Supper by Matteo Ponzoni. To
ie east of the monastery is the summer
ouse of playwright and judge Hanibal
ucić (1485–1553), author of the play
obinja (*The Slave Girl*). The coves and
ne-fringed beaches of PAKLENI OTOCI,
f the coast of Hvar, are probably the
ain attractions of these islands.

TARIGRAD. The urban layout
iplemented by the independent *polis*
f Pharos is well preserved ● *54* and still
sible. The town was surrounded by a
iassive wall, partially preserved in later
uildings. In the southeastern part, the
oet and aristocrat Petar Hektorović
uilt the Tvrdalj in 1520. Hektorović only
ft this fortified stronghold, surrounded
y a garden and a seawater fishpond (*top*
ght), for a short period during the Turkish attack of 1539.
here are inscriptions in Croatian, Latin and Italian engraved
n many of the stones of this house. The Dominican monastery
ouses a collection of paintings including a remarkable
ntombment by Tintoretto (16th century). The Nautical and
rcheological Museum is housed in the Bianchini Palace.

RBOSKA. This town was founded in the 15th century to
rve as a port for Vrbanja, the birthplace of Matija Ivanić
445–1523), who led the revolt – suppressed by the Venetian
eet – by the commoners of Hvar against the aristocracy
510–14). The fortified church of Sv. Marija (St Mary, *top*
t) has been a dominant feature of the small town since the
te 16th century. The baroque church of Sv. Lovro
t Lawrence) contains a polyptych by Veronese
6th century) and paintings by Venetian
asters from the 16th and
7th centuries.

**PETAR HEKTOROVIĆ
(1487–1572)**
In his most important
work *Ribanje I
Ribarsko Prigovaranje*
(1568, *Fishing and
Fishermen's Talk*), the
poet and patrician
relates the three-day
journey he made
between Starigrad
and Nečujam (Šolta
▲ 229) in the company
of two fishermen. His
observations on the
landscape, fishing
methods, fishermen's
conversations and
even the notes of
their songs are
recorded in
minute
detail.

The novelist and playwright, Ranko Marinković, was born in Vis in 1913.

SPLIT

Vis

Komiža○ ○Vis

Polje○

Biševo

Vis Island ◆ C C4

The colony of Issa was founded on the site of present-day Vis Town by Dionysius The Elder, the tyrant of Syracuse, in the first half of the 4th century BC. It soon became the most important Greek town in the Adriatic. After the civil war between Julius Caesar and Pompey, the town was relegated to the rank of *oppidum civium Romanorum*. A dependency of Hvar Town from the 15th century, the island shared its fate until the Napoleonic Wars. During World War Two, it served as an advance base for the Allies. Assigned to the Yugoslav navy between 1945 and 1989, it was closed to tourism, which has meant that its landscape remains relatively unspoiled.

VIS TOWN. The present-day town was formed by the merging of two towns around a bay – Luka in the west and Kut in the east. The nobility of Hvar built their summer houses here. The most representative is the Renaissance Gariboldi Palace, with its inscription of 1522. In the 17th century, the town was fortified with four towers, the most elegant of which is the Perasti Tower (1617). The church of Gospa od Spilica (Our Lady of Spilica), built in the 16th and 17th centuries, contains a Rococo reredos by the Venetian painter Giambattista Pittoni. In Kut, the church of Sv. Ciprijan (St Cyprian) was remodeled in baroque style in the 18th century, while that of the Sv. Duh (Holy Spirit) in Luka dates from the early 17th century. The Franciscan monastery was built in the early 16th century over the remains of a Roman theater.

KOMIŽA. The inhabitants of this small port overlooked by a fortified monastery were sailors and fishermen who used to ply their trade on board *falkušas*, traditional fishing boats with a triangular sail. The church of Gospa Gusarica (Our Lady of the Pirates) is formed of three medieval churches, whose single naves are linked by wide arcatures. Heading out of Vis, the remarkable Pre-Romanesque church of Sv. Mihovil (St Michael) can be seen perched above a pass.

BIŠEVO. The Modra Špilja (Blue Cave) was discovered on this small island, 3 miles (5 km) from Komiža, in 1881. Like the Blue Grotto in Capri, it owes its fame to a phenomenon caused by light refraction: around midday, the sun's rays striking an underwater entrance cause light to flood in, illuminating the blues and mauves of the walls and casting a silvery tinge over submerged objects.

ISSA
Surrounded by a trapezoidal wall, Issa ● *54* was built on a hillside. Despite the sloping terrain, the streets intersected at right angles. The Agora, later the site of the Roman Forum whose niched north wall can still be seen, extended along the seafront. Nearby stood a massive Roman baths, some of whose rooms were paved with mosaics (2nd century). There are submerged remains of the Greek port around the Prirovo peninsula, which was the site of the Roman theater. The western necropolis, at Mrtvilo, has some surviving Hellenistic tombs.

Dubrovnik

Dubrovnik, *234*
The Elaphite Islands, *242*
Northwest of Dubrovnik, *244*
The Pelješac Peninsula, *245*
Korčula, *246*
The Župa Region, *248*
The Konavle Region, *249*
Mljet, *250*
Lastovo, *252*

◆ F

A VALUABLE MESSAGE
'Non bene pro toto libertas venditur auro' ('Liberty cannot be sold for all the gold in the world'). The city's motto can be found over the main entrance to the Lovrijenac Fortress.

SUMMER GAMES
A music and drama festival has been held in Dubrovnik between July 10 and August 25 every year since 1950. There are open-air performances in the squares of the old town while concerts are held in the churches or palace courtyards and the first night takes place on the Luža Square.

AROUND THE RAMPARTS ★
The route around the top of the ramparts is just over a mile (2km) long and takes about two hours. You climb up via a narrow stairway which is beside the Pile Gate. If you like, you can interrupt the tour to descend near the Church of St Savior, from where there is a majestic view over the Stradun. The walk offers a panoramic view of the honey-coloured roofs of the town, and the blue sea that pounds the sides of Fort Bokar.

Dubrovnik's motto, *Libertas* ('liberty'), is on view all over the city: in the palaces, on the ramparts, where officers stood ready to resist enemy attacks and in the port, where the merchants chartered galleys that sailed to the four corners of the world. This freedom was not won with gold, arms or defensive walls, but with that unique combination of shrewd diplomacy and bravery which has always been the strength of the people of Dubrovnik.

History of Dubrovnik

TENTATIVE BEGINNINGS. At the turn of the 7th century, Roman Epidaurum (now Cavtat ▲ 248, one of the busiest trading ports in the southern Adriatic), was sacked by invading Slavs. The people of Cavtat took refuge on a small rocky island which had been inhabited by fishermen since ancient times: Ragusium. Slavs settled in the surrounding areas and gradually the two peoples mingled. Under attack in the 8th and 9th centuries from seafaring Arabs, the people of Ragusium equipped their ships and requested aid from the Byzantines, who made them part of Dalmatia. In the 12th century, the name of Dubrovnik appeared in the archives, from *dubrava*, meaning 'wood'. As early as 1161, the Arab geographer Al-Idrisi (1100–65/66) marveled at the burgeoning fleet which, in 1191, was granted the right of free trade in all states governed by the Byzantine Basileus.
THE RISE OF A CITY-STATE. In 1204, Venice conquered Constantinople and took control of Dubrovnik. The nobles of Ragusa invented an original political system, modeled on the Italian city-states, which was a type of Republican oligarchy ruled by a Knez (Rector) ▲ 239. The Venetian

> 'Oh beautiful, oh sweet, oh beloved liberty,/
> divine gift which embraces every treasure,/true source of all our
> glory,/sole adornment of this venerable city,/your pure beauty
> cannot be bought/by silver, gold, or spilled blood.'

Ivan Gundulić

SKILLED NEGOTIATORS
In order to boost the growth of their city without becoming embroiled in costly wars, the governors of Dubrovnik developed mutual assistance relationships with neighboring powers in the 11th century, expanded their merchant fleet and signed free trade agreements with the inhabitants of Omiš ▲ 224 in 1190 and other cities in eastern Dalmatia. Having become the main intermediary between Europe and the Balkans, they signed agreements with Ancona, Ravenna and, most importantly, Pisa, Venice's age-old rival, to protect themselves from the rapacious Venetian Republic.

Republic undermined the city's independence but could do nothing to check its trade. In 1358, after conquests by Louis I of Anjou, Dubrovnik became part of the Hungaro-Croatian Kingdom and acquired the official title of Republic in the 15th century. Its territory extended from the Konavle region ▲ 249 to the Pelješac Peninsula ▲ 245, and its merchants were already traveling as far as Spain and Syria.

THE GOLDEN AGE. The city signed a treaty with the Turks in 1430, which guaranteed peace in exchange for a tribute. Dubrovnik continued to trade with Asia Minor and expanded what was the third largest cargo fleet in the Mediterranean. Its power rested on its salt monopoly, the exportation of silver from Bosnian and Serbian mines and shipbuilding. The city opened trading posts in Tangiers, Lisbon, Algeria and Palermo and twice fought off attacks by Venice.

A TIME OF CHANGE. In 1667, Dubrovnik was destroyed by an earthquake which claimed the lives of 4,000 inhabitants. Hard hit by the growth in transatlantic trade, the city was forced to cede lands to the Ottomans in 1699 and 1718 in order to avoid falling into the clutches of Venice. Napoleon invaded the city in 1806, proclaimed that 'the Republic of Ragusa had ceased to exist' in 1808 and made it part of the Illyrian Provinces a year later. It was restored to Austrian control in 1814 and once more became part of the province of Dalmatia. This marked the end of Dubrovnik's independence. The city was made part of the Kingdom of Serbs, Croats and Slovenes in 1918, and became part of Tito's Yugoslavia after World War Two. Tourism began to develop in 1950, which ushered in a new era of prosperity.

THE WAR OF INDEPENDENCE
In 1991, after the proclamation of Croatian Independence, Dubrovnik was besieged by the Yugoslav army and repeatedly bombed. Architects and restorers are working hard to erase the battle scars of the city, designated a Unesco World Heritage Site.

Two monasteries, one Franciscan and the other Dominican, were built next to the city's Pile and Ploče gates. This was no coincidence. Their position reflected the aim of the monks to welcome travelers and protect the city from undesirables.

AN ANCIENT SYNAGOGUE

On Žudioska Street (Street of the Jews), at the northern end of the Stradun, Dubrovnik's synagogue is the second oldest functioning in Europe, after the one in Prague. It occupies a 14th-century building whose baroque interior dates from 1652 (Torah, fabrics, silver and gold). Jews were recorded in Dubrovnik for the first time in 1324, but most of them arrived in the late 15th century after their expulsion from the Iberian peninsula. They made a huge contribution to the economic development of the Republic and the flowering of arts and sciences.

ONOFRIO'S FOUNTAINS

Two fountains stand at the eastern and western ends of the Placa. The Big Fountain (1438) is very plain and takes the form of a polygonal tank topped by a dome. The water gushes out through 16 carved heads. The Small Fountain (1440–1), on Luža Square, is decorated with sculptures by the Milanese sculptor Pietro di Martino. Both were built in 1438 by the Neapolitan architect, Onofrio della Cava. Onofrio took his inspiration from ancient towns, preferring to draw water from a lake 7 miles (12 km) from Dubrovnik instead of collecting rainwater, which was common practice in most medieval towns.

The walls

The top of the walls provides a stunning view of Dubrovnik's churches, steep lanes, flights of steps and narrow passageways, as well as the city's layout: an irregular and sprawling tangle of streets in the south and a strict grid of streets in the more compact northern sector, laid out according to a statute of 1298. These two halves are divided by a main thoroughfare, the Placa, also known as the Stradun, which runs from east to west. The walls, which were begun in the 13th century and acquired their present appearance in the 15th and 16th centuries, are remarkable for the juxtaposition of different structures. The square Gothic towers in the west and north (*above*) were reinforced by semicircular Renaissance bastions after the fall of Constantinople in 1453. The walls, 82 feet (25 meters) high, are 20 feet thick in places and the corners are guarded by four forts. Access by land was protected by a moat and a second rampart, while attacks from the sea were combated by the oldest fort, the Lovrijenac Fortress (12th century). The western Pile Gate leads into the covered way. There is a statue of St Blaise, the patron saint of Dubrovnik, in a niche above the Renaissance arch. The Minčeta Tower, which looms above the fortifications, has two pepper boxes that were added (1461–5) by the Florentine architect Michelozzo di Bartolomeo, and Juraj Dalmatinac ▲ 202. At the northeast corner, the Revelin Fort (16th century) defends the Ploče Gate. The port is protected by two fortresses: St Luke in the north and St John in the south, rebuilt in the 16th century by Paskoje Milićević; a chain and a wooden barrier were erected between them at night. The well-proportioned Bokar Fortress, built between 1461 and 1463 by Michelozzo Michelozzi and later remodeled, stands at the southwestern corner of the city.

Milićević Square ◆ F A2

The Pile Gate leads into Milićević Square, which is bordered by churches built of golden stone and is the site of the huge Onofrio Fountain.

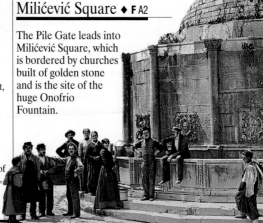

FRANCISCAN MONASTERY. Standing at the northeast corner of the square, this monastery was built between the early 14th century and the late 15th century and its church, destroyed by the earthquake of 1667, was rebuilt in baroque style. The only original element is the south portal with its tympanum carved by the Petrović brothers, Leonardo and Petar (1499); the figure of God the Father is seen above a *Pietà* who is flanked by St John the Baptist and St Jerome. The treatment of the volumes prefigures the Renaissance. The church contains the tomb of the poet Ivan Gundulić ▲ *240* and a high altar with jasper marble columns carved by Celio of Ancona in 1712. The beautifully proportioned monastery cloister, realized in the mid-14th century by Miho Brajkov, is a Romanesque-Gothic gem. Its arches with slender twin pillars run the length of four galleries. In the center of the garden stands a Gothic well topped with a statue of St Francis.

CONVENT OF ST CLAIRE. This convent was for young noblewomen who wanted to complete their education. The buildings, constructed in the late 13th century, had to be rebuilt after the earthquake of 1667. The orphanage founded in 1432 near the convent was one of the first in Europe. There is still a house on Dominko-Zlatarić street with an inscription above the door: where the window used to be, on the left, anonymous mothers would leave their newborn babies in one of the niches designed expressly for that purpose.

THE FRANCISCAN PHARMACY
Founded in 1317, this pharmacy has been continually in use ever since. It is the third oldest pharmacy in Europe.

CHURCH OF ST SAVIOR. The City Council decided to appease divine wrath by building this church after the earthquake of 1520. Petar Andrijić, an architect from Korčula, drew up the plans. He designed the façade decorated with a rose window and the interior in Renaissance style. The church's main attraction is *The Resurrection* painted by Pier Antonio Plermini of Urbino (1527–8).

STRADUN OR PLACA. Originally called the Placa, the main street was renamed the Stradun, from the Venetian *stradon*, meaning 'main street'. Since the earthquake of 1667, it has been lined with identical merchants' houses, whose harmonious façades reflect the same baroque principles.

THE COLLECTIONS IN THE FRANCISCAN MONASTERY
Exhibits include paintings from between the 15th and 17th centuries, modern works, a Paleochristian sarcophagus (5th–6th centuries), silver and gold objects, and sacerdotal vestments. The library contains musical scores and the most extensive collection of ancient Croatian literature.

ORLANDO'S COLUMN
This column was the symbol of the city's independence and the Republic's white flag flew from its top for four centuries. Carved by Bonino da Milano in collaboration with Antun Dubrovčanin, it was erected on Luža Square in 1419. Since the cult of Orlando (or Roland) was better known in Northern Europe, it might seem surprising to find a statue of this hero in Dubrovnik. However, according to legend, Orlando vanquished one of the city's Saracen enemies in the early Middle Ages. The column is also doubtless a homage to the Hungaro-Croatian ruler, King Sigismund of Luxembourg ● *32*. The statue itself played a key role in Ragusan trade: its forearm, which was 20 inches (51.2 cm) long, served as a standard for merchants, and was called the 'Ragusan Cubit'.

THE FESTIVAL OF ST BLAISE
This is celebrated on February 3 every year. St Blaise, bishop of Sebasta in Armenia, was martyred in 316 by the Romans. According to legend, he appeared in a dream to the Rector, in the 10th century, to warn him of a Venetian attack. The city was saved and he was made their patron saint.

On Luža Square ♦ **F** B2

Luža ('Loggia') Square, situated at the eastern end of the Stradun, was the hub of the medieval city's public life. There was a gate here providing access to the port. The view from this square takes in the city, the lush islet of Lokrum ▲ *248* and the deep blue Adriatic Sea.

THE GRADSKI ZVONIK. This white clock tower, 102 feet (31 meters) tall, has been a symbol of the civil liberties cherished by the inhabitants of Ragusa since 1444. Two heavy bronze statues nicknamed *Zelenci* ('the Greenies'), because of the greenish patina they had acquired over the years, used to strike the clock bell every hour. The tower, which was leaning too much to one side, was shortened in 1906, then demolished. An identical copy was rebuilt in 1928. Next to it stands the Main Guard House, once the home of the city admiral, whose classical façade boasts a monumental baroque doorway by Marino Gropelli (1708). The former palace of the Great Council, now the Town Hall, forms a continuation of this building. Gutted by a fire in 1817, the original mansion was rebuilt in 1867 in neo-Renaissance style.

SPONZA PALACE ● *63*. This mansion on the north side of the square used to be the customs house and mint. Its architecture is an example of combined Gothic-Renaissance style (1516–21). The plans were designed by

After the explosion at the Rector's Palace in 1463, Salvi di Michele, a Renaissance artist from Florence, carried out the restoration while the Milanese sculptor, Pietro di Martino, carved the portal, some of the capitals and the portrait of Asclepius which graces the column at the southeastern corner of the porch.

askoje Milićević and the statues are partly the work of he Andrijić brothers, stonecutters from Korčula ▲ 246. he façade is a skillful fusion of the two styles: the porch as elegant arcades and classical columns, the second floor ports arched Gothic windows and the top floor has a Renaissance pediment. Over the lintel of the main arch of he inner courtyard, a Latin inscription provides an insight nto the Ragusans' ethical approach to business: 'Our weights revent us from cheating or being cheated. When I weigh he goods, God Himself weighs me.' The palace now contains he State Archives, which include manuscripts in Latin, talian, Croatian and Turkish.

HURCH OF ST BLAISE. The highly ornamental façade of his church forms a contrast with the plain Renaissance style hat prevails in Luža Square. Destroyed in a fire in 1706, the Gothic church was rebuilt between 1707 and 1715 by Marino Gropelli, who drew his inspiration from Venetian baroque hurches. This church is a baroque showcase with friezes nd cherubs on the portal, polychromatic marble altars, mnipresent gilding and light slanting among the majestic olonnades. The statue of St Blaise on the high altar is the nly 15th-century masterpiece, produced by the city's silver- nd goldsmiths. In his left hand, the saint is holding a model f the city as it would have looked before the earthquake of 667, providing historians with much valuable information.

To the South of the Stradun ◆ F B-C2-3

HE RECTOR'S PALACE. This building has had a checkered istory: destroyed by fire in 1435 then rebuilt by Onofrio ella Cava, it was damaged by an exploding powder keg in 463, and again by the earthquake of 1667. Although Onofrio's Gothic inspiration can still be seen in the general ayout of the building, the Renaissance spirit that inspired alvi di Michele, Juraj Dalmatinac and Marko Andrijić revails in the design of the porch arcades and the light-filled trium. A touch of baroque elegance is added by the alustraded staircase leading from the courtyard to the econd floor, which housed the Rector's apartments, as well as rooms for meetings and for receiving foreign iplomats. The palace is now home to the City Museum, hose collections of furniture, costumes and paintings ecreate a powerful sense of the past.

'OBLITI PRIVATORUM PUBLICA CURATE.'
This inscription – 'Forget your private concerns for the general good' – engraved on the lintel of the door to the Council Room, is a good indication of the city's political philosophy, founded on mutual surveillance and total commitment to the community. The Republic of Dubrovnik was an oligarchy in which power was held by the aristocrats, as was the case in most of the free cities in the Mediterranean. There were three councils: the Great Council, which was open to the nobility, who elected the members of the other administrative bodies for a year and passed the laws; the Small Council, which was the supreme court of justice; and the Senate, which controlled diplomatic staff, financial affairs and domestic administration. The Rector had executive power. He was appointed for just a month and was not permitted to leave the palace during that period, except for affairs of state. His post carried no privileges.

GUNDULIĆ SQUARE
This square, to the right of the Rector's Palace, is dominated by the bronze statue of Ivan Gundulić, cast in 1892 by Ivan Rendić. A picturesque market is held here every morning.

▲ Dubrovnik

THE HUMANIST PERIOD
In the late 15th century, Dubrovnik's cathedral became the seat of literary and philosophical debates attended by the city's nobility and clergy. In the 16th century, an Academy of the Unanimous was founded by a group of poets on the second floor of the Sponza Palace. The main exponents of this spiritual and artistic revival, supported by the cultural authorities, were Marin Držić (1508–67) and Ivan Gundulić (1589–1638). Držić, a Mannerist playwright nicknamed the Croatian Shakespeare, wrote about ten plays providing an ironic portrait of his time. Gundulić (*below*), a poet, was the most famous author in the Ragusan Parnassus. His main works included the epic poem *Osman*, a sort of Croatian *Legend of the Centuries*, the pastoral play *Dubravka* and *The Tears of the Prodigal Son*.

A LEARNED JESUIT
Dubrovnik physicist and astronomer Ruđer Bošković (1711–87) invented the achromatic telescope and was a forefather of atomic science. The square in front of St Ignatius is named for him.

KATEDRALA. Dubrovnik's cathedral, whose light-hued façade is reminiscent of some baroque church in Rome. It was rebuilt between 1672 and 1713 over the ruins of a Romanesque church with a donation, according to legend, from Richard the Lionheart. It replaced a Byzantine basilica dating from the 6th–9th centuries. Vestiges of the two earlier buildings can still be seen under the nave. Many architects helped rebuild the cathedral to a Latin cross plan with three naves: Andreotti and Pier Antonio Bazzi (Genoa Andrea Buffalini (Urbino), Tomaso Napoli (Palermo) and Ilija Katičić (Dubrovnik). They were assisted by a prestigiou Ragusan, Stjepan Gradić (1613–83), a diplomat, scholar and poet, who was advisor to Pope Alexander VII. The cathedra has a magnificent treasury and is lavishly furnished with paintings by Titian and Padovanino, violet or polychrome marble altars and touching icons.

THE FORT OF ST JOHN. This baroque fortress houses the Maritime Museum and the Institute of Biology, whose aquarium boasts 34 tanks containing examples of flora and fauna from the Dalmatian coast. The museum illustrates the role played by the sea in Dubrovnik's history, with models of galleasses – large Venetian galleys with sails and oars.

THE JESUIT COLLEGE. A stately flight of steps by Pietro Passalacqua (1735), modeled on the baroque staircases in th Piazza di Spagna, in Rome ● 66, leads up to the austere Jesu College, founded in 1658. Dubrovnik's great scholars and writers studied here. The church of St Ignatius, built (1699–1725) to plans by Jesuit architect Andrea Pozzo, displays a spare baroque style. Only the trompe-l'oeil frescos by Spanis artist Gaetano Garcia, which cover the ceiling and walls of the apse, provide some relief from the verticality of the lines

THE CATHEDRAL TREASURY

Mentioned by Shakespeare in *Twelfth Night*, the treasury boasts one of the city's most precious works of art: a 12th-century reliquary containing the skull of St Blaise (*left*), fashioned in gold and silver with Byzantine enamels.

HEADING WEST. Strossmayerova Street leads into the district of St Mary, which is the site of the 16th-century grain warehouse nicknamed the Rupe, 'the Holes', for the 15 storage pits which are carved out of bare rock. Grain was stored here at a constant temperature of 63°F (17°C). The building, sometimes also called the 'grain cathedral' because of its monumental vaults, has been converted into an Ethnographic Museum which provides information about traditional techniques of agricultural production, as well as regional costumes. Further along lies the district known as Za Rokom, meaning 'behind St Roch', a small church where a Humanist engraved this wise warning in 1597: *Pax vobis – Memento mori qui ludetis pilae* ('Peace be with you – Remember that you will also die, you who are playing ball').

Toward the Ploče Gate ♦ F B-C1-2

The steep streets in the northern part of the city are crossed by Prijeko Avenue which runs parallel to the Stradun. To the east stands the small church of St Nicholas, which still has its 11th-century Romanesque chevet. The nearby Renaissance church of St Sebastian houses a gallery of modern art.

THE DOMINICAN MONASTERY. Not only the finest cultural attraction in Dubrovnik, this monastery is also one of its strategic buildings. Its construction, begun in the 14th century, received financial aid from the government, and the building was constructed against the walls to improve the fortification of the northeastern part of the city. The complex was remodeled on several occasions in the 15th and 16th centuries. Its austere walls enclose various treasures of art and architecture. The cloister, designed by the Florentine architect, Massa di Bartolomeo, was constructed between 1456 and 1483 by Dubrovnik's master builders. Extending around a garden of palm trees, its triple arches have spandrels decorated with delicate trefoils. The treasury is full of interesting exhibits, including paintings by the famous Renaissance school of Ragusa, and the remarkable library has 239 incunabula and illuminated manuscripts. The Romanesque south portal of the monastery church was reinterpreted in Lombard Gothic style by Bonino da Milano around 1420. The richly decorated interior contrasts with the simple plan. The floor is paved with engraved tombstones because the building was used as a burial place for the city's inhabitants. Above the high altar hangs a large wooden crucifix painted in 1358 by one of the most eminent artists of the time, Paolo Veneziano.

THE RAGUSA SCHOOL

Many artists' studios opened in Dubrovnik in the 15th and 16th centuries. Most of their works were lost in fires and earthquakes, but what survives shows the quality of their output. The Treasury in the Dominican Monastery contains polyptychs by Lovro Dobričević (mid 15th century), who heightened the expressiveness of medieval hieratic figures. There are also some 16th-century works by Mihajlo Hamzić and Nikola Božidarević, who combined two major trends of the Italian Renaissance: his landscapes were Umbrian in style while his figures displayed a more Venetian influence (*below*).

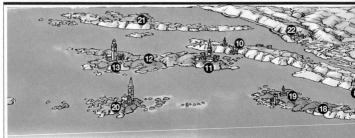

1. DUBROVNIK ★   **2.** KOLOČEP   **3.** LOPUD   **4.** ŠIPAN   **5.** RIJEKA DUBROVAČKA   **6.** TRSTENO   **7.** SLANO

The Elaphite Islands ♦ C A-B5-6

The string of 14 islands that lie between Dubrovnik and the Pelješac peninsula are blessed with lush vegetation, abundant crops and a rich architectural heritage. They are believed to have been inhabited since prehistoric times and are mentioned by Pliny the Elder (1st century AD) in his *Historia Naturalis* where they are first referred to as the Elaphites (Deer Islands), from the ancient Greek *elaphos* ('deer'). They passed under the aegis of Dubrovnik in the 10th century and have some lovely pre-Romanesque chapels and dozens of 15th–16th century churches and villas in a blend of Gothic and Renaissance styles ● *64*. The villages of the archipelago display the influence exerted by Dubrovnik. Only the largest islands (Šipan, Lopud and Koločep) are inhabited. Others, such as Daksa and Sveti Andrija, are crowned by lighthouses.

KOLOČEP. This wooded island, with an area just under a square mile (2.35 km²) has a number of ancient remains, including three pre-Romanesque chapels dedicated to Sv. Antun Padovanski (St Anthony of Padua), Sv. Nikola (11th century) and Sv. Trojstvo (the Holy Trinity, 12th century). Built a little later, the chapel of Sv. Antun Opat (St Anthony of Egypt) has a polyptych (1434) by the Ragusan artist Ivan Ugrinović. Donje Čelo, one of the island's two villages (the other is Gornje Čelo), has a 13th–15th century parish church and the remains of a fortress built following the Turkish attack of 1571.

LOPUD. With an area of 1½ square miles (4.63 km²), Lopud – the ancient Greek island of Delphodia – is about twice the size of Koločep. It has a number of ruined villages dating from the 11th

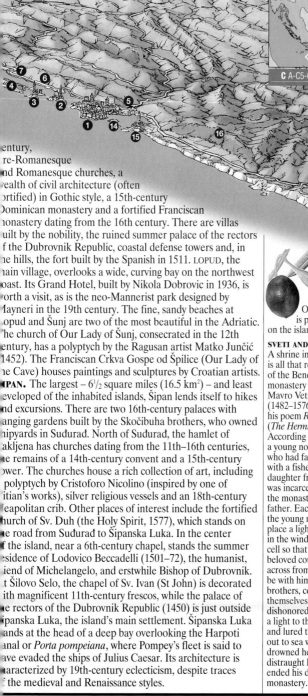

C A-C5-6

entury,
re-Romanesque
nd Romanesque churches, a
vealth of civil architecture (often
ortified) in Gothic style, a 15th-century
Dominican monastery and a fortified Franciscan
monastery dating from the 16th century. There are villas
uilt by the nobility, the ruined summer palace of the rectors
f the Dubrovnik Republic, coastal defense towers and, in
he hills, the fort built by the Spanish in 1511. LOPUD, the
main village, overlooks a wide, curving bay on the northwest
oast. Its Grand Hotel, built by Nikola Dobrovic in 1936, is
vorth a visit, as is the neo-Mannerist park designed by
Mayneri in the 19th century. The fine, sandy beaches at
opud and Šunj are two of the most beautiful in the Adriatic.
The church of Our Lady of Šunj, consecrated in the 12th
entury, has a polyptych by the Ragusan artist Matko Junčić
1452). The Franciscan Crkva Gospe od Špilice (Our Lady of
he Cave) houses paintings and sculptures by Croatian artists.
ŠIPAN. The largest – $6\frac{1}{2}$ square miles (16.5 km²) – and least
eveloped of the inhabited islands, Šipan lends itself to hikes
nd excursions. There are two 16th-century palaces with
anging gardens built by the Skočibuha brothers, who owned
hipyards in Suđurad. North of Suđurad, the hamlet of
akljena has churches dating from the 11th–16th centuries,
e remains of a 14th-century convent and a 15th-century
ower. The churches house a rich collection of art, including
 polyptych by Cristoforo Nicolino (inspired by one of
itian's works), silver religious vessels and an 18th-century
eapolitan crib. Other places of interest include the fortified
hurch of Sv. Duh (the Holy Spirit, 1577), which stands on
e road from Suđurad to Šipanska Luka. In the center
f the island, near a 6th-century chapel, stands the summer
esidence of Lodovico Beccadelli (1501–72), the humanist,
iend of Michelangelo, and erstwhile Bishop of Dubrovnik.
t Šilovo Selo, the chapel of Sv. Ivan (St John) is decorated
ith magnificent 11th-century frescos, while the palace of
e rectors of the Dubrovnik Republic (1450) is just outside
ipanska Luka, the island's main settlement. Šipanska Luka
ands at the head of a deep bay overlooking the Harpoti
anal or *Porta pompeiana*, where Pompey's fleet is said to
ave evaded the ships of Julius Caesar. Its architecture is
aracterized by 19th-century eclecticism, despite traces
 the medieval and Renaissance styles.

Olive oil
is produced
on the islands.

SVETI ANDRIJA
A shrine in the rock
is all that remains
of the Benedictine
monastery where
Mavro Vetranović
(1482–1576) wrote
his poem *Remeta*
(*The Hermit*).
According to legend,
a young nobleman,
who had fallen in love
with a fisherman's
daughter from Lopud,
was incarcerated in
the monastery by his
father. Each evening,
the young man would
place a lighted candle
in the window of his
cell so that his
beloved could swim
across from Lopud to
be with him. The girl's
brothers, considering
themselves
dishonored, attached
a light to their boat
and lured their sister
out to sea where they
drowned her. The
distraught lover
ended his days in the
monastery.

Northwest of Dubrovnik ♦ C B5

THE GLORY OF THE SORKOČEVIĆ FAMILY
The villa built by the Sorkočević family at Komolac during the 16th, 17th and 18th centuries was transformed into a sailing club in 1956. It has a distinctive baroque staircase that once led down into the sea. The interior of their summer palace in Gruž is decorated with murals on mythological themes painted in the second half of the 16th century.

A DELIGHTFUL PLACE TO STAY
It was not by chance that Nikola Vitov chose the gardens of Ivan Gučetić's Trsteno villa as the setting for his *Dialogue on Beauty* (1581), between his wife and Cvijeta Zuzorić, a famous Ragusan society woman of the Renaissance period. The villa's fountain (1736) is fed by an aqueduct and adorned with statues of Neptune and nymphs, and it is said that it 'did not have its like between Trieste and the Dardanelles'. Over the centuries, many famous artists, including Titian and Lord Byron, are reputed to have stayed in the villa.

RIJEKA DUBROVAČKA. The deep, narrow inlet known as the Rijeka Dubrovačka ('river of Dubrovnik') that stretches for 3 miles (5 km) to the north of the city is bordered by small villages and modern coastal resorts. It became a possession of the former city-state of Ragusa in the 9th century and, from the 15th century onward, acquired the beautiful summer villas built by Dubrovnik's nobles, shipowners and sea captains at Batakovina, Čajkovići, Komolac, Rožat and Mokošica. Built in an arid landscape, these villas were surrounded by walls enclosing gardens that echoed to the murmur of fountains ● *64*. Today, they are in a sorry state, with the exception of the villas of the Sorkočević family in Komolac and Gruz, a western suburb of Dubrovnik, and the summer villa of the Gučetić-Durđević family, near Mokošica. In 1814, this villa hosted the last session of the parliament of Ragusan nobles.

THE COAST. The coast north of the Rijeka Dubrovačka, known as the Dubrovačko primorje, produces olives and medicinal plants. The region is also famous for its *lindo* ● *43* or 'jumping dance'. Two huge plane trees mark the approach to TRSTENO and its beautiful arboretum. The first trees were planted in the early 16th century, when Dubrovnik noble Ivan Gučetić built a villa here. At the head of a bay, the site of SLANO has been inhabited since prehistoric times, as evidenced by the barrows in the surrounding area. The Franciscan monastery, built in the 15th century and since renovated, stands next to a 16th-century church that houses several major works of art.

The Pelješac Peninsula ◆ C E-F4-5

This narrow, mountainous peninsula, about 40 miles (65 km) long, is barren along its northwest coast where it is swept by the Bura ■ 17, while the southeast coast is planted with vines and orange trees. In prehistoric times, it was inhabited by the Illyrians and, from the 7th and 8th centuries, by the Croats. It became a possession of Ragusa in 1333 and enjoyed its golden age in the 18th century, with the development of the Dubrovnik Republic's maritime activities. As well as churches and villas, the Pelješac also has some excellent red wines – dingač and postup.

TON AND MALI STON. The twin settlements of Ston and Mali Ston, linked by a 3¹/₂ mile (5.5km) fortification wall surmounted by towers, are part of a remarkable medieval defensive system. In 1333, the Republic of Dubrovnik began building a defensive system to control access to the Pelješac Peninsula. This system included two fortresses with a regular grid layout – the salt-producing town of Ston, and Mali Ston, originally one of the bastions of Ston's fortifications – that stood on either side of the isthmus linking the peninsula to the mainland. Ston was badly damaged in the earthquake of 1996 but still has its fortress, chancellery, Sorkočević Palace, Archbishop's Palace and Franciscan monastery (1349), whose late Romanesque church has a crucifix painted by Blaž Jurjev Trogiranin ▲ 209. At the other end of the fortifications, Mali Ston and its delightful 15th-century port still have their salt storehouse, a reminder of the time when the saltpans (still in use today) were central to the prosperity of Ragusa. Today, oysters and mussels are farmed in the bay and kanal of Mali Ston, which are part of a protected nature park. Not far from Ston are the ruins of several pre-Romanesque churches, including the well-preserved church of Sv. Mihailjo (St Michael) which dates from the 9th century and has very old murals.

OREBIĆ. Orebić, in the northwest of the peninsula, was the center of Ragusa's maritime activity. It has had shipyards since the 16th century, and played a key commercial role, since its merchant fleet accounted for much maritime trade between the Ottoman empire and western Europe. The city enjoyed its golden age in the 18th century, as shown by the beautiful baroque villas surrounded by gardens that were built on the waterfront by shipowners and sea captains. Various paintings, models and documents evoke this history in the town's Pomorski muzej (Maritime Museum).

A WELL-DEFENDED PENINSULA
The fortifications (top), built by the Dubrovnik Republic across the isthmus linking the Pelješac to the mainland, controlled access to the peninsula. They were built by the same architects and builders who worked on the ramparts of Ragusa – Michelozzo Michelozzi, Juraj Dalmatinac, Onofrio della Cava and Paskoje Milićević, among others. The work spanned a period of almost 300 years.

OREBIĆ'S PLAQUES
About 1¹/₂ miles (2 km) west of Orebić, a Franciscan monastery (above) stands in spectacular landscape. Inside are commemorative plaques – small paintings on wood, often representing a storm survived by the donor – dating from the 16th–19th centuries. The Virgin Mary or a patron saint is in one corner.

▲ The Southern Dalmatian coast

Split   Split/Hvar
Vela Luka
Korčula
Korčula
Lastovo   Dubro

A MINIATURE DUBROVNIK ★
The town of Korčula is like a miniature version of Dubrovnik, apart from the fact that it no longer has its ramparts. A few hours are enough to stroll its narrow streets, protected from the wind, and visit its palaces and churches. At sunset, sitting on the beautiful terrace of the Korčula Hotel, you can enjoy a magnificent view of the port and the sea beyond.

The cathedral of Sv. Marko (St Mark) is in the heart of the town in a square of the same name. The name is a reminder that Venice seized the island and occupied it for almost four centuries.

Korčula ◆ C D-E4-5

The island of Korčula has a surface area of 104 square miles (270 km²) and an irregular coastline indented with coves. The mild climate favors a varied vegetation, from conifer forests to scrubland and meadows of wildflowers. The inhabitants live by fishing, boat building and stone quarrying, as well as cultivating vines and olive, orange, fig and almond trees. Inhabited during the Stone Age, colonized by the Greeks in the 6th century BC and conquered by the Romans in the 1st century AD, Korčula, like the rest of Dalmatia, has always been disputed territory. Between the 7th and 10th centuries, the island was part of the kingdom of Croatia, then occupied by the Venetians, in 1000, before falling into the hands of various masters. Between 1420 and 1797, Korčula was once again a Venetian possession and was subsequently occupied by the French, English and Austrians until 1918, when it became part of the Kingdom of Serbs, Croats and Slovenes.
KORČULA TOWN. The island's main town occupies a small promontory opposite the Pelješac Peninsula, a strategic position from which to control the sea route to the Adriatic. In the 13th century, its layout was redesigned according to a 'fishbone' plan to make the maximum use of the space. Side streets converge on the main street (or backbone), Korčulaskog Statuta, which runs along a north-south axis. Squares are small and the houses have several stories, while churches and public buildings occupy the high ground. In the 14th century, the town was fortified with high walls which, with the exception of the south wall and some towers, were demolished in the 19th century. The old town has a number of houses built between the 15th and 17th centuries by architects from Korčula and Dubrovnik, using stone quarried on the neighboring islands. At the time, quarrying and shipbuilding were Korčula's principal activities. The only entrance to the town by land is via an elegant 19th-century flight of steps leading to the 14th-century Kopnena vrata (Land Gate) dominated by the 15th-century Revelin tower. On the town side, the gate is in the form of a triumphal arch erected in 1650 to honor the Venetian general and military governor of Dalmatia, Leonardo Foscolo, who led Venetian forces against the Turks in the Candia War (1645–9). The main square – Trg bracé Radića – is dominated by a 16th-

century column and bounded on one side by the Renaissance town hall and, on the other, by the 15th–17th century church of Sv. Mihovil (St Michael). The church houses an 18th-century painting by the Venetian artist Francesco Maggioto. Founded in the 13th and rebuilt in the 15th century, the cathedral of Sv. Marko (St Mark) is the town's pride and joy. It was built on a triple-nave basilical plan, in Apulian Gothic style, and embellished with Renaissance elements. Its magnificent porch flanked by two lions is the work of Bonino da Milano (1412). Other parts were the work of local craftsmen, including stonemason Marko Andrijić. The high altar has an early altarpiece by Tintoretto (1550), while a chapel dedicated to Sv. Rok (St Roch) and added in the 16th century houses wooden statues (1575) by sculptor Franjo Čučić, a native of Korčula. The town's cultural heritage can be seen in the Bishop's Treasury, the Gradski muzej (Town Museum) and Crkva svih vetih (All Saints' Church).

THE ISLAND. LUMBARDA, one of the island's eight villages, is situated near a vineyard that

MARCO POLO
According to tradition, the navigator Marco Polo was born in the town of Korčula in 1254. In 1298, he was involved in a naval battle off the coast of the island between the Venetians and Genoese and taken prisoner. The house in which he was born is near the cathedral, to the right of the bell tower.

LIVING TRADITIONS
The *moreška* has been performed in the town of Korčula since the 15th century. It is a warlike dance that re-enacts a battle against the Turks and culminates with a young island girl

produces the sweet, syrupy wine known as *grk*. In the 17th century, RAČIŠĆE, in the north, was inhabited by refugees fleeing the Turks. Today, it is a community of farmers and fishermen. ČARA is built on the south-facing slopes of a hill overlooking a vast vineyard that cultivates the *pošip* grapes used to produce the wine of the same name. Its pilgrim church, Crkva Gospa Čarskog Polja (Our Lady of the Fields) has a strange Gothic altar made from Nottingham alabaster. In the village of Blato, the Crkva svih svetih (All Saints' Church) still houses the relics of Saint Vincenza, a martyr and local saint. The island's most recently built village, Vela Luka, was founded in the 19th century on a broad bay at the western end of Korčula, near the neolithic site of Vela Špilja.

being liberated. The palace and churches provide a majestic setting for performances throughout the festival season. During religious festivals in the villages of Žrnovo, Pupnat, Čara, Smokvica and Blato, young men perform a dance known as the *kumpanija* or *moštra* (*above*).

247

A crystal-clear sea,
pine forests and paths
lined with cypresses
and oleanders – it will
come as no surprise
that the tiny island of
Lokrum, which lies 20
minutes by boat to the
east of Dubrovnik, is
also a nature park.
Its Benedictine
monastery, built in
the 11th century, was
abandoned in 1798
following an accord
between the Pope and
the Republic of
Dubrovnik. It was
rediscovered in 1859
by Maximilian,
Archduke of Austria,
who had it rebuilt in
Historicist style. He
used to come here
with his wife to escape
the pressures and
constraints of court
life, as did Rudolf,
Archduke and Crown
Prince of Austria,
before meeting his
tragic end at
Mayerling. Today
Lokrum is a popular
tourist venue. At its
northernmost tip, the
fort built by Napoleon
I and extended by the
Austrians, offers a
panoramic view of the
island.

The Župa region ◆ C B6

As you leave Dubrovnik via the eastern suburbs, you come to
the Župa, a region that belonged to the Republic during the
early Middle Ages. Here, pebble beaches and scrub contrast
with mountains scattered with forests and waterfalls. The
villages have their own sites of historic interest – Roman
remains in Spilan and Gradac, pre-Romanesque chapels and
funerary steles (*stećci* ▲ *225*) in Brgat, Gothic-Renaissance
villas built by high-ranking Ragusans ● *64* in the hinterland,
and an 800 year-old tileworks in Kupari.
CAVTAT. Situated at the south end of the Župa Dubrovcka
(Bay of Župa), Cavtat provides a link between the Župa and
Konavle regions. The site was originally occupied by an
Illyrian settlement that was superseded by the Roman (or
some say a Greek) colony of Epidaurum. All that remains of
this period are the ruins of a theater, a few tombs and some
engraved paving stones. When the town was destroyed by the
Avars and Slavs in the early 7th century, its inhabitants fled
to Dubrovnik ▲ *234*. The Ragusan authorities developed

The mausoleum was
built for this family of
shipowners and
bankers by Ivan
Meštrović in 1920–3
▲*222*. The hillside
cemetery of Sv. Rok
(St Roch) offers a
beautiful view of
Cavtat.

Cavtat in the second half of the 15th
century, building fortifications but also
turning it into a pleasant coastal resort.
It gradually became a small commercial
and maritime port and, in the 20th
century, a tourist resort. At the entrance
to the old town stands the former
Knežev dvor (Rector's Palace), a mid-
16th century Renaissance building
renovated in 1958 to house the Baltazar
Bogišić Collection. Exhibits include pre-
1500 books from Bogišić's vast library,
drawings, coins and documents relating
to the life of this internationally
renowned lawyer and cultural activist
(1834–1908). The lapidarium houses an
altar dedicated to Mithra, god of light,
who was widely worshipped during the
Roman empire – a similar altar is carved
in the rock of the cave of Močići. Near
the statue of Bogišić on the quay is the

VLAHO BUKOVAC
(1855–1922) ● *78*
The portraitist and
father of modern
Croatian art was born
in Cavtat, where his
house and studio, and
also a gallery, are
open to the public.
Cavtat was also the
birthplace of the
public law specialist,
Frano Supilo
(1870–1917), who
advocated a union of
South Slav states with
equal rights for all
ethnic groups.

**COSTUMES OF THE
KONAVLE REGION**
The women of the
Konavle region
proudly wore a
costume decorated
with sumptuous silk
embroidery. On
festivals and special
occasions, the
inhabitants of Cilipi
dress in traditional
costume and perform
folk dances ● *42*.

aroque church of Sv. Nikola (St Nicholas) whose presbytery
houses paintings dating from the 16th–20th century. At the
northern end of the quay stands the Franciscan monastery of
Samostan snježne Gospe (Our Lady of the Snow), founded
in 1484 and rebuilt several times. The double-nave church
has a polytypch by Vičko Lovrin (1509), a member of the
Ragusa Renaissance school ▲ *241*, a *Madonna and Child* by
Božidar Vlatković (1494), and *Our Lady of Cavtat* by Vlaho
Bukovac (*top*, *right*).

The Konavle Region ◆ C C6

An autonomous region during the Middle Ages, Konavle
passed under Bosnian control and then the jurisdiction of
several overlords before becoming part of Ragusa in the
15th century. The region comprises a long karstic plain, with
an area of 77 square miles (200 km²), bounded by two ranges
of hills dotted with 30 or so villages. The coastal cliffs are
inaccessible, except at Molunat, the only village on the coast,
built in the second half of the 15th century. Further inland,
Snježnica (4,049 ft/1,234 m), Southern Damatia's highest
peak, offers a spectacular view.

PRIDVORJE. Pridvorje was formerly the administrative
center of the Konlave region and seat of the rectorate. Many
Dubrovnik nobles, including the poet Ivan Gundulić ▲ *240*,
occupied the palace during their time as rector. The church
of Sv. Vlaho (St Blaise) adjoining the Franciscan monastery
(1429–38) has a large wooden crucifix by Juraj Petrović (mid-
15th century). Just before you get to Pridvorje, GABRILLI has
the largest collection of *stećci* ▲ *225* in the region, near the
pre-Romanesque church of Sveti Mitar. Carry on through
DUBRAVKA, once the regional capital, and take the road
toward Herzegovina. You'll come to a cliff surmounted by
the ruined Ragusan fortress of Soko, abandoned in 1673,
which played a key role in repelling Turkish attacks.

THE EASTERN KONAVLE. Near GRUDA, on the banks of
the Ljuta, the Konavoski dvori offer a pleasant excursion
in a Mediterranean landscape crossed by mountain streams.
OŠTRI RT, a headland at their most southeasterly point,
offers a magnificent view of the deep, narrow inlets of
the Boka Kotorska in Montenegro.

Trstenik/.
Korčula
Sobra
Mljet
Dubrovnik

AN ISLAND
OF LEGENDS
According to legend,
the winds of Poseidon
drove Odysseus
ashore on the island
of Mljet, where he
was entertained for
seven years by
Calypso, who tried
to make him forget
Ithaca. Legend also
has it that, having
been exiled to the
island, Agesilas built
the largest palace in
Dalmatia in the
village Polače, where
he lived with his son,
the poet Oppian,
author of the
Halieutica, a
collection of tales,
myths, scientific facts
and folklore on the
subject of fish
(2nd century AD).
Historians are still
discussing whether
Saint Paul's shipwreck
off the island of
Melita refers to Mljet
or Malta. Whichever
it was, the inhabitants
of Mljet pray
regularly to the saint
and use a number of
expressions involving
his name. A medieval
legend recounts that,
during a battle
between the armies
of two knights on
St John's Day, blood
flowed freely,
covering the ground
with a purple carpet.

Mljet ◆ C F5

Mljet, which has a surface area of $38\frac{1}{2}$ square miles
(100 km²), is the most southerly of Croatia's large islands,
separated from the Pelješac peninsula by the Mljetski kanal.
Mljet was once an important staging post on the shipping
routes linking the Strait of Otranto (between southern Italy
and Albania) with the northern Adriatic. It was cited by
Greek chroniclers and, although there are no traces of Greek
settlements on the island, a great many amphora have been
recovered off the coast. The Illyrians built *oppida* on the hill
and the Romans built an impressive palace near Polače
(the Croatian word for 'palace'). Most settlements were
established away from the coast to protect them from
unwelcome visitors. Although Mljet was part of the
principality of Neretva in the 10th century, and came under
the control of the dukes of Zahumlje (Land of Hum) in the
11th century, the island enjoyed relative administrative
autonomy. In the 14th century, it came under the aegis of the
Republic of Dubrovnik, which reorganized the Benedictine
community and brought the island's development into line
with its own needs. Mljet's mild climate and high average
annual temperatures, its lush vegetation (over 70 percent of
the island is wooded), fertile soil and the wealth of fish in
the sea and eels in the lakes, make it an Adriatic paradise.
THE EASTERN END OF THE ISLAND. BABINO POLJE, the
island's largest village, has two Romaneque chapels
dedicated to Sv. Pankracije (St Pancras) and Sv. Durad
(St George), and the Renaissance palace of the rector of
Mljet. The Gothic church of Sv. Trojstvo (the Holy Trinity)
in PROŽURA, built by the Benedictines of Lokrum ▲ *248*,
has a Romanesque bronze crucifix. About $1\frac{1}{2}$ miles (3 km)
above MARANOVIĆI stands the Renaissance-style church of
Sv. Marija od brda (St Mary of the Mount). The southeastern
part of the island, with its sandy beaches and woods of
Aleppo and umbrella pines, is now a nature reserve. For
centuries, sand for the construction of houses was exported
to Dubrovnik from the magnificent bay of SAPLUNARA.
THE MLJET NATIONAL PARK. The park at the western end
of the island harbors a rich architectural heritage. POLAČE
has the remains of the *villa rustica* ● *56*, built in the 3rd or
4th century AD for the island's Roman governor, and of a
Paleochristian church. In 1151, this part of the island was
bestowed by Desa, Prince of Zahumlje, on the Benedictine
monks who had come to Mljet from Apulia. They built a
monastery on Otok svete Marija (St Mary's Island) in the
Veliko jezero (Big Lake), which was rebuilt several
times, finally in Renaissance style (*right*).
Extended in the 16th century, the
Romaneque church with its single nave
and three bays has stylistic elements
that reflect the Apulian influence
● *60*. Many scientists and artists
stayed in the monastery, including
Ignjat Durđevic (1675–1737) who
wrote about it with great humor in
one of his poems.

THE LOGGERHEAD
TURTLE
This turtle, which
lives in warm seas, is
on the verge of
extinction on Mljet.

A PROTECTED NATURAL SETTING

In the second half of the 19th century, the Austrian authorities took steps to ensure the protection of the natural environment and scientific observation of geological phenomena, in particular earth tremors. Mljet National Park, created in 1960, covers one-third of the island. Its vegetation, in spite of a predominance of Aleppo pines, scrub and jasmine, is extremely diverse. Nestling between forested slopes are the island's two lakes – Malo jezero (Small Lake), 59 acres (24 hectares) and 95 feet (29 meters) deep, and Veliko jezero (Big Lake), 358 acres (145 hectares) and 151 feet (46 meters) deep. Because they are linked to each other and the sea by narrow channels, the strong currents flowing through them change direction every six hours with the tide. Their waters, which have lower salt levels but a much wider range of temperatures than the sea, constitute a remarkable habitat. However, Malo jezero suffers from the phenomenon known as eutrophication – i.e. the lake is rich in nutrients and plant life and poor in oxygen – which, in the long term, runs the risk of destroying this habitat.

Lastovo ◆ **C** D-E5

DOBRIĆ DOBRIČEVIĆ (BONINUS DE BONINIS)
This printer of incuncabula was born in Lastovo in 1457 or 1458 and is the most famous descendant of the island's great families. He wrote introductions to the works of Catullus, Virgil, Plutarch and Dante which he published in Padua, Brescia and Lyons. Above the altar in the little church of Gospe od polja (Our Lady of the Fields), in the cemetery of Lastovo, is a painting by Francesco Bissolo (1516). It was donated by Dobričević, who is thought to be one of the figures represented.

Lastovo – a tiny, wooded island with fertile fields of vines, olive and fruit trees – is about 6 miles (10 km) long from east to west and lies south of Korčula across the Lastovski kanal. The island was inhabited in prehistoric times, as shown by the caves of Rača and Pozalica. Since ancient times, when it was known as Ladesta, the island's position has enabled it to control the shipping routes of the Adriatic. In the early 12th century, as an island in the kingdom of Croatia, it was part of the Hungaro-Croatian union, but in the mid-13th century passed under the control of Dubrovnik. A statute in 1310 gave Lastovo a certain autonomy but this did not prevent the inhabitants driving out their Ragusan rector and offering their island to Venice during the rebellion of 1602–6. The Republic of Dubrovnik negotiated to regain possession of the island, which it kept until its own dissolution, when Lastovo shared the republic's fate and became part of the Austrian empire. Between 1920 and 1943, the island belonged to Italy before rejoining the modern republic of Croatia.

LASTOVO. Situated in the southeast of the island, away from the coast, Lastovo Town is the result of a series of reconstructions. On the main square stands the Gothic church of Sv. Kuzma i Damjan (SS Cosmas and Damian), built in the mid-15th century. The lateral naves were added in the 16th and 17th centuries, and the bell tower in 1942. A symbol of the sovereignty of Dubrovnik, the church that stands at the entrance to the town is dedicated to Sv. Vlaho (Saint Blaise), the patron saint of the former city-state. There is a spectacular view from the fort built above the town by the French (1809), on the site of a fortress destroyed by the Ragusans in 1606 after the islanders' revolt. Apart from LASTOVO and UBLI, a port founded in the 20th century on the site of a Roman town, the tiny harbors of Sveti Mihovil and Zaklopatica, on the northern coast, and the bay of Skrivena Luka (Hidden Port) to the south, are within easy reach.

THE LASTOVO ARCHIPELAGO. The waters around Lastovo, scattered with 46 tiny islands and rocky islets, are said to have the widest variation and highest concentration of marine flora and fauna in the Adriatic. In the past, coral was harvested here, but today underwater fishing is prohibited.

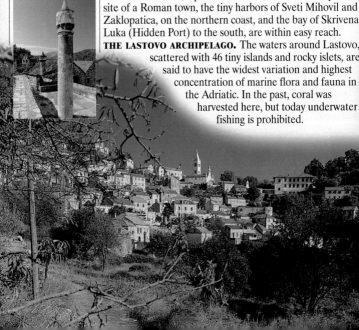

Practical information

254 Before you go
255 Croatia from A to Z
260 Festivals
261 Hotels, restaurants
and cafés
267 Glossary
268 Addresses and opening times
of places to visit
281 Bibliography
282 List of illustrations
286 Index
289 Map section

USEFUL ADRESSES

→ CROATIAN EMBASSY

■ IN THE UNITED STATES
2343 Massachusetts Ave NW, Washington D.C. 20008-2853
Tel. (202) 588 5899

■ IN THE UK
21 Conway Street London W1P 5HL
Tel. 0870 005 6709

→ CROATIAN NATIONAL TOURIST OFFICES

■ IN THE US
350 Fifth Avenue, Suite 4003,
New York 10118
Tel. (212) 279 8672
www.croatia.hr

■ IN THE UK
2 The Lanchesters, 162-164 Fulham Palace Rd,
London W6 9ER
Tel. (020) 8563 7979
www.croatia.hr

CLIMATE

■ ADRIATIC COAST
Mild winters and hot, dry summers.

■ MOUNTAINS
Heavy rain throughout the year. Cold with snowstorms in winter.

■ INLAND
Harsh winters and hot, humid summers.

→ WHEN TO GO
Spring and fall to avoid the hottest days of the summer. July–August to make the most of the beaches and wide range of water sports available.

TOUR OPERATORS
For vacations, cruises and packages that include travel and accommodation, contact the Croatian Tourist Office for information.

TIME DIFFERENCE
Croatia is one hour ahead of GMT (six hours ahead of New York).

FORMALITIES
■ Citizens of EU countries need a valid passport for stays of up to 90 days.

■ US citizens need a valid passport for stays of up to 90 days. For longer stays, a visa is required and should be obtained in advance from the Croatian Embassy in the US.

Note
The road to Dubrovnik crosses Bosnian territory but there is a border corridor that enables drivers to avoid any additional formalities.

HEALTH
Medical treatment is free to nationals of other countries if a reciprocal health care agreement has been signed between Croatia and their country of origin. This applies to most EU countries, but not to the US. US citizens need valid health insurance.

TELEPHONE

→ CALLING CROATIA FROM THE US OR UK

■ LANDLINE
011 (US) or 00 (UK) + 385 (Croatia) + area code (without the 0) followed by the 6- or 7-digit number.

■ MOBILE PHONES
00 385 + the number, which will be preceded by either 091, 098 or 099. Croatia uses GSM 900/1800 which is compatible with the rest of Europe. Tri- or Quad-band cell phones with the GSM system will work in Croatia, but many domestic US cellular phone plans will not include Croatian service. Croatia's leading GSM operator, T-Mobile, has many active agreements with international networks, and you may be able to arrange for service. Check their webpage at www.t-mobile.hr/ english/default.asp

TRAVEL

→ BY PLANE
Croatian airports include: Dubrovnik, Zagreb, Split, Pula, Zadar, Rijeka, Osijek, Brac, Losinj, Vrsar, and Zagreb-Lucko.

■ FROM THE US
There are regular flights from New York to Croatia via connections in major European cities. The following carriers offer connecting services to Croatia with affiliate partner Croatia Airlines. Prices start at $700.

◆ CONTINENTAL
Tel. (800) 231-0856
www.continental.com

◆ DELTA AIRLINES
Tel. (800) 241-4141
www.delta.com

◆ UNITED AIRLINES
Tel. (800) 538-2929
www.united.com

◆ LUFTHANSA AIRLINES
Tel. (800) 399-5838
www.lufthansa.com

◆ CROATIA AIRLINES
Connections with Croatia Airlines can be made in Brussels, Amsterdam, London, Frankfurt, Munich, Paris, Prague, Rome, Vienna and Zurich, offering travel to the Croatian cities of Dubrovnik, Zagreb, Split, Pula and Zadar.

■ FROM THE UK
There are regular direct flights from London to Zagreb, Dubrovnik and Split. Flights to Croatia's other airports are less regular and often require connections inside Croatia, usually from Zagreb. Prices start at £180.

◆ BRITISH AIRWAYS
Tel. 0870 850 9 850
www.ba.com

◆ CROATIA AIRLINES
Tel. (020) 8563 0022
www.croatiaairlines. com

◆ LUFTHANSA AIRLINES
Tel. 0870 8377 747
www.lufthansa.com

→ ONLINE BOOKING
www.expedia.com
www.orbitz.com
www.travelocity.com

www.lastminute.com
www.cheapflights.co

→ BY TRAIN
■ LONDON–PARIS
Eurostar from London-Waterloo to Paris-Gare du Nord (from £70 return).

Information
◆ Eurostar (London)
Tel. 08705 186 186
www.eurostar.com
◆ Rail Europe (UK)
Tel. 08705 848 848
www.raileurope.co.u

■ PARIS–ZAGREB
There are two daily links between Paris and Zagreb, via Germany or Switzerland.

■ SNCF
Tel. 08 92 35 35 35
www.sncf.com

→ BY CAR
■ DISTANCE
London to Paris: 210 miles (338 kms) From there
-to Zagreb: 978 mile (1,574 kms);
-to Split: 1,209 mile (1,946 kms);
-to Dubrovnik: 1,33 miles (2,153 kms)

■ FORMALITIES
At the border, you will need to show a valid driving license vehicle registration documents and the green insurance car listing Croatia, other wise you will have t pay for insurance at the border.

→ BY BOAT
■ FROM ANCONA
Links to Zadar and Sibenik (7 hours and 8 hours) or by ferry (4 hours), Split (9 to 10 hours).

■ FROM BARI, TRIESTE AND VENICE
Links to Dubrovnik

■ JADROLINIJA
Main ferry company in Croatia
◆ In Rijeka
Riva 16
Tel. 051 330 899 and 051 214 483
◆ In Zagreb
Zrinjevac 20
Tel. 01 421 777
Fax 01 427 820
www.jadrolinija.hr

rports	255
rline	
:ompanies	255
:ccommodation	255
ating out	256
ectric current	256
nergency	
numbers	256
ail	256
oney	256
ature parks	257
ational parks	257
pening times	258
ublic holidays	258
orts	258
lephone	259
ansportation	259
seful	
ddresses	259

RPORTS

DUBROVNIK
. 020 773 377
www.airport-
brovnik.hr
egular bus
nnections to the
y center (11 miles;
prox. 20 mins)

PULA
Itursko polje
. 052 530 105
egular bus
nnections to the
y center (4 miles;
prox. 10 mins)

SPLIT
. 021 203 506
www.split-airport.hr
egular bus
nnections to the

city center (14 miles;
approx. 35 mins)

■ **SUPETAR**
ON BRAČ ISLAND
Tel. 021 648 615

■ **ZADAR**
Tel. 023 313 311
www.zadar-airport.hr
Regular bus
connections to the
city center (9 miles;
approx. 15 mins)

■ **ZAGREB**
Tel. 01 626 52 22
www.zagreb-airport.hr
Bus connections to
the city center every
30 mins (11 miles;
approx. 30 mins and
25 kn). Taking a taxi
will cost around
150 kn.

AIRLINE COMPANIES

The following
airlines travel to
Croatia: Aeroflot,
Air Bosna, Alitalia,
Australian Airlines,
Air France, British
Airways, Crossair,
Lufthansa, Swissair
and Turkish Airlines.

■ **CROATIA AIRLINES**
◆ Zrinjevac 17
10000 Zagreb
Tel. 01 481 96 33
www.croatiaairlines.
com
◆ At the airport
Tel. 01 616 45 82

ACCOMMODATION

→ **INFORMATION AND
RESERVATIONS**
At travel agencies
and local tourist
offices (see p. 268)
and through their
websites:
www.croatia.com
www.dalmacija.net
www.dubrovnikportal.
com
www.istra.com
www.kvarner.hr
www.visitsplit.com
www.zadar.hr
www.zagreb-
touristinfo.hr

→ **YOUTH HOSTELS**
Only in the main
towns. Popular with
Croatian students,
so they are often full
in summer. Contact
the local tourist office
for details.

→ **CAMPSITES**
Over 300 campsites
throughout the
country. Drinking
water, electricity,
bathroom facilities
and designated
parking areas.
■ **CATEGORIES**
From I (for the most
basic) to III. This
grading system is
also supplemented
by stars.

■ **PRICES**
3–8 €/US$ 4–10
(per pers.), around
4 €/US$ 5 for a car.
■ **RESERVATIONS**
www.camping.hr
or through the
Croatian Camping
Association.
Pionirska 1
52440 Poreč
Tel. 052 451 324

→ **PRIVATE ROOMS**
15–30 €/US$ 20–40
(for 2 pers.) This type
of accommodation
(sobe in Croatian)
is found along the
coast and it tends
to be less expensive
than staying in a
hotel. As the main
foreign languages
spoken in Croatia
(apart from English)
are German and
Italian you'll often see
often the words
camere and Zimmer
signposted on the
roads.

→ **HOTELS**
Although Croatia is
starting to adopt the
European star
system, hotels are
still often graded by
letter (A, B, C, D).
Room price usually
includes breakfast.

The amount of tourist tax payable depends on the category of the hotel and the season.

■ **CATEGORY A**
60–110 €/
US$ 80–145
(double room)
High standard of comfort, restaurant, bar, night club, swimming pool, wide range of sports activities (tennis, sailing, etc.), occasionally boutiques.

■ **CATEGORY B**
40–60 €/US$ 50–80
(double room)
Same services as hotels in Category A, although there isn't always a swimming pool and there are fewer sports facilities.

■ **CATEGORY C**
30–40 €/ US$ 20–50
(double room)
Rooms with shower and toilet, but basic standard of comfort. Often some distance from the beach.

■ **CATEGORY D**
15–30 €/ US$ 20–40
(double room)
Basic standard of comfort, shared shower on the landing, no breakfast.

EATING OUT
Croatian cuisine reflects a wide variety of influences: Austro-Hungarian in the north, Italian and Balkan on the coast. Meals begin with soup (*juha*), which is followed by cold dishes such as salads or cold meats. Smoked ham (*pršut*) is very popular. Hot main courses include fish (sardines and mackerel), squid and grilled peppers on the coast and salted *Štrukli* ● *50*, in the north. Shellfish also feature widely in the menu: clams, prawns, shrimps, scampi, etc. The variety of fish means that there is a wide

selection of main courses. You can often pick the fish you want and determine how it is cooked. Meat (lamb, beef and pork) is often barbecued. There are also many dishes served in a sauce. Cheese tends to be eaten as a starter or dessert.

■ **MEALS**
Except in coastal areas, it can be hard to find somewhere for lunch. Bars opening at noon do

PLITVICE LAKES

MLJET NATIONAL PARK

not serve food. In summer, markets provide a cheap alternative with fresh produce and local color, ideal for picnicking.

■ **PRICES**
Much cheaper than in the UK and slightly less expensive than the rest of Europe.

■ **TIPPING**
It is customary to tip 10–15 percent of the total bill.

ELECTRIC CURRENT
220 volts AC, 50Hz Most plugs have two round pins, European-style, so bring a plug adaptor and transformer for essential electrical equipment.

EMERGENCY NUMBERS
Police: 92
Fire: 93
Ambulance: 94
Vehicle breakdown service: 987

For embassy details, see p. 259

MAIL
Post offices have a yellow and blue sign with the lettering HPT.

■ **OPENING TIMES**
Mon-Fri 7am–7pm, Sat 7am–1pm
During the summer, certain post offices in the main towns and tourist sites stay open until 10pm.

■ **STAMPS**
Available from post offices, tobacconists and news kiosks.

MONEY
→ **CURRENCY**
The Croatian kuna (HRK), divided into 100 lipa.

■ **COINS**
1, 2, 5, 10, 20, 50 lipa and 1, 2 and 5 kuna.

■ **NOTES**
5,10, 20, 50,100, 200, 500 and 1,000 kuna.

→ **EXCHANGE**
1 € = around 7.50 Kn
1 US$ = around 5.60 Kn
£1 = around 10 Kn

(at the time of going to press).
Currency can only be exchanged while in Croatia, in banks, foreign exchange offices, post offices, most tourist offices, hotels and campsites.

→ **ATMS**
These machines, called *mjenjačnica* or *bankomat*, are found in main towns by the entrance to banks. A commission is charged on each cash withdrawal.
Note
Take a supply of cash to tide you over when the banks are closed.

→ **METHODS OF PAYMENT**
■ **CASH**
The most usual method of payment in stores.

■ **INTERNATIONAL CREDIT CARDS**
Accepted in most hotels, restaurants and stores. You can make cash withdrawals in most banks and from ATMs (in the main towns) using a credit card.

→ **CREDIT CARDS**
■ **CARDS FROM THE U**
None of the major credit card companies have toll-free numbers in Croatia. If you need customer assistance, or to report a lost or stolen card, call your card company collect at the following American number, and they will cover the bill:
VISA:
    (410) 581-9994
MASTER CARD:
    (636) 722-7111
AMERICAN EXPRESS:
    (336) 393-1111
■ **CARDS FROM THE U**
VISA:
    1442 422 929
MASTER CARD:
    1636 722 7000
AMERICAN EXPRESS:
    (0)1273 689955

NATURE PARKS

Croatia's national and nature parks, which take in mountains, islands, coastal areas and rivers, provide a fascinating insight into the country's varied habitats and beautiful landscapes. Croatia has eight national parks and ten nature parks, four of which have been designated very recently: Mounts Učka, Žumberak and Papuk and Lake Vranjsko.

THE BIOKOVO MOUNTAINS ▲ 226

Magnificent karst mountains (5,781 ft/ 1,762 meters at their highest) looming above the tourist region of Makarska. The slopes of the Biokovo afford fabulous panoramic views over the coast and Adriatic sea.
Information
Tel. and fax
021 616 924
www.biokovo.com

THE KOPAČKI RIT ▲ 147

The vast swampland of the Kopački Rit lies at the convergence of the Drava and Danube rivers, to the east of the town of Osijek in Slavonia. A lush habitat which boasts a wide variety of plants and is home to many zoological species, including fish, marsh birds, stags and wild boar.
Note: The Kopački Rit is mined. Don't try to explore this park without a guide.
Information
Tel. 031 750 855
www.kopacki-rit.com

THE LONJSKO POLJE ▲ 134

One of the most extensive wetlands in Europe, situated near the Sava river between the towns of Sisak and Nova Gradiška. Extensive stretches of oak forest.
Information
Tel. and fax
044 672 080

THE MEDVEDNICA ▲ 116

Massif situated to the north of Zagreb. Vast forests of ancient beech and pine trees. Caves, waterfalls and gorges make this park popular with the inhabitants of Zagreb.
Information
Tel. 01 458 63 17
www.pp-medvednica.hr

THE TELAŠĆICA ▲ 199

Situated in the southwestern part of Dugi Otok Island in central Dalmatia, near the Kornati National Park. The park encompasses several small islands and draws a great many sailors. Interesting natural attractions include a small saltwater lake near the coast and some impressive cliffs which climb to an altitude of 459 feet (140 meters) above sea level.
Information
Tel. and fax
023 377 096
www.telascica.hr

THE VELEBIT ▲ 186

Because of its wide variety of plant and animal species, the highest mountain in Croatia has become the largest protected area in the country (772 square miles/ 2,000 km²). Designated an International Biosphere Reserve in 1978, it encompasses the Paklenica and Northern Velebit National Parks ▲ 257.
Information
Tel. 053 560 450
www.velebit.hr

PAPUK ▲ 151

Slavonia's highest mountain chain.
Information
Tel. 034 313 030
www.pp-papuk.hr

UČKA

The mountain range dividing the Kvarner region from central Istria.
Information
Tel. 051 293 753
www.pp-ucka.hr

VRANSKO JEZERO

Located near Zadar, this is Croatia's largest lake.
Information
Tel. 023 386 455
www.vransko-jezero.hr

ŽUMBERAK ▲ 136

Samoborsko Gorje The range of hills to the west of Zagreb.
Information
Tel. 01 332 38 48
www.pp-zumberak-samoborko-gorje.hr

NATIONAL PARKS

BRIJUNI ISLANDS ▲ 164

Two large islands and twelve smaller ones off the coast of Pula.
Area: 14 square miles (36 km²), including the surrounding sea. Renowned for their Mediterranean vegetation, safari park and cultural and historical heritage dating from the Roman and Byzantine periods.
Information
52214 Brijuni
Tel. 052 525 888
www.np-brijuni.hr

KORNATI ISLANDS ▲ 200

Extensive group of islands off the coast of Šibenik, the highest number in the Mediterranean (about 150). Area: about 96 square miles (250 km²), including the surrounding sea. One of the most popular destinations for yachting. Nine marinas, the largest of which is Piškera.
Information
Butina 2
22243 Murter
Tel. and fax
022 434 662
www.kornati.hr

THE KRKA RIVER ▲ 204

Area: 39 square miles (102 km²). Along the Krka river between Knin and Skradin. The river, which winds its way through a karst landscape for 47 miles (75 km²), is famous for its sequence of deep gorges and waterfalls, including the magnificent Skradinski buk and Roski Slapovi. Between the two, the river widens to form a lake, at the center of which lies the small island of Visovac, the site of a Franciscan Cloister.
Information
Trg Pavla II 5
22000 Šibenik
Tel. 022 217 720
www.npkrka.hr

MLJET ISLAND ▲ 250

To the southwest of Dubrovnik.
Area: 12 square miles (30 km²) in the western part of the island and 8 square miles (20 sq. km) of sea. The two deeply indented bays resemble lakes as they are only linked to the sea by narrow channels. A small island is the site of a 12th-century Benedictine Cloister.
Information
Pristanište 2
20226 Govedari
Tel. 020 744 041
www.mljet.hr

PAKLENICA ▲ 186

In the Southern Velebit, this park extends from the foot of the range, near the coast, to its highest peaks.
Area: 39 square miles (102 km²). There are

◆ Croatia from A to Z

Opening times – public holidays – sports

two breathtaking gorges, the Velika and the Mala Paklenica. The Anica Kuk rock face is a great favorite with mountaineers.

Information
Jadranska cesta
23244 Starigrad
Tel. 023 369 155
www.paklenica.hr

THE PLITVICE LAKES
▲ *138*
Designated a World Heritage Site by Unesco. Near the Zagreb-Zadar road. Area: 114 square miles (296 km²). Sixteen lakes are linked by waterfalls in a forest of beech and pine trees. Guided tour in panoramic trains and electric boats.

Information
53231 Plitvice
Tel. 053 751 015
www.np-plitvicka-jezera.hr/

THE RISNJAK ▲ *140*
To the north of Rijeka.
Area: 25 square miles (64 km²). Wooded mountains (over 4,922 feet/ 1,500 meters in altitude) in one part, the source of the Kupa river in the other (max. 984 feet/ 300 meters in altitude). This region is the gateway to the Dinaric Alps. Numerous animal species, particularly brown bears, lynx, chamois and stag. A popular area with hikers.

Information
51317 Crni Lug
Tel. 051 836 133
and 051 836 246
www.np-risnjak.hr
www.archaeology.net/ risnjak

THE NORTHERN VELEBIT
The most beautiful part at the summit of the Velebit, including the Hajduk and Rožan peaks, Zavratnica Bay,

the gorges of the Zrmanja river and the finest cave in Croatia, the Cerovačke Pećina.

Information
Tel. and fax
053 884 552
www.np-sjeverni-velebit.hr

OPENING TIMES

■ **BANKS**
Mon–Fri 7am–7pm.
Sat 7am–1pm.

■ **HOTELS AND RESTAURANTS**
Opening times vary depending on the level of custom they are experiencing. In high season, most establishments open daily from noon to midnight.

■ **STORES**
Mon–Fri 8am–8pm
Sat 8am–3pm

■ **MUSEUMS AND CHURCHES**
See p. 268 for addresses and opening hours.

■ **PHARMACIES**
Mon–Sat 9am–7pm

■ **PUBLIC SERVICES**
Mon–Fri 8am–4pm

PUBLIC HOLIDAYS

January 1
January 6
    (Epiphany)
Easter Monday
May 1 (Labor Day)
Corpus Christi
    (second Thursday
    after Whit Sunday)
June 22 (Anti-Fascist
    Struggle Day)
June 25 (Day of
    Croatian Statehood)
August 5 (National
    Thanksgiving Day)
August 15 (Feast of
    the Assumption)
October 8
    (Independence Day)
November 1
    (All Saints' Day)
December 25–26.

SPORTS

→ **CLIMBING**
This is an increasingly popular sport in the Gorski Kotar, the Velebit, the Biokovo Mountains, the Žumberak hills and the Medvednica massif.

Information
◆ Croatian
Mountaineering
Association
Kozarčeva 22
10000 Zagreb
Tel. 01 482 41 42
◆ Zagreb Climbing
Federation
Ribnjak 2
10000 Zagreb
Tel. 01 481 85 51

→ **SEA FISHING**
You can fish in many places along the Adriatic coast, except in the protected areas of marine parks and certain off-limit zones. You will also need a license.

Information
Croatian Association
for Fishing
Matije Gupca 2a
51000 Rijeka
Tel. 051 212 196

→ **WINDSURFING**
The best spots in Croatia are: Bol (Brač Island), Punat and Baška (Krk Island), Buškamen (near Omiš), Viganj (Pelješac) and Korčula Island.

Information
Croatian Surfing
Association
Obala hrvatskog
preporada 3/II
21000 Split
Tel. 021 345 788
Fax 021 585 881

→ **DIVING**
Equipment hire and diving lessons along the coast and on the islands. A special annual permit must be bought from tourist agencies and diving clubs, but this is only issued to those who have internationally recognized diving qualifications.

Information
Croatian Diving
Federation
Dalmatinska 12
10000 Zagreb
Tel. 01 484 87 65
www.diving-hrs.hr/ gb.html

→ **RAFTING**
There is whitewater rafting on the rapids of the Dobra and Cetina rivers, while canoeing or kayaking is popular along the Kupa, Korana, Mrežnica, Cetina and Una rivers.

Information
Croatian Canoeing &
Kayaking Association
Dalmatinska 12
10000 Zagreb
Tel. 01 484 86 45
Fax 01 585 87 65

→ **SKIING**
The main ski resorts are in the Gorski Kotar: Platak (3,645 ft/1,111 meters), Delnice (3,389 ft/1,033 meters), Begovo Razdoblje (3,537 ft/ 1,078 meters) and Bjelolasica (4,593 ft/ 1,400 meters). Last but not least, the Medvednica massif (3,389 ft/1,033 meters) to the north of Zagreb. These resorts are not easily accessible and the facilities cannot compete with those in the Alps. However, they do have the advantage of being peaceful.

Information
Croatian Ski
Association
Trg Sportova 11
10000 Zagreb
Tel. 01 350 584
www.platak.hr
www.bjelolasica.hr
www.sljeme.hr

→ **SAILING AND YACHTING**
Some of the 48 marinas along the Croatian coast stay open all year round. Sailors must pay a daily tax for the use of water and electricity (water for washing the boats is extra). There are also several sailing schools open throughout the year.

Information
◆ ACI Club
M. Tita 221

1410 Opatija
Tel. 051 271 288
www.aci-club.hr
◆ Association of
Nautical Tourism
Oslobodjenja 23
51000 Rijeka
Tel. 051 209 147
◆ Croatian Yachting
Association
Trg Sportova 11
10000 Zagreb
Tel. 01 350 555

→ **TENNIS**
Available in many
of the hotels on
the coast. Small
tournaments are
organized for
amateurs in the
summer.
Information
Croatia Tennis
Association
Gunduliceva 3/II
10000 Zagreb
Tel. 01 443 615
Fax 01 481 12 56
www.hts.hr

TELEPHONE
■ **CALLING THE US OR
UK FROM CROATIA**
Dial 00 + 1 (US) or
00 + 44 (UK) then
the area code and
number (without the
initial 0, for UK
numbers).
■ **WITHIN CROATIA**
In the same area, dial
the 6 or 7 digits of
the number and omit
the code. From one
area to another,
dial the 0 then the
area code followed
by the number.
■ **PUBLIC
TELEPHONES**
These can only be
operated with
phonecards which
are available at post
offices, news kiosks
and tobacconists.
■ **USEFUL NUMBERS**
Directory enquiries
(national) 988
(international) 902
Main area codes:

Dubrovnik	020
Osijek	031
Pula	052
Rijeka	051
Split	021
Sibenik	022
Varaždin	042
Zadar	023
Zagreb	01

TRANSPORTATION
→ **AROUND TOWN**
Trams in Zagreb and
buses in the other
towns are an
affordable means of
getting around. Taxis
are fairly expensive
so you should only
use them for traveling
short distances.

→ **BY CAR**
■ **CAR RENTAL**
It's fairly expensive to
rent a car in Croatia.
All the major rental
companies have
offices in the airports
and Zagreb but you
can book from the
US and UK.
■ **SPEED LIMITS**
30 mph (50 km/h) in
built-up areas,

TRAMWAY IN ZAGREB

BATEAU-TAXI IN OPATIJA

PULA MARINA (ISTRIA)

50 mph (80 km/h)
on normal roads,
80 mph (130 km/h)
on freeways.
■ **TRAFFIC
INFORMATION**
01 464 08 00
■ **SERVICE STATIONS**
Open 7am–8pm,
10pm in summer.
Note:
*Fill your tank before
leaving for the islands,
as not all of them
have service stations.*

→ **BY BOAT**
The Jadrolinija ferry
company runs most
services between the
mainland and the
islands and from
island to island. In
summer, ferries
generally sail

between 5am and
2am. Book ahead or
queue on the day.
Information
◆ In Rijeka
Riva 16
Tel. 051 330 899
and 051 214 483
◆ In Zagreb
Zrinjevac 20
Tel. 01 421 777
www.jadrolinija.hr

→ **BY COACH**
The best way to
travel between towns.
■ **ZAGREB BUS
STATION**
Tel. 01 615 7983
www.akz.hr/Eng/Time
-table/time-table.html

→ **BY TRAIN**
The railroad system
is not extensive in
Croatia. There are no
trains south of Split.
Information
Tel. 060 333 444
www.hznet.hr

USEFUL ADDRESSES
→ **EMBASSIES**
■ US Embassy
in Zagreb:
2 Thomas Jefferson St
Tel. 01 661 2200 or
01 661 2300
(consular services)
www.usembassy.hr
■ British Embassy
in Zagreb:
Ivana Lucica 4
Tel. 01 600 9100
british.embassyzagreb
@fco.gov.uk
■ British Consulate
in Split:
Obala Hrvatskog
Narodnog
Preporoda 10/III
Tel. 021 346 007
■ British Consulate
in Dubrovnik:
Buniceva Poljana 3
Tel. 020 324 597

→ **TOURIST OFFICES**
In all the main towns.
See p. 268 for their
addresses and
opening hours.
■ National Tourist
Office in Zagreb
Iblerov trg 10
Importanne Galleria
Tel. 01 4556 455
www.croatia.hr
Mon-Fri. 8.30am–
8pm, Sat 10am–6pm,
Sun 10am–2pm

◆ Festivals

FEBRUARY	SAMOBOR	**FAŽNIK** *Carnival parade.*
SHROVE TUESDAY	RIJEKA	**CARNIVAL** *Croatia's most important festival with carnival parades, theater performances, balls, exhibitions etc.*
MAY	OSIJEK	**MUSIC FESTIVAL FROM CROATIA AND GAMBURA** *Groups from all over Croatia.*
JUNE	SLAVONSKI BROD	**FOLKLORIC DANCING** *Brodsko Kolo.*
	PAZIN	**JULES-VERNE DAYS** *Dedicated to the hero of Mathias Sandorf ▲ 162.*
JUNE-JULY	ŠIBENIK	**INTERNATIONAL CHILDREN'S FESTIVAL** *Children exhibit their work. Puppet shows, collage and art workshops, and shows organized by older children.*
JULY-AUGUST	ZAGREB	**ZAGREB SUMMER FESTIVAL** *Croatian folklore described through song and dance.Organ recitals in Zagreb Cathedral. The festival combines recitals of classical music, theater and various open-air cultural events.*
JULY	ĐAKOVO	**DAKOVO EMBROIDERY AND TRADITIONAL COSTUMES** *Traditional song-and-dance performances by folkloric societies from the Baranja and Slavonia.*
	PULA	**PULA FILM FESTIVAL** *Screenings of films in the city's historic Roman arenas* www.pulafilmfestival.hr
	ZAGREB	**FOLK FESTIVAL** *Traditional song-and-dance performances by folk groups from all over the country.*
JULY-AUGUST	DUBROVNIK	**DUBROVNIK SUMMER FESTIVAL** *Croatia's largest cultural event incorporates folklore opera, classical music and dance. This festival features on the program of the European Festival Association, along with 63 other festivals organized in European cities, and also in Ankara, Jerusalem and Osaka.* www.dubrovnik-festival.hr
	KORČULA (Korčula island)	**MOREŠKA** *Performances of war-like dances through the streets of the town, on Mondays and Thursdays at 9pm.*
	OSOR	**OSOR MUSICAL NIGHTS (ISLAND OF CRES)** *Traditional music interpreted by modern Croatian artists.*
	POREČ	**CLASSICAL MUSIC FESTIVAL** *In the Basilica of Euphrasius.*
	SPLIT	**SUMMER OF SPLIT** *Opera, drama, ballet and classical music in the open air* www.splitsko-ljeto.hr
	ZADAR	**MUSICAL EVENINGS IN SAINT-DONAT** *Concerts of classical music in the beautiful historical church of St Donat (Sv. Donatu), in Zadar ▲ 193.* www.kuz.hr
AUGUST	SINJ	**ALKA DE SINJ ('THE RING OF SINJ')** *Tilting the ring – a competition during which horsemen in traditional costume try to spear a metal ring on the end of a lance, at full gallop, against a background of music and cannon fire ▲ 212.*
	VELA LUKA (Korčula island)	**KLAPA FESTIVAL** *The songs of seafarers played on pipes.*
SEPTEMBER	VINKOVCI	**VINCOVCI FALL FESTIVAL** *A two-day festival: Croatian traditional costume against a background of music and dance*
SEP-OCT	VARAŽDIN	**FESTIVAL OF BAROQUE MUSIC** *Baroque music (opera and chamber music) played by the country's leading musicians.*
DECEMBER	VIS	**FEAST OF ST NICHOLAS** *A fishing boat is burned in Komiža.*

Places preceded by the symbol ✪ are our favorites

Brač, Island of	261
Dubrovnik	261
Hvar, Island of	262
Konavle	262
Korčula, Island of	262
Opatija	262
Osijek	263
Poreč	263
Pula	263
Rovinj	263
Samobor	263
Šibenik	264
Split	264
Ston	265
Varaždin	265
Zadar	265
Zagreb	265

BRAČ (ISLAND OF)

▲ 228

HOTEL

✪ VILLA GIARDINO ***
C D3
Novi Put 2, Bol
Tel. 021 635 286
Fax 021 635 566
This delightful hotel occupies an ordinary house slightly set back from the harbor. A large, carefully tended garden leads down to a terrace with a wonderful view out across the Adriatic. Breakfast is served beneath an arbor, there's an outdoor bar screened by shrubbery, and an array of sun loungers inviting you to relax. The rooms are light and spacious, attractively furnished, and all of them open onto the garden.
14 rooms.
480–620 Kn

DUBROVNIK

▲ 234

HOTELS

ARGENTINA*** F C1
Frana Supila 14
Tel. 020 440 555
www.hoteli-argentina.hr
Situated a few hundred yards from the Pile Gate and only five minutes' walk from the old town. The hotel was built in 1922, extended in 1963 and renovated in 2003. From the street, the building is fairly unattractive, but the façade facing the sea (the old part) has a splendid view of the city's ramparts. In summer, dinner is served on the terrace overlooking the magnificent garden. A flight of stone steps leads down to a salt-water swimming pool. Beyond the pool, there's a little beach hidden amongst the rocks.
155 rooms.
1,150–2,100 Kn

EXCELSIOR **** F C1
Frana Supila 12
Tel. 020 414 222
www.hotel-excelsior.hr
The Excelsior is next door to the Argentina and shares the same ideal location, within easy walking distance of the old town. The two wings added in the 1960s spoiled the charming façade of the original building (1918), but on the side facing the sea, the harmony has been preserved. The restaurant opens onto a vast terrace offering a magnificent view of the ramparts of Dubrovnik. The beach below shares the same view, as do the terrace of the bar and the rooms facing the sea. The hotel was completely renovated in 1998 and all the rooms are the epitome of comfort. Even so, try and get a room in the old part of the hotel.
172 rooms.
1,360–2,300 Kn

STARI GRAD ***
F A2
Od Sigurate 4
Tel. 020 321 373
The hotel occupies a narrow building on one of the narrow streets leading up to the ramparts and only a stone's throw from the Stradun – a prime location in the heart of Dubrovnik. The rooms are rather cramped but there's a cozy sitting room behind the reception area. 695–995 Kn

THE PUCIĆ PALACE
**** F B2
Ulica od Puća 1
Tel. 020 324 111
www.thepucicpalace.com
The first luxury boutique hotel in Dubrovnik is also the only one in the old town. It opened in 2002 and is housed in a baroque building, slightly set back from the Gunduliceva poljana square, where Dubrovnik's fruit and vegetable market is held every morning. The luxurious rooms are furnished with period furniture and have olive-wood parquet floors, Italian-mosaic bathrooms and high ceilings. A yacht, moored in the old port, is available for the use of guests who like sailing.
19 rooms.
1,150–2,150 Kn

✪ VILLA DUBROVNIK **** F C1
Vlaha Bukovca 6
Tel. 020 422 933
www.villa-dubrovnik.hr
A boutique hotel near the Pile Gate, at the end of an avenue bordered by elegant 1920s villas set in beautiful gardens. The vegetation partially masks the modern architecture of the hotel, which stands on a rock directly overlooking the sea. The large bay windows ensure that the rooms and sitting rooms are light and airy. The décor is restrained but elegant. Boat shuttle service to the marina.
40 rooms.
1,200–1,500 Kn

VILLA ORSULA ****
F C1
Frana Supila, 14
Tel. 020 440 555
www.hoteli-argentina.hr
The Villa Orsula adjoins the Argentina and shares the gardens leading down to the sea. This elegant 1920s villa was converted into a hotel in 1989 and is very tastefully decorated. The restaurant opens onto a terrace shaded by wisteria and offering a magnificent view of the ramparts and the island of Lokrum.
15 rooms. 1,400 Kn

RESTAURANTS

DOMINO F A3
Ulica od Domina 6
Tel. 020 432 832
The restaurant stands on a square in the old town, away from the hustle and bustle of the crowds strolling along Stradun. The terrace takes up a large part of the sidewalk but places are limited, so, if you want to eat outside, you need to get there early. Otherwise you'll have to make do with the vaulted basement dining room whose stone walls have the advantage of keeping it cool. Domino is a place for lovers of red meat: the menu offers a choice of 15 different steaks but hardly any fish.
150–200 Kn

JADRAN F A2
Tel. 020 428 672
or 020 423 547
Only a stone's throw from Onofrio's Large Fountain and near Dominko-Zlataric, this restaurant occupies the cloister of the Convent of the Poor Clares that Napoleon I transformed into an arsenal. The menu is not particularly original (omelets, fries and salads) but it's ideal for a light lunch away from the main tourist routes.
80 Kn

◆ Hotels, restaurants and cafés

Towns and islands are listed alphabetically. The symbol ▲ refers to the Itineraries.
A A1 are the coordinates for the map on the front endpaper.

✪ NAUTIKA
F A1
Brsalje 3
Tel. 020 442 526
Today, Dubrovnik's former Naval School houses the city's most elegant restaurant (booking essential). The top-floor terrace, flanked by the Lovrijenac and Bokar fortresses, offers a sweeping view out across the Adriatic. The gastronomic menu has a wide choice of fish and seafood cooked on the grill. Guests can enjoy an after-dinner drink on the terrace and take in the view.
280 Kn

✪ PROTO
F B2
Široka 1
Tel. 020 323 233
Between the Pile Gate and Stradun, the Proto has just reopened after being closed for 15 years. Founded in 1886, it is one of Dubrovnik's oldest restaurants. Edward VIII is said to have dined here with Mrs Simpson shortly after his abdication. Old photographs decorate the walls of the restaurant, which opens onto a terrace. The menu gives pride of place to seafood – the stuffed squid (pujenje lignje) is absolutely delicious and there's an excellent white wine (Pošip) on the wine list.
180 Kn

CAFÉ

GRADSKA KAVANA **F** C2
Luža
One of the terraces of the 'town café', which occupies the former city arsenal, looks out onto the old port and the other onto Luža Square. Early in the morning, they are the preserve of the inhabitants of Dubrovnik who, as the day wears on, are replaced by tourists. In the evening, the terraces are assailed by the city's young set. The café's Edwardian décor is worth a visit.

✪ HEMINGWAY BAR
F C2
Pred Dvorom
This bar opposite the Rector's Palace is dedicated to the author of The Old Man and the Sea and his Croatian muse, Adriana Ivančić. Old photographs pay homage to their memory, while the names of the cocktails evoke the life and work of the US novelist.

HVAR (ISLAND OF)
▲ 230   **C** D4

HOTEL

HOTEL PALACE***
Hvar
Tel. 021 741 966
Fax 021 742 420
The hotel is situated behind the Hectorovic Palace on the port, not far from the town's main square. Built in 1898, it was one of the first luxury hotels on the Dalmatian coast and welcomed such 19th-century travelers as French writer and diplomat Paul Morand (1888–1976), who can be seen in the black-and-white photos that hang in the corridors. In spite of the alterations made during the Tito era, traces of which can still be seen in the restaurant, the hotel has retained its characteristic elegance.
300–560 Kn

RESTAURANTS

HANIBAL
Trg Sv. Stjepana 12
Tel. 021 742 760
The restaurant stands on the main square (Trg Sv. Stjepana) opposite the cathedral of Sv. Stjepan (St Stephen). Its décor is inspired by marine architecture – the walkway across the dining room imitates a ship's gangway, a duckboard covers the pebbles on the floor, and the ceiling lights are model yachts. The steak with figs is the most original specialty on the menu, but the regulars tend to prefer the pasta with prawns or lobster.
150 Kn

✪ KONOBA MENEGO
Gruda
Tel. 021 742 036
On one of the narrow streets leading to the fortress, this cozy first-floor restaurant is steeped in tradition – Dalmatian ham carved at the table and local wine drawn from a barrel. Although listed as an appetizer, the very generous assortment of Dalmatian cooked meats, marinated fish and ewe's-milk cheeses could equally well be a main course. If you're partial to desserts, you'll love the figs with almonds and brandy.
120 Kn.

KONAVLE
▲ 249   **C** C6

RESTAURANTS

✪ KONAVOSKI DVORI
Ljuta
Near Gruda
Tel. 020 791 039
About 23 miles (37 km) from Dubrovnik and 6 miles (10 km) from Cavtat – the restaurant will arrange transport. The rural setting is rather unexpected given its proximity to the coast. This country inn, once a water mill, nestles at the foot of a mountain stream, its terrace is shaded by centuries-old trees. The menu features exclusively local produce – trout caught in the river and cooked on a wood fire, just below the terrace. The homemade bread is also baked on a wood fire. The waitresses are dressed in the costume of the Konavle region.
150–200 Kn

KORČULA (ISLAND OF
▲ 246   **C** E

HOTEL

HOTEL KORČULA**
Šetalište Frana Krsinica 12
Tel. 020 711 078
Fax 020 711 746
The Korčula was opened in 1912, in a former warehouse. Its neo-Renaissance façade gives it the air of a Venetian palace, but its décor is rather perfunctory and the basic comfort of its rooms is reminiscent of the days when it was part of the socialist republic of Yugoslavia. A terrace shaded by palm trees offers a splendid view of the port. The local inhabitants sit here early in the morning and even in the evening, when there are a few spare tables.
470–670 Kn

▲ 178   **B** B

HOTEL

KVARNER
Park 1- Maja 4
Tel. 051 271 233
Fax 051 271 202
Built on Lungomare, in 1884, this was the very first luxury hotel on the Adriatic coast. Taking their lead from Francis Ferdinand, Archduke of Autria-Este, many of the crowned heads of Europe stayed here. Since then, the hotel has lost much of its luster, although the high ceilings still lend it a certain air of majesty. You have to

Hotels, restaurants and cafés ◆

100 Kn = $18 or £10

For restaurants the price given is for a standard meal, drinks excluded. For hotels we have given the minimum and maximum price for a double room (2 persons), depending on the season.

...sk to be shown the impressive ballroom which today hosts conferences. But be warned: some of the rooms are very small. 50 rooms.
600–800 Kn

OSIJEK

▲ 142   A F3

HOTEL

HOTEL CENTRAL *
Trg Ante Starčevića 6
Tel. 031 283 399
Fax 031 283 891
Situated on the busiest street in the upper town. The main entrance hall and café have an appealing Art Deco décor. The rooms have been renovated and are now reasonably comfortable with ultra-modern bathrooms.
39 rooms.
272–420 Kn

RESTAURANT

SLAVONSKA KUĆA
Firingera 26
Tel. 031 208 277
This restaurant is in Tvrda, the oldest of Osijek's three town centers. Enjoy the specialties of Slavonia – cooked meats and the famous kulen (a type of spicy paprika sausage) – in a rustic setting. Also on the menu, goulash and marinated meats reflect the Hungarian influence. Try the paprikas stew – the restaurant serves a version prepared with fish (riblji paprikas).
100 Kn

POREČ

166   B A2

HOTEL

HOTEL JADRAN *
Obala Maršala Tita, 15
Tel. 052 400 800
The Hotel Jadran occupies an attractive 20th-century residence on the edge of the port. Completely

renovated in 2001, it has a great deal more style than the very modern hotel to which it is attached. The rooms are high and very spacious and all have good views over the port. The hotel terrace faces the open sea and is a pleasant place to sit in the evening.
400–600 Kn

RESTAURANT

PETEROKRATNA KUĆA
Decumenus 1
Tel. 052 451 378
The restaurant occupies a 15th-century pentagonal tower (for which it is named) on the edge of the Roman decumanus.
As well as tastefully decorated and incontestably charming surroundings, the restaurant offers a complete range of gourmet cuisine from Istria. Fish and seafood are sometimes prepared with truffles gathered in the inland regions of the peninsula. There's an excellent selection of wines – and the red Merlot produced in Poreč goes well with most things.
200 Kn

CAFÉ

LAPIDARIJ
Svetog Maura, 10
This delightfully romantic café is an ideal place to enjoy a drink in the evening, outside in the courtyard or inside where the old furniture has been worn smooth over the years.

PULA

▲ 157   J

HOTEL

HOTEL RIVIERA *
J C1
Splitska Ulica 1
Tel. 052 211 166
Fax 052 219 117

www.arenaturist.hr
Situated about 100 yards from the Amphitheater, and five minutes' walk from the old town. Built in 1908, the hotel is a fine example of Austro-Hungarian tourist resort architecture. Its broad staircases and high ceilings still give it an air of lofty splendor. However, its décor is somewhat faded, in spite of a recent but rather tentative attempt to 'freshen it up'. Only the 5th-floor rooms have been completely renovated.
80 rooms.
370–405 Kn

RESTAURANTS

VALSABBION
Pješčana Uvala 26
Tel. 052 218 033
This restaurant, situated about 1½ miles (3 kms) from Pula, is not only renowned throughout Istria but has been voted one of the best in Croatia by food critics. The chef reinterprets traditional dishes based on nouvelle cuisine. Try his Istrian version of carpaccio – delicious Dalmatian ham accompanied by truffles and Parmesan cheese.
300 Kn

ROVINJ

▲ 165   B A3

HOTEL

HOTEL SOL INN ADRIATIC *
Obala Budicin bb.
Tel. 052 815 088
Fax 052 813 573
www.istra.com/jadran turist
This elegant villa with its yellow roughcast walls is slightly set back from the port, at the point where the maze of Rovinj's busiest narrow streets opens onto the waterfront. The hotel was built in

1912 and has always been carefully maintained. A stone staircase with beautiful wrought-iron banisters forms the centerpiece of the main entrance hall. The rooms are pleasantly large and have been renovated with such attention to detail that they can now be described as luxurious.
27 rooms.
330–450 Kn

RESTAURANT

AMFORA
Rismondo 23
Tel. 052 815 525
This waterfront restaurant is famous for serving the best crawfish in Istria. Even so, the fish prepared in autumn with local truffles is a regional specialty not to be missed. The excellent seafood risotto is also highly recommended.
150 Kn

CAFÉ

❂ **VALENTINO**
Santa Croce 28
Tel. 052 838 683
The café is perched on a cliff overlooking the sea, at the end of the quay. The bar is a huge rock, while cushions have been placed on other, smaller rocks that serve as seats. If you feel like a swim, you can simply climb down the ladder attached to the cliff face. Cocktails are served in a thatched hut below the café.

SAMOBOR

▲ 136   A A3

RESTAURANTS

PRI STAROJ VURI
Giznik 2
Tel. 01 33 60 548
About 50 yards from the main square, this traditional restaurant serves truly delicious cuisine – the ham 'turnover' and smoked trout are the house specialties.

263

◆ Hotels, restaurants and cafés

The restaurant's owner usually recommends Portugiec to go with your meal, a red wine reminiscent of Beaujolais.
100 Kn

ŠIBENIK
▲ 202   I A2

HOTEL
HOTEL JADRAN **
E A2
Obala
Oslobodenija 52
Tel. 022 212 644
Fax 022 212 480
www.rivijera.hr
A recently renovated, modern hotel ideally situated on the waterfront, on the edge of the old town. Its rooms are comfortable, but not the height of luxury. The restaurant opens onto a huge terrace which, in the evening, is a favorite meeting place for Šibenik's trendy young set.
400–600 Kn

RESTAURANTS
GRADSKA VIJEĆNICA
Trg Republike Hrvatske 3
Tel. 022 213 605
This restaurant occupies the first floor of the old town hall, near the cathedral of Sv. Jakova (St James) – in fact, its terrace spills onto the parvis in summer. The columns and wood paneling of the interior attract an elegant clientele. The service is meticulous and the cuisine extremely stylish. The crawfish in wine are absolutely delicious.
150–200 Kn

TINEL
Trg Pučkih Kapetana 1
Tel. 022 331 815
The restaurant occupies three floors in a small house in the old town, with a different décor in each room. Among the entrées, the

cheese from the island of Pag is an absolute must. Follow your main course – the chef has a predilection for fish in breadcrumbs – with figs in wine, a Dalmatian speciality all too rarely featured on dessert menus.
80–120 Kn

SPLIT
▲ 214   E

HOTELS
✪ HOTEL BELLEVUE
E A2
Bana Josipa Jelačića 2
Tel. 021 347 499
Fax 021 362 383
The Bellevue is ideally situated, at the far end of the Riva, on the edge of the old town. The building dates from the time of the Austro-Hungarian empire and the façade has retained its lofty splendor. By contrast, the 1970s interior is in need of renovation but, even so, the rooms are remarkably comfortable. The hotel's main attraction is its terrace on Trg Republike (Republic Square), overlooking the palm trees on the Riva.
46 rooms.
600-680 Kn

HOTEL PARK ***
E C3
Šetalište Bacevice
Tel. 021 40 64 00
www.hotelpark-split.hr
The hotel is ten minutes' walk from Diocletian's Palace and the neighboring food market. Built in c.1920 and completely renovated in 2001, it is the only elegant hotel in Split. The terrace shaded by palm trees at the front of the hotel is particularly charming. The rooms are all air conditioned and extremely comfortable,

although their décor could have been a little more subdued.
750–990 Kn

RESTAURANTS
BOTA ŠARE
E C3
Bavice b.b.
Tel. and fax 021 488 648
This restaurant overlooks the beach and picture windows offer a sweeping view of Bacvice Bay. Ceiling drapes add a touch of exoticism to the tasteful décor, accentuated by the foliage of many palm trees. The cuisine makes brilliant use of Mediterranean flavors – the fish, accompanied by a bottle of sweet, syrupy white wine from Korčula (grk), is a must try.
250 Kn

KONOBA VAROŠ
E A1
Ban Mladenova 7
Tel. 021 396 138
This tavern, which lies behind the Riva, to the west of Diocletian's Palace, is typical of the old districts of Split. Checked tablecloths and wooden benches create an unpretentious setting. The prawn risotto is highly acclaimed; grilled meat and fish are the other house specialty. On the wine list, try the Plavac (red) from the island of Brač.
100–140 Kn

ŠPERUN
E A1
Šperun, 3
Tel. 021 346 999
A really traditional restaurant, only a stone's throw from the arcades of Trg Republike (Republic Square). The walls are decorated with oars, while an upturned fishing boat serves as an hors-d'œuvre buffet

(Dalmatian cheeses and hams, marinated sardines). The brujet, a Dalmatian-style fish soup, is the uncontested house specialty. It is best accompanied by the Plavac, a red wine from the island of Korčula, served in a pitcher. For dessert, the warm peaches in maraschino syrup are delicious.
100 Kn

✪ ŠUMICA
E C3
Put Furula 6
Tel. 021 389 897
This elegant restaurant, on the edge of the old town, occupies a pavilion nestling beneath the pines – šumica means 'small forest'. The terrace overlooks an unspoiled bay. The pasta with salmon is a house specialty; entrées include a delicious fish terrine.
180 Kn

ZLATNA VRATA
E A2
Dioklecianova 7
Tel. 021 345 015
This charming pizzeria is actually inside Diocletian's Palace. The courtyard with its smattering of tables is set off by the remains of Roman columns. Inside, the vaulted restaurant is pleasantly cool. Pizzas are available in three sizes.
35 Kn for the biggest

CAFÉ
✪ LUXOR
E B2
Peristil
Tel. 021 346 768
You can't visit Split without taking time out on the terrace of the Luxor, at the foot of the sphinx for which the café is named, and directly opposite the cathedral.

Hotels, restaurants and cafés ◆

Places preceded by the symbol ✪ are our favorites

STON
▲ 245　　　　　C A5

RESTAURANTS

TAVERNA BOTA
Tel. 020 754 482
The restaurant
occupies an elegant
stone building
opposite the port of
Mali Ston. Inside, the
walls are hung with
old cooking utensils.
The authentic
Dalmatian cuisine
includes the famous
black risotto (crni
ižot) that features on
all menus, and
delicious home-
baked bread. The
wine list gives pride
of place to the
Dingac wines from
the Pelješac
peninsula. But be
warned, it's best to
book as the Taverna
Bota has become a
gastronomic staging
post on the road to
Dubrovnik.
180–200 Kn

VILLA KORUNA
Tel. 020 754 359
A large bay window
overlooks the oyster
beds in the bay of
Ston, so oysters are
something of a must
(ordered individually).
Mussels cooked in
white wine are the
town's other
specialty. The
restaurant, renowned
for the quality of its
seafood, prides itself
on serving one of the
best squid- or
calmary-juice risottos
on the Dalmatian
coast.
60–180 Kn

VARAŽDIN
▲ 127　　　　　A B1

HOTEL

TURIST HOTEL
Aleja Kralja
Zvonimira, 1
Tel. 042 105 105
www.hotel-turist.hr
The modern façade
lacks charm and the
functional rooms
have a modest décor.
But this is the most
comfortable hotel in
Varaždin and
conveniently located
only a few minutes'
walk from Trg Kralja
Tomislava, the main
town square. The
hotel also accepts
pets – there's a
kennels in the
outbuildings.
500–800 Kn

RESTAURANTS

ZLATNA GUSKA
Jurija Habdelka, 4
Tel. 042 213 393
During the
Inquisition, trials
were held in the
cellars of the
Zakmardi Palace.
Today, they house a
chic restaurant
whose décor evokes
a less turbulent
history. The tables
bear the coats of
arms of the Zagorje's
most prestigious
families and the
menu also reflects
the heritage of the
region's old nobility –
for example,
escalopes 'Marquis
de Brandebourg' or
cutlets 'Chevalier',
washed down with a
subtle Croatian
Chardonnay.
200 Kn

PARK
Juraja Habdelica, 6
Tel. 042 211 499
The terrace opens
directly onto the
municipal gardens
and, in summer, its
tables seem to be set
amongst the flowers,
shrubs and bushes.
Grilled meats occupy
pride of place on the
menu – try the 'Park'
escalope, filled with
ham and cheese, and
accompanied by
delicious
mushrooms. If you
have a more modest
appetite, the
'Varaždin' salad –
chicken breasts,
red sweet peppers,
apples, walnuts and
mayonnaise – comes
highly recommended.
It is really delicious.
At the Park, a white
wine from the
Zagorje region – for
example a Grasevina
– is an absolute must.
170 Kn

CAFÉ

KAFANA KORZO
Trg Kralja Tomislava, 2
Tel. 042 390 914
The café has an
old-fashioned
atmosphere and a
traditional cloakroom.
The morning papers
– suspended,
Viennese style,
from a wooden
hanger – are available
for customers, while
the pastries arranged
on a trolley add
another Viennese
touch. During
summer, the Korzo
has the excellent
idea of allowing its
tables to spill out
onto Tomislav
Square.

ZADAR
▲ 190　　　　　H

HOTEL

HOTEL KOLOVARE *
Bože Perića 14
Tel. 023 203 200
www.hotel-kolovare-
zadar.htnet.hr
This waterfront hotel,
in a suburb of Zadar,
is only a few minutes'
walk from the old
town. It has been
extensively – and
expensively –
renovated and the
rooms (all air
conditioned) are
extremely
comfortable and
tastefully decorated.
Unfortunately, the
restaurant where
breakfast is served
lacks atmosphere,
but the service is
extremely efficient
and friendly. The
hotel has a swimming
pool near the beach.
237 rooms.
640–730 Kn

RESTAURANTS

✪ FOŠA
H C3
Kralj Dmitra
Zvonimira 2
Tel. 023 314 421
The restaurant is only
a few yards from the
Kopnena vrata (Land
Gate) that once gave
access to the town.
The terrace
overlooking the Foša
sis canal and its
peaceful little port is
packed on summer
evenings, so make
sure you book. The
interior is rather old
fashioned but not
without charm. On
the menu – grilled,
fried or stuffed squid
(lignje) and all kinds
of risottos. The fish is
prepared at your
table.
150–180 Kn

KONOBA MARTINAC
H B2
Aleksandra
Paravjera, 7
Tel. 091 7202 748
An unpretentious
family restaurant,
ensconced in one of
the quiet, narrow
streets of the old
town. The dining
room opens onto a
flower-filled terrace.
The father is in
charge of the
kitchens, while his
sons take care of the
service. The house
specialty is an
original combination
of veal escalopes and
tuna. The restaurant
has also put Sansveta
Tosja – Zadar's
traditional
maraschino-flavored
gateau – back on the
menu. Diners are
offered a glass of
maraschino to round
off their meal,
courtesy of the
management.
80 Kn

ZAGREB
▲ 100　　　　　D

HOTELS

HOTEL DUBROVNIK *
D C3
Gajeva 1
Tel. 014 873 555
The hotel's ideal
location – on a
pedestrian street only
a few yards from the
Trg bana Jelačića –
makes up for its
unprepossessing
appearance.

265

◆ Hotels, restaurants and cafés

Towns and islands are listed alphabetically. The symbol ▲ refers to the Itineraries.
A A1 are the coordinates for the map on the front endpaper.

However, once inside, this imposing tower block has a pleasant and relaxed atmosphere, and its comfortable bar invites you to linger over a drink. The restaurant overlooking the square is always busy in the evening.
262 rooms.
900–990 Kn

ESPLANADE **
D D6
Mihanovićeva 1
Tel. 014 566 666
Fax 014 577 907
Built in 1925 near the railway station (the Orient Express used to stop here), this is the capital's luxury hotel. The Art Deco entrance hall alone is worth a visit. The rooms, divided between the hotel's six floors, are all spacious and some have a balcony. They were all renovated in 2004 and are now extremely comfortable with a sober décor. Zin Fandel, the Esplanade's restaurant, is one of the best in Zagreb.
209 rooms.
1,050–1,400 Kn

HOTEL PALACE
D D5
Strossmayerov trg 10
Tel. 01 48 14 611
Fax 014 48 11 358
The Palace stands on one of the main squares in the heart of the city. Behind the elegant 19th-century façade, the hotel has retained much of its former character due to the impressive marble staircase that dominates the entrance hall. In spite of their slightly old-fashioned décor, the rooms are both charming and comfortable. Try and get one overlooking the park. 130 rooms.
800–1,000 Kn

RESTAURANTS

BOBAN
D C4
Gajeva 9
Tel. 014 811 549
The location of this fashionable restaurant – between Kaptol and the Lower Town – partly explains its success. The patio bar is extremely popular with the Zagreb smart set, while the vaulted, basement restaurant serves delicious pasta, original salads and even pizzas.
80 Kn

CANTINETTA
D C4
Teslina Ulica 14
Tel. 014 811 335
Closed on Sundays
Situated between the Dolac market and the Trg bana Jelačića, the restaurant has an elegant interior, decorated with frescos, and a pleasantly relaxed atmosphere. The cuisine is both elegant and inventive – try the chicken stuffed with cheese or the turkey with prunes.
150 Kn

DUBRAVKIN PUT
D B1
Dubravkin Put 2
Tel. 014 834 975
The best fish and seafood restaurant in Zagreb occupies a pavilion in a lush setting on the edge of Tuskanac park forest, at the foot of the Upper Town. Succulent grilled squid is just one of the many Dalmatian specialties on the menu, served in a pale wood décor.
250 Kn

KAPTOLSKA KLET
D D2
Kaptol 5
Tel. 014 817 838
This restaurant is so close to the cathedral that, in summer, its terrace spills onto the parvis. In fact, the vaulted, wood-paneled interior is rather reminiscent of a sacristy. The cuisine is traditional, with duck and turkey served with every kind of sauce. Lamb cooked on skewers is the house specialty, although sausages also feature prominently on the menu. White wines from Slavonia (Traminac and Silvanac) are recommended by the wine waiter.
150 Kn

LENUĆI
D D4
Zrinjevac 16
Tel. 014 873 091
Closed on Sundays
On the edge of the gardens that form part of the famous Lenuci's Horseshoe. A designer décor (you could find the same thing in Edinburgh or Rotterdam), a cuisine that combines French and Italian influences, and a wine list that gives pride of place to chiantis from Tuscany (although there's also a small selection of Croatian wines). The restaurant is popular with the young smart set and sometimes local celebrities.
150 Kn

PAVILJON
D D6
Trg Kralja Tomislava 22
Tel. 014 813 066
Zagreb's most elegant restaurant stands in a garden setting, near the railway station. It occupies a 19th-century exhibition pavilion and is popular with the city's businessmen and women. The service is impeccable and the presentation that of the dishes meticulous. The extremely stylish cuisine reflects Italian influences (pasta, carpaccio). In summer, you can dine at tables set out on the delightful flower-filled terrace.
180 Kn

STARA VURA
D C2
Opatička 20
Tel. 014 851 368
Dine in the cellars of the Museum of Zagreb, with their beautiful brick vaults, soft lighting, tasteful décor and elegant clientele. The restaurant has a reputation for its meats, prepared according to traditional recipes, but the menu also offers a selection of grilled fish.
180–220 Kn

CAFÉS

GRADSKA KAVANA
D C3
Trg bana Jelačića 10
One of the oldest cafés in Zagreb is extremely 'Viennese' in style. In winter, customers read their newspaper over a cup of hot chocolate. There is also a choice of pastries and delicious strudels. In summer, the terrace on the Trg bana Jelačića is always packed.

KAZALIŠNA KAVANA
D B4
Maršala Tita 1
Tel. 014 855 851
The terrace of Zagreb's other historic café faces the Narodni Kazalište (National Theater). Its regulars call it the KavKaz ('theater café'). It is popular with students who meet over a coffee or a glass of warm wine when the weather is particularly cold.

PRONUNCIATION

Not as difficult as it looks!

c = ts (as in hats)
č = tch (as in chucrh)
ć = t (as in nature)
đ = dj (as in juice)
e = è (as in bed)
g = gu (as is guest)
j = y (as in young)
lj = li (as in million)
r = always rolled
š = ch (as in shore)
u = ou (as in food)
ž = j (as in pleasure)

EVERYDAY PHRASES

Yes: da
No: ne
Good morning: dobro jutro, dobar dan
Good evening: dobra večer
Good night: laku noć
How are you?: kako ste ?
Goodbye: doviđenja
Please: molim
Thank you (very much): hvala (lijepo)
Excuse me: ispričavam se
am ill: Ja sam bolestan
don't understand: ne razumijem
don't speak Croatian: ne govorim hrvatski
would like: htio bi
s it possible to: je li moguće
When?: kada ?
What time is it?: koliko je sati ?
How: sada
Today: danas
Tomorrow: sutra
Big: velik
Old: star
Small: mali, malen
Lower: donji
Upper: gornji

GETTING AROUND

On/To the right: lijevo
On/To the left: desno
Far from: daleko od
Where is?: gdje se nalazi ?
Near: blizu
Straight on: ravno
Address: adresa
Airport: aerodrom, zračna luka
Travel agent: putnička agencija
Return (ticket/ journey): tamo i natrag
Arrival: dolazak
Bus: autobus
Plane: avion
Luggage: prtljaga
Boat: brod
Driving licence: vozačka dozvola
Departure: polazak
Station: kolodvor
Bus station: autobusna stanica
Road: cesta
Street: ulica
Gas station: benzinska pumpa
Cab: taxi
Car: auto
To travel: putovati

THE RESTAURANT

Addition: račun
Butter: maslac, putar
Beer: pivo
Bread: kruh
Breakfast: doručak
Cake: kolač
Cheese: sir
Chicken: pile
Chocolate: čokolada
Coffee, black (white): kava (s mlijekom)
Dinner, to have: večerati
Drink, to: piti
Eat, to: jesti
Fruit: voće
Ice cream: sladoled
Ham: šunka
Fruit juice: voćni sok
Egg: jaje
Fish: riba
Potatoes: krumpir
Glass: čaša
Lunch, to have: ručati
Meat: meso
Menu: jelovnik
Milk: mlijeko
Plate: tanjur
Restaurant: restoran
Rice: riža
Salad: salata
Sandwich: sendvič
Soup: juha
Tea: čaj
Tip: napojnica
Vegetables : povrće
Water: voda
Wine (white, red, rosé): vino (bijelo, crno, crveno)

ACCOMMODATION

Bathroom: kupaonica
Bed: krevet
Camp, to: kampirati
Hotel: hotel
House: kuća
Room (in hotel): soba
Shower: tuš
Toilets: WC, zahod

MONEY, SHOPPING

It's too expensive: preskupo je
How much is it?: koliko košta ?
Money: novac
Bank: banka
Cheap: jeftino
Credit card: kreditna karta
Exchange: mjenjačnica
Expensive: skupo
Bill: račun
Store: dućan
Price: cijena

SIGHTSEEING

Open: otvoreno
Closed: zatvoreno
Church: crkva
Fortress: tvrđava
Island: otok
Monastery : samostan
Museum: muzej
Tourist office: turistički ured
Palace: palača
River: rijeka
Village: selo
Town: grad

MAIL

Post office: pošta
Postcard: razglegnica, dopisnica
Envelope: omotnica, koverta
Letter: pismo
Telephone, to: telefonirati
Stamp: poštanska marka

FIRST NAMES

Anne: Ana
Andrew: Andrija
Anthony: Antun, Ante
Blaise: Blaž, Vlaho (in Dubrovnik)
Catherine: Katarina
Charles: Karlo
Claire: Klara, Vedrana
Étienne: Stjepan
Francis: Franjo
Guy: Vid
John: Ivan
Joan: Ivana
Joseph: Josip
Luke: Luka
Mary: Marija
Mark: Marko
Martin: Martin
Paul: Pavao, Pavle
Peter: Petar
Vincent: Vinko

DAYS, MONTHS AND SEASONS

Monday: ponedjeljak
Tuesday: utorak
Wednesday: srijeda
Thursday: četvrtak
Friday: petak
Saturday: subota
Sunday: nedjelja
January: siječanj
February: veljača
March: ožujak
April: travanj
May: svibanj
June: lipanj
July: srpanj
August: kolovoz
September : rujan
October: listopad
November: studeni
December: prosinac
Fall: jesen
Summer: ljeto
Winter: zima
Spring: proljeće

NUMBERS

Zero: nula
One: jedan
Two: dva
Three: tri
Four: četiri
Five: pet
Six: šest
Seven: sedam
Eight: osam
Nine: devet
Ten: deset
Eleven: jedanaest
Twelve: dvanaest
Thirteen: trinaest
Fourteen: četrnaest
Fifteen: petnaest
Sixteen: šesnaest
Seventeen: sedamnaest
Eighteen: osamnaest
Nineteen: devetnaest
Twenty: dvadeset
Twenty-one: dvadeset i jedan
Thirty: trideset
One hundred: sto
One thousand: tisuća
First: prvi
Second: drugi

◆ Addresses and opening times of places to visit

Towns and villages are listed alphabetically.
The symbol ▲ refers to the relevant Itinerary section.
A X0 are map coordinates and refer to the Map section at the end of this guide.

ALJMAŠ	31205 (ZIP CODE)	TO 032 344 034	A F3
CASTLE		Only the exterior can be visited	▲ 147
CHURCH OF OUR LADY OF REFUGE		Only the exterior can be visited	▲ 147

BALE	52211	TO 052 824 270	B A3
PARISH CHURCH		Open daily 9am–1pm, 5–8pm	▲ 164

BARBAN	52207	TO 052 855 560	B B3
CHURCH OF ST NICHOLAS		Visits by appt (Tel. 052 567 173)	▲ 160

BELEC	49254	TO 049 460 040	A A2
OUR LADY OF THE SNOWS		Visits by appt (Tel. 049 460 040)	▲ 119

BERAM	52000	TO 052 622 460	B A2
CHURCH OF OUR LADY OF THE ROCKS		Open daily 9am–7pm	▲ 163
CHURCH OF ST MARTIN		Visits by appt (Tel. 052 622 088)	▲ 163

BRIBIR	51253	TO 051 248 730	B C3
CHURCH OF ST PETER AND ST PAUL		Visits by appt (Tel. 051 248 510)	▲ 177

BUZET	52420	TO 052 662 343	B B2
CHURCH OF ST ROCH		Open daily 5–6pm	▲ 170

CAVTAT	20210	TO 020 479 025	C B6
FRANCISCAN MONASTERY		Open daily 9am–7pm	▲ 249
CHURCH OF ST NICHOLAS		Open daily 8am–6pm	▲ 249
RECTOR'S PALACE/ BOGIŠIĆ MUSEUM		Open daily 10am–1pm	▲ 248

CRIKVENICA	51260	TO 051 241 867	B C3
CHURCH		Open daily 9am–7pm	▲ 177
SPA Gajevo šetalište 21 Tel. 051 785 018		Open daily Pools are closed in July-Aug.	▲ 177

ČAKOVEC	40000	TO 040 313 319	A B1
CASTLE Trg Republike 5 Tel. 040 313 285		Open Tue.–Fri. 10am–3pm, Sat.–Sun. 10am–1pm	▲ 130
CHURCH OF ST NICHOLAS		Open daily 6.30am–noon and 5–7pm	

ĆILIPI	20213	TO 020 479 025	C B6
KONAVLE MUSEUM		Open Apr.-Oct.: Sun. and by appt (Tel. 020 771 007)	▲ 249

DARDA	31326	TO 031 740 201	A F3
CASTLE		Only the exterior can be visited	▲ 147
CHURCH OF ST JOHN THE BAPTIST		Damaged. Only the exterior can be visited	▲ 147
CHURCH OF ST MICHAEL		Only the exterior can be visited	▲ 147

DONJA STUBICA		TO 049 287 467	A A2
CHURCH OF THE HOLY TRINITY		Visits by appt (Tel. 049 286 020)	▲ 117

DONJI MIHOLJAC	31540	TO 031 633 103	A E3
MANOR HOUSE		Open May-Sep: Tue.–Sat. 9am–1pm	▲ 147

DRNIŠ	22320	TO 022 219 072	C C2
CHURCH OF ST ANTHONY		Open daily 8am–7pm	▲ 206
CHURCH OF OUR LADY OF THE ROSARY		Visits Sun. and by appt (Tel. 022 886 137)	▲ 206

DUBROVNIK	20000	TO 020 323 887	F
TOURIST OFFICE Cvijeta Zuzorić Tel. 020 323 725		Open Mon.–Sat. 8am–4pm	F B2
CATHEDRAL Kneza Damjana Jude 1		Open daily 9am–7pm	▲ 240 F B3
JESUIT COLLEGE Poljana Rudera Boškovića 6		Open daily 8am–7pm	▲ 240 F B3
DOMINICAN MONASTERY Sv. Dominika 4		Open daily 9am–6pm	▲ 241 F C1
FRANCISCAN MONASTERY Braće Andrijića 7		Open daily 9am–6pm	▲ 237 F A1

CONVENT OF ST CLAIRE Poljana Paška Miličevića 1	Jadran Restaurant in the cloister	▲ 237 F A2
CHURCH OF ST BLAISE Luža	Open daily 8am–7pm	▲ 239 F B2
FORT OF ST JOHN Tel. 020 426 465 (museum) Tel. 020 427 937 (aquarium)	Maritime Museum: open daily 9am–6pm Aquarium: open daily 9am–6pm	▲ 240 F C2-3
ETHNOGRAPHIC MUSEUM Od Rupa 3 Tel. 020 323 018	Open Mon.–Sat. 9am–2pm	▲ 241 F A2
CITY MUSEUM Pred dvorom 3 Tel. 020 321 422	Open Mon.–Sat. 9am–2pm (Rector's Palace)	▲ 239 F C2
SPONZA PALACE – STATE ARCHIVES Sponza Tel. 020 321 032	Open Mon.–Sat. 9am–3pm	▲ 238 F C2

OVIGRAD	**52540**	**TO 052 825 003**	**B** A3
BASILICA	Visits by appt (Tel. 052 825 115)		▲ 162

ĐAKOVO	**31400**	**TO 031 812 313**	**A** E4
CATHEDRAL Strossmayerov trg	Open 7am–noon and 3–7pm		▲ 148
ALL SAINTS' CHURCH	Visits by appt (Tel. 031 812 313)		▲ 148
LIPPIZANER STUD FARM Augusta Šenoe 33 Tel. 031 813 286	Open daily 9am–4pm		▲ 148

GORNJA BISTRA	**49000**	**TO 013 310 309**	**A** A2
CASTLE	Visits by appt (Tel. 013 390 032)		▲ 117

GORNJA STUBICA	**49250**	**TO 049 289 282**	**A** A2
ZAGORJE MUSEUM Sanci 64 Tel. 049 587 887	Open Jan.–May: daily 8am–4pm; June–Oct.: 8am–8pm		▲ 118

GRAČIŠĆE	**52403**	**TO 052 622 460**	**B** B2
BISHOP'S CHAPEL	Open daily		▲ 161
CHURCH OF ST MARY	Visits by appt (Tel. 052 89687 111)		▲ 161

HLEBINE	**48323**	**TO 048 836 139**	**A** C2
MUSEUM-GALLERY Trg Ivana Generalića 15 Tel. 048 836 075	Open Mon.–Fri. 10am–4pm, Sat. 10am–2pm		▲ 131

HRVATSKA KOSTAJNICA	**44430**	**TO 044 851 800**	**A** B4
FORTRESS	Temporarily closed		▲ 135

HUM	**52420**	**TO 052 662 343**	**B** B2
CHURCH OF ST JEROME	Visits by appt (Tel. 052 660 005)		▲ 170

ILOK	**32236**	**TO 032 344 034**	
FRANCISCAN MONASTERY AND **CHURCH OF ST JOHN OF CAPISTRANO**	Visits by appt (Tel. 032 590 073)		▲ 149
ILOK MUSEUM Šetalište oca Mradena Barbarica Tel. 032 590 065	Closed for alterations		▲ 149

IMOTSKI	**21260**	**TO 021 841 125**	**C** E3
FORTRESS	Only the exterior can be visited		▲ 225

JANUŠEVEC	**10290**	**TO 010 203 755**	**A** A3
CASTLE **AND NATIONAL ARCHIVES** Zagrebačka 4	Only the exterior can be visited		▲ 120

JASTREBARSKO	**10450**	**TO 01 628 11 15**	**B** E1
CASTLE Ulica Zrinsko-frankopanska	Only the exterior can be visited		▲ 136

◆ Addresses and opening times of places to visit

Towns and villages are listed alphabetically.
The symbol ▲ refers to the relevant Itinerary section.
A X0 are map coordinates and refer to the Map section at the end of this guide.

KARLOVAC	47000	**TO 047 615 115**	**B** E2
CHURCH OF ST NICHOLAS		*Closed for restoration*	▲ 137
CHURCH OF THE HOLY TRINITY		*Open daily 7am–noon, 5–7pm*	▲ 137
TOWN MUSEUM Strossmayerov trg 7 Tel. 047 615 980		*Open Mon.–Fri. 8am–4pm, Sat.–Sun. 10am–noon*	▲ 137

KAŠTEL-GOMILICA	21213	**TO 021 227 933**	**C** C3
CASTLE		*Only the exterior can be visited*	▲ 209
CHURCH OF ST JEROME		*Only the exterior can be visited*	▲ 209

KAŠTEL-KAMBELOVAC	21214	**TO 021 227 933**	**C** C3
TOWER		*Only the exterior can be visited*	▲ 209

KAŠTEL-LUKŠIĆ	21215	**TO 021 227 933**	**C** C3
CHURCH OF ST JOHN		*Visits by appt (Tel. 021 227 557)*	▲ 209
VITTURI PALACE – REGIONAL MUSEUM		*Open daily 9am–noon, plus 6–9pm in summer*	▲ 209

KAŠTEL-NOVI	21215	**TO 021 227 933**	**C** C3
CASTLE		*Only the exterior can be visited*	▲ 209

KAŠTEL-STARI	21216	**TO 021 227 933**	**C** C3
CASTLE		*Open to the public*	▲ 209

KAŠTEL-SUĆURAC	21212	**TO 021 227 933**	**C** C3
GOTHIC VILLA AND MUSEUM Tel. 021 224 221		*Open Mon.–Sat. 5–8pm*	▲ 209

KAŠTEL-ŠTAFILIĆ	21215	**TO 021 227 933**	**C** C3
CASTLE		*Only the exterior can be visited*	▲ 209
CHURCH		*Open daily 6am–8am and 5–6pm*	▲ 209

KLANJEC	49290	**TO 049 550 235**	**A** A2
CHURCH		*Visits by appt (Tel. 049 550 032)*	▲ 120
MUSEUM AND GALLERY ANTUN AUGUSTINČIĆ Tel. 049 550 343		*Open daily 9am–5pm*	▲ 120

KLENOVNIK	42244	**TO 042 791 090**	**A** A2
CASTLE		*Only the exterior can be visited*	▲ 127

KLIS	21231	**TO 021 240 578**	**C** D3
FORTRESS		*Open Oct.-Apr.: Mon.-Sat. 10am–5pm; May-Sep: daily 9am–7pm*	▲ 212

KLOŠTAR		**TO 052 441 187**	**B** A3
MONASTERY OF ST MICHAEL		*Only the exterior can be visited*	▲ 165

KNIN	23400	**TO 022 664 822**	**C** C1
CHURCH OF ST SAVIOR		*Visits by appt (Tel. 021 827 460)*	▲ 206
FORTRESS		*Open daily 8am–5pm*	

KRAPINA	49000	**TO 049 371 330**	**A** A2
FRANCISCAN MONASTERY		*Visits by appt (Tel. 049 371 455)*	▲ 123
ARCHEOLOGICAL SITE AND MUSEUM Šetalište Vilibalda Sluge		*Open April-Oct.: daily 9am–5pm (3pm Nov-March)*	▲ 123

KRIŽEVCI	48260	**TO 048 681 199**	**A** B2
CHAPEL OF OUR LADY OF CARINTHIA		*Visits by appt (Tel. 048 711 210)*	▲ 131
CHAPEL OF ST FLORIAN		*Visits by appt (Tel. 048 711 210)*	▲ 131
CHURCH OF THE HOLY CROSS		*Visits by appt (Tel. 048 711 210)*	▲ 131
FRANCISCAN MONASTERY		*Visits by appt (Tel. 048 711 210)*	▲ 131

KUMROVEC	49295	**TO 049 502 044**	**A** A2
ECOMUSEUM Tel. 049 553 107		*Open May-Sep.: daily 9am–7pm (4pm Oct.-April)*	▲ 122

KUTJEVO	34340	**TO 034 255 107**	**A** D4
MANSION Zdenka Turkovića 2		*Visits by appt with the TO*	▲ 151

TH: town hall
TO: tourist office

MONASTERY **OF ST NICHOLAS OF REMETA**	*Visits by appt (Tel. 098 482 244)*		▲ 151
LABIN	52220	*TO 052 855 560*	B B3
MUSEUM Tel. 052 852 477	*Open daily 10am–1pm, 3–8pm (midnight Wed.-Thu. in June-Sept.)*		▲ 161
LEPOGLAVA	42250	*TO 042 791 090*	A A2
MONASTERY **AND CHURCH OF ST MARY** Trg Hrvatskoga Sveučilišta 3	*Visits by appt (Tel. 042 791 190)*		▲ 126
LINDAR	52000	*TO 052 622 460*	B B2
CHURCH OF ST CATHERINE	*Visits by appt (Tel. 052 640 006)*		▲ 161
FORTRESS	*Visits by appt (Tel. 052 640 006)*		▲ 161
LOVRAN	51415	*TO 051 291 740*	B B2
CHURCH OF ST GEORGE	*Open Mon., Wed. and Fri. 7–9pm*		▲ 177
LUDBREG	42230	*TO 042 810 690*	A B2
CHURCH OF THE HOLY TRINITY	*Open daily 7am–8pm*		▲ 131
LUKAVEC	10410	*TO 01 622 23 78*	A A3
CASTLE	*Visits by appt (Tel. 01 622 2378)*		▲ 133
LUŽNICA	10211	*TO 01 331 03 09*	A A3
CASTLE	*Visits by appt (Tel. 01 331 0118)*		▲ 120
MAKARSKA	21300	*TO 021 612 002*	C E3
CATHEDRAL OF ST MARK Kačićev trg 1	*Open daily 7–11am, 5–8pm*		▲ 226
FRANCISCAN CLOISTER Franjevački put 1	*Open daily 7–11am and by appt (Tel. 021 616 681)*		▲ 226
CHURCH OF ST PHILIP NERI Kralja Tomislava	*Visits by appt (Tel. 021 611 365)*		▲ 226
MARIJA BISTRICA	49246	*TO 049 468 380*	A A2
CHURCH OF ST MARY OF BISTRICA Ivana Pavla 2	*Open daily 7am–7pm*		▲ 119
MARUŠEVEC	42243	*TO 042 729 696*	A A2
CASTLE Tel. 042 759 312	*Visits by appt (Tel. 042 759 312)*		▲ 127
MEDVEDGRAD	10000	*TO 01 481 40 51*	A A2
FORTRESS	*Only the exterior can be visited*		▲ 117
METKOVIĆ	20350	*TO 020 681 899*	C F4
ORNITHOLOGICAL MUSEUM Stjepana Radića 4 Tel. 020 681 110	*Open Mon.–Fri. 8am–2pm*		▲ 227
MILJANA	49217	*TO 049 502 044*	A A2
CASTLE	*Only the exterior can be visited*		▲ 122
MOTOVUN	52424	*TO 052 617 480*	B A2
CHURCH OF ST STEPHEN	*Open daily 8am–8pm*		▲ 170
NAŠICE	34500	*TO 031 614 951*	A E3
CASTLE AND MUSEUM Pejačevićev trg 5 Tel. 034 313 414	*Open Mon.–Fri. 8am–1pm*		▲ 151
NIN	23232	*TO 023 265 247*	B D6
CHURCH OF ST AMBROSE	*Visits by appt (Tel. 023 264 162)*		▲ 197
CHURCH OF ST ANSELM	*Open daily 10am–noon and 6–8pm*		▲ 197
CHURCH OF ST NICHOLAS	*Visits by appt (Tel. 023 264 162)*		▲ 196
CHURCH OF THE HOLY CROSS	*Visits by appt (Tel. 023 264 162)*		▲ 197
NOVA GRADIŠKA	35400	*TO 035 361 494*	A C4
CHURCH OF ST TERESA	*Only the exterior can be visited*		▲ 152

◆ Addresses and opening times of places to visit

Towns and villages are listed alphabetically.
The symbol ▲ refers to the relevant Itinerary section.
A X0 are map coordinates and refer to the Map section at the end of this guide.

NOVI DVORI ZAPREŠIĆ	10211	*TO 01 331 63 09*	**A** A3
CASTLE AND MATIJA SKURJENI GALLERY Novi dvori Tel. 01 331 05 40	*Open Tue. and Thu. 9am–2pm, Wed. and Fri. 1–8pm, Sat. 9am–1pm and Sun. 9am–noon*		▲ 120

NOVIGRAD	52466	*TO 052 757 075*	**B** A2
CHURCH OF ST PELAGIUS	*Open daily 8am–8pm (entrance on the side)*		▲ 167
GALLERY OF MODERN ART Velika ulica 5 Tel. 052 757 790	*Open daily 6–9pm when there are exhibitions*		▲ 167

NUŠTAR	32100	*TO 032 344 034*	**A** F4
CASTLE	*Only the exterior can be visited*		▲ 149

OMIŠ	23310	*TO 021 861 350*	**C** D3
CHURCH OF ST MICHAEL	*Open daily 7am–8pm*		▲ 224
CHURCH OF ST PETER	*Visits by appt (Tel. 021 864 888)*		▲ 225
CHURCH OF ST ROCH	*Visits by appt (Tel. 021 861 264)*		▲ 225

OPATIJA	52428	*TO 051 271 310*	**B** B2
CHURCH OF ST HELEN 3 miles from Opatija toward Kastav	*Open daily 8am–noon*		▲ 176

OPEKA	42000	*TO 042 394 100*	**A** A1
CASTLE	*Damaged. Castle grounds open to the public*		▲ 127

OPRTALJ	52428	*TO 052 644 077*	**B** A2
CHURCH OF ST MARY	*Visits by appt (Tel. 052 644 200)*		▲ 170
CHURCH OF ST GEORGE	*Visits by appt (Tel. 052 644 200)*		▲ 170

OPUZEN	20355	*TO 020 681 899*	**C** F4
FORTIS OPUS FORTRESS	*Visits by appt through TO*		▲ 227
BRŠTANIK FORTRESS	*Visits by appt through TO*		▲ 227

OREBIĆ	20250	*TO 020 713 718*	**C** E4
FRANCISCAN MONASTERY	*Open daily 9am–noon and 4–6pm*		▲ 245
MARINE MUSEUM Trg Mimberi Tel. 020 713 009	*Closed for renovation*		▲ 245

OSIJEK	31000	*TO 031 203 755*	**A** F3
TOURIST OFFICE Županijska 2 Tel. 031 203 755	*Open Mon.–Sat. 7am–4pm*		
LIBRARY 24, avenue de l'Europe Tel. 031 211 218	*Open Mon.–Fri. 8am–7.30pm*		▲ 146
CHURCH OF ST JAMES MAJOR Kapucinska ulica 41	*Open daily 7am–noon and 5–7pm*		▲ 146
CHURCH OF ST MICHAEL Križanićev trg	*Open daily 7–11am and 5–8pm*		▲ 145
CHURCH OF ST PETER AND ST PAUL Trg Marina Držića	*Open daily 7am–noon and 5–7pm*		▲ 146
GALLERY OF FINE ARTS 9, avenue de l'Europe Tel. 031 213 587	*Open Mon.–Fri. 10am–6pm, Sat.–Sun. 10am–1pm*		▲ 146
MUSEUM OF SLAVONIA Trg Svetog trojstva 6 Tel. 031 208 501	*Open Tue–Sun 10am–1pm*		▲ 145

PAKRAC	34550	*TO 034 411 133*	**A** C4
CHURCH OF THE HOLY TRINITY	*Badly damaged. Only the exterior can be visited*		▲ 152
CHURCH OF OUR LADY OF THE ASSUMPTION	*Open daily during office hours*		▲ 152
BARON VON TRENK'S PALACE	*Undergoing restoration. Only the exterior can be visited*		▲ 152
COUNT JANKOVIĆ'S PALACE	*School. Only the exterior can be visited*		▲ 152
BISHOP'S PALACE	*Damaged. Only the exterior can be visited*		▲ 152

PAZIN	52000	TO 052 622 460	B B2
CASTLE AND ETHNOGRAPHIC MUSEUM Trg istarskog razvoda 1 Tel. 052 625 040	Open Tue.–Fri. 10am–6pm		▲ 162
CHURCH OF ST NICHOLAS	Open daily 8am–8pm		▲ 162
PEROJ	52215	TO 052 511 700	B A3
BASILICA OF ST FOŠKA	Open Sun. 2–6pm and by appt (Tel. 052 511 420)		▲ 164
PETRINJA	44250	TO 044 815 431	A B4
GAVRILOVIC PORK BUTCHER'S Duga ulica 59	Open to customers only		▲ 135
PIČAN	52332	TO 052 855 199	B B3
CHURCH OF THE ANNUNCIATION	Only the exterior can be visited		▲ 161
PISAROVINA	10424	TO 016 291 616	B F1
OPEN-AIR MUSEUM	Only the exterior can be visited		▲ 136
POREČ	52440	TO 052 451 293	B A2
EUPHRASIAN BASILICA	Open daily 7am–7pm		▲ 166
POŽEGA	34000	TO 034 274 900	A D4
CHURCH OF ST THERESA OF AVILA	Visits by appt (Tel. 034 274 321)		▲ 151
MONASTERY OF ST MICHAEL OF RUDINA	Only the exterior can be visited		▲ 151
MUSEUM OF POŽEGA Matice Hrvatska 6 Tel. 034 272 130	Open Mon.–Fri. 8am–3pm		▲ 151
PRIDVORJE	20271	TO 020 479 025	C C6
FRANCISCAN MONASTERY	Open daily 8am–7pm		▲ 249
PULA	52100	TO 052 212 987	J
TOURIST OFFICE Tel. 052 219 197	Open Mon.–Sat. 8am–4pm		J A2
AMPHITHEATER	Open daily Oct.-Apr.: 9am–5pm; May–Sept.: 8am–9pm		▲ 159 J C1
CATHEDRAL Trg sv. Tome 2	Open June-Sep: daily 10am–7pm		▲ 158 J B1
CHAPEL OF ST MARY Flaciusova ulica	Only the exterior can be visited		▲ 158 J A3
FRANCISCAN MONASTERY Ulica sv. Franje	Open daily 10am–1pm, 4–7pm		▲ 158 J A-B2
CHURCH OF ST NICHOLAS	Only the exterior can be visited		▲ 158 J B2
ARCHEOLOGY MUSEUM Carratina 3	Open May-Sep: Mon.–Fri. 9am–8pm, Sun. 10am–3pm.		▲ 157 J B-C2
MUSEUM OF ISTRIAN HISTORY Gradski uspon 6	Oct-April: Mon.–Fri. 9am–2pm Open daily 9am–7pm		▲ 158 J B2
RAKALJ	55208	TO 052 571 098	B B3
CHURCH OF ST GEORGE THE ELDER	Visits by appt (Tel. 052 571 098)		▲ 160
RIJEKA	51000	TO 051 213 145	G
TOURIST OFFICE Korzo 13 Tel. 052 335 882	Open Mon.–Sat. 8am–4pm		G B2
CATHEDRAL OF THE ASSUMPTION Frankopanski trg 12	Open daily 7am–7pm		▲ 175 G C2
CHURCH OF ST VITUS	Open daily 7am–noon and 4–8pm		▲ 175 G B2
CHURCH OF ST NICHOLAS	Open daily 7am–noon and 4–8pm		▲ 174 G B3
MODERN ART GALLERY Dolac 1/II Tel. 051 334 280	Open Tue.–Sat. 10am–1pm and 5–8pm		▲ 175 G A2
HISTORY AND MARITIME MUSEUM Muzejski trg 1 Tel. 051 335 772	Open Mon.–Fri. 9am–2pm and 5–8pm, Sat. 9am–1pm		▲ 175 G A-B2

◆ Addresses and opening times of places to visit

Towns and villages are listed alphabetically.
The symbol ▲ refers to the relevant Itinerary section.
A X0 are map coordinates and refer to the Map section at the end of this guide.

NATURAL HISTORY MUSEUM Lorenzov prolaz 21 Tel. 051 213 145	Open Mon.–Sat. 9am–7pm	**G** B1
NATIONAL THEATER Verdijeva	Open during performances	▲ 174 **G** C3

ROČ	**52425**	**TO 052 662 343**	**B** B2
CHURCH OF ST ANTHONY	Visits by appt (Tel. 052 666 462)		▲ 170

SOLIN	**21210**	**TO 021 210 048**	**C** D3
ARCHEOLOGICAL SITE OF SALONA	Open daily 7am–7pm		▲ 210

SAMOBOR	**10430**	**TO 013 366 714**	**A** A3
CHURCH OF ST ANASTASIA Ulica sv. Ane	Visits by appt (Tel. 013 363 861)		▲ 136
CHURCH OF ST MARY Milana langa 18	Visits by appt (Tel. 013 360 010)		▲ 136

SELA	**44273**	**TO 044 522 655**	**A** B3
CHURCH OF ST MARY MAGDALEN	Open daily 8am–7pm		▲ 134

SENJ	**53270**	**TO 053 881 068**	**B** D3
CATHEDRAL ST MARY	Open daily 8am–7pm		▲ 185
CHURCH OF ST MARY	Visits by appt (Tel. 053 881 043)		▲ 185
TOWN MUSEUM Ogrizovićeva 7 Tel. 052 881 141	Open Mon.–Fri. 7am–3pm and 6–8pm; Sat. 7am–noon		▲ 185

SINJ	**21230**	**TO 021 826 352**	**C** D2
FRANCISCAN CLOISTER	Open daily 8am–noon and 4–8pm		▲ 212

SISAK	**44000**	**TO 044 522 655**	**A** B3-4
CHURCH OF THE HOLY CROSS Trg ban J. Jelačića	Open daily 8am–7pm		▲ 134
FORTRESS Brkljača Erdelija	Undergoing restoration; only the exterior can be visited		▲ 134

SLANO	**20232**	**TO 020 871 236**	**C** A5
FRANCISCAN MONASTERY	Open daily 8am–6pm		▲ 244

SLAVONSKI BROD	**35000**	**TO 035 447 721**	**A** D-E4
FRANCISCAN MONASTERY Trg sv. Trojstva	Open daily 8am–6pm		▲ 150

SOŠICE	**10457**	**TO 01 336 00 44**	
CHURCH OF ST PETER AND ST PAUL	Visits by appt (Tel. 013 387 600)		▲ 136

SPLIT	**21000**	**TO 021 348 600**	**E**
TOURIST OFFICE Peristyle Tel. 021 348 600	Open Mon.–Sat. 8am–2pm		**E** B2
CATHEDRAL	Open daily 8am–8pm		▲ 215 **E** B2
BAPTISTERY OF ST JOHN In Diocletian's Palace	Open daily 8am–8pm		▲ 218 **E** B2
FRANCISCAN MONASTERY Trg Franja Tudmana 1	Open daily 7am–7pm		▲ 220
CHURCH OF OUR LADY OF GRACE IN POLJUD Topuska 4	Visits by appt (Tel. 021 301 377)		▲ 220
CHURCH OF ST NICHOLAS Čopova ulica	Visits by appt (Tel. 021 394 636)		▲ 221
FORTRESS	Only the exterior can be visited		▲ 220
NATIONAL ART GALLERY Lovretska ulica 11 Tel. 021 480 149	Open Tue.–Sat. 9am–noon and 5–7pm		▲ 220
MEŠTROVIĆ GALLERY Šetalište I. Meštrovića 46 Tel. 021 340 800	Open Tue.–Sat. 9am–4pm, Sun. 10am–3pm		▲ 222
DOMINICAN MONASTERY Hrvojeva 2	Visits by appt (Tel. 021 341 378)		▲ 219 **E** C3

TH: town hall
TO: tourist office

ARCHEOLOGICAL MUSEUM Zrinsko Frankopanska 25 Tel. 021 318 714	*Open Tue.–Sat. 9am–2pm, Sun. 10am–1pm*	▲ 220
TOWN MUSEUM Papalićeva 1 - Tel. 021 344 917	*Open Tue.–Fri. 9am–4pm and Sat.–Sun. 10am–noon*	▲ 218 **E** C1-2
MUSEUM OF CROATIAN ARCHEOLOGICAL MONUMENTS Meštrovićeva šetalište 18 Tel. 021 358 455	*Open Mon.–Fri. 9am–4pm, Sat–Sun. 10am–1pm*	▲ 219
AUGUBIO PALACE *In Diocletian's Palace*	*Only the exterior can be visited*	▲ 218 **E** B2
ĆINDRO PALACE *In Diocletian's Palace*	*Only the exterior can be visited*	▲ 219 **E** B1-2
DIOCLETIAN'S PALACE	*Tour of the Subterranean Halls 8am–9pm*	▲ 216 **E** A-C1-3
STON	**20230** **TO** *020 754 452*	**C** A5
FRANCISCAN MONASTERY, CHURCH AND BISHOP'S PALACE	*Visits by appt (Tel. 020 754 474)*	▲ 245
STUBIČKI GOLUBOVEC	**49240** **TO** *049 286 463*	**A** A2
CASTLE	*Visit Mon.–Fri. 9am–4pm*	▲ 118
STUBIČKE TOPLICE	**49244** **TO** *049 282 727*	
BATHS AND SPA	*Open daily 8am–8pm*	▲ 117
SVETI VINČENAT	**52343**	**B** A3
ABBEY CHURCH OF ST VINCENT	*Visits by appt (Tel. 052 560 004)*	▲ 163
SVETI LOVREČ	**52448** **TO** *052 448 195*	**B** A3
CHURCH OF ST MARTIN	*Visits by appt (Tel. 052 448 172)*	▲ 165
LAPIDARY MUSEUM	*Free entry*	▲ 165
ŠIBENIK	**22000** **TO** *022 212 075*	**I**
TOURIST OFFICE Fausta Vrančića 18	*Open Mon.–Sat. 8am–8pm*	**I** B2
FORT ST ANNE Trg Republike Hrvatske	*Open daily 9am–7pm*	▲ 202 **I** A2
CITADEL ST ANNE	*Only the exterior can be visited*	▲ 203 **I** A1
CHURCH OF ST FRANCIS Trg Nikole Tomazzea 1	*Open daily 8am–7pm*	▲ 203 **I** B3
CHURCH OF ST NICHOLAS	*Open daily 10am–noon*	▲ 203 **I** A3
TOWN LOGGIA Trg Republike Hrvatske	*Only the exterior can be visited*	▲ 203 **I** A2
TOWN MUSEUM Gradska vrata 3 Tel. 022 213 880	*Open daily 10am–1pm and 7–10pm*	▲ 203 **I** A2
BISHOP'S PALACE	*Only the exterior can be visited*	▲ 203 **I** A2
TRAKOŠĆAN	**42254** **TO** *042 210 987*	**A** A2
CASTLE Tel. 042 796 281	*Open June–Sep: daily 9am–6pm* *Oct.–May: daily 9am–3pm*	▲ 126
TROGIR	**21220** **TO** *021 881 412*	**C** C3
CATHEDRAL OF ST LAWRENCE Trg Ivana Pavla II	*Open daily 9am–7pm*	▲ 207
CHAPEL OF ST JOHN OF TROGIR	*Open daily 9am–7pm*	▲ 208
CHURCH OF ST JOHN THE BAPTIST	*Open Mon.–Fri. 9.30am–1.30pm, 4–6pm*	▲ 208
MONASTERY OF ST NICHOLAS	*Open Mon.–Fri. 10am–noon*	▲ 209
TRSAT	**51000** **TO** *051 213 145*	**B** C2
CASTLE Tel. 051 217 714	*Open daily 9am–5pm*	▲ 176
TRŠKI VRH	**49230** **TO** *049 371 330*	**A** A2
CHURCH	*Visits by appt (Tel. 049 371 456)*	▲ 124

◆ Addresses and opening times of places to visit

Towns and villages are listed alphabetically.
The symbol ▲ refers to the relevant Itinerary section.
A X0 are map coordinates and refer to the Map section at the end of this guide.

VALPOVO	31500	TO 031 656 200	A E3
BIZOVAČKE TOPLICE Sunčana 39	Thermal spa open to the public (Tel. 031 585 100)		▲ 147
CASTLE	Open Mon.–Fri. 8am–2pm and by appt (Tel. 031 650 490)		▲ 147
VALPOVO MUSEUM	Undergoing restoration		▲ 147

VARAŽDIN	42000	TO 042 210 987	A B1-2
TOURIST OFFICE Ivana Padovca 3	Open Mon.–Fri. 8am–4pm,		
CHURCH OF THE ASSUMPTION	Open daily 7am–noon and 4–7.30pm		▲ 128
CHURCH OF THE HOLY TRINITY	Open daily 6am–noon and 5.30–7pm		▲ 129
CHURCH OF ST FLORIAN Vladimira Nazora	Open Sun. 8am–noon		▲ 127
CHURCH OF ST JOHN THE BAPTIST Franjevački trg	Open daily 6.30am–noon, 7–8pm and by appt (Tel. 042 213 167)		▲ 128
CHURCH OF ST NICHOLAS Trg slobode 11	Open during services Mon.–Fri. 6pm, Sun 10am		▲ 129
TOWN HALL Aleja Kralja Zvonimira 1	Open to the public		▲ 128
RITZ HOUSE	Open to the public		▲ 128
URSULINE CONVENT Uršulinska 3	Open daily 7am–7.30pm and by appt (Tel. 042 211 808)		▲ 129
TOWN MUSEUM Strossmayerovo šetalište 7 Tel. 042 210 399	Open Tue.–Fri. 10am–3pm and Sat.–Sun. 10am–1pm		▲ 128
PALACE OF THE COUNTS OF VARAŽDIN	Only the exterior can be visited		▲ 128
DRAŠKOVIĆ PALACE Trg Kralja Tomislava 3	Only the exterior can be visited		
ERDÖDY PALACE Tel. 042 213 123	Conservatory of Music		▲ 129
HERTZER PALACE – MUSEUM Franjevački trg 6 Tel. 042 210 474	Open June-Sep: Tue.–Fri. 10am–5pm, Sat.–Sun. 10am–1pm; Oct.–May: Tue.–Fri. 10am–3pm		▲ 129
KLEGEVIĆ PALACE Vladimira Nazora	Croatian Academy of Sciences and Arts		▲ 127
PATAČIĆ PALACE Franjevački trg 5	Only the exterior can be visited		▲ 128
SERMAGE PALACE – MUSEUM Stančićev trg 3 Tel. 042 214 172	Open Tue.–Fri. 10am–3pm and Sat.–Sun. 10am–1pm		▲ 128
ZAKMARDI PALACE J. Habdalića 4	Houses a restaurant		▲ 128
THEATER Auusta Cesarca 1	Open during performances		▲ 129
VARAŽDINSKE TOPLICE Trg slobode 16 Tel. 042 633 133	Spa open to the public		▲ 128

VELIKA GORICA	10410	TO 01 622 16 66	A A3
TUROPOLJE MUSEUM Trg Kralja Tomislava 1 Tel. 01 622 13 23	Open Tue.–Fri. 10am–6pm and Sat.–Sun. 10am–1pm		▲ 133

VELIKI TABOR		TO 049 343 052	A A2
CASTLE	Open daily May-Sep: 10am–6pm (3pm Oct.–April)		▲ 122

VINAGORA	49219	TO 049 377 050	A A2
ST MARY OF THE VISITATION	Open daily 7am–8pm		▲ 123

VINKOVCI	30210	TO 032 334 653	A F4
CHURCH OF ST EUSEBIUS	Open to the public		▲ 148
TOWN MUSEUM Tel. 032 332 504	Open Tue.–Fri. 10am–1pm and 5–7pm and Sat.–Sun. 10am–1pm		▲ 148

VIROTIVICA	33000	TO 033 726 069	A C3
CHURCH OF ST ROCH	Open daily 8am–noon and 5–7pm		▲ 151
TOWN MUSEUM Trg Bana Jelačića Tel. 033 722 127	Open Mon., Wed. and Fri. 9am–2pm; Tue. and Thu. 9am–7pm and Sat. 9am–noon		▲ 151

TH: town hall
TO: tourist office

VIŠNJAN	TO 052 451 293	B A2
PARISH CHURCH	Only the exterior can be visited	▲ 167
VODNJAN	52515 TO 052 511 672	B A3
CHURCH OF ST BLAISE	Open daily 9am–7pm	▲ 163
VRSAR	52450 TO 052 441 187	B A3
CHURCH OF ST MARY	Open daily 11am–1pm and 6–9pm	▲ 165
VUKOVAR	32100 TO 032 442 889	A F4
FRANCISCAN MONASTERY	Open daily 10am–noon and 3–5pm	▲ 149
CHURCH OF ST NICHOLAS	Visits by appt (Tel. 032 441 662)	▲ 149
CHURCH OF ST PHILIP AND ST JAMES	Open daily 5.30pm–7 and by appt (Tel. 032 441 381)	▲ 149
TOWN MUSEUM ve Lole Ribara 2	Open Mon.–Sat. 9am–3pm and by appt (Tel. 032 441 270)	▲ 149
ZADAR	23000 TO 023 315 316	H
TOURIST OFFICE Smiljanića, 5 Tel. 023 212 222	Open Mon.–Sat. 8am–4pm	H C2
CATHEDRAL OF ST ANASTASIA Trg Sv. Stošije 1	Open daily at 6pm	▲ 193 H B2
CHURCH OF ST CHRYSOGONUS Ulica Brne Krautiža	Open only for concerts	▲ 194 H B1-2
CHURCH OF ST DONAT Forum	Open daily 9am–1pm and 5–7.30pm	▲ 193 H B2
CHURCH OF ST FRANCIS Trg Sv. Frane 1	Open daily 8am–noon and 5–6pm	▲ 194 H A1
CHURCH OF ST SIMEON Trg Šime Budinića	Open daily at 8am and 6pm	▲ 194 H C2
PERMANENT EXHIBITION OF CHURCH ART Trg Opatice ćike, 1 Tel. 023 211 545	Open daily 10am–1pm and 6–8pm	▲ 194 H B2
FACULTY OF LETTERS AND SOCIAL SCIENCES Obala kralja Petra Krešimira IV. 2	Only the exterior can be visited	▲ 195
ARCHEOLOGICAL MUSEUM Trg Opatice ćike Tel. 023 212 447	Open Mon.–Fri. 9am–1pm and 5.30–7.30pm	▲ 192 H B2
BISHOP'S PALACE	Closed to the public	▲ 192 H B2
ZAGREB	10000 TO 01 489 85 55	D
TOURIST OFFICE Kaptol 5 Tel. 01 489 85 55	Open Mon.–Fri. 8am–4pm	D D3
NATIONAL TOURIST OFFICE blerov trg 10, Importanne Galleria Tel. 01 455 64 55 Fax 01 455 78 57	Open Mon.–Fri. 8.30am–8pm, Sat. 10am–6pm and Sun. 10am–2pm	DC4
CROATIAN ACADEMY OF SCIENCES AND ARTS Trg N. Šubića Zrinskoga 11 Tel. 01 456 90 83	Open Mon.–Fri. 8am–4pm	▲ 112 D D5
MEŠTROVIĆ ATELIER Mletačka 8	Open Tue.–Fri. 9am–2pm and Sat. 10am–6pm	▲ 105 D B2
CROATIAN STATE ARCHIVES Marulićev trg 21 Tel. 01 480 19 99	Open Mon.–Fri. 8am–4pm	▲ 113 D A-B6
NATIONAL LIBRARY Hrvatske bratske zajednice Tel. 01 616 41 11	Open Mon.–Fri. 8am–9pm and Sat. 8am–3pm	▲ 115
CATHEDRAL Kaptol	Open daily 9.30am–3pm	▲ 108 D D3
FRANCISCAN MONASTERY andriževa 21	Open Mon.–Sat. 8am–6pm and Sun. during services (7am, 10am, 11.30am and 6pm)	▲ 110 D C2
MIROGOJ CEMETERY Mirogoj 10	Open daily 8am–7pm	▲ 115

◆ Addresses and opening times of places to visit

Towns and villages are listed alphabetically.
The symbol ▲ refers to the relevant Itinerary section.
A X0 are map coordinates and refer to the Map section at the end of this guide.

CHURCH OF ST BLAISE Prilaz Đure Deželića 64	*Open daily 7–8.45am and 6.30–7.15pm*	▲ 114
CHURCH OF ST MARK Trg sv. Marka	*Open daily 7am–7pm*	▲ 103 **D** B2
CHURCH OF ST CATHERINE Katarinin trg	*Open daily 7am–8pm*	▲ 104 **D** C3
CHURCH OF ST MARY Dolac 2	*Open daily 8am–11am*	▲ 110 **D** C3
MODERN ART GALLERY Hebrangova 1 Tel. 01 492 23 68	*Undergoing restoration*	▲ 113 **D** C5
STROSSMAYER GALLERY Trg Nikola Šubića Zrinskoga 11 Tel. 01 489 51 17	*Open Tue. 10am–1pm and 5–7pm,* *Wed.–Sun. 10am–1pm*	▲ 112 **D** D5
BOTANICAL GARDENS Marulićev trg 9a	*Open Tue.–Sun. 9am–7pm*	▲ 113 **D** B6
ARCHEOLOGICAL MUSEUM Trg N. Šubića Zrinskoga 19 Tel. 01 487 31 01	*Open Tue.–Fri. 10am–6pm and Sat.–Sun. 10am–1pm*	▲ 112 **D** C4
MUSEUM OF MODERN ART Katarinin trg 2 Tel. 01 485 18 08	*Open Tue.–Sat. 11am–7pm and Sun. 10am–1pm*	▲ 104 **D** B3
MUSEUM OF NAÏVE ART Ćirilometodska 3 Tel. et fax 014 851 911	*Open Tue.–Fri. 10am–6pm and Sat.–Sun. 10am–1pm*	▲ 104 **D** B2-3
CROATIAN SCULPTURE MUSEUM Medvedgradska 2 Tel. 01 466 70 05	*Open Mon.–Fri. 11am–7pm and Sat.–Sun.10am–2pm*	▲ 115
ZAGREB TOWN MUSEUM Opatička 20 Tel. 01 485 13 64	*Open Tue.–Fri. 10am–5pm and Sat.–Sun. 10am–1pm*	▲ 106 **D** C1
MUSEUM OF ARTS AND CRAFTS Trg maršala Tita 10 Tel. 01 482 80 86	*Open Tue.–Fri. 10am–6pm and Sat.–Sun. 10am–1pm*	▲ 114 **D** A4-5
NATURAL HISTORY MUSEUM Demetrova 1 Tel. 01 485 17 00	*Open Tue.–Fri. 10am–5pm and Sat.–Sun. 10am–1pm*	▲ 105 **D** B2
CROATIAN HISTORICAL MUSEUM Matoševa 9 Tel. 01 485 19 90	*Open Tue.–Thu. 9am–1pm and 5–7pm and* *Fri.–Sun. 9am–1pm*	▲ 105 **D** B2
ETHNOGRAPHIC MUSEUM Mažuranićev trg 14 Tel. 01 455 85 44	*Open Tue.–Thu. 10am–6pm and Fri.–Sun. 10am–1pm*	▲ 113 **D** A5
MIMARA MUSEUM Rooseveltov trg 5 Tel. 01 482 81 00	*Open Tue.–Wed. and Fri.–Sat. 10am–5pm,* *Thu. 10am–7pm and Sun. 10am–2pm*	▲ 113 **D** A5
ZOO Maksimirski perivoj	*Open Apr.-Oct.: daily 9am–8pm and* *Nov.-March: daily 9am–4pm*	▲ 115
ART PAVILION Trg kralja Tomislava 22 Tel. 01 484 10 70	*Open Mon.–Sat. 11am–7pm and Sun. 10am–1pm*	▲ 112 **D** D6
NATIONAL THEATER Trg maršala Tita 15	*Open during performances (which start around* *7.30pm)*	▲ 113 **D** A-B5

ZAOSTROG	21334	**TH 021 629 050**	**C** E4

FRANCISCAN CLOISTER	*Open daily 9am–noon and 4–8pm*	▲ 226
CHURCH OF ST MARGARET	*Open to the public*	▲ 226

ŽMINJ	52341	**TH 052 825 003**	**B** A3

CHAPEL OF ST ANTHONY	*Visits by appt (Tel. 052 846 318)*	▲ 163
CHAPEL OF THE HOLY TRINITY	*Visits daily 8am–6pm*	▲ 163

THE ISLANDS

BRAČ ISLAND	21240	**TO 021 490 032**	**C** C-D3

MONASTERY (BLACA)	*Visits Tue–Sun 9am–6pm*	▲ 229
GALLERY OF MODERN ART (BOL)	*Open Mon.–Sat. 6–10pm*	▲ 229
CHURCH OF ST HELEN (ŠKRIP)	*Open 15 June–15 Sep: daily 9am–noon and 5–9pm*	▲ 228

TH: town hall
TO: tourist office

CHURCH OF ST MARY (NEREŽIŠĆA)	Visits by appt ((Tel. 021 637 147)		▲ 229
CHURCH OF ST PETER (NEREŽIŠĆA)	Visits by appt (Tel. 021 637 147)		▲ 229
KAŠTEL RADOJKOVIĆ AND MUSEUM (ŠKRIP) Tel. 021 646 325	Open 15 June–15 Sep: daily 9am–noon and 5–9pm		▲ 228
ČIOVO ISLAND	**21224**	**TO 021 887 311**	**C** C3
MONASTERY OF THE HOLY CROSS (ARBANIJA)	Visits by appt (Tel. 021 881 412)		
MONASTERY OF ST ANTHONY (ČIOVO)	Visits by appt (Tel. 021 881 412)		
CHURCH OF ST MARY (PRIZIDNICA)	Visits by appt (Tel. 021 881 412)		
CRES ISLAND	**51557**	**TO 051 571 535**	**B** B-C3-55
CHURCH OF ST ISIDORE (CRES)	Only the exterior can be visited		▲ 180
CHURCH OF ST MARY OF THE SNOW (CRES)	Open during services Mon.–Sat. 8am and 6pm		▲ 180
CATHEDRAL (OSOR)	Visits by appt (Tel. 051 237 112)		▲ 180
CHURCH (VALUN)	Open during services Sun. 11am		▲ 180
DUGI OTOK ISLAND	**23281**	**TO 023 377 094**	**B** D6
CHURCH OF ST MARY (SALI)	Open July-Aug. daily 8am–7pm		▲ 198
CHURCH OF ST PEREGRINE (SAVAR)	Visits by appt (Tel. 023 377 181)		▲ 198
CHURCH OF ST MICHAEL (ZAGLAV)	Visits by appt (Tel. 023 378 700)		▲ 198
HVAR ISLAND	**21450**	**TO 021 741 059**	**C** D-E4
CATHEDRAL OF ST STEPHEN (HVAR)	Open daily 8–9am and 7–8pm		▲ 230
CHURCH OF SS COSMAS AND DAMIAN (HVAR)	Open daily 8–9am and 7–8pm		▲ 230
THEATER (HVAR)	Open during performances 9.30am–1pm and 5–9pm		▲ 231
KASTEL TVRDALJ (STARI GRAD)	Open to the public: June 15-Sep 15: 10am–1pm and 5–9pm		▲ 231
DOMINICAN MONASTERY (STARI GRAD)	Open June-Sep: 10am–1pm and 5–9pm		▲ 231
NAUTICAL AND ARCHAEOLOGICAL MUSEUM (STARI GRAD)	Open June-Sep: 9am–noon and 7–10pm		▲ 231
CHURCH OF ST MARY (VRBOSKA)	Open daily 10am–noon and 7–9pm		▲ 231
CHURCH OF ST LAWRENCE (VRBOSKA)	Open daily 10am–noon and 7–9pm		▲ 231
Ž ISLAND	**23284**	**TO 023 88 491**	**C** A1
ROTUNDA CHURCH OF ST MARY	Visits by appt (Tel. 023 88 491)		▲ 198
KOLOČEP ISLAND	**20221**	**TH 020 757 025**	**C** C6
CHAPEL OF ST ANTHONY OF PADUA	Visits by appt (Tel. 020 757 000)		▲ 242
CHAPEL OF ST ANTHONY OF THE DESERT	Visits by appt (Tel. 020 757 000)		▲ 242
CHAPEL OF ST NICHOLAS	Visits by appt (Tel. 020 757 000)		▲ 242
CHAPEL OF THE HOLY TRINITY	Visits by appt (Tel. 020 757 000)		▲ 242
KORČULA ISLAND	**20260**	**TO 020 715 867**	**C** D-E4-5
CHURCH OF OUR LADY OF THE FIELDS (ČARA)	Visits by appt (Tel. 020 831 044)		▲ 247
CATHEDRAL OF ST MARK (KORČULA)	Open daily 8am–noon and 4–7pm		▲ 247
CHAPEL OF ST ROCH (KORČULA)	Open daily 8am–noon and 4–7pm		▲ 247
ALL SAINTS' CHURCH (KORČULA)	Open daily 10am–1pm and 5–7pm		▲ 247
CHURCH OF ST MICHAEL (KORČULA)	Open daily 9am–1pm and 5–7pm		▲ 246
TOWN MUSEUM (KORČULA) Tel. 020 711 420	Open daily 9am–1pm and 5–7pm (9am–9pm in July-Aug)		▲ 247
KRK ISLAND			
CHURCH OF ST STEPHEN (DOBRINJ)	Visits by appt (Tel. 051 852 107)		▲ 182
CATHEDRAL (KRK)	Open daily 9am–1pm and 6–8pm		▲ 183
CHAPEL OF ST DUNAT (KRK)	Only the exterior can be visited		▲ 183
BISHOP'S PALACE (KRK)	Closed to the public		▲ 183
CHURCH AND MONASTERY (GLAVOTOK)	Visits by appt (Tel. 051 862 102)		▲ 183
CHURCH OF ST LUCY (JURANDVOR)	Open daily 10am–2pm and 5–8pm		▲ 183
CHURCH OF THE ASSUMPTION (OMIŠALJ)	Open daily 8am–8pm		▲ 182
CHURCH OF ST MARY (VRBNIK)	Open daily 8am–8pm		▲ 183

◆ The islands

LASTOVO ISLAND	20290	TO 020 801 018	C E5
CHURCH OF OUR LADY OF THE FIELDS	Open by request (Tel. 020 801 043)		▲ 252
CHURCH OF ST BLAISE	Open by request (Tel. 020 801 043)		▲ 252
CHURCH OF SS COSMAS AND DAMIAN	Open Mon.–Sat. 7–8pm and Sun 10am–noon		▲ 252
CHURCH OF ST LUKE	Open by request (Tel. 020 801 043)		▲ 252
FORTRESS	Only the exterior can be visited		▲ 252
LOKRUM ISLAND	20000	TO 020 323 887	C B6
BENEDICTINE MONASTERY	Closed to the public		▲ 248
LOPUD ISLAND	20222	TO 020 759 038	C B5
DOMINICAN MONASTERY	Open daily 8am–7pm and by appt (Tel. 020 759 038)		▲ 242
FRANCISCAN MONASTERY	Open daily 8am–7pm and by appt (Tel. 020 759 038)		
CHURCH OF ST MARY	Visits by appt (Tel. 020 759 038)		
LOŠINJ ISLAND	51550	TO 051 231 547	B C4-5
CHURCH OF THE NATIVITY (MALI LOŠINJ)	Open daily 8am–8pm		▲ 181
CHURCH OF ST MARTIN (MALI LOŠINJ)	Visits by appt (Tel. 051 231 731)		▲ 181
CHURCH OF ST ANTHONY (VELI LOŠINJ)	Visits by appt (Tel. 051 236 247)		▲ 181
MLJET ISLAND	20225	TO 020 744 086	C A5-F5
CHAPEL OF ST GEORGE (B. POLJE)	Only the exterior can be visited		▲ 250
CHAPEL OF ST PANCRAS (B. POLJE)	Only the exterior can be visited		▲ 250
CONVENT OF ST MARY (B. POLJE)	Open daily 9am–6pm		▲ 250
CHURCH OF ST MARY OF THE MOUNT	Open daily 9am–6pm		▲ 250
CHURCH OF THE HOLY TRINITY (B. POLJE)	Visits by appt (Tel. 020 745 200)		▲ 250
RECTOR'S PALACE (BABINO POLJE)	Only the exterior can be visited		▲ 250
PAG ISLAND	23250	TO 023 611 301	B D5
COLLEGIATE CHURCH OF ST MARY	Open to the public		▲ 188
CHURCH OF ST MARGARET	Open to the public		
ARCHEOLOGICAL SITE OF CASKA	Not open to the public		▲ 188
PAŠMAN ISLAND	23262	TO 023 260 155	C A1
FRANCISCAN MONASTERY (KRAJ)	Open Mon.–Fri. 4–7pm		▲ 198
BENEDICTINE MONASTERY (TKON)	Open Mon.–Sat. 4–6pm		▲ 198
RAB ISLAND	51280	TO 051 724 064	B C4
ABBEY CHURCH OF ST PETER	Visits by appt (Tel. 051 776 112)		▲ 184
CATHEDRAL OF ST MARY THE GREAT	Open daily 10am–noon and 7–9pm		▲ 184
BENEDICTINE MONASTERY	Open daily 7.30–8am		▲ 184
CHURCH OF ST JOHN	Open daily 8am–8pm		▲ 184
FRANCISCAN CONVENT OF ST EUPHEMIA	Open July-Aug.: 10am–noon and 7–9pm, the rest of the year by appt (Tel. 051 724 195)		▲ 184
ŠIPAN ISLAND		TO 020 758 084	C A5
CHAPEL ST JOHN (ŠILOVO SELO)	Visits by appt (Tel. 020 758 015)		▲ 243
CHURCH OF THE HOLY SPIRIT (PAKLJENO)	Visits by appt (Tel. 020 758 015)		▲ 243
RECTOR'S PALACE (ŠIPANSKA LUKA)	Only the exterior can be visited		▲ 243
UGLJAN ISLAND		TO 023 288 011	C A1
PALEOCHRISTIAN BASILICA (MULINE)	Ruins		▲ 198
FORTRESS OF ST MICHAEL (UGLJAN)	Ruins		▲ 198
MONASTERY OF ST JEROME (UGLJAN)	Visits by appt (Tel. 023 288 091)		▲ 198
VIS ISLAND	21480	TO 021 717 017	C C4
FRANCISCAN MONASTERY (LUKA)	Visits by appt (Tel. 021 711 146)		▲ 232
CHURCH OF OUR LADY OF THE PIRATES	Visits by appt (Tel. 021 713 219)		▲ 232
CHURCH OF OUR LADY OF SPILICA	Visits by appt (Tel. 021 711 146)		▲ 232
CHURCH OF ST CYPRIAN (KUTA)	Visits by appt (Tel. 021 711 146)		▲ 232
CHURCH OF THE HOLY SPIRIT (LUKA)	Visits by appt (Tel. 021 711 146)		▲ 232
CHURCH OF ST MICHAEL	Visits by appt (Tel. 021 713 219)		▲ 232
GARIBOLDI PALACE	Only the exterior can be visited		▲ 232
VRGADA ISLAND		TO 021 539 14 81	C A-B2
CHURCH OF ST ANDREW	Visits by appt (Tel. 023 371 052)		▲ 198

GENERAL

◆ *A Concise atlas of the Republic of Croatia and of the Republic of Bosnia and Hercegovina,* The Miroslav Krleža Lexicographical Institute, Zagreb, 1993

◆ *Croatia Tourist Guide,* The Miroslav Krleža Lexicographical Institute Masmedia, Zagreb, 1998

◆ *Croatian Coast Insight Fleximap,* Insight Fleximaps, 2000

◆ *The Natural Heritage of Croatia,* Buvina Ltd., Zagreb, 1995-1996

◆ BOUSFIELD, JONATHAN *Rough Guide to Croatia,* Rough Guides, 2003

◆ SCHEIN, MOSHE *Travels in Undiscovered Country,* University of Alberta Press, 2003

HISTORY AND LANGUAGE

◆ ALMOND, MARK *Europe's Backyard War,* William Heinemann, London, 1994

◆ AUTY, PHYLLIS *Tito,* Viking Press, 1970

◆ BANAC I. *The National Question in Yugoslavia : Origins, History, Politics,* Cornell University Press, Ithaca, New York, 1984

◆ BENNETT, CHRISTOPHER *Yugoslavia's Bloody Collapse: Causes, Course and Consequences,* New York University Press, 1996

◆ BRACEWELL, CATHERINE WENDY *The Uskoks of Senj: Piracy, Banditry and Holy War in the 16th-century Adriatic,* Cornell University Press, 1992

◆ DRAKULIČ, SLAVENKA *Café Europa,* Archipelago Books, 2004

◆ GLENNY, MISHA *The Fall of Yugoslavia,* Penguin Books, London, 1996

◆ GOLDSTEIN, IVO *Croatia,* C. Hurst & Co., 1999

◆ HALL, BRIAN *The Impossible Country: A Journey Through the Last Days of Yugoslavia,* Penguin Books, London, 1995

◆ HAWKESWORTH C. *Split. Thousand Years of Literacy,* PEN Centre/ Matica Hrvatska, Zagreb, 1997

◆ KAČIČ M. *Le croate et le serbe, illusions et falsifications,* Honoré Champion, Paris, 2000

◆ KREKIČ, BARIŠA *Dubrovnik in the 14th and 15th Centuries: A City Between East and West,* University of Oklahoma Press, 1972

◆ LAMPE, JOHN R. *Yugoslavia as History: Twice there was a Country,* Cambridge University Press, 2004

◆ MAGAŠ, BRANKA *The Destruction of Yugoslavia: Tracking the Break-up 1980–1992,* Verso Books, London, 1993

◆ OMRCANIN I. *Diplomatic and Political History of Croatia,* Dorrace and Cie pub., Philadelphia, 1972

◆ RUSSELL, ALEC *Prejudice and Plum Brandy,* Michael Joseph, London, 1993

◆ SELL, LOUIS *Slobodan Milosevic and the Destruction of Yugoslavia,* Duke University Press, 2003

◆ SILBER, LAURA AND LITTLE, ALAN *The Death of Yugoslavia,* Penguin Books, London/New York, 1996

◆ SIMMS, BRENDAN *Unfinest Hour: Britain and the Destruction of Bosnia,* Allen Lane, London, 2001

◆ TANNER, MARCUS *Croatia – a Nation Forged in War,* Yale University Press, New Haven/London, 1997

◆ VRATOVIČ V. *Croatian Latinity and the Mediterranean Constant,* PEN Centre/ DKH, Zagreb, 1993

ARTS AND ARCHITECTURE

◆ CAMBI N. *Diocletian and his Palace,* PEN Centre, Zagreb/Split, 1997

◆ CHAPMAN C., SHIEL R., BATOVIČ S., *The Changing Face of Dalmatia-Archaeological and Ecological Studies in a Mediterranean Landscape,* Leicester University Press, London, 1996

◆ GOSS V. *Early Croatian Architecture – a Study of the Pre-Romanesque,* Duckworth, London, 1987

◆ IVANČEVIĆ R. *Trésor artistique de la Croatie,* ITP Motovun, Zagreb, 1993

◆ KIPČIČ V., ED. *Croatian Folk Embroidery-Designs and Techniques,* Van Nostrand Reinhold pub., New York/ London, 1976

◆ MALEKOVIĆ, V., ED. *Biedermeier in Kroatien,* Muzej za umjetnost i obrt, Zagreb, 1997

◆ MALEKOVIĆ, V and TONKOVIĆ, M. EDS.: *Photography in Croatia, 1848–1951,* Muzej za umjetnost i obrt, Zagreb, 1994

◆ MOHOROVIČIČ A. *Architecture in Croatia,* Croatian Academy of Sciences and Arts, Zagreb, 1994

◆ WOLFF, LARRY *Venice and the Slavs: The Discovery of Dalmatia in the Age of Enlightenment,* Stanford University Press, 2003

LITERATURE

◆ ANDRIČ, IVO *The Bridge on the Drina,* Harvill Press, London/New York, 1995

◆ DRAKULIČ, SLAVENKA *How we Survived Communism and Even Laughed,* Harper Perennial, 1993

◆ DRAKULIČ, SLAVENKA *A Novel about the Balkans,* Penguin Books, London, 2001

◆ JUNGER, ERNST *Atlantische Fahrt [Atlantic Voyage],* 1947

◆ KAPLAN, ROBERT *Balkan Ghosts,* St Martin's Press, New York, 1993

◆ KRLEZA, MIROSLAV *The Return of Philip Latinowicz,* Quartet Books, London, 1990

◆ MATOŠ, ANTUN GUSTAV *Kod Kuce [At Home],* 1909

◆ ROMAINS, JULES *Les Hommes de Bonne Volonté [Men of Goodwill],* Le 7 Octobre, Vol. 27, Éditions Flammarion, Paris, 1958

◆ ŠENOA, AUGUST *Zlatarovo Zlato [The Goldsmith's Gold],* 1871

◆ ŠOLJAN, ANTUN *Luka [The Port],* Grafički Zavod Hravatske, Zagreb, 1974

◆ UGREŠIČ, DUBRAVKA *Culture of Lies,* Phoenix Paperbacks, 1999

◆ UGREŠIČ, DUBRAVKA *The Museum of Unconditional Surrender,* Phoenix Paperbacks, 1999

◆ UGREŠIČ, DUBRAVKA *Thank You For Not reading,* Essays on Literary Trivia, Dalkey Archive, 2004

◆ WEST, REBECCA *Black Lamb and Grey Falcon,* Canongate, Edinburgh, 1993

◆ YOURCENAR, MARGUERITE *Oriental Tales,* trans. by Alberto Manguel, Aidan Ellis Publishing, UK, 1985

DUBROVNIK

◆ BARBER, ANNABEL *Dubrovnik Visible Cities,* Visible Cities, 2004

◆ CARTER F. *Dubrovnik (Ragusa): a Classic City-State,* Seminar, New York/ London, 1972

◆ COOK, WHITFIELD *Taxi to Dubrovnik,* Delacorte Press, 1981

◆ FORETIČ M. *Dubrovnik,* Croil, Split, 1997

◆ LETCHER, PIERS *Dubrovnik,* BRADT Travel Guides, 2004

◆ NOVAK, S.P., ED. *Dubrovnik/ Raguse,* Most-Relations coll., DKH, Zagreb, 1991

◆ STUARD S. *A State of Deference: Dubrovnik in the Medieval Centuries,* University of Pennsylvania Press, Philadelphia, 1992

◆ TRAVIRKA A. *Dubrovnik: History, culture, art heritage,* Forum, Zadar, 1998

◆ List of illustrations

Front cover
Rijeka, Lorenzo Butti, 1840, oil/canvas © History & Maritime Museum, Rijeka.

Front endpaper
Infographie, Édigraphie. Zagreb, tramway on Tomislav square © René Mattès. Varaždin © Maja Strgar. Plitvice waterfalls © Maja Strgar. Pula amphitheater © Ivo Pervan. Poreč, façade of a Gothic palace on Decumanus street, 1473 © Ivo Pervan. Saint-Donat © Ivo Pervan. Aerial view of cathedral and loggia © Damir Fabijanić. Street of Trogir © Ivo Pervan. Aerial view of Split © Damir Fabijaniç. Hvar harbor, the arsenal and cathedral © Giovanni Siméone/Diaf. Historical center and cathedral © Giovanni Siméone/Diaf. Aerial view of Korčula © Ivo Pervan.
Back endpaper
Infographie, Édigraphie.

1 Illustration by Pierre-Marie Valat.
10-11 *Our Daily Bread*, August Frajtić, photo, 1939, Museum of Arts and Crafts coll., Zagreb.
12-13 *The port of Split*, photo, c.1890 © A.K.G., Paris.
14 *Wine barrels*, I. Pariš, photo, c.1920, Museum of Arts and Crafts coll., Zagreb.
16 *The plain of Slavonia* © Marin Topić.
The red earth of Istria © Maja Strgar. Hrvastko zagorje © idem.
Underwood in the Gorski kotar © idem.
17 Otok © Croatian Tourist Board, illus. Alban Larousse.
18-19 *The oak forests of Slavonia*, illus. François Desbordes, Jean Chevallier, Claire Felloni/Gallimard. Flooded forest, R.R.
20-1 Kopački Rit, illus. François Desbordes, Jean Chevallier/Gallimard. Kopački Rit © Croatian Tourist Board.
22-3 Conifer forests in the Gorski kotar, illus. F. Desbordes, C. Felloni, C. Lachoud/Gallimard. Gorski kotar © Damir Fabijanić.
24-5 Mediterranean forest/Gallimard.
26-7 Marine life, illus. François Desbordes/

Gallimard.
28 Karst, illus. Alban Larousse/Gallimard. Cave © Ivo Pervan. Lapiaz © Bios.
29 *The History of the Croats*, Ivan Meštrović, bronze sculpture, 1932 © Meštrović Foundation, Zagreb.
30 Scene from the Exodus of the Hebrews, sarcophagus from Manastrine (nr Salona), Roman art, Archeological Museum coll., Split © Dagli-Orti.
31 Roman coins (1st century AD), Archeological Museum coll., Zagreb. Greek vases, Vis © Ivo Pervan.
32 *King Zvonimir*, relief from the small temple in the Baptistery of St John in Split, late 11th c. © Ivo Pervan.
33 *Louis II of Hungary*, Hans von Krell, 1522, Habsburg's Portrait Gallery coll., Schloss Ambas, Innsbruck © A.K.G., Paris. Saint Blaise holding a model of Dubrovnik, bronze © Ivo Pervan *The Battle of Sisak*, colored lithograph, 1593, coll. Iva Babaja, Zagreb.
34 *Fran Krsto Frankopan and Nikola Zrinski*, Croatian postage stamps, priv. coll. *The Treaty of Vienna*, 1815, lithograph by J. Zutz © A.K.G., Paris.
35 *The Croatian National Revival*, Vlaho Bukovac, 1896, House of Croatian Artists coll., Zagreb. *Soldiers*, M. Kraljević, photo, 1916, Museum of Arts and Crafts coll., Zagreb.
36 Stjepan Radić, Historical Museum of Croatia coll., Zagreb. *Rob Nikada!* ('never slaves'), Ustaše propaganda poster, Historical Museum of Croatia coll., Zagreb. Portrait of Tito, National Library coll., Zagreb, neg. Maja Strgar/Gallimard.
37 Elections in Zagreb, 1990 © R. Rajtić/Wostok. Vukovar, December 28, 1991 © Michel Anglade/ Sygma. President Tuđman on the rostrum of the U.N.O. © Croatian presidency. Croatian soldiers outside Dubrovnik © Zoro/Magnum.
38 Zagreb, young men in top hats, photo, 1890, Museum of Arts

and Crafts coll., Zagreb.
39 Missal of Juraj of Topusko, Zagreb Cathedral treasure, late 15th c. © Giraudon. Bilingual program for the Monopol movie theater in Osijek, March 1913, Museum of Slavonia coll., Osijek, neg. Maja Strgar/Gallimard. *Café Corso*, F. Mosinger, photo, 1932, Museum of Arts and Crafts coll., Zagreb.
40 Baška Tablet, detail © Damir Fabijanić. Glagolitic calendar, 1495, and missal, 1483, R.R.
41 *Rural landscape of Delovo*, Krsto Hegedušić, 1934, coll. Modern Gallery, Zagreb © Alinari/Giraudon.
42 Tambura © Historical Museum of Croatia, Zagreb. Lijerica player © M. Pavić.
42-3 *Stjepan Radić with villagers* © Historical Museum of Croatia, Zagreb.
43 Kolo © Igor Michieli, Institute for Ethnology and Folklore Research, Zagreb. Sopila players © idem. Donji Andrijevci © Jean-Denis Joubert/Hoa-Qui.
44 Traditional sandals, Institute for Ethnology and Folklore Research coll., Zagreb. Sinjska alka, coll. © idem. Tanac, Krk © Damir Fabijanić.
44-5 *Slunjanka*, Vjekoslav Karas, oil/canvas, 1848 © Luka Mjeda/ Modern Gallery, Zagreb.
45 Costume of Slavonia © Croatian Tourist Board. Embroidery, Baranija © Damir Fabijanić. Zoomorphic design, Museum of Slavonia coll., Osijek, neg. Maja Strgar/Gallimard.
46-7 Harvest in the Zagorje region © Maja Strgar.
46 Costume of Slavonia © Jean-Denis Joubert/Hoa-Qui.
47 Decorated gourds, coll. Museum of Slavonia, Osijek, neg. Maja Strgar/Gallimard. Domestic activities, Institute for Ethnology and Folklore Research coll., Zagreb.
48 Port of Cres © Giovanni Simeone/Diaf. Fishermen, Brela © Ivo Pervan. Fishermen, Hvar © Roger-Viollet.
49 Zvončari © Igor Michieli/Institute for

Ethnology and Folklore Research, Zagreb. Sheep shearing, Institute for Ethnology and Folklore Research coll., Zagreb. Vineyards on the island of Hvar © Ivo Pervan.
50-51 Recipe for Štrukli © Eric Guillemot/Gallimard.
51 Dolac market, Zagreb © Jean-Denis Joubert/Hoa-Qui.
52 Wine cellar, Krk © Jean-Denis Joubert/Hoa-Qui. Croatian specialties © Patrick Léger/Gallimard.
53 Church of St Donat, Zadar, illus. Philippe Candé/Gallimard.
54-5 Ancient architecture, illus. Claude Quiec/Gallimard.
56-7 idem.
58-9 Pre-Romaneque architecture, illus. Ph. Candé/Gallimard.
60-1 Romanesque architecture, illus. J.-S. Roveri/Gallimard.
62-3 Gothic and Renaissance architecture, illus. J.-F. Pénau.
64-5 Renaissance villas of Dubrovnik, illus. M. Pommier/Gallimard.
66-7 Baroque architecture, illus. A. Soro.
68-9 Rural architecture, illus. M. Pommier/Gallimard.
70-1 Neoclassical and Modernist architecture, illus. Ph. Biard/Gallimard.
72 idem.
73 *Zagreb, Trg bana Jelačića*, Menci Klemen Crnčić,1911, oil/canvas Museum Gallery Center coll., Zagreb.
74-5 *The Taking of Zadar*, Tintoretto, 16th c., Doge's Palace coll., Venice © Cameraphoto Arte, Venice.
74 *The Battle of Sisak*, Hans von Aachen, 17th c., coll. Heeresgeschichtliches Museum, Vienna © Erich Lessing/ Magnum.
75 *The Madonna flanked by Saint Blaise and Saint Francis*, Antonio de Bellis, 17th c., Dominican Monaster coll., Dubrovnik © Božo Đukić.
76-7 *Heathland*, Mato Celestin Medović, 1911 oil/canvas © Luka Mjeda/Modern Gallery, Zagreb. *Rain*, Menci Klement Crnčić, 1914–18, oil/canvas ©

List of illustrations ◆

idem. *Zagorje landscape*, Ljubo Babić, 1937 © idem. *Rijeka*, Lorenzo Butti, 1840, oil/canvas, © History & Maritime Museum, Rijeka.

78-9 *Hlebine*, Krsto Hegedušić, 1931, oil/canvas, Modern Gallery coll., Zagreb © Alinari/Giraudon *Portrait of the Katalinić children*, Vlaho Bukovac, oil/canvas, c.1885 © Museum of Modern Art, Zagreb. *Ana Krešić*, Vjekoslav Karas, oil/ canvas, 1853 © Luka Mjeda/Modern Gallery, Zagreb. *Croatian peasant*, Ljubo Babić, oil/canvas, 1926 © idem.

80 *Motif in Dalmatia*, Zoran Mušić, oil/canvas, 1950, Cà Pesaro coll., International Gallery of Modern Art, Venice © Osvaldo Böhm, Venice. *Deserted Landscape*, Frano Šimunović, 1987, oil/canvas © Luka Mjeda/Modern Gallery, Zagreb.

81 Fishing boat, P. Salcher, photo,1890, Museum of Arts and Crafts coll., Zagreb.

82 Agave © Maja Strgar.

83 Brač © Maja Strgar.

84 Dalmatian fishermen, photo © Roger-Viollet.

86-7 Market scenes in Dubrovnik, photo © Roger-Viollet.

87 Panorama of Dubrovnik, photo, c.1890 © Roger-Viollet.

88-9 Zagreb, lithograph, 1858, Historical Museum of Croatia coll., Zagreb.

90 *Ilica*, Nasta Rojc, oil/canvas, c.1910, Museum of Zagreb coll.

91 *Zagreb, passageway*, S. Pavić, photo, 1951, Museum of Arts and Crafts coll., Zagreb.

92 *Vukovar*, Josef Koudelka, photo, 1992 © Koudelka/Magnum.

93 Zagorje landscape © Maja Strgar.

94 Varaždin © Maja Strgar. The roofs of Kaptol, Zagreb © Jean-Denis Joubert/Hoa-Qui.

95 Trg Republike (Republic Square), Split © Jean-Denis Joubert/Hoa-Qui. Tourist Office, Zagreb © Maja Strgar.

96 Aerial view of Hvar, off the coast of Hvar © Ivo Pervan. Brela © idem.

97 Port of Valun, Cres © Giovanni Simeone/ Diaf.

Port of Preko, Ugljan © Ivo Pervan.

98 Lacemakers in Pag © Damir Fabijanić. Terraced vineyard, Korčula © Ivo Pervan. Diocletian's Palace, Split © idem.

99 Trams on Tomislav Square, Zagreb © René Mattès.

100-1 Postage stamps commemorating Zagreb's 900th anniversary, priv. coll.

100 Map of Zagreb, 1521–9 © Museum of Zagreb. *The Bishop of Zagreb, Toma of Debrenthe presenting Pope Pius II with a document thanking him for his financial aid during the struggle against the Turks*. Illumination in Latin manuscript 7844, fol 1, 15th c. © B.N.F., Paris.

101 Bela IV, oil/canvas, 18th c. © Museum of Zagreb.

102 Aerial view of Gradec © Ivo Pervan. Auntun Gustav Matoš, Ivan Kozari, bronze, 1978 © Zagreb Tourist Board.

102-3 View of Gradec, watercolor, 1792 © Museum of Zagreb.

103 Seal of Gradec, 14th c. © Museum of Zagreb. Radićeva ulica © Jean-Denis Joubert/ Hoa-Qui. Ban's Palace © H. Jolivet/Hoa-Qui.

104 Marble sculpture by Ivan Meštrović, Ivan Meštrović Foundation coll. © Damir Fabijanić Gornji Grad © Maja Strgar. Church of St Catherine © Alfred Wolf/ Hoa-Qui.

105 Drašković Palace © Zvonimir Tadić. Publicity figurine for Penkala fountain pens, 1916 © Museum of Zagreb.

106-7 Photos © Museum of Zagreb.

108 Aerial view of Kaptol © Radovan Ivančević. Hermann Bollé, photo © idem.

108-9 Cathedral, watercolor of the façade elevation and layout of the square, Hermann Bollé © idem.

109 Cathedral treasure, crook of Bishop Oswalda Thuza, 15th c. © Krešimir Tadić. Cardinal Alojzije Stepinac during his trial in 1946 © Museum of Zagreb.

110-11 Trg bana Jelačica © René Mattès.

110 *Josip Jelačić*, J.

Kriehuber, oil/canvas, Historical Museum of Croatia coll., Zagreb.

111 Tkalčićeva © Jean-Denis Joubert/Hoa-Qui. August Šenoa © Maja Strgar.

112 Ilica, photo, c. 1930 © Roger-Viollet. Aerial view of Lenuci's Horseshoe © Damir Fabijanić.

113 *Liber Linteus Zagrebiensis*, Archeological Museum coll., Zagreb, neg. Abbeg Stiftung Riggisberg, Switzerland. Zrinjevac © Maja Strgar. Façade of the Archeological Museum © Nenad Kobasić/ Archeological Museum, Zagreb. *The Dream of Gundulić*, Vlaho Bukovac, oil/canvas, 1894 © Luka Mjeda/ Modern Gallery, Zagreb.

114 The National Theater, façade © Maja Strgar. The National Theater, auditorium and balconies © Tourist Board, Zagreb. Glass 'fish' lamp, 18th c. © Museum of Arts and Crafts, Zagreb.

115 Fountain of *The Source of Life*, detail, Ivan Meštrović, bronze, 1905 © Damir Fabijanić. Mirogoj cemetery © H. Jolivet/Hoa-Qui.

116 Views of Mount Medvenica © Maja Strgar.

117 Fortress of Medvegrad © Damir Fabijanić.

118 Gornja Stubice © Jean-Denis Joubert/ Hoa-Qui. *Marija Bistrica*, postcard, National Library coll., Zagreb neg. Maja Strgar/ Gallimard. Marija Bistrica © Maja Strgar.

119 Belec, interior of Our Lady of the Snow © Nikola Vranić. Gingerbread heart © Damir Fabijanić.

120 Wayside shrine © Nikola Vranić. Sculpture by Antun Augustinčić © Jean-Denis Joubert/ Hoa-Qui.

121 Landscapes and details of the Zagorje region © Maja Strgar.

122 Kumrovec © Maja Strgar. Palace of Miljana © Ivo Pervan. Fresco in the Palace of Miljana, 1172, detail © Nikola Vranić.

122-3 Castle of Veliki Tabor © Maja Strgar.

123 *Ljudevit Gaj*, engraving, priv. coll.

124-5 St Mary of Jerusalem, Trški Vrh,

illus. A. Soro/ Gallimard.

126 Castle of Trakošćan, armory © Maja Strgar. Castle of Trakošćan, postcard, National Library coll, Zagreb, neg. Maja Strgar/Gallimard.

126-7 Saint Elizabeth, Aleksje Königer, wood, 1770, Lepoglava © Nikola Vranić.

127 Lepoglava © Maja Strgar.

128 Low relief of the baths of Varaždin © Damir Fabijanić. The old town of Varaždin © Maja Strgar. The castle © Damir Fabijanić.

128-9 Trg kralija Tomislava © Jean-Denis Joubert/Hoa-Qui.

129 Cathedral, Baroque altarpiece © Damir Fabijanić.

130 *Čakovec*, Croatian postage stamp, priv. coll. Križevca, detail of the marble altar of Sv. Križ (the Holy Cross), Francesco Robba, 1756, R.R.

131 *Funeral of Stéf Halacek*, Ivan Generalić, 1935, oil/canvas, Modern Gallery coll., Zagreb © Alinari-Giraudon. Hlebine, room in the Galerija Hlebine © Damir Fabijanić.

132 Turopolje landscape © Nikola Vranić.

133 Velika Mlaka, Church of St Barbara, illus. M. Pommier/ Gallimard.

134 Aerial view of the castle of Sisak © Croatian Tourist Board. Roman statuette, bronze © Archeological Museum, Zagreb

135 *Nikola Subić Zrinski*, Croatian postage stamp, priv. coll. Lonsjko Polje, illus. A. Larousse/Gallimard.

136 *Samobor*, postcard, coll. Maja Strgar. *Udovica Kupinec*, *Woman from Jastrebarsko*, photo, 1922, Institute for Ethnology and Folklore Research coll., Zagreb.

137 Aerial views of Karlovac © Croatian Tourist Board. Bosiljevo © Nikola Vranić.

138 Waterfalls at the Plitvice Lakes © Maja Strgar. Map of the Plitvice Lakes © Vincent Brunot/Gallimard. Aerial view of the Plitvice Lakes National Park © Maja Strgar.

139 Plitvice Lakes, illus. F. Desbordes/Gallimard.

140 Japode helmet,

◆ List of illustrations

Archeological Museum coll., Ante Starčević © Historical Museum of Croatia, Zagreb.
141 Costume of Slavonia © Croatian Tourist Board.
142 The Croatian plain, River Danube © Marin Topić.
143 Vukovar, November 22, 1991 © Antoine Gyori/Sygma.
144-5 Tvrđa, Osijek's fortress, illus. Amato Soro/Gallimard.
146 Aerial view of Osijek © Croatian Tourist Board. Commemorative coin, Museum of Slavonia, Osijek coll., neg. Maja Strgar/Gallimard. Baranja, woman sitting beneath red peppers © Marin Topić.
147 Kopački Rit © Marin Topić. Fortress of Erdut © idem.
148 *Josip Juraj Strossmayer*, oil/canvas, 1871 © Historical Museum of Croatia, Zagreb. Đakovo, chevet of the cathedral © Jean-Denis Joubert/Hoa-Qui.
149 *The Vučedol Dove*, a ceramic vase, 2600 BC, Archeological Museum coll., Zagreb © K. Tadić. Vineyard © Marin Topić.
150 Romanesque sculpture, Town Museum coll., Požega © Marin Topić. Ivana Brlić-Mažuranić, photo, National Library coll. Zagreb, neg. Maja Strgar/Gallimard. Castle of Kutjevo © Croatian Tourist Board.
151 Aerial view of Kutjevo © Croatian Tourist Board. Jankovac © Marin Topić.
152 Sarcophagus from Veliki Bastaji, Archeological Museum coll., Zagreb. Nova Gradiška © Marin Topić. Lippizaners © idem.
153 Kažun © Ivo Pervan.
154 Motovun © René Mattès.
155 Roman sculpture, coll. Archeological Museum, Pula © Ivo Pervan.
156 *Map of Istria*, by Antonio Magini in Bologna, 1620, Novak coll. © S.Tadić.
156-7 *Pula*, photo c. 1930, National Library coll., Zagreb, neg. Maja Strgar/Gallimard.
157 *James Joyce*, photo, 1934 © Roger-Viollet.
158 Mosaics, Archeological Museum coll., Pula © Ivo Pervan. Pula, windows and Ulica Giardini © Maja Strgar.
159 Aerial view of the amphitheater, Pula © Ivo Pervan. Amphitheater, Pula © Damir Fabijanić. Amphitheater, Pula © Ivo Pervan.
160-1 Landscape near the village of Gračišće © Maja Strgar.
160 Labin and details © Maja Strgar.
161 *Mathias Flacius Illyrius* (Matija Vlacić Illirik), engraving, 16th c., coll. of the Société de l'Histoire du Protestantisme Français, Paris. Plomin © René Mattès.
162 Dvigrad © Maja Strgar. Panorama of Pazin © René Mattès.
163 *The Beram Cycle, Dance of Death* © René Mattès. Vodnjan © Maja Strgar.
164 Conference of nonaligned countries, July 19, 1956 in Veli Brijun. From left to right: Nasser, Nehru, Tito © J.B. Archives / A.F.P. Paris. Aerial view of the Brijuni Islands © Croatian Tourist Board. Aerial view of Rovinj © Ivo Pervan.
165 Street in Rovinj © Ivo Pervan. Port of Rovinj © René Mattès.
166 Istrian wine © Damir Fabijanić. Poreč, façade of a Gothic palace on the Decumanus, 1473 © Ivo Pervan.
167 Archeological collection of the Regional Museum of the Poreština © S. Tadić. Goran Ivanišević at the Roland-Garros tournament, 1997 © Franck Séguin/Temp Sport. Street in Umag © Ivo Pervan. Rampart, Novigrad © Maja Strgar.
168-9 Basilica of Poreč, illus. M Pommier/Gallimard. Fish, mosaic © Ivo Pervan. Visitation, mosaics © Hell/Artephot. Chancel and stucco decoration © Bruno Lenormand/Gallimard.
169 Vault of the apse © Hell/Artephot.
170 Buje © Ivo Pervan. Grožnjan © Maja Strgar. Fresco and Glagolitic graffiti, Hum © Agnès Gattegno.
171 Sveta Nedjelja © Damir Fabijanić.
172 Brsec © René Mattès. Mali Lošinj © Jean-Denis Joubert/Hoa-Qui.
173 Morčići, R. R.
174 Lovro Matačić, photo, National Library coll., Zagreb, neg. Maja Strgar/ Gallimard. Korso gradski Torava, Rijeka © Damir Fabijanić.
175 Aerial view of the port of Rijeka © Ivo Pervan. Carnival, Rijeka © idem.
176 Crikvenica © Damir Fabijanić. Our Lady of Trsat © Damir Fabijanić. Lovran, tourist poster, National Library coll., Zagreb, neg. Maja Strgar/Gallimard.
177 Lovran © Ivo Pervan. Julije Klović, engraving, National Library coll., Zagreb, neg. Maja Strgar/ Gallimard.
178-9 *Opatija*, color postcards, National Library coll., Zagreb, neg. Maja Strgar/ Gallimard.
178 *Theodor Billroth*, lithograph, Library of the School of Medecine, Paris.
179 Hotels in Opatija © Damir Fabijanić.
180 *Map of the islands of Cres and Lošinj*, 16th c., National Library coll., Zagreb, neg. Maja Strgar/Gallimard. Griffon vulture © Damir Fabijanić.
180-1 Lubenice, island of Cres © Giovanni Simeone/Diaf.
181 Port of Cres © Giovanni Simeone/ Diaf. Lošinj © idem.
182-3 Port of Krk © René Mattès.
182 Krk, cathedral altarpiece, P. Kalor,1477 © Lauros-Giraudon.
183 Krk, Church of St Donat, 9th c. © Agnès Gattegno. Vrbnik, island of Krk © Jean-Denis Joubert/Hoa-Qui. Baška, island of Krk © René Mattès.
184 Rab Island © Ivo Pervan.
185 Port of Senj © Jean-Denis Joubert / Hoa-Qui. Vinjerac, in the foreground © idem. Fortress of Senj © idem. Main road © idem.
186-7 The Tulove Grede © Ivo Pervan.
186 Meteorological station © Petar Strmečki. Veliki Lubenovac © Damir Fabijanić.
187 Paklenica © Ivo Pervan. Rosijeva Koliba © Petar Strmečki. Marked track © idem.
188 Church of St Mary, Pag © Maja Strgar. View of Pag © Giovanni Siméone/Diaf. Pag lace © Damir Fabijanić. Traditional headdress, Pag © idem.
189 Aerial view of one of the Kornati Islands © Ivo Pervan.
190 Aerial view of Zadar © Ivo Pervan. *The emperor Augustus*, marble, AD 37, Archeological Museum coll., Zadar © Ivo Pervan.
191 *The Taking of Zadar*, Micheli Andrea (1539–1614), Doge's palace coll., Venice © Scala.
192 Façade of St Anastasia, Zadar © Ivo Pervan. Collections of the Archeological Museum, Zadar © Ivo Pervan.
192-3 The Forum © Ivo Pervan.
193 Maraschino, neg. Patrick Léger/Gallimard. Church of St Donat © Ivo Pervan.
194 Reliquary of Saint Simeon, hammered silver, 1380 © Ivo Pervan. Reliquary bust of Saint Anastasia, commissioned in Venice,1622, Permanent Exhibition of Church Art, Zadar © idem.
195 Crucifix, 12th c., Franciscan Monastery coll. © Giraudon. The Foša sis canal © Giovanni Siméone/ Diaf.
196 Church of St Nicholas © Ivo Pervan. Reliquary of Saint Ambrose © idem.
197 Church of the Holy Cross, Nin © Damir Fabijanić.
199 Aerial views © Ivo Pervan.
200-1 Aerial views of the Kornati Islands © Ivo Pervan.
201 Krune © Damir Fabijanić.
202 Juraj Dalmatinac © Ivo Pervan. View of Šibenik © Maja Strgar. Aerial view of the cathedral and loggia © Damir Fabijanić.
203 Frieze of the baptistery © Ivo Pervan. Baptistry © idem.
204 Bunch of grapes © Gallimard. *Krka river*, color postcard, National Library coll., Zagreb, neg. Maja Strgar/ Gallimard. Slapovi vrile © Maja Strgar.

List of illustrations ◆

205 Island of Visovac © Maja Strgar.
206 *Knin*, Croatian postage stamp, priv. coll.
206-7 Trogir, island of Čiovo © Ivo Pervan.
206 Street in Trogir © Ivo Pervan.
207 The Radovan portal and detail © Ivo Pervan.
208 Chapel of St John © S. Tadić. Saint John the Baptist © idem.
209 Kairos, god of opportunity © Ivo Pervan. Kastel Gomilica © Radovan Ivančević. Kastel Štafilić © Ivo Pervan.
210-11 Amphitheater © Damir Fabijanić.
210 Young woman from Salona, colored marble, 3rd c. AD, Archeological Museum coll., Zagreb © Ivo Pervan.
211 Sarcophagus of the Good Shepherd, 4th c. AD © Ivo Pervan. *Trano Bulić*, photo, National Library coll., Zagreb, neg. Maja Strgar/ Gallimard. Ciborium, 11 c., Archeological Museum coll., Split © Ivo Pervan.
212 Sinjska alka © Damir Fabijanić. Our Lady of Sinj © idem. Klis © Ivo Pervan.
213 Diocletian's Palace, detail © René Mattès.
214 Aerial view of Split © Damir Fabijanić. View of the port, Split © René Mattès.
215 Coin stamped with the effigy of the emperor Diocletian © Croatian Tourist Board. Sphinx © Ivo Pervan.
216-17 Diocletian's Palace, illus. Ph. Biard/ Gallimard.
218 Baptistery, illus. Ph. Biard/Gallimard. Cathedral door © Damir Fabijanić.
219 Diocletian's Palace © René Mattès. *Marko Marulić*, Ivan Meštrović, bronze © Ivo Pervan.
220 Sarcophagus, detail, Archeological Museum coll., Split © Ivo Pervan. Split stadium © Damir Fabijanić.
221 Prince Višelav's baptismal font, Archeological Museum coll., Split © Ivo Pervan.
220-1 View of Split from the Marjan peninsula © Bruno Barbier/Hémisphères.
222 Meštrović Gallery, Split © Ivo Pervan. *Contemplation or Psyche*, Ivan Meštrović,

marble, 1923, Meštrović Gallery coll., Split © Ivo Pervan. *Moses*, Ivan Meštrović marble 1918 © Meštrović Foundation, Zagreb.
223 Ivan Meštrović in Geneva, *Crucifixion*, photo, 1916 © Meštrović Foundation, Zagreb. *Djevojka lutnjom*, Ivan Meštrović, bronze, 1918 © Foundation Meštrović, Zagreb. *Gregory of Nin*, Ivan Meštrović, bronze, Split © Jean-Denis Joubert/Hoa-Qui. *The Madonna and Child*, Ivan Meštrović, wood, Atelier Meštrović, Zagreb © Damir Fabijanić.
224 Omiš © Ivo Pervan.
225 Church of St Peter, Omiš © Ivo Pervan. Modro jezero (Blue Lake) © idem.
226 Shell, Museum of Markaska coll. © Ivo Pervan.
226-7 Markaska © Ivo Pervan.
227 The Neretva Delta © Jean-Denis Joubert/ Hoa-Qui. Mrala river © idem.
228 Bol © Giovanni Siméone/Diaf.
229 Views of Brač © Maja Strgar. The Dragon's Cave © Ivo Pervan. Monastery of Blaca, library of the observatory © Damir Fabijanić.
230 Hvar lace © Damir Fabijanić.
230-1 The port of Hvar, arsenal and cathedral © Giovanni Siméone/Diaf.
231 The fortified Church of St Mary © Radovan Ivancević. The Tvrdalj built by Hektorović in Strarigrad © Ivo Pervan. Theater © idem.
232 Artemis, sculpture discovered in Vis, 4th c. BC © Ivo Pervan. Komiža © Maja Strgar.
233 Door of the Rector's Palace © Ivo Pervan.
234-5 Aerial view of Dubrovnik © Lavaud & Lechenet/Altitude.
234 Libertas festival © Ivo Pervan.
235 Saint Paul and Saint Blaise, detail of the triptych by Nikola Božidarević, early 16th c., Dominican Monastery coll., Dubrovnik © S. Tadić.
236 Pile Gate, detail of three heads © Ivo Pervan. The ramparts © Radovan Ivančevič.
236-7 Onofrio's Large

Fountain, tinted photo, c.1890 © Roger-Viollet.
237 The cloister of the Franciscan Monastery © Damir Fabijanić. Pharmacy © Ivo Pervan.
238 The Stradun © Croatian Tourist Board. Orlando's Column © Jean-Denis Joubert/ Hoa-Qui.
239 Sponza Palace © Damir Fabijanić. The market © Ivo Pervan.
240 Cathedral treasure, reliquary of Saint Blaise, c.1200 © A. Held/ Artephot. The historic center and cathedral © Giovanni Siméone/ Diaf. Ivan Gundulić, lithograph, National Library coll., Zagreb, neg. Maja Strgar/ Gallimard.
241 Street in Dubrovnik © René Mattès. *The Madonna and Child*, detail, 16th c. © S.Tadić.
242 Views of Lopud © Damir Fabijanić.
244 Sorkočević Palace, staircase © Damir Fabijanić. Fountain of Ivan Gučetić 's villa, Trsteno © idem.
245 Aerial view of Ston, the saltpans © Lavaud & Lechenet/Altitude. Orebić © Ivo Pervan. *Fishing boat in a storm*, commemorative plaque, tempera, 1613, coll. Monastery of Our Lady of the Angels, Orebić.
246 Aerial view of Korčula © Ivo Pervan. Balcony © idem. Cathedral © Jean-Denis Joubert/Hoa-Qui.
247 *Marco Polo*, wood engraving, Nuremberg, 1477 © Ronald Sheridan, London. Vineyard on the island of Korčula © Ivo Pervan. Blato © idem.
248-9 Cavtat © René Mattès.
248 Cavtat © Jean-Denis Joubert/Hoa-Qui. The Račić Mausoleum, Ivan Meštrović © Damir Fabijanić.
249 *Self-portrait*, Vlaho Bukovac © Ivo Pervan. *Costume of the Konavle* region, watercolor in Album N. Arsenovica, 19th c., Institute for Ethnology and Folklore Research coll., Zagreb.
251 Aerial view of Mljet © Giovanni Siméone/ Diaf. St Mary's Island © idem. St Mary's Island © Ivo Pervan. The monastery © Damir Fabijanić.
252 *The Dance of Death*, wood engraving in 'The Hours of the

Virgin Mary', printed in Lyon by Bonin de Boninis in 1499, Musée de l'Imprimerie, Lyon. Lastovo © Ivo Pervan.
Practical information
255 Historical center and cathedral, Zagreb © Giovanni Siméone / Diaf. Zagorje landscape © Maja Strgar. Otok © Croatian Tourist Board. Jelačića square © René Mattès.
257 Aerial views of the Plitvice Lakes and Mljet © Croatian Tourist Board.
258 Market in Dubrovnik © Réné Mattès. The marina, Pula © Ivo Pervan.
259 Tramway, Zagreb © René Mattès. Water taxi, Opatija © Ph. Jolivet/Hoa-Qui.

ACKOWLEDGMENTS

"The War" by Vesna Parun, translated by Daniela Gioseffi with Ivana Spalatin, from *Women on War: An International Anthology of Writings from Antiquity to the Present*, edited by Daniela Gioseffi, copyright 2003, The Feminist Press at CUNY.

We have not been able to trace the heirs or publishers of certain documents. An account is being held open for them in our offices.

◆ Index

A

Aachen, Hans von 75
Abbazia 179
Accommodation **256**
Alagović, Aleksander (bishop) 110, 114
Albertal, Ivan 109
Aleši, Andrija 202, 207, 208
Aljmaš 147
Anastasia, Saint 211, 215
Ancient architecture 54–7
Ancona, Celio of 237
Andautonia(ns) 132
Andrijić, Marko 239, 247
Aquileia 156, 170
Argonauts, legend of the 181
Augustinčić, Antun 119, 120

B

Babić, Ljubo 77, 78, 80, 104
Babino Polje 250
Bale 164
Ban 32
Banovina 135
Baratin, Luka (bishop) 109
Barban 160
Baredine Cave 167
Baroque architecture 66–7
Bartolomeo, Massa di 241
Bartolomeo, Michelozzo di 236
Baška 183
Baška tablet 40, 183
Bauer, Antun 109
Bazzi, Andreotti and Pier Antonio 240
Béla IV 101, 132, 215
Belec 69, 119
Beli 180
Belje 146
Bellis, Antonio de 75
Beram 163
Biedermeier 77, 78
Bijele stijene Nature Reserve 140
Bilje 147
Biograd 197
Biokovo 226
Birkett, Dea 91
Biševo 232
Biskupija 206, 221
Blaca 229
Blaise, Saint 238
Blato 247
Blue Grotto 232
Blue Lake (Modro jezero) 225
Bogišic, Baltazar 248
Boka Kotorska 249
Bol 229
Bollé, Herman 103–5, 108–10, 112, 115, 119, 131, 151
Boninis, Boninus de 205, 252
Bosančica 39, 224
Bosiljevo 137
Bošković, Ruđer 39, 240
Bozdari, Villa 65
Božidarević, Nikola 241

Brač, island of 228
Brajkov, Miho 237
Branimir 32, 59
Branjug, Juraj (bishop) 110, 115
Brela 226
Brezovica 133
Bribir 177, 205
Brijuni Islands 56, 164, 165
Brlić-Mažuranić, Ivana 150
Brseč 172
Brtonigla 261
Budičić, Andrija 204
Budislavić, Ivan 207
Buffalini, Andrea 240
Buje 170
Bukovac, Vlaho 78, 114, 249
Bukovica 196
Bulić, Frane 211
Bura 17, 52, 173
Buševec 133
Butti, Lorenzo 77
Buvina, Andrija 218
Buzet 170

C

Carpaccio, Vittore 194
Cassiodore 164
Catarino 194
Cava, Onofrio della 236, 245
Cavtat 223, 248
Celesti 230
Cerovac caves 140
Cetina 59, 206, 212, 224, 225
Chakavian 38, 39
Climate 12, 254
Clovio, Giulio 177
Communism 36, 37
Costumes, traditional 44–5, 46
Cres 180
Cres, island of 180
Crijevic, Ilija 39
Crikvenica 177
Crna Mlaka 136
Crnčić, Menci Klement 77
Croatia, kingdom of 31, 58, 196, 206
Croatian language 38
Crveno jezero (Red Lake) 225
Currency **254**, **255**

Č

Čakovec 130
Čara 247
Česmički, Ivan 117
Čiovo, island of 206
Čučić, Franjo 247

D

D'Annunzio, Gabriele 174
Dalj 147
Dalmatinac, Juraj (George the Dalmatian) 62, 188, 202, 203, 207, 209, 219, 236, 239, 245
Dandolo, Enrico (doge) 190

Dante 81, 157
Danube 18, 20, 147, 149
Darda 143, 147
Daruvar 152
Delnice 147
Diocletian 215, 216
Diocletian's Palace 55, 56, 57, 214, 216–7
Dobričević, Dobrić 205, 252
Dobričević, Lovro 241
Dobrinj 182
Dolac market 110
Domnius, Saint 211, 215
Donat, Bishop of Zadar 193
Donja Lomnica 133
Donja Stubica 117
Donji Miholjac 147
Drava 18, 20, 142, 144
Draganić-Vrančić family 204
Drava 18, 20, 142, 144
Draškovic, Juraj 126
Drivenik 177
Drniš 205
Držić, Marin 39, 240
Držislav 221
Dual monarchy of Austria-Hungary 35
Dubrovačka, Rijeka 244
Dubrovčanin, Antun 238
Dubrovnik 34, 66, 75, 86, 234–41, 248, 261
Dubrovnik river 244
Dubrovnik, villas of 64
Dugi Otok 198, 201
Duknović, Ivan 208, 209
Dvigrad, castles of 162

Đ

Đakovo 45, 71, **148**
Đurđević (Ignjat) 250

E

Elaphite Islands 242
Eltz, counts of 149
Empire, Byzantine 31
Empire, Western Roman 31
Erdödy, Toma Bakač 109
Erdödy, Šimun 109
Erdut 147
Eszterházy barons 147
Eugene of Savoy, Prince 146
Euphrasius, Bishop 168

F

Fažana 164
Felbinger, Bartol 70, **105**, 120, 131
Fellner 113, 129, 174
Ferrari, Pietro 218
Filipović, Franjo 108
Firentinac, Nikola ('Nicholas of Florence') 62, 203, **208**, 209, 230
Fiume 173
Flacius Illyricus, Mathias 161
Forest, Mediterranean 24–5
Forests of Slavonia, oak 18–19, 142, 148
Forests, mountain 22–3
Foscolo, Leonardo 212, 246

Franciscus Patricius 180
Frangeš-Mihanovic, Robert 112, 120
Frankopan 140, 173, 177, 182
Frankopan, Fran Krsto 34, 109, 182

G

Gabrili 249
Gaj, Ljudevit 35, 123
Garcia, Gaetano 241
Gata 224
Gavrilović (pork butcher's) 135
Generalić, Ivan 131
Glagolitic script 39, 40, 172
Glavotok 183
Glina 135, 137
Gornja Bistra 67, 117
Gornja Stubica 118, 120
Gorski kotar 16, 69, 137, 140
Gospić 140
Gosseau d'Heneff, Maximilian (colonel) 144, 149
Gracac 140
Gračišće 161
Gradac 226
Gradec 101, **102–5**, 106
Gradić, Stjepan 240
Grič 102
Grižane 177
Gropelli, Marino 238, 239
Grožnjan 170
Gruda 249
Gruz 244
Gualdo, Andrija 209
Gubec, Matija 118
Gundulic, Ivan 39, 237, 240

H

Habsburg 33, 34, 35
Hajdučki (nature reserve) 187
Hamzić, Mihajlo 241
Hauszmann, Alajos 175
Heathland 24
Hegedušić, Krsto 78, 131
Hektorović, Petar 39, 231
Helmer 113, 129, 174
Historicism 70
Histri 31, 154, 155, 157
Hlebine 78, 131
Hotels 261
Hrvatska Kostajnica 135
Hum 170, 262
Hungary 33, 34, 35
Hvar 13, 230
Hvar, island of 230, 262

I

Ibrišimović, Luka 150
Illyrian 31, 140, 172, 173, 190, 250
Illyrian provinces 34, 195, 220, 235
Illyrianism 35, 39, 101, 123
Iločki family 149

Ilok 149
Ilovik, island of 180
Imotski 225
Independence, struggle for 37, 143, 191, 235
Issa 31, 54, 232
Istarski razvod 162, 170
Istria 16, **154–70**
Ivanić, Matij 231
Ivanić Grad 134
Iž, island of 198

J

Jacobello del Fiore 163
Jadera 54, 190, 192
Janković family 152
Januševec 70, 120
Jasenovac 135
Jastrebarsko 136
Javornik, Josip 125
Jelačić, Josip 35, 103, 105, 110, 120, 144
Jezero Mir (Mir Lake) 199
Josipdol 140
Joyce, James 157
Jünger, Ernst 82
Jurandvor 183

K

Kačić Miošić, Andrija 226
Kajkavian 38, 39
Kamenjak, Cape 160
Kampor Bay 184
Kanfanar 162
Kanižlić, Antun 150
Kaplan, Robert 90
Kaprije, island of 204
Kaptol 101, 106, **108–10**
Karađorđević 36
Karas, Vjekoslav 78
Karga, Cape 160
Karlobag 185
Karlovac 62, 69, 137
Karst 28, 187
Kastav 176
Katančić, Matija Petar 145
Katičić, Ilija 240
Kavanjin, Jerolim 220, 229
Kaštel Gomilica 209
Kaštel Lukšić 209
Kaštel Novi 209
Kaštel Sućurac 209
Kaštel Štafilić 209
Kaštel Stari 209
Kazun 69, 163
Kingdom of Serbs, Croats and Slovenes 36
Klanjec 120
Klape 43
Klenovnik 127
Klis 185, 212
Kljaković, Jozo 103
Kloštar 165
Klović, Julije 177
Knin 206
Kolo 43
Koločep, island of 242
Koloman 32, 190, 194
Komiža 232
Konavle 249, 262
Köninger, Aleksije 127
Kopački Rit Nature Park 20, 147

Koprivnica 131
Korčula 80, 246
Korčula, island of 246, 262
Kornati Islands 200–1
Košljun, island of 183
Kovačić, Viktor 72, 114
Kraljevica 177
Krapanj, island of 204
Krapina 123
Križevci 130, 131
Krk 13, 61, 183
Krk, island of 182, 262
Krka 203, 204
Krstjani 225, 226, 245
Kukuljević Sakcinski, Ivan 39
Kumrovec 122
Kunc, Zinka 114
Kupa 134, 136
Kutjevo 151
Kušan, Fran 186
Kvarner **172**, 182

L

Labin 161
Lastovo 252
Lastovo, island of 252
Leisure 13, 261
Lenuci, Milan 111
Lepoglava 126
Lerchinger, Anton 118, 122, 124
Lika 69, 140, 186
Limski Kanal 165, 262
Lindar, fortress of 161
Lipik 152
Lippizaner 148, 152
Lisinski, Vatroslav 115
Ližnjan 160
Lokrum, island of 248
Longhena, Baldassare 66, 194, 230
Lonjsko polje 134
Lopud, island of 242
Lošinj, island of 180, 181, 263
Lotto, Lorenzo 221
Louis I of Anjou 32, 182, 191, 194, 197, 235
Lovran 177
Lovreć 60
Lovrin, Vicko 249
Lower Town (Zagreb) 107, 109–15
Lubenice 180
Lubynski, Rudolf 71, 113
Lučić, Hanibal 231
Lučić, Ivan 209
Ludbreg 131
Lukačić, Ivan 220
Lukavec 133
Lumbarda 247
Lun peninsula 188
Luzzo, Lorenzo 194
Lužnica 120

M

Macanović, Ignacije 209
Maček, Vlatko 36
Maggioto, Francesco 247
Majlath family 147
Makarska 69, 225
Mala Paklenica 187
Mali Lošinj 181
Mali Ston 245

Maranovići 250
Maraschino 52, 193
Marčana 160
Marija Bistrica 119
Marine life 26–7
Marinković, Ranko 232
Marmont (Marshal of France) 219
Martino, Pietro di 236, 239
Martinšćica 180
Marulić, Marko 39, 219, 220
Maruševec 127
Mašković, Yusuf (vizir) 197
Matačić, Lovro 174
Matoš, Antun Gustav 89, 102
Maur, Saint 168
Mažuranić , Ivan 177
Medovic, Mato Celestin 77
Medulin 160
Medvedgrad 117
Medvednica, Mount 116
Međimurje 130
Mersi, Anton 124
Meštrović, Ivan 104, 105, 114, 115, 206, 219, 221, **222–3**, 248
Metković 227
Metzinger, Valentin 136
Michele, Salvi di 239
Michelozzi, Michelozzo 245
Mikulić, Aleksander (bishop) 109
Milan, Ivan Petrov de 194
Milano, Bonino da 203, 219, 238, 241, 247
Milano, Pietro da 219
Milićević, Nikola 229
Milićević, Paskoje 236, 239, 245
Military Frontier 33, 35, 132, 135, 140, 145, 148
Miljana 122
Milna 228
Mir Lake (Jezero Mir) 199
Mirogoj 71, 115
Mljet, island of 60, 250
Modernism 70, 72
Modro jezero (Blue Lake) 225
Molunat 249
Morčići 173
Moreška 247
Morlaiter, Giovanni Maria 219
Morrison, Fynes 87
Mosor 224
Motovun 154, 170, 263
Mraz, Franjo 131
Mrežnica 140
Murter, island of 199
Music and dance 42–3
Mušić, Zoran 80
Mutvoran, fortress of 160

N

Napoli, Tomaso 240
Narona 226
Narodna stranka (National Party) 35
Našice 151
National anthem 12, 120
Nazor, Vladimir 105, 228

Nelipić 205
Neretva 227
Nerežišća 229
Nesactium 155, 160
New Objectivity (Neue Sachlichkeit) 3, 78
Nicolino, Cristoforo 243
Nin 196
Nonaligned movement 36, 164
Nova Gradiška 152
Novalja 188
Nova Vas 167
Novigrad 167, 196, 263
Novi Vinodolski 177
Nuštar 149

O

Obrovac 196
Ogulin 137, 140
Omiš 224, 235
Omišalj 182
Opatija 176, 177, **178–9**, 263
Opeka 127
Oprtalj 170
Opuzen 227
Orebić 245
Osijek 66, 72, **142–6**, 263
Osor 180
Oštarije pass 185
Oštri rt (headland) 249
Otavice 206, 222
Otočac 69, 140
Otto, Master 214
Ottoman 32, 34, 75, 100, 102, 134, 137, 143, 146, 173, 185, 191, 235
Ozalj 136

P

Padua, Saint Anthony of 170
Pag 52, 188
Pag, island of 188
Paklenica National Park 187
Pakleni otoci 231
Pakrac 152
Palladio, Andrea 55, 66, 157, 170
Pannonia 16, 18
Pannonius, Janus 117
Papuk 151
Parler, Ivan 103
Partisans 36
Party, Croatian Peasant 36
Party, National (Narodna stranka) 35
Party of Rights, Croatian 35, 140
Parun, Vesna 84, 204
Paški sir 52
Pašman, island of 198
Pauline Order 119, 126, 163, 177
Pavelić, Ante 36
Pazin 162
Pejačević, Dora 151
Pelješac peninsula 77, **245**
Penkala, Slavoljub 105
Pepys, Samuel 85
Peroj 164
Petar Krešimir IV 32, 193, 202, 221

◆ Index

Petrić, Franjo 180
Petrinja 69, 135, 137
Petrović, Leonardo 237
Petrović, Petar 237
Pharos 54, 230
Pićan 161
Pirovac 204
Pisarovina 136
Plermini, Pier Antonio 237
Pleso 133
Plitvice Lakes 138–9
Ploče 227
Plomin 161
Podravina 131
Polače 56, 250
Poljica 224
Polo, Marco 247
Ponzoni, Matteo 218, 231
Poreč **166–7**, 263
Poreč, Basilica of 57, **168–9**
Poreština 167
Posavina 132
Postira 228
Pozzo, Andrea 240
Požega 150
Premantura 160
Premužić, Ante 187
Pre-Romanesque architecture 58–9
Pribislavić 202
Pridvorje 249
Prožura 250
Pršut 50, 52, 170
Psunj 152
Public holidays 256
Pula **157–9**, 264
Pula, amphitheater of 55, 159
Punat 183

R

Rab 184
Rab Island 184
Račišće 247
Radić, Stjepan 36
Radovan (master-mason) 61, 207
Ragusa 234–41
Rakalj 160
Rakija 47
Ranger, Ivan **115**, 119, 127, 131
Rastić, Villa 65
Ravni kotari 196
Red Lake (Crveno Jezero) 225
Remete 115
Renaissance architecture 62–5
Restaurants 261
Revival, Croatian National 35, 39, 101, 123
Rijeka 49, 66, 77, **172–6**
Risnjak National Park 140
Riečina 172, 174
Robba, Francesco 104, 130, 134
Roč 170
Romains, Jules 85
Roman empire 31, 54, 155, 160, 180
Romanesque architecture 60–1
Rösner, Karl 71, 148
Rovinj 165, 264

Rožanski kukovi (nature reserve) 187
Rural architecture 68–9
Ružička , Lavoslav 149

S

Sabor 32, 102, 103
St Michael of Rudina, monastery of 151
Salona 54, 57, 210–11, 212, 214
Samobor 136, 265
San Marino, republic of 184
Sanmicheli, Gian Girolamo 203
Sanmicheli, Michele 195
Saplunara 250
Sava 18, 101, 132, 134
Savudrija, Cape 167
Scarpa, Iginio 176, 178
Sela 134
Senj 185
Serbs 33, 35, 36, 37
Sergians, Arch of the 55, 157
Shaw, George Bernard 200
Sinj 44, 212
Sisak 33, 75, 101, 109, **134**
Sitno 224
Skradin 205
Skradinski buk 204, 205
Slano 244
Slavenski, Josip 130
Slavonia 16, 18, 46, **142–152**
Slavonic, Old Church 39, 40
Slavonski brod 150
Slunj 140
Soko, fortress of 249
Solin 212, 221
Sopila 43
Sorkočević 65, 244
Split **214–23**, 265
Srijem 149
Starčević, Ante 35, 140
Stari Grad 231
Stepinac, Alojzije 109
Stokavian 38, 39
Ston 58, 245, 265
Straub, Filip Jacob 124
Strossmayer, Josip Juraj 35, 71, 112, 148
Stubičke Toplice 117
Stubički Golubovec 118
Suleyman the Magnificent 33
Sumpetar 224
Supetar 228
Supetarska Draga 184
Supilo, Frano 249
Susak, island of 180
Sutivan 228
Sveti Andrija, island of 243
Sveti Juraj 185, 186
Sveti Lovreč 165
Sveti Petar u Šumi 163
Svetvinčenat 163

Š

Šćitarjevo 132
Šenoa, August 88, 103, 111
Šibenik **202-3**

Šimunović, Frano 80
Šipan, island of 243
Škrip 228
Šoljan, Antun 83
Šolta, island of 229
Šubić 135, 205, 206
Štrukli 50

T

Tahi, Franjo 117, 118
Telašćica Bay of 199
Telephone 254, 259
Tesla, Nikola 140
Tintoretto 75, 231
Tito 36, 122, 164
Tomislav 32, 112, 219
Topusko 135
Tourism 13, 178, 179
Trakošćan 126
Transport 254, 259
Travarica 52
Trenk, Franz von 150, 151, 152
Tribalj 177
Tribunj 204
Trnina, Milka 114
Trogir 61, 62, **206–9**
Trogiranin, Blaž Jurjev 209, 220, 245
Trogiranin, Petar 184
Trpimir 32
Trsat 176
Trsteno 244
Trški Vrh 67, **124–5**
Truhelka, Jagoda 146
Trumbić, Ante 220
Tuđman, Franjo 37
Turopolje 69, 132, 133

U

Ubli 252
Učka, Mount 177
Ugljan, island of 48, 198
Umag 167
Uniate 136
Unije 180
Upper Town (Zagreb) 102–5, 106
Uskok 136, 185
Ustaše (Rebels) 36, 135

V

Valle d'Augusto 181
Valpovo 147
Valun 180
Varaždin 127–9
Varaždinske Toplice 56, 128
Vela Luka 247
Velebit 69, 140, 185, **186–7**
Veli Brijun 164
Velika Gorica 133
Velika Kapela 177
Velika Mlaka 133
Velika Paklenica 187
Veliki Tabor 122
Veli Lošinj 69, 181
Veneziano, Antonio 195
Veneziano, Paolo 194, 231
Venice 32, 34, 75, 173, 180, 191, 234
Vernes, Jules 162
Vid 226

Villehardouin, Geoffroi de 190
Vinagora 123
Vinkovci 47, 148
Vinodol 177
Vinodol 177
Virovitica 151
Vis 232
Vis, island of 232
Visovac, island of 205
Visovačko, Lake 205
Višnjan 167
Vlačić Ilirik, Matija 161
Vodice 204
Vodnjan 163
Volosko 177
Vrana 197
Vrančić, Antun 39
Vrančić, Faust 204
Vratnik pass 140, 186
Vrbnik 183
Vrboska 231
Vrgada, island of 198
Vrhovec, Maksimilijan 114, 117, 118
Vrsar 165
Vučedol 149
Vuka 69, 149
Vukelić, Vilma 146
Vukotić, Dušan 106
Vukovar 92, 143, 149
Vušković, Dujam 219

W–Y

Weissmann 72
West, Rebecca 89
Wine 6, 49, 52, 151, 166, 230
Yourcenar, Marguerite 86
Yugoslavia 36, 37, 39

Z

Zadar 59, 60, 61, 75, **190–5**
Zagorje 16, 77, **120–9**
Zagreb 67, 70, 71, 72, 88, **100–15**, 132, 265
Zajc, Ivan 174
Zaostrog 226
Zaprešić 120
Zara 191
Zemlja ('Earth') 78, 120, 131
Zlarin, island of 204
Zlatni rat 229
Zoranić, Petar 39, 191
Zrin 135, 205
Zrinski 130, 135, 177
Zrinski, Petar 34, 109
Zrmanja 186
Zvonimir 32, 183, 211

Ž

Žirje, island of 204
Žminj 163
Žumberak 136
Županja 47

Map section

A   ZAGORJE, BANOVINA,
    PODRAVINA, SLAVONIA
B   ISTRIA,
    CENTRAL CROATIA
C   DALMATIA
D   ZAGREB
E   SPLIT
F   DUBROVNIK
G   RIJEKA
H   ZADAR
I   ŠIBENIK
J   PULA

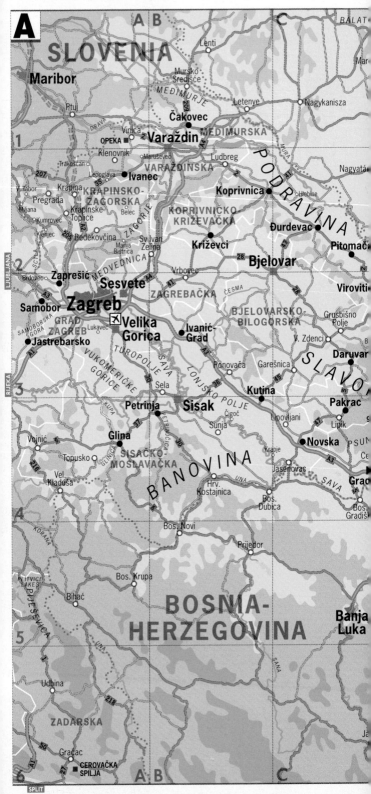

Tomási

Kalocsa

Kaposvár

Dombóvár

Baja

1

HUNGARY

Pécs

Mohács

2

FEDERATION
OF SERBIA
AND
MONTENEGRO

**Beli
Manastir**

Sombor

**Donji
Miholjac**

Knezevi-
Vinogradi

BARANJA

212

DANUBE

atina

Valpovo

P O D R A V I N A

Darda

Apatin

OVITIČKO-
DRAVSKA

Cačinci

Bizovac

Bilje

DRAVA

Erdut

Orahovica

Durdenovac

2

KOPAČKI
RIT

213

PUK

KRNDIJA

Kaptol

Našice

VUKA

Ajmaš

Osijek

Aljmaš

3

OSJEČKO-
BARANJSKA

Dalj

ŽEŠKO-
AVONSKA

Kutjevo

53

51

53

Trpinja

Vukovar

Požega

Đakovo

Ivankovo

Nuštar

S L A V O N I A

Vinkovci

Petrovo
Selo

BRODSKO-
POSAVSKA

St. Mikanovci

St. Jankovci

2

Oriovac

**Slavonski
Brod**

Vprolje

Cerna

BOSUT

Tovarnik

or

Sibinj

D. Andrijevci

55

VUKOVARSKO-
SRIJEMSKA

Komletinci

Bos. Brod

Županja

4

Derventa

Bos.
Samac

Bošnjaci

Snačva

A3

BELGRADE

Gunja

Gradačac

SAVA

Brčko

Bijeljina

Doboj

5

**BOSNIA-
HERZEGOVINA**

Tuzla

BOSNIA

Zenica

25 miles

0

20

40 km

Travnik

D

E

F

1/1 370 000 · 1 cm : 8 miles

6

◆ Istria

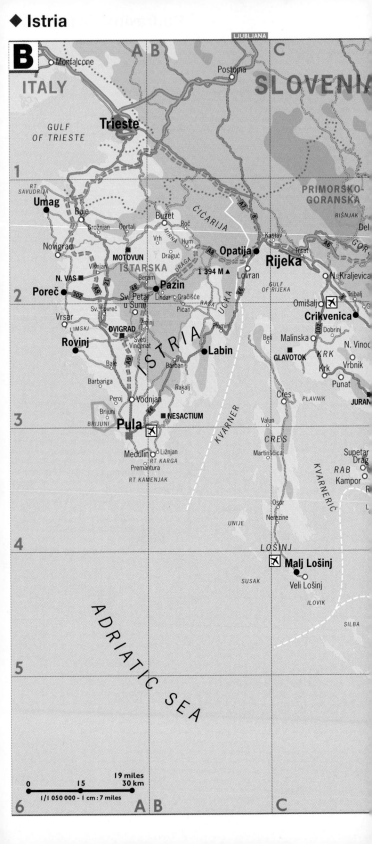

B

LJUBLJANA

ITALY
Monfalcone
Postojna

SLOVENIA

GULF OF TRIESTE

Trieste

PRIMORSKO-
GORANSKA

1

RT SAVUDRIJA
Umag
Buje
Buzet
ČIČARIJA
RIŠNJAK
Del

Grožnjan
Oprtalj
Roč
Kaštav

Novigrad
Vrh
Hum
Trsat

MIRNA
DRAGA
Opatija
Rijeka
GOR

MOTOVUN
Dragúc
R8
Lovran
N. Kraljevica

N. VAS
ISTARSKA
Beram
Pazin
1 394 M ▲
GULF OF RIJEKA
Tribalj

2
Poreč
302
R8
R8
Sv. Petar
Lindar
Gračišče
RAŠA
UČKA
Omišalj ✈ R8
Crikvenica

Višnjan
u Šumi
Pićan
Pičan
Pirmir
Dobrinj

Vrsar
Sv. Lovreč
Žminj
Beli
Malinska
N. Vinod

LIMSKI
DVIGRAD
Sveti
Labin
GLAVOTOK
KRK
Vrbnik

Rovinj
Vinčenat
Barban
Krk
Punat

Bale
Rakalj
Cres
JURAN

Barbariga
PLAVNIK

Peroj
Vodnjan
KVARNER
Valun

Brijuni
R8
NESACTIUM
CRES

3
BRIJUNI
Pula ✈
Martinšćica
Supetar
Drag

Medulin
Ližnjan
RAB
Kampor

Premantura
RT KARGA
Osor
Nerezine

RT KAMENJAK
UNIJE
KVARNERIĆ

4
LOŠINJ

Malj Lošinj ✈
SUSAK
Veli Lošinj
ILOVIK
SILBA

ADRIATIC

5
SEA

0   15   19 miles / 30 km
1/1 050 000 - 1 cm : 7 miles

6   A   B   C

LJUBLJANA

D

E

F

KRKA

Novo
Mesto

SV. GERA
1 178 M.

ŽUMBERAČKA GORA

Samobor

Zaprešić

Sesvete

Zagreb

A3

SAMOBORSKA GORA

Velika
Gorica

Lukavec

evje

ZAGREBAČKA

GRAD
ZAGREB

BELGRADE

Jastrebarsko

VUKOMERIČKE GORICE

A1

Ozalj

Pisarovina

30

KUPA

1

Karlovac

Bosiljevo

Duga Resa

SISAČKO-
MOSLAVAČKA

A6

Vrbovsko

KUPA

37

MREŽNICA

KORANA

Vojnić

6

Glina

Topusko

GLINICA

Ogulin

VELIKA KAPELA

Jasenak

23

Jopsidol

Vel.
Kladuša

2

AR

KARLOVAČKA

Modruš

Plaški

Slunj

KORANA

BOSNIA-
HERZEGOVINA

3

Brinje

MALA KAPELA

VRATNIK
694 M.

GACKA

50

217

Boš. Krupa

raj

Otočac

504

M. RAJINAC
1 699 M.

LIČKO-
SENJSKA

52

PLITVICE
LAKES

Bihać

UNA

Štirovača

LIKA

KRUŠĆIČKO
JEZ.

Lički Osik

1

PLJEŠEVICA

4

valja

VELEBIT

Smiljan

Karlobag

Gospić

Udbina

218

OŠTARIJSKA
928 M.

LIKA

Pag

VAGANSKI VRH
1 757 M.

PAG

106

PAKLENICA

A1

50

Gračac

5

8

Nin

Posedarje

54

Obrovac

27

CEROVAČKA
SPILJA

Novigrad

1

Ugljan

Zadar

502

D. Zemunik

ZADARSKA

UGLJAN

Preko

56

Savar

Veli-Iž

Bibinje

Benkovac

Knin

IŽ

Sukošan

DUGI
OTOK

PAŠMAN

Kistanje

KRKA

Zaglav

Sali

D

Biograd

Vrana

E

58

F

6

SPLIT

◆ Dalmatia

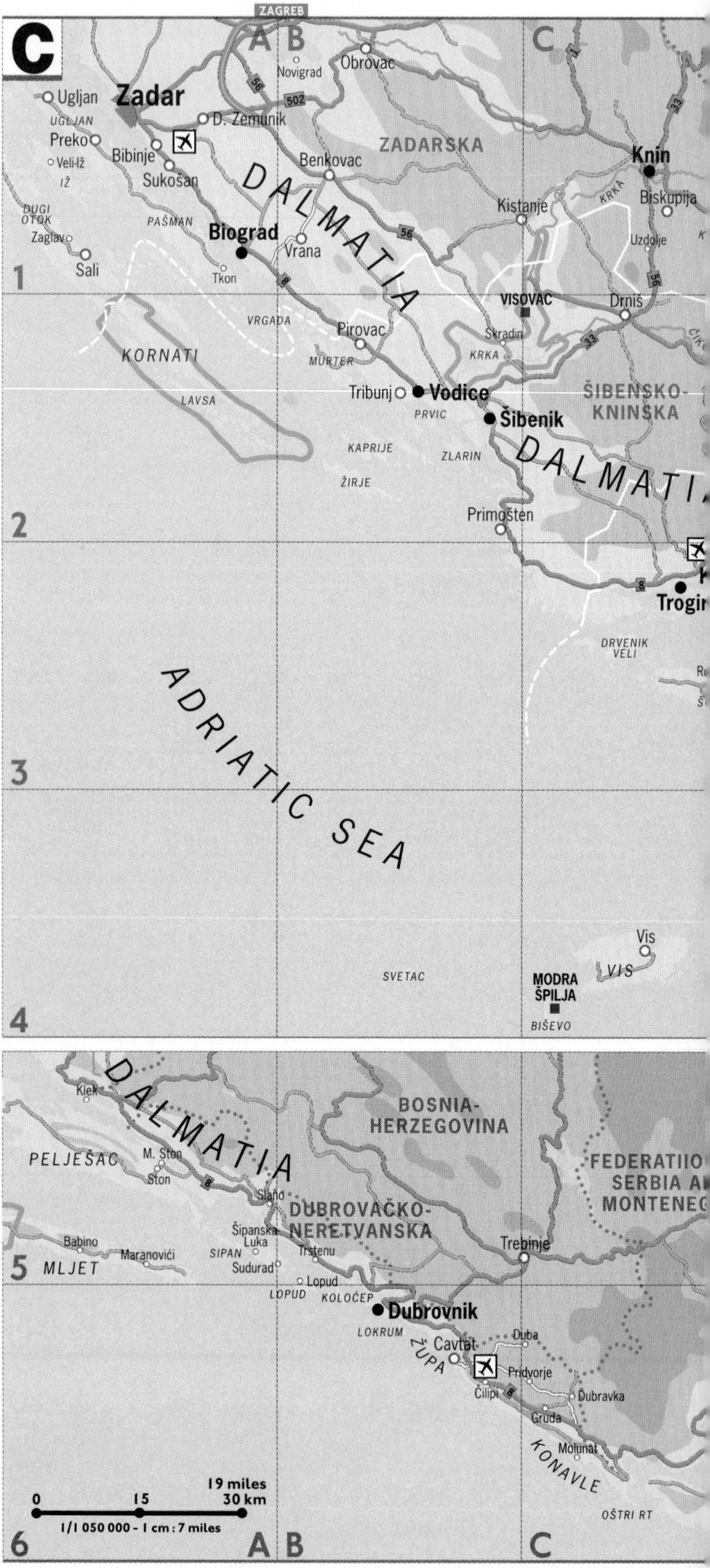

ZAGREB

C

A B C

Ugljan
Zadar
Novigrad
Obrovac
UGLJAN
502
D. Zemunik
56
Preko
Bibinje
ZADARSKA
Knin
Veli-Iž
Sukošan
Benkovac
Biskupija
IŽ
PAŠMAN
Kistanje
Uzdolje
DUGI
OTOK
Zaglav
56
Biograd
Drniš
Sali
Tkon
Vrana

1

VRGADA
Pirovac
Skradin
VISOVAC
KORNATI
MURTER
KRKA
33
LAVSA
Tribunj
Vodice
PRVIC
ŠIBENSKO-
KNINSKA
KAPRIJE
Šibenik
ŽIRJE
ZLARIN
D A L M A T I

2

Primošten

DRVENIK
VELI
Trogir

A D R I A T I C   S E A

3

Vis
SVETAC
**MODRA
ŠPILJA**
VIS
BIŠEVO

4

D A L M A T I A
BOSNIA-
HERZEGOVINA
Klek
M. Ston
PELJEŠAC
Ston
Slano
DUBROVAČKO-
NERETVANSKA
FEDERATIIO
SERBIA A
MONTENEG
Babino
Maranovići
Šipanska
Luka
Trstenu
Trebinje
MLJET
SIPAN
Sudurađ
Lopud

5

LOPUD
KOLOČEP
Dubrovnik
LOKRUM
Duba
ŽUPA
Cavtat
Pridvorje
Čilipi
Dubravka
Gruda
Molunat
KONAVLE
OŠTRI RT

6

0   15   19 miles
30 km
1/1 050 000 – 1 cm : 7 miles

A B C

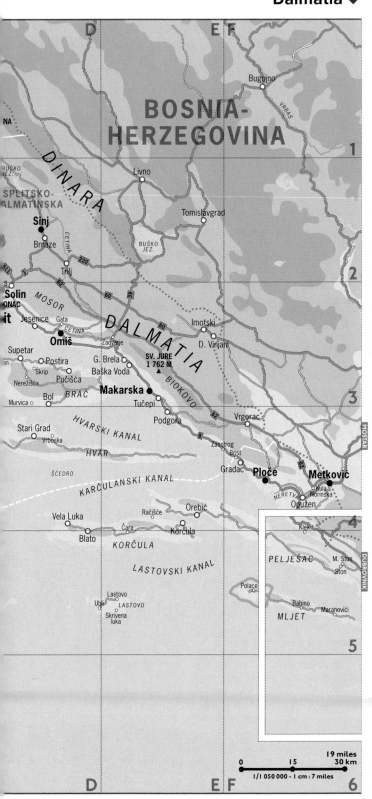

BOSNIA-
HERZEGOVINA

Bugojno

VRBAS

NA

DINARA

RUŠKO
JEZ.

Livno

1

SPLITSKO-
DALMATINSKA

Tomislavgrad

Sinj

Brnaze

CETINA

BUŠKO
JEZ.

Trilj

220

2

Solin

MOSOR

60

39

DONAC

it

Jesenice

Gata

CETINA

DALMATIA

Imotski

60

Omiš

Zadvarje

D. Vinjani

Supetar

Postira

G. Brela

SV. JURE
1 762 M ▲

MOSTAR

Škrip

Baška Voda

BIOKOVO

Nerežišća

Pučišća

Murvica

Bol

BRAČ

Makarska

Tučepi

3

Stari Grad

Vrboska

HVARSKI KANAL

Podgora

Vrgorac

52

62

HVAR

Zaostrog

Brist

Gradac

Ploče

Metković

ŠĆEDRO

KARČULANSKI KANAL

NERETVA

Kula
Norinska

Opuzen

DUBROVNIK

Vela Luka

Račišće

Orebić

Klek

4

Čara

PELJEŠAC

M. Ston

Blato

Korčula

Ston

KORČULA

LASTOVSKI KANAL

Polače

Lastovo

Babino

Maranovići

Ubli

LASTOVO

Skrivena
luka

MLJET

5

19 miles
30 km

0

15

1/1 050 000 · 1 cm : 7 miles

D

E

F

6

◆ Zagreb

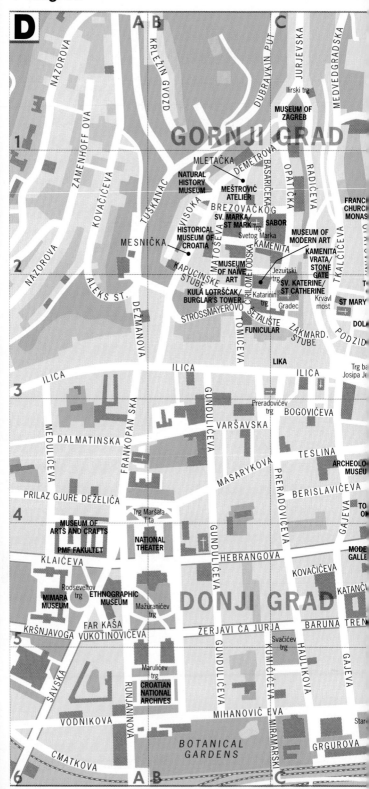

D

A B C

NAZOROVA

KRLEŽIN GVOZD

DUBRAVKIN PUT

JURJEVSKA

MEDVEDGRADSKA

ZAMENHOFF OVA

Ilirski trg

MUSEUM OF ZAGREB

GORNJI GRAD

1

KOVAČIĆEVA

TUŠKANAC

MLETAČKA

DEMETROVA

BASARIČEKA

OPATIČKA

RADIĆEVA

NATURAL HISTORY MUSEUM

VISOKA

BREZOVAČKOG

MEŠTROVIĆ ATELIER

SV. MARKA/ ST MARK trg **SABOR**

Svetog Marka

FRANC CHURCH MONAS

HISTORICAL MUSEUM OF CROATIA

MESNIČKA

MUSEUM OF MODERN ART

KAMENITA

TKALČIĆEVA

NAZOROVA

ALEKS ST.

DEŽMANOVA

KAPUCINSKE STUBE

MESOLA

MUSEUM OF NAÏVE ART

ĆIRILOMETODSKA

Jezuitski trg

KAMENITA VRATA/ STONE GATE

2

KULA LOTRŠĆAK/ BURGLAR'S TOWER

Katarinin trg

SV. KATERINE/ ST CATHERINE

Gradec

Krvavi most

ST MARY

STROSSMAYEROVO

ŠETALIŠTE

ZAKMARD. STUBE

DOLA

PODZID

TOMIĆEVA

FUNICULAR

LIKA

ILICA

ILICA

Trg ba Josipa Je

3

ILICA

ILICA

Preradovićev trg

BOGOVIĆEVA

GUNDULIĆEVA

VARŠAVSKA

MEDULIĆEVA

DALMATINSKA

FRANKOPANSKA

MASARYKOVA

TESLINA

PRERADOVIĆEVA

ARCHEOLO MUSEU

BERISLAVIĆEVA

PRILAZ GJURE DEŽELIĆA

Trg Maršala Tita

GAJEVA

TO O

4

MUSEUM OF ARTS AND CRAFTS

NATIONAL THEATER

GUNDULIĆEVA

HEBRANGOVA

MODE GALLE

PMF FAKULTET

KLAIĆEVA

KOVAČIĆEVA

KATANČI

Rooseveltov trg

MIMARA MUSEUM

ETHNOGRAPHIC MUSEUM

Mažuranićev trg

DONJI GRAD

BARUNA TREN

KRŠNJAVOGA

FAR KAŠA

VUKOTINOVIĆEVA

ŽERJAVI CA JURJA

Svačićev trg

GAJEVA

5

SAVSKA

RUNJANINOVA

Marulićev trg

CROATIAN NATIONAL ARCHIVES

GUNDULIĆEVA

KUMIČIĆEVA

HAULIKOVA

VODNIKOVA

MIHANOVIĆ EVA

MIRAMARSKI

Stare

GRGUROVA

CMATKOVA

BOTANICAL GARDENS

6

A B C

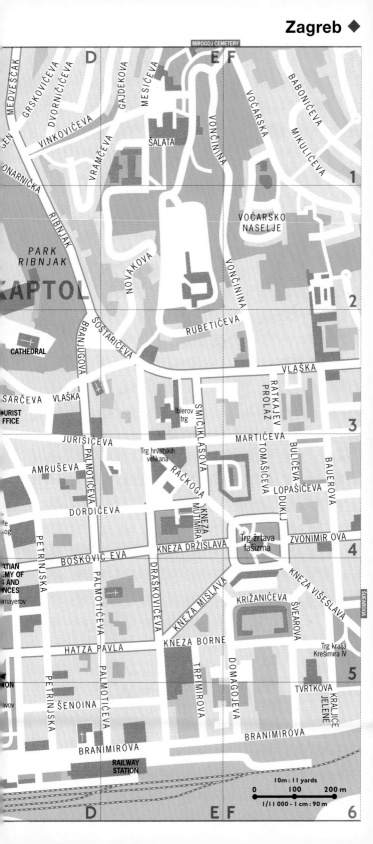

Zagreb ◆

◆ Split/Dubrovnik

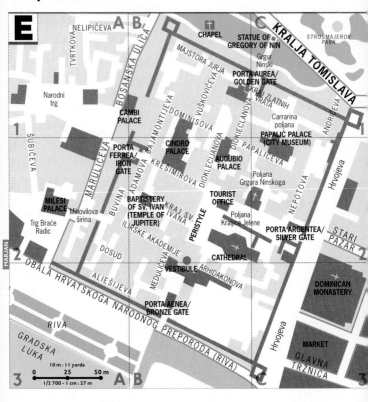

E

NELIPIĆEVA
TVRTKOVA
Narodni trg
BOSANSKA ULICA
CHAPEL
STATUE OF GREGORY OF NIN
Grgur Ninski
STROSMAJEROV PARK
KRALJA TOMISLAVA
MAJSTORA JURJA
CAMBI PALACE
PORTA AUREA/ GOLDEN GATE
KRALJ ZLATNIH VRATA
ŠUBIĆEVA
MARULIĆEVA
VUŠKOVIĆEVA
DOMINISOVA
BAJAMONTIJEVA
Carrarina poljana
ANDRIĆEVA
PORTA FERREA/ IRON GATE
CINDRO PALACE
KREŠIMIROVA
DIOKLECIANOVA
PAPALIĆ PALACE (CITY MUSEUM)
PAPALIĆEVA
HRVOJEVA
ADAMOVA
AUGUBIO PALACE
MILESI PALACE
Mihovilova širina
BUVINA
KRALJ SV. IVANA
TOURIST OFFICE
Poljana Grgura Ninskoga
NEPOTOVA
Trg Braće Radić
BAPTISTERY OF SV. IVAN (TEMPLE OF JUPITER)
ILIRSKE AKADEMIJE
PERISTYLE
DIOKLECIANOVA
Poljana Kraljice Jelene
PORTA ARGENTEA/ SILVER GATE
STARI PAZAR
MARJAN
DOSUD
MEDULIĆEVA
ARHIDAKONOVA
CATHEDRAL
VESTIBULE
OBALA HRVATSKOGA NARODNOG PREPORODA (RIVA)
ALIEŠIJEVA
PORTA AENEA/ BRONZE GATE
DOMINICAN MONASTERY
RIVA
GRADSKA LUKA
Hrvojeva
MARKET
GLAVNA TRŽNICA

10 m : 11 yards
0 25 50 m
1/2 700 - 1 cm : 27 m

F

ĐURA PALICA
SRENDNJI KONO
UZ POSAT
IZMEĐU VRTA
PUT IZA GRADA
MINČETA TOWER
ZAGREBAČKA
M. PERIĆA
PETRA KREŠIMIRA IV.
PLOČE
HVARSKA
PILE
Poljana Dr. Vinka Foretića
OD SIGURATE
OD MEDU
MISPOD MINČETE
PELINE
AN JUNINSK
PELINE
FRANCISCAN MONASTERY
NALJ ESKOVIĆE
H. LUCIĆA
DOMINICAN MONASTERY
REVELIN FORT
PILE-CRUZ
PILE GATE
ST SAVIOR
OD DOMINA
PALMOTIĆE
KUNIĆE
PETI OVR ENC
PRIJEKO
VETRANIĆA
PLOČE GATE
Brsalje
ONOFRIO FOUNTAIN
Poljana P. Miličevića
PLAČA (STRADUN)
BOŠKOVIĆA
ST SEBASTIAN
FORTRESS OF ST LUKE
CONVENT OF ST CLAIRE
ZLATARIĆEVA
GETALDIĆEVA
ĐORĐIĆEVA
IZMEĐU POLAČA
ZAMANJIN
DROPČEVA
ŽUDIOSKA
ST NICHOLAS
KLATARS
BOKAR FORTRESS
ST ROCH
ZA ROKOM
GARIŠTE
UZ JEZUITE
UZA VRA
MIHA PRACATA
ZUZORIĆ EVA
Luža
SPONZA PALACE
Ribarnica
ORLANDO'S COLUMN
NA ANDRIJI
PUZLJIVA
OD RUPA
OD DOMINA
N. BOŽIDAREVIĆA
USKA
TOURIST OFFICE
ST BLAISE
OLD PORT
RUPE (ETHNOGRAPHIC MUSEUM)
OD SORTE
ZA ROKOM
SVETE MARIJE
OD PUČA
MAROJICE KABOGE
UZ POLAČE
RANJINE
ZELJARICA
RECTORS' PALACE
Ponta
OD PUSTIJERNE
OD KAŠTELA
N. RANJINE
GUČETIĆEVA
Gundulićeva poljana
CATHEDRAL
Poljana Marina Držića
FORTRESS OF ST JEAN
IVANA RABLJANINA
STROSSMAYEROVA
Bunićeva poljana
KNEZA DAMJANA JUDE
Poljana Mrtvo Zvono
SV. SIMUNA
UZ JEZUITE
ST IGNATIUS
STULINA
ILIJE SARAKE
POBIJANA
RESTIĆEVA
DUBRA BELJAVI
ANDRIĆA
MARGARITE
CRIJEVIĆEVA
Poljana R. Boškovića
KNEZA HRVAŠA
POBIJANA
ISPOD MIRA
STAJEVA
JESUIT COLLEGE

0 50 100 m
1/4 850 - 1 cm : 48,5 m

A B C

ADRIATIC SEA

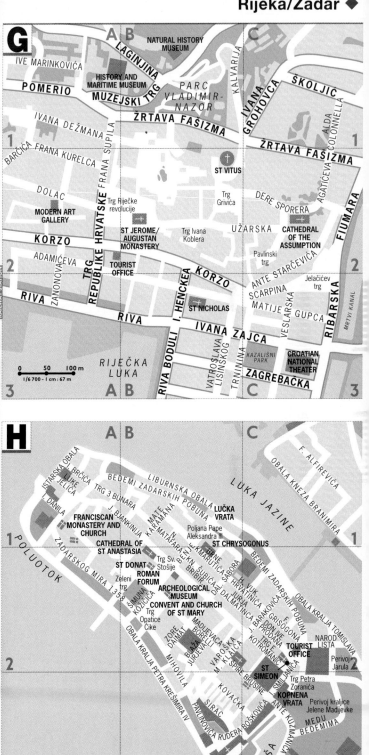

Rijeka/Zadar ◆

G

NATURAL HISTORY MUSEUM

IVE MARINKOVIĆA

LAGINJINA

POMERIO

HISTORY AND MARITIME MUSEUM

MUZEJSKI TRG

PARC VLADIMIR-NAZOR

KALVARIJA

IVANA GROHOVCA

ŠKOLJIĆ

ŽRTAVA FAŠIZMA

ALDA COLONNELLA

1

IVANA DEŽMANA

ŽRTAVA FAŠIZMA

1

BARČIĆA FRANA KURELCA

FRANA SUPILA

ST VITUS

Trg Grivića

DERE SPORERA

AGATIĆEVA

FIUMARA

DOLAC

Trg Riječke revolucije

HRVATSKE

MODERN ART GALLERY

ST JEROME/ AUGUSTAN MONASTERY

Trg Ivana Koblera

UŽARSKA

CATHEDRAL OF THE ASSUMPTION

KORZO

Pavlinski trg

FIUMARA

ADAMIĆEVA

TRG REPUBLIKE HRVATSKE

TOURIST OFFICE

KORZO

ANTE STARČEVIĆA

Jelačićev trg

2

ZANONOVIĆA

I. HENCKEA

SCARPINA

VESLARSKA

MATIJE GUPCA

RIBARSKA

MRTVI KANAL

RIVA

RIVA

ST NICHOLAS

IVANA ZAJCA

RIVA BODULI

Kazališni PARK

VATROSLAVA LISINSKOG

TRNINNA

CROATIAN NATIONAL THEATER

3

RIJEČKA LUKA

ZAGREBAČKA

3

0   50   100 m
1/6 700 – 1 cm: 67 m

A   **B**   **C**

H

F. ALFIREVIĆA

OBALA KNEZA BRANIMIRA

ISTARSKA OBALA

LUKE BRĆIĆA

JELIĆA

TRG 3 BUNARA

BEDEMI ZADARSKIH POBUNA

LIBURNSKA OBALA

LUKA JAZINE

I. DANILA

J. BJANKINIJA

MATE KARMANA

LUČKA VRATA

POLUOTOK

FRANCISCAN MONASTERY AND CHURCH

ZADARSKOG MIRA 1358

N. MATAFARA

BRIBIRA

Poljana Pape Aleksandra III

ST CHRYSOGONUS

BEDEMI ZADARSKIH POBUNA

OBALA KRALJA TOMISLAVA

1

CATHEDRAL OF ST ANASTASIA

BENJ. ŠUPIČIĆA

Trg Sv. Stošije

 I. KMARUTIČA

DON IVE PRODANA

1

ST DONAT

Zeleni trg

DAL. SABORA

DAL. HRVATSKA

JURJA DALMATINCA

BARAKOVIĆA

GRIŠOGONA

TRG I. KOTROMANIĆ

ROMAN FORUM

ŠIMUNA KOŽIČIĆA

ARCHEOLOGICAL MUSEUM

V. YUK

CONVENT AND CHURCH OF ST MARY

Trg Opatice Čike

MADIJEVACA

NARODNI LISTA

TOURIST OFFICE

Perivoj Jarula

ZORE DALMAT.

BLAŽA JURJEVIĆ

BORELLI

VAROŠKA

M. KLAIĆA

SPIRE BRUSINE

SIMIČLANICA

2

MIHOVILA

KOVAČKA

ST SIMEON

Trg Petra Zoranića

2

KOPNENA VRATA

Perivoj kraljice Jelene Madijevke

ANTE KUZMANIĆA

OBALA KRALJA PETRA KREŠIMIRA IV

ŠIRAC

PAVLINOVIĆA

RUDERA BOŠKOVIĆA

MEDU BEDEMIMA

FOŠA

KRALJA DMITRA ZVONIMIRA

3

0   100   200 m
1/13 300 – 1 cm: 133 m

A   **B**   **C**

◆ Šibenik/Pula

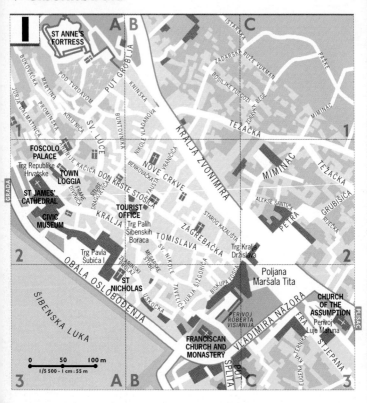

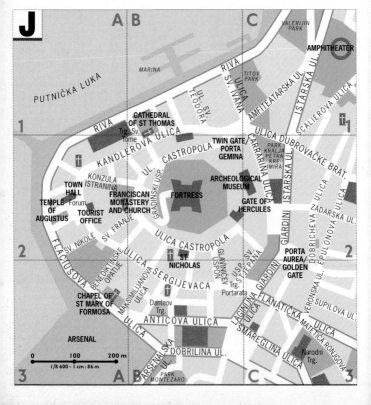

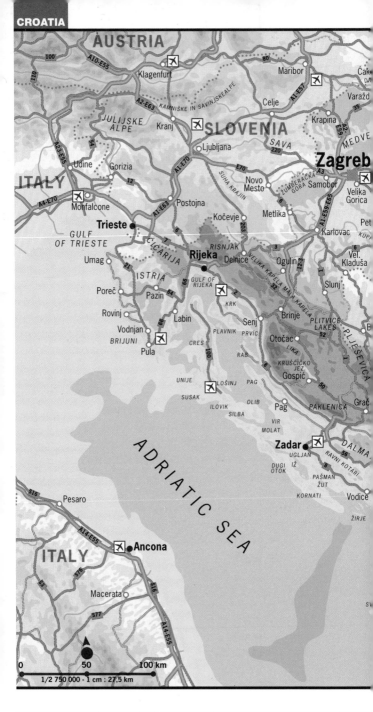

■ **SURFACE AREA**
54,318 square miles (35,180 square miles of land,19,138 square miles of sea); 1,102 miles of coastline; 1,185 islands.

■ **POPULATION**
4,440,000 of which 56.5 percent live in urban areas.

■ **DENSITY**
131 habitants/ square mile.

■ **CAPITAL**
Zagreb (800,000 inhab.)

■ **MAIN CITIES**
Split (190,000 inhab.), Rijeka (145,000 inhab.), Osijek (115,000 inhab.), Zadar (73,000 inhab.), Dubrovnik (50,000 inhab.).

■ **BORDERS**
Slovenia to the northwest; Hungaria to the northeast; Bosnia to the southeast; Serbia and Montenegro to the east.

■ **LANGUAGE**
Croatian

■ **ADMINISTRATIVE DIVISION**
21 counties (županija)

■ **ETHNIC DISTRIBUTION**
90 percent Croats, 4.5 percent Serbs, 0.5 percent Bosnians and Albanians, 5